COLLECTI
AND OTHER

FRANÇOIS DE LA ROCHEFOUCAULD, a member of a prominent French aristocratic family, was born in Paris in 1613. He was married at the age of 14 and took part in his first military campaign the following year. For the next quarter of a century he participated actively in military life, supporting the interests of the hereditary French aristocracy not only against foreign armies, but at times also against the king and his chief minister (Richelieu under Louis XIII, Mazarin under Louis XIV). When Louis XIV finally gained control of Paris in 1652, La Rochefoucauld retired from public life. In 1657–8 he began to compose the sayings published in 1664 as *Réflexions ou Sentences et Maximes morales* (*Moral Reflections or Sententiae and Maxims*). The work was carefully revised several times, its fifth and final authorized edition appearing in 1678. La Rochefoucauld died in Paris in 1680. Many further maxims, and the nineteen essays now known as the *Réflexions diverses* (*Miscellaneous Reflections*), were published posthumously from his manuscripts.

E. H. and A. M. BLACKMORE and FRANCINE GIGUÈRE have translated *Twelve Plays by Alfred de Musset* and George Sand's *Five Comedies* and *The Devil's Pool and Other Stories*. E. H. and A. M. Blackmore have also edited and translated nine other volumes of French literature, including, in Oxford World's Classics, *Six French Poets of the Nineteenth Century*, *The Essential Victor Hugo*, and Stéphane Mallarmé's *Collected Poems and Other Verse*. Their work has been awarded the American Literary Translators' Association Prize and the Modern Language Association Scaglione Prize for Literary Translation. Their other publications include literary criticism and studies in psycholinguistics and grammatical awareness.

OXFORD WORLD'S CLASSICS

*For over 100 years Oxford World's Classics have brought
readers closer to the world's great literature. Now with over 700
titles—from the 4,000-year-old myths of Mesopotamia to the
twentieth century's greatest novels—the series makes available
lesser-known as well as celebrated writing.*

*The pocket-sized hardbacks of the early years contained
introductions by Virginia Woolf, T. S. Eliot, Graham Greene,
and other literary figures which enriched the experience of reading.
Today the series is recognized for its fine scholarship and
reliability in texts that span world literature, drama and poetry,
religion, philosophy and politics. Each edition includes perceptive
commentary and essential background information to meet the
changing needs of readers.*

OXFORD WORLD'S CLASSICS

FRANÇOIS DE LA ROCHEFOUCAULD

Collected Maxims
and Other Reflections

Translated with an Introduction and Notes by
E. H. AND A. M. BLACKMORE
and FRANCINE GIGUÈRE

OXFORD
UNIVERSITY PRESS

OXFORD
UNIVERSITY PRESS

Great Clarendon Street, Oxford OX2 6DP

Oxford University Press is a department of the University of Oxford.
It furthers the University's objective of excellence in research, scholarship,
and education by publishing worldwide in

Oxford New York

Auckland Cape Town Dar es Salaam Hong Kong Karachi
Kuala Lumpur Madrid Melbourne Mexico City Nairobi
New Delhi Shanghai Taipei Toronto

With offices in

Argentina Austria Brazil Chile Czech Republic France Greece
Guatemala Hungary Italy Japan Poland Portugal Singapore
South Korea Switzerland Thailand Turkey Ukraine Vietnam

Oxford is a registered trade mark of Oxford University Press
in the UK and in certain other countries

Published in the United States
by Oxford University Press Inc., New York

British Library Cataloguing in Publication Data

Data available

Library of Congress Cataloging in Publication Data

La Rochefoucauld, François, duc de, 1613–1680.
[Maximes, English]
Collected maxims and other reflections / François de la Rochefoucauld ;
translated with an introduction and notes by
E. H. and A. M. Blackmore and Francine Giguère.
(Oxford world's classics)
Includes bibliographical references and index.
I. Blackmore, E. H. II. Blackmore, A. M. III. Giguère, Francine. IV. Title.
PQ1815.A72 2007 848'.402—dc22 2006019481

ISBN 978–0–19–954000–6

21

Typeset in Ehrhardt
by RefineCatch Limited, Bungay, Suffolk
Printed and bound in Great Britain by Clays Ltd, Elcograf S.p.A.

CONTENTS

PRINCIPAL ABBREVIATIONS

I   *Réflexions ou Sentences et Maximes morales*, first (1664–5) edition

II   *Réflexions ou Sentences et Maximes morales*, second (1666) edition

III   *Réflexions ou Sentences et Maximes morales*, third (1671) edition

IV   *Réflexions ou Sentences et Maximes morales*, fourth (1674–5) edition

V   *Réflexions ou Sentences et Maximes morales*, fifth (1678) edition

VIs   *Réflexions ou Sentences morales*, supplement to the sixth (1693) edition

L   Liancourt manuscript, *c.*1659–63
PV124   Maxims sent to Jacques Esprit, *c.*1660
PV158   Maxims sent to Madame de Sablé, 1667
RD   *Réflexions diverses*
RDA   Addenda to the *Réflexions diverses*
SL   Smith-Lesouëf manuscript, 1663

Further information can be found in the Note on the Text and Translation (p. xxxiii).

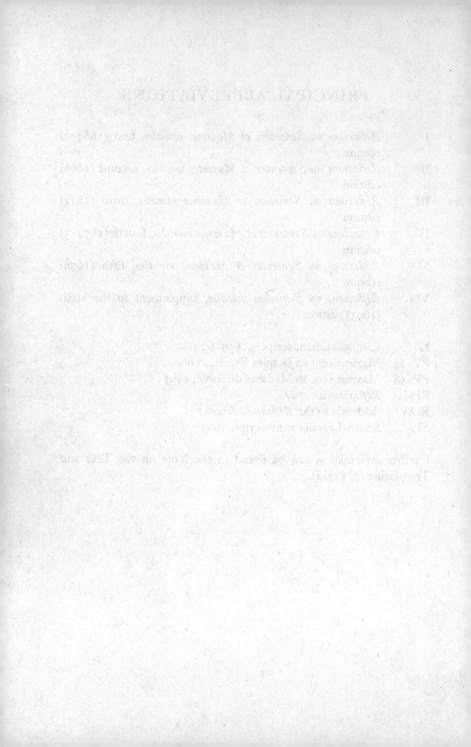

PRINCIPAL ABBREVIATIONS

I   Réflexions ou Sentences et Maximes morales, first (1665) edition.

II   Réflexions ou Sentences et Maximes morales, second (1666) edition.

III   Réflexion ou Sentences et Maximes morales, third (1671) edition.

IV   Réflexions ou Sentences et Maximes morales, fourth (1675) edition.

V   Réflexions ou Sentences et Maximes morales, fifth (1678) edition.

VI   Réflexions ou Sentences morales, supplement to the sixth (1693) edition.

L   La Rochefoucauld, p. 670 sq.
M   Manuscrit in Jacques Esprit, 1080.
HvdB   Versus von de Madame de Sablé, 1097
SP   Sorbière 1095
RO   Liancourt rope, Portland, 1000.
S   Smith, Lettres manuscript, 1097.

Further abbreviations can be found in the Note on the Text and Translation, p. xxviii.

INTRODUCTION

'Neither the sun nor death can be looked at steadily,' declares La Rochefoucauld (v: 26). The same may be said of his *Moral Reflections or Sententiae and Maxims*. Few books as widely read have provoked as much resistance. Most of us can no more look at it without wavering than we could the sun. We cannot bear the thought that it might be true; the consequences would be too painful. So, to shut our eyes to it, to avoid facing it, we rely on every psychological defence we can muster. The book is a work of cynicism, pessimism, scepticism, Jansenism, or some other limited and limiting -ism; we ourselves are much wiser, and take a broader, more balanced view of humanity. Or it is inconsistent, and contains its own refutation. Or it is true only of La Rochefoucauld himself (how corrupt he must be, to be capable of thinking *us* corrupt!). Or it may be true of many people, but it is not true of us. Or if it is, it is true of us only in our worst moments, or only in some details. Or if we do happen to entertain the thought that it might be wholly true, we entertain that thought only while actually reading it; a few minutes later we put the book aside and turn our minds to other, more comfortable things; we live, in practice, as if we had never read it.

More curiously still, those defences are employed almost as often by La Rochefoucauld's admirers as by his opponents. Even the author of *La Princesse de Clèves*—Madame de La Fayette, who cannot be dismissed as stupid or hostile—reacted against the *Maxims* at first. 'Oh, Madame, how much corruption a person must have in his mind and heart to be capable of imagining all those things!' she exclaimed in an undated letter to Madame de Sablé. At the present day, subtle unconscious resistances to the book can be discerned even in the writings of La Rochefoucauld's most committed advocates. Such resistances will probably be visible in the very pages of this Introduction; it is uncannily difficult to avoid slipping into them.

La Rochefoucauld himself was well aware of this effect of his work. 'The reason why we argue so much against the maxims that expose the human heart, is that we ourselves are afraid of being exposed by them,' he wrote—but did not publish (L 245).

So profoundly unsettling a book might have been extraordinary at

any time and in any place. Perhaps it is not the less extraordinary for being the work of a leisured seventeenth-century French aristocrat with no significant literary training or experience.

Life and Writings of La Rochefoucauld

François, Prince de Marcillac, was born in Paris in 1613. He came from an ancient aristocratic French family, which had been prominent since the eleventh century; five of his ancestors had borne the same first name, and therefore he is sometimes termed 'François VI'. He became Duc de La Rochefoucauld in 1650, on the death of his father, who had been granted that dukedom in 1622.

At the age of 14 years and 4 months, in 1628, he was married to Andrée de Vivonne. 'There are good marriages, but there are no rapturous ones,' he wrote thirty years later (V: 113). Their first seven children were born between 1634 and 1646, their eighth and last in 1655. Between 1646 and 1651 La Rochefoucauld conducted an affair with the Duchesse de Longueville (the cousin of Louis XIV and sister of the Great Condé, 'the Prince' of the *Maxims* and *Miscellaneous Reflections*), by whom he had one child, born in 1649. Nevertheless Jean de Segrais, in *Segraisiana* (1721), reported that 'Monsieur de La Rochefoucauld used to say that he had found love only in novels; he had never felt it himself'. That was also Madame de Sévigné's impression; 'I don't think he has ever been what is called "in love",' she wrote in a letter of 7 October 1676. In his own memoirs, La Rochefoucauld retrospectively depicted his affair with Madame de Longueville as motivated more by pride, ambition (a wish to conquer a woman, a wish to triumph over other men), and political motives (a wish to advance his personal interests) than by affection or desire. Here again, his experience may be obliquely reflected in some of his maxims, such as 'What is least often found in love affairs is love' (V: 402).

At the age of 15 he began to participate actively in the political and military life of his country. He fought with the French army against Spain, first in Italy (1629) and later in the Netherlands (1635). At home, however, he was not always a loyal supporter of his government. During the first half of the seventeenth century France underwent a complex series of political struggles; broadly speaking, the traditional French aristocracy gradually lost power, which

became more exclusively vested in the king (Louis XIII from 1610 to 1643, Louis XIV for the rest of the century) and his chief minister (Richelieu from 1624 to 1642, Mazarin from 1643 to 1659). Like many noblemen of the time, the young Prince de Marcillac strenuously opposed some of these developments. As early as 1635 he was exiled from court for reasons that are not fully clear. In 1637 he took part in an abortive conspiracy led by the Duchesse de Chevreuse; this earned him a short imprisonment in the Bastille and a further period in exile. During the civil wars of the Fronde (1649–53), La Rochefoucauld sided with Condé and fought against the forces of Louis XIV and Mazarin. Twice, in these wars, he was seriously— almost fatally—wounded: at Lagny during the siege of Paris in February 1649, and at the battle of the Faubourg Saint-Antoine in July 1652. In October 1652 the king issued a general pardon to the rebels. La Rochefoucauld took little further part in the public life of his country; but as late as the 1670s, when he wished to cite examples of great men, it was natural for him to think primarily of military leaders (RD 14).

He had already written a short manuscript defence of his conduct—the *Apologie de M. le prince de Marcillac*—in 1649. Now, in his retirement, he began to write his memoirs. The main part of the work was drafted between 1653 and 1659; two long preliminary sections were added in 1661–2, and apparently the text was still being revised in the final years of his life (the paragraph on Godefroy d'Estrades must have been updated in or after 1675; La Rochefoucauld's portraits of Cardinal de Retz and Madame de Montespan, written around the same time, may also have been intended as supplements to the *Mémoires*).

So far there had been little in La Rochefoucauld's private or public life to set him apart from his contemporaries. Many other seventeenth-century French aristocrats dabbled in politics, fought against the Spaniards, took part in the Fronde, and wrote memoirs to justify their conduct privately to their friends and families. But during the late 1650s La Rochefoucauld's career took a new turn: he became part of a small social and literary group that also included Jacques Esprit (1611–78) and Madeleine de Souvré, Marquise de Sablé (1599–1678). Neither Esprit nor Madame de Sablé had yet published anything significant, but both were well known in fashionable literary circles: the former had been a member of France's most

illustrious literary body, the Académie Française, since 1639, while the latter had been praised as Parthénie in Madeleine de Scudéry's immensely popular novel *Le Grand Cyrus* (1649–53). Esprit's fellow Academician Chapelain characterized him as follows in 1660: 'His strong point is theology; he has little depth outside that area. Imagination and style he has in abundance, and he writes French elegantly in both prose and verse.' Madame de Sablé lived at Port-Royal des Champs, a Jansenist community outside Paris, where she was visited by some of the most eminent people in the realm (including Monsieur, the king's brother).

For some years the three friends profoundly influenced each other's thoughts and writings. In 1657 or 1658 they began to compose short epigrammatic or proverbial sayings, which they called *sentences, maximes*, or *réflexions*. At first there seems to have been relatively little question of individual ownership; maxims or small groups of maxims were circulated freely in manuscript among the various members of Madame de Sablé's circle, who discussed them and sometimes suggested modifications to them. As time passed, however, La Rochefoucauld's series of maxims began to separate from the others. The surviving documents suggest that there may have been several reasons for this. By 1660 Esprit had married, and some time later he left Paris, after which he had little direct contact with the others. Madame de Sablé began to feel that her own maxims were substantially inferior to La Rochefoucauld's and were dwarfed by being juxtaposed with his. Perhaps, too, she may have been conscious of differences in outlook and philosophy (though there are fewer such differences than people used to think in the days when most of her writings were unpublished or unread). Finally, there was a simple difference in productivity: La Rochefoucauld generated maxims far more copiously than either of the others. Whatever the reasons, the three strands eventually appeared separately. Madame de Sablé's surviving *Maximes*, eighty-one in number, were issued very shortly after her death in 1678; Jacques Esprit's grew into an imposing systematic treatise, *La Fausseté des vertus humaines* (*The Falsehood of Human Virtues*), published in 1677. No admirer of La Rochefoucauld should neglect those two books; their value for the appreciation of his work can scarcely be exaggerated.

La Rochefoucauld's own maxims had appeared in print much earlier. During 1663 he prepared a manuscript collection entitled

Sentences et Maximes de Morale (*Sententiae and Maxims on Morality*); copies of this were circulated privately among his friends, and one such copy—or a very similar document—found its way to Holland, where a somewhat garbled pirate edition was issued, without any author's name, late in 1663 or very early in January 1664.

La Rochefoucauld was understandably alarmed. A similar Dutch edition of his *Mémoires*, which had appeared a year earlier, had provoked a certain amount of public hostility. That piracy he had simply disowned (he never did authorize the publication of his memoirs); but for the maxims he chose a different policy—perhaps because they were potentially more dangerous, perhaps because their subject matter was less private or less personal. He decided to issue an accurate authorized edition, polished as carefully as the pressure of time would permit, and prefaced by a long defensive essay written by the lawyer Henri de La Chapelle-Bessé. Certainly he needed to act rapidly and tread cautiously: in his world an attack on the pretence of virtue could easily be taken for an attack on virtue itself, as the troubled fortunes of Molière's comedy *Tartuffe* (first performed at Versailles on 12 May 1664, and promptly banned) vividly demonstrated.

The first authorized edition of the maxims appeared on 27 October 1664, with the title *Réflexions ou Sentences et Maximes morales* (*Moral Reflections or Sententiae and Maxims*). Its textual history shows the haste with which it was prepared. In its original state, three maxims were accidentally duplicated, two were assigned the same number, several contained obvious textual errors, and at least one politically dangerous remark was allowed to slip through into print (I: 284[1], 'The education given to princes gives them a second dose of self-love'). Most of these matters were corrected while the volume was passing through the press.

La Chapelle-Bessé's prefatory defence was arranged partly on lines drafted by La Rochefoucauld in an important letter to Jacques Esprit's brother Thomas on 6 February 1664: 'As the plan of both [Jacques Esprit and La Rochefoucauld himself] was to prove that the old pagan philosophers' virtue, which they trumpeted so loudly, was built on false foundations, and that man—no matter how persuaded he may be of his own merit—has in himself only deceptive appearances of virtue, with which he dazzles other people and often deceives himself (unless faith plays any part in the matter), it seems

to me, I say, that there has been no gross exaggeration of the miseries and contradictions of the human heart, humiliating the absurd pride that fills it, and showing it that it needs to be supported and buttressed in all respects by Christianity. It seems to me that the maxims in question pursue that aim pretty well and are not committing any crime, since their purpose is to attack pride—which, from what I have heard, is not necessary for salvation.' La Rochefoucauld concludes by asking that his letter be shown to La Chapelle-Bessé: 'you will spare me the trouble of rewriting it for him'. Nevertheless, a letter to the Jesuit René Rapin on 12 July shows that La Rochefoucauld was not entirely happy with La Chapelle-Bessé's finished essay. He was anxious not to offend his supporters—'sooner than cause any pain to those who have undertaken to defend' the maxims, he declared, 'I would prefer a thousand times that they never appeared at all'—and therefore he did allow the essay to stand at the head of the first authorized edition; but he never reprinted it when his maxims were reissued.

The October 1664 edition attracted considerable attention, and seems to have sold out within a couple of years. La Rochefoucauld's maxims were much read in fashionable French society, and widely discussed—not always favourably, but there was no serious outcry and no attempt to ban them. By the time of the second authorized edition (1 September 1666) the work needed no serious defence. La Rochefoucauld's preliminary address 'To the Reader' was rewritten and considerably abridged; La Chapelle-Bessé's introduction was dropped. The text of the work itself was extensively revised. Forty-four new maxims were introduced, but sixty maxims present in the previous edition were omitted, while many of those that were carried over were altered—and often abridged. The new volume was tighter, terser, more direct, less concerned to explain or justify itself.

The third (after February 1671) and fourth (17 December 1674) authorized editions differed from the second mainly in the addition of new maxims. The fifth and final authorized edition (26 July 1678) contained more substantial revisions (numerous deletions and alterations as well as additions). Nearly all subsequent printings of La Rochefoucauld's maxims reproduce the text published in 1678, often supplemented by material from the earlier editions and/or from manuscripts.

The so-called *Réflexions diverses* (*Miscellaneous Reflections*),

nineteen essays on various—mainly moral—subjects, date from the last decade of his life (after 1673), though they may well incorporate earlier material. There is no evidence that La Rochefoucauld himself intended to publish them, or even that he considered them a unitary work; none of the known manuscripts gives them any overall title (they were first named *Réflexions diverses* in 1789). Seven of them were published in 1731, the other twelve in 1863.

During the final phase of his life La Rochefoucauld also collaborated with Jean Regnault de Segrais and Madame de La Fayette on the novel *Zayde* (published 1669–71). He was in almost daily contact with Madame de La Fayette during the years when she was writing *La Princesse de Clèves* (1672–7); thus he may well have influenced that novel—and, conversely, she may well have influenced the last three editions of his maxims. It would be impossible to issue any precise *Collected Works of La Rochefoucauld*; at various points his own writings merge insensibly into those of other authors.

La Rochefoucauld died in Paris on 17 March 1680.

Background and Sources

La Rochefoucauld did read ('I like reading in general; I like best the kind that contains something to shape the mind and strengthen the soul,' he wrote in his 1656–8 self-portrait), but he did not read widely. 'It is more vital to study men than books,' declares one of his maxims (VIS: 17). 'It's incomprehensible how you know everything so perfectly without having studied,' Madame de Sablé told him in an undated letter of the early 1660s. 'Monsieur de La Rochefoucauld had not studied; but he had remarkable good sense, and he knew the world perfectly,' wrote Segrais in *Segraisiana* (1721).

Parallels to some of the maxims can be found in many earlier writers (see the Explanatory Notes); but any influence may well be indirect rather than direct. La Rochefoucauld must have heard or read many passages from the Latin Vulgate Bible, some of them frequently; but even here, similarities may be due simply to general cultural factors, and not to specific reminiscence. Beyond that, there is no proof that he had *first-hand* acquaintance with the writings of any ancient or contemporary philosopher, theologian, or moralist— even Seneca, the one author mentioned by name in the *Maxims*. Proverbial material is so frequently repeated (both orally and in

written form), generation after generation, that it is notoriously hard to identify direct sources in this field. Not everyone who quotes 'A rose by any other name . . .' has opened a volume of Shakespeare or seen a performance of *Romeo and Juliet*.

The form and content of La Rochefoucauld's maxims are clearly modelled, directly or indirectly, consciously or unconsciously, on the wisdom literature in the Hebrew Scriptures (Job, Proverbs, Ecclesiastes) and the Apocrypha (notably the Wisdom of Jesus Son of Sirach). This similarity was immediately recognized by the book's first readers. An unknown correspondent remarked to Madame de Schomberg in 1663 that many of La Rochefoucauld's maxims 'tallied perfectly with the *sententiae* of Sirach'. 'Please give my compliments to Monsieur de La Rochefoucauld, and tell him that the Book of Job and his Maxims are my only reading,' Madame de Maintenon wrote to Ninon de Lenclos in a letter of March 1666.

Another obvious influence was proverbial folk wisdom, a topic that interested many seventeenth-century writers (in English, we might recall George Herbert's *Outlandish Proverbs*). One popular saying, *la pelle se moque du fourgon*, literally 'the coal shovel mocks the fire poker' (a French Renaissance analogue of modern English 'the pot calling the kettle black'), formed the basis of La Rochefoucauld's manuscript maxim L 121; but when he came to publish it, he substituted the less earthy 'Everyone objects to something in other people that they object to in him' (I: 33). Like most of his contemporaries, La Rochefoucauld was concerned in public to maintain a literary dignity and decorum that he did not always observe in private.

La Rochefoucauld referred repeatedly to 'the philosophers' ('the old pagan philosophers' of the 6 February 1664 letter already cited), but always to oppose, or at least (in L 62) to correct, their views. They were therefore partly, if not predominantly, a negative influence. The only philosopher mentioned by name in the *Maxims* is Seneca (I: 105), and his pagan Stoicism may have been one of La Rochefoucauld's principal targets; certainly Seneca and Stoicism are attacked repeatedly in Esprit's *Fausseté des vertus humaines*. Several leading Rochefoucaldian scholars (including Jean Marchand, Jean Lafond, and Laurence Plazenet) have suggested that Esprit and La Rochefoucauld may have been particularly provoked by Jean Puget

de La Serre's book *L'Esprit de Sénèque* (*The Spirit of Seneca*), which was published in 1657—probably just about the time when La Rochefoucauld and his friends began to compose their own maxims—and which contained over a thousand brief 'precepts' derived from the writings of the ancient Stoic. Puget de La Serre's preface declared 'that Seneca's morality has comforted as many sufferers as his political thought has made men wise', and that 'the most illustrious preachers and most famous lawyers' had learnt their art from him. Esprit and La Rochefoucauld may well have seen this book—its popularity is attested by the facts that a second edition was required in 1660 and that a companion collection of precepts from Tacitus followed in 1664. But they would have encountered Senecan Stoicism in many other contexts too; it was as fashionable in seventeenth-century France as in seventeenth-century England. La Rochefoucauld himself had been under its spell; his early self-portrait is framed largely in the Stoic terms he was soon to reject: 'All my passions are fairly gentle and fairly well regulated; I have hardly ever displayed a fit of anger. . . . I am not troubled by ambition at all. I am not afraid of many things, and I have absolutely no fear of death.' Maxims written only a very few years later revealed a radical change in some of his attitudes: 'every man who is able to see [death] as it really is, finds it a terrifying thing', he declared in v: 504. By that time he had apparently come to regard Stoicism as a comforting but delusive drug, which soothes us with the claim that it is in our power to lead virtuous lives, while allowing all our innate vices to flourish undetected. The frontispiece to the October 1664 edition of the *Maxims* depicts the Love of Truth removing a calm beautiful mask from Seneca's face, and revealing the tormented ugly reality.

The direct or indirect influence of Plutarch (most conspicuous in RD 14) has perhaps been underestimated. We naturally tend to look for La Rochefoucauld's sources mainly in overtly moral or philosophical works; yet Plutarch's *Lives* are surely among the writings that La Rochefoucauld is most likely to have known. It is scarcely thinkable that a seventeenth-century French aristocrat immersed in military and political activity, and mildly interested in literature, would not have read Amyot's translation of at least the lives of Alexander and Julius Caesar—which are precisely the *Lives* most often echoed in La Rochefoucauld's writings. There are fewer passages

suggestive of the *Moralia*, and we have noticed none that would require first-hand knowledge.

Traces of more recent writings can also be found in the *Maxims*. Montaigne is virtually quoted in 1: 134, though once again the influence might of course be indirect (both of La Rochefoucauld's collaborators, Madame de Sablé and Jacques Esprit, were clearly familiar with Montaigne's writings). Other widely read philosophical or moralistic works that appear to be echoed in the *Maxims* include *De la sagesse* (*Wisdom*, 1601), by Montaigne's disciple Pierre Charron, and *Oráculo manual y arte de prudencia* (*The Art of Worldly Wisdom*, 1647), a collection of three hundred maxims by the Jesuit Baltasar Gracián. Like Seneca, these writers may have provoked more disagreement than agreement in La Rochefoucauld's circle.

Collections of brief or fragmentary prose writings were popular during the seventeenth century. We have already noted two such collections, Puget de La Serre's *L'Esprit de Sénèque* and Gracián's *Oráculo manual*; these, and/or many similar works, could have influenced the form of La Rochefoucauld's book. Between mid-1657 and mid-1658, at the time when La Rochefoucauld and his friends were beginning to write maxims, Blaise Pascal was drafting the discontinuous notes in defence of Christianity ultimately published as his *Pensées* (1670). Both Jacques Esprit and Madame de Sablé had close ties with the Port-Royal religious community supported by Pascal; Madame de Sablé knew Pascal particularly well (indeed, one of her maxims was long mistaken for the work of Pascal and incorporated in the *Pensées*). There is no reason to suppose that La Rochefoucauld ever saw Pascal's manuscripts or borrowed from them, but the two writers were akin in their ways of thinking and modes of expression, as their contemporaries were quick to realize — see, for instance, the famous comparison between the *Maxims* and the *Pensées* in the introductory discourse to Jean de La Bruyère's *Les Caractères* (1688). 'When sin came, man lost his first love; and, in this great soul capable of an infinite love, only self-love remained. That self-love spread out and overflowed into the void that the love of God had left, and so he loved only himself, and all things for the sake of himself,' wrote Pascal in a much-quoted letter of 17 October 1651. Here we seem almost on the brink of the great meditation on self-love that stands at the start of La Rochefoucauld's first edition

('Self-love is the love of oneself, and of all things for the sake of oneself . . .'; 1: 1).

Sententiae were also popular in more extended writings—poems, novels, plays—and were often set out in boldface or italics, or identified by marginal marks, in printed editions of such works. The pungent and unillusioned observations on human behaviour in the plays of Pierre Corneille are likely to have been a particularly significant influence. When, in his letter of 6 February 1664, La Rochefoucauld discussed 'the clemency of Augustus toward Cinna' (finding in it 'a desire to try a new remedy, a weariness of so much useless bloodshed, and a fear of consequences, to which people have preferred to give the name of virtue instead of dissecting all the crannies of the heart'), he was certainly thinking specifically of Corneille's *Cinna, ou le Clémence d'Auguste* (1642). La Rochefoucauld knew Corneille personally, and heard the dramatist read his latest play, *Pulchérie*, in January 1672 (its remarkable treatment of love in old age must have struck a responsive chord in a maxim writer increasingly preoccupied with such themes; V: 418, first published in 1678, might almost stand as an epigraph to the play). His library apparently contained a 1664 edition of Corneille's collected dramatic works, as well as many other plays (by Thomas Corneille, Molière, Racine, and others) and novels (especially those of Madeleine de Scudéry); most of these, judging from their dates, were bought during the late 1650s, 1660s, and 1670s. During the years when he was working on his maxims, his reading may have consisted as much of fiction and drama as of philosophy or theology.

But many of the factors that shaped La Rochefoucauld's thought must lie in undocumented regions: in private conversations and public speeches; in the examples—positive and negative—set by the people around him; in a casual remark heard after a battle, in an oration at the funeral of a relative or a family friend. Such things may have been the most important influences of all; but they have left no written traces, and inevitably remain beyond our reach.

Form and Content

In all five authorized editions, the work's full title is *Réflexions ou Sentences et Maximes morales* (*Moral Reflections or Sententiae and Maxims*). The adjective *morales* is to be taken as modifying all three

nouns, because the brief form of the title, appearing after the introductory address to the reader and in running heads at the top of each
page, is *Réflexions morales* (*Moral Reflections*).

La Rochefoucauld's writings do not draw any clear distinction
between the words *réflexions*, *sentences*, and *maximes*; indeed, in his
correspondence he applies all three terms to the work as a whole—
sentences being used mainly during the early years (1658–62), and
maximes later (perhaps under the influence of Madame de Sablé and
others who were favouring that word). Definitions in the French
dictionaries compiled by Antoine Furetière (1690) and the Académie
Française (1694) may help us to appreciate the significance that these
terms would have had for the book's first readers. *Réflexion* is defined
by Furetière as 'meditations on some topic' ('the *Moral Reflections* of
Monsieur de La Rochefoucauld' being cited as an example of this
meaning), and by the Académie as 'the act of the mind when it
reflects; serious meditation, attentive consideration of something'.
Furetière defines *sentence* as 'noteworthy saying, remark that contains a great truth, a fine moral saying, apophthegm uttered by some
great man; the Proverbs of Solomon are all *sententiae*', and the
Académie defines *maxime* as 'general proposition that serves as principle, foundation, rule in some art or science'; in each case the defin-
ition in the other dictionary is very similar though briefer. Thus the
three words were not exact synonyms. By applying all of them to his
book, La Rochefoucauld was evoking a richer and more diverse
range of associations than any one of them could have conveyed—a
richer and more diverse range than some of his contemporaries were
willing to grant—though it is evident that, in all five authorized
editions, he wished the term *réflexion* to be pre-eminent.

La Rochefoucauld's maxims were products of French Classicism,
exact contemporaries of Racine's secular plays (1664–77) and Boi-
leau's *Art poétique* (1674). Their vocabulary is simple and economical,
shunning archaisms and neologisms, and using few rare or technical
terms. Imagery is relatively infrequent (the commonest source being
health and disease: V: 182, 188, 193, 194, 271, 300, 392, 459; I: 1, 21,
305) and is phrased in general terms: we hear of 'rivers' and 'the sea'
(V: 171), 'the flowers' and 'the fruits' (V: 274), 'every kind of tree' (I:
138). Nonetheless, La Bruyère, in his introductory discourse to *Les
Caractères* (1688), could praise La Rochefoucauld's 'variety of
expression'. To some extent this is another typical Classicist trait, a

dislike of stylistic monotony, but La Rochefoucauld displays far more than the usual Classical ingenuity in avoiding repetition and finding new ways to say almost the same thing: consider, for instance, how many different methods he employs in 1: 1 to express the all-pervasiveness of self-love.

Though the individual words are easily comprehensible, the sense was sometimes found difficult even by La Rochefoucauld's contemporaries. In a letter of 1663, Madame de Schomberg noted that 'many people find obscurity in some parts' of the *Maxims*. (Madame de Sablé herself was sometimes among them; in an undated letter to La Rochefoucauld she remarked of L 210, 'I don't fully understand it.') La Chapelle-Bessé, in his introductory discourse to the October 1664 edition, observed that 'many people find obscurity in the sense and expression of these reflections', and commented that 'you must take the time to penetrate the sense and power of the words; your mind must traverse the full range of their significance, before it can come to rest and appraise them'. Many of the maxims leave unsaid something that must be added before the sense can be grasped. To understand 'Our self-love is sure to prevent the person who flatters us from ever being the one who flatters us most' (1: 157), we must answer the question 'Who is the one who flatters us most?'; to appreciate the full significance of 'The reason why lovers are never bored with each other's company is because they are always talking about themselves' (V: 312), we must answer the question 'Why is it never boring to talk about oneself?' These are simple gaps, which the mind quickly fills; in other cases—as with 'The end of good is an evil thing; the end of evil is a good thing' (L 210), which so puzzled Madame de Sablé—the gaps are more extensive and could conceivably be filled in several different ways, so that the ultimate sense of the maxim is more elusive. Sometimes the very lucidity of the vocabulary and clarity of the syntax may act as snares, seducing us into a false belief that the point of a given maxim must be perfectly simple and straightforward.

In this respect La Rochefoucauld's maxims stand in the tradition of many ancient proverbs, which were designed partly to tease the mind, or even to be incomprehensible to the unenlightened. 'Wise people hide their wisdom' (Proverbs 10: 14). 'A scoffer seeks wisdom and does not find it; knowledge is easy to a sensible man' (Proverbs 14: 6). 'To you', Jesus told his disciples, 'it is given to know the

mystery of the kingdom of God; but to those who are outside, all
things are done in parables, in order that, seeing, they may see and
not perceive, and hearing, they may hear and not understand' (Mark
4: 11–12). And Blake wrote to John Trusler, in a letter dated 23
August 1799, 'the wisest of the ancients considered what is not too
explicit as the fittest for instruction, because it rouses the faculties to
act'.

The first edition's 'Note to the Reader' characterizes the work as
'a portrait of man's heart'. Its characteristic technique is description,
not exhortation: usually it states what is ('Self-love is the greatest
flatterer of all'; v: 2), very rarely what should be ('To know things
well, we must know the details . . .'; v: 106). Here again La Rochefoucauld's method is in line with certain familiar strands of
seventeenth-century thought: the purpose of at least one art, says
Hamlet, is 'to hold, as 'twere, the mirror up to nature; to show virtue
her own feature, scorn her own image, and the very age and body of
the time his form and pressure'. Of course an explicit description
often carries an implicit exhortation; when scorn is shown her own
image, it is usually with some hope of changing her. But in La
Rochefoucauld such hopes tend to be particularly guarded; even his
few overt exhortations tend to carry some acknowledgement that
they will not fully cure the problem (v: 106 continues 'and as they
are almost infinite, our knowledge is always superficial and
imperfect').

The scope of the phrase 'portrait of man's heart' is ambiguous:
how much of the human race does the term 'man' encompass? In La
Rochefoucauld's usage it sometimes clearly includes women, sometimes clearly excludes them, and sometimes hovers indefinitely
between those two meanings; a statement (e.g. 'All these qualities are
found in man'; RD 11) may seem applicable to all humanity, yet its
discussion may be framed in exclusively or predominantly masculine
terms. In the same way, his remarks about 'man' or 'men' tend to
address themselves mainly or solely to adults, members of the upper
classes, inhabitants of France, and so on, without necessarily exclud-
ing other members of the human race. Indeed the scope of a statement may alter when the text is revised. A maxim aimed in manuscript primarily at 'the French' addresses itself simply to 'men' in
the final edition (v: 14); a maxim initially concerned with 'all men'
subsequently has more limited reference (1: 174). La Roche-

foucauld's uses of *on* ('one'), *nous* ('we'), and *vous* ('you') contain similar ambiguities; sometimes, indeed, he glides from one to another in the course of a single maxim, as if they were interchangeable. A remark may be qualified with 'often', 'usually', 'almost always', 'perhaps', or 'it seems'. Here too its scope may change when it is revised: 'was' becomes 'may merely have been' (v: 7), 'always' becomes 'almost always' (v: 10), 'is' becomes 'is often merely' (v: 15), and so on. (As these examples show, most of La Rochefoucauld's revisions narrow the frame of reference, though a few expand it.) In the final state of his preliminary address 'To the Reader' he says explicitly that his maxims do not apply to 'those people whom God preserves from such things by special grace'—but the nature and extent of that 'grace' were much debated in the seventeenth century, as every reader of Pascal's *Provinciales* (1656–7) will know. All these techniques ambiguously and ironically leave room for each individual reader to dissociate himself or herself from the work's judgements. The strategy is made explicit in the 1664 'Note to the Reader': 'The reader's best policy is to start with the premiss that none of these maxims is directed specifically at him, and that he is the sole exception to them, even though they seem to be generally applicable. After that, I guarantee that he will be the first to subscribe to them.'

Yet the limiting and qualifying phrases need not be merely ironic. Few statements are universally true of such diverse and intricate creatures as human beings; to most generalizations about them, there will be some exceptions. A book filled with unqualified universal assertions is likely to be less rich, less complex, less true than one that acknowledges the existence of possible alternatives. Thus the hinted reservations and loopholes, the *oftens* and *usuallys* and *almost alls*, may function to deepen and strengthen La Rochefoucauld's text, making it broader and more all-embracing. Perhaps a given maxim *is* 'almost always' true; perhaps you *are* one of the very few exceptions to it. The notion is comforting, but that does not necessarily make it wrong. So the book incessantly teases your mind, acknowledging that you could just possibly be better than it says, but declaring that you will probably think yourself better even if (like almost all of us) you are not.

Like all writers, La Rochefoucauld has his favourite terms and favourite themes. The October 1664 edition assigns special promin-

ence to *amour-propre* ('self-love'): that is the subject of the edition's
massive opening maxim (1: 1), and it is also given particular attention
in the preliminary 'Note to the Reader'. Self-love has often been seen
as a connecting thread, either in the work as a whole (Voltaire's *Le
Siècle de Louis XIV* (1751) declares that La Rochefoucauld's book
contains only one theme, 'that self-love is the motive behind everything'—this single idea being presented in 'many varied forms'), or
in certain parts of it (in his *Journal* for 30 September 1921, André
Gide distinguishes between 'the maxims dealing with self-love' and
'those that are not associated with any theory or thesis'). Self-love
had been an important concept in Western philosophical and moralistic writing ever since the days of ancient Greece; the theme can be
pursued through Plato, Cicero, Augustine, Gregory the Great, Montaigne, Erasmus, and post-Renaissance writers of many different
schools (Neoplatonic, Jansenist, devotional . . .). Still, we must not
necessarily assume that La Rochefoucauld uses the word in the same
sense as his predecessors or contemporaries (some of the latter
objected that he was attaching an idiosyncratic meaning to it). He
describes self-love as 'love of oneself, and of all things for the sake of
oneself' (1: 1). In the same maxim he sees it as all-pervasive ('It exists
at every stage of life and in every walk of life. It lives everywhere; it
lives off everything—or nothing; it adapts to anything—or the loss
of anything'), endlessly variable, and fundamentally beyond human
comprehension ('No one can fathom the depth of its chasms, or
penetrate their darkness'; compare V: 3). It cannot be defeated: it 'is
cleverer than the cleverest man in the world' (V: 4). Other maxims
trace its relationship to kindness (V: 236), loyalty (V: 247), self-
interest (L 270), love (V: 262), jealousy (V: 324), and the various
passions (PV158: 1). Like Pascal, La Rochefoucauld presents it as
ultimately a punishment imposed on the human race because of
sin—a punishment from which there is no escape: 'To punish man
for original sin, God has allowed him to make a god of his self-love,
so that it may torment him in every deed he ever does' (L 256). At
best, it can merely be kept in check. RD 10 speaks of 'some people'
whose 'self-love and temperament are not overriding their innate
enlightenment. All their faculties act in concert and have the same
tone. This harmony makes them judge things soundly.' The passage
goes on to observe that such people are 'few'.

Nevertheless, other statements suggest that other concepts may be

almost equally central. The 1666–78 address 'To the Reader' draws special attention to the term *intérêt* ('interest' or 'self-interest'), declaring that La Rochefoucauld 'most often' uses it to mean 'an interest in honour or glory'. 'Men are born with self-interest' (RD 17); it, no less than self-love, is multifarious and many-sided (V: 39); it too pervades much of human behaviour: 'self-interest is the sole cause of friendship' (V: 85); 'we never praise anyone without some motive of self-interest' (V: 144). Yet two late maxims (V: 390, 486) acknowledge the existence of people who are 'without self-interest', and an incidental remark in RD 5 also suggests that it is possible to act without self-interest.

In La Rochefoucauld's indexes, however, neither *amour-propre* nor *intérêt* takes pride of place. The topics indexed most frequently are *vices* ('vices'; eighteen index entries in 1665, ten in 1678) and *défauts* ('faults'; subsumed under *vices* in 1665, eighteen entries in 1678), *amour* ('love'; sixteen entries in 1665, twenty-six in 1678), and *amitié* ('friendship'; seven entries in 1665, twenty in 1678). The first of these subjects is further given prominence by the book's epigraph ('Our virtues are, most often, only vices in disguise'); the last two may remind us not to define La Rochefoucauld's interests too narrowly. Taken in isolation, such terms as 'a portrait of the human heart', 'self-love', and 'self-interest' might suggest a predominantly introspective, solitary attitude. However, the large numbers of index entries under 'love' and 'friendship' show us that the maxims are extensively concerned with interpersonal relations—not only love and friendship, but also (compare RD 2) social contact in general. Often, when the book does discuss self-love and self-interest, it is contemplating not their effect on the isolated human soul, but their effect on interactions between human beings.

The *Miscellaneous Reflections* are more diverse in form and content. In form some of them are not very different from the longer maxims, but others are multi-paragraph prose meditations up to several thousand words long, recalling the essays of Seneca or Montaigne. In style they are less consistently elegant than the *Maxims*, with some notable clumsinesses of wording and even lapses of syntax. Perhaps this is simply because La Rochefoucauld had not yet polished them, or because he had no intention of publishing them; but it may also be that he was less at home with the longer, less concise format (even within the *Maxims*, the longer pieces tend to be

less stylistically poised than the very short ones). Their outlook is consistent with that of the *Maxims* wherever the two can be compared, but they deal with many matters that the published book avoids; and even when they cover similar terrain (as with RD 2, 'Social Contact', and RD 4, 'Conversation'), they are more willing to tell us how people should behave, and not only how people do behave.

Critical Reception

La Rochefoucauld's maxims attracted immediate attention and provoked considerable difference of critical opinion, not only in France, but throughout Europe. Because of their author's social status, they were pondered by people of exceptional influence and unusually exalted rank. The first edition was read by Louis XIV's mistress Madame de Maintenon, the third by Queen Christina of Sweden; each was impressed by what she read, and each was in a position to influence public opinion and critical taste. The work exerted a profound, and widespread, effect on the French literature of its age—in verse as well as prose. Writers as distinguished as La Bruyère and La Fontaine (who lavished exceptionally high praise on La Rochefoucauld and dedicated two of his *Fables* to him) openly acknowledged their debt to it.

La Rochefoucauld's influence can also be seen in the work of many subsequent philosophers and moralists: Voltaire and Nietzsche are particularly obvious examples. Yet it can be identified in some more surprising quarters. Scholars have traced the impact of La Rochefoucauld on the thinking of Marcel Proust and Charles de Gaulle. Even in Balzac there are sentences that could scarcely have been written but for the *Maxims*: 'We are accustomed to judge others by our own standard; and if we absolve them of our faults indulgently enough, we condemn them severely for lacking our merits,' in *Le Médecin de campagne* (1833), for instance. Labiche's ever-popular comedy *Le Voyage de Monsieur Perrichon* (1860) is essentially a witty extension of the observation that men 'hate those to whom they are obliged' (V: 14). Conan Doyle knew the maxims well enough to quote V: 451 (in French, and from memory—the citation is slightly inexact) in *The Sign of (the) Four* (1890); they are one of the models from which he drew the dry, incisive sayings of Sherlock Holmes

('Singularity is almost invariably a clue'; 'The lowest and vilest alleys of London do not present a more dreadful record of sin than does the smiling and beautiful countryside').

Indirectly, the work's heritage has spread even further. Blake may never have read La Rochefoucauld, but he certainly studied La Rochefoucauld's eighteenth-century followers, whose influence can be discerned in much of *The Marriage of Heaven and Hell* (1790–3) and 'Auguries of Innocence' ('It is easier to forgive an enemy than to forgive a friend')—and, still further afield, in the writings of Blake's admirer George Bernard Shaw, especially the 'Revolutionist's Handbook' appended to *Man and Superman* (1901). Nor should we overlook a more diffuse influence on popular culture in general. In the Hollywood cinema, for instance, La Rochefoucauld—like Confucius—became a recognized dispenser of proverbial wisdom of any and every kind. 'As Rochefoucauld 'as said, "When a man 'as something on 'is mind, 'e wants nothing in 'is stomach," ' remarks a character in Norman Tokar's *Big Red* (1962).

This is not the place for a detailed survey of critical responses to La Rochefoucauld's work; we shall simply mention a few general trends.

According to one school of interpretation, the book consists of heterogeneous detached observations, without any consistency of viewpoint. Alexandre Vinet, in his *Essais de philosophie morale* (1837), wrote that La Rochefoucauld 'did not connect the components of his work according to any general guiding principle; no scientific stance is apparent in this product of a courtier; as befits such a man, it consists of little flashes of thought, sententiae that are ingenious and sometimes profound, but brief and disconnected. . . . There is no guiding principle in his work because there was none in his life.' More recently, in 'La Rochefoucauld et les morales substitutives' (*Nouvelle Revue française*, 28 (1966), 16–33, 211–29), Jean Starobinski argued that the book is fundamentally inconsistent and self-contradictory, and not only has no centre but 'cannot have any centre': the maxims' 'deliberate disorder, their aristocratic refusal to organize themselves into a coherent system, form an apt transcription of the inner discontinuity of man'.

Such accounts have the advantage of drawing attention to the way La Rochefoucauld presents his views: as a series of detached reflections, a 'heap of diverse thoughts' (his own description, in a letter to

Thomas Esprit, 6 February 1664) the truth and validity of which are to be weighed individually, without reference to any previously established line of argument or any system of philosophy—whether or not such a system may originally have generated them. And in practice this is how most of La Rochefoucauld's correspondents and other contemporary readers (such as Queen Christina) responded to them, accepting one maxim and rejecting another, without feeling that the book's items were logically interdependent and must stand or fall together. The 1664 'Note to the Reader' gave haste as the main reason for the lack of order, but in subsequent editions this argument was abandoned, and, far from seeking a more orderly presentation, La Rochefoucauld strove to heighten the appearance of discontinuity: maxims were progressively abridged, removing supportive arguments and leaving them more terse, more naked and exposed; sequences of maxims on similar topics were removed or disrupted. Perhaps his most startling change was the insertion of the maxim on humility (V: 358), which produces a sudden unprepared dissonance like the unexpected intrusion of a visitor from some alien universe. 'I was very surprised to find humility there,' Madame de Rohan wrote to La Rochefoucauld in a letter of the early 1670s. 'I confess I was so little expecting it that, although I had been thoroughly familiar with [this maxim] for a long time, I had all the trouble in the world recognizing it in the midst of everything that precedes and follows it.'

Nevertheless, if we focus too exclusively on the heterogeneity of La Rochefoucauld's work, we may underestimate its complexity (see, for instance, E. D. James, 'Scepticism and Positive Values in La Rochefoucauld', *French Studies*, 23 (1969), 349–61). Many would question whether it is even possible for an author to write in a way that lacks 'any' centre and obliterates 'all' internal consistency (to use Starobinski's terms). And in La Rochefoucauld's particular case, heterogeneity is counterbalanced by the employment of a narrow repertoire of stylistic devices, the recurrent use of favourite words and phrases, and the pervasive sense of a highly individual (and highly coherent) speaking voice. Indeed the imposition of maxim form throughout is itself a homogenizing device: it ensures that the book always looks at its subject from a particular angle, or at least a particular range of angles. Thus, if it is valuable to recognize that there is a heterogeneity in La Rochefoucauld's work, it is also valuable to recognize that there is a certain consistency.

Two contrasting schools of thought have attempted to define the nature of that consistency.

According to one, the work expresses an Augustinian or Jansenist view of human nature. In his later years Augustine (354–430) argued that, ever since the original sin of Adam and Eve, all human beings have been born totally depraved, unable to perform any true good deed by their own efforts, though God graciously chooses to save some (a small minority) from this fate—as a free gift, not in response to any merit of their own. Cornelius Jansen's provocative study of Augustine's teachings, *Augustinismus* (1640), was widely read in seventeenth-century France, and those who were supposed to be influenced by it became known as 'Jansenists'; both Madame de Sablé and Jacques Esprit had close ties with the leading Jansenist community at Port-Royal. (Even at Port-Royal, however, beliefs differed considerably; Madame de Sablé herself radically disagreed with the classic Augustinian position summarized above. 'Jansenism' was in some respects a French analogue of the seventeenth-century English term 'Puritanism', and was as variously applied.)

Some of La Rochefoucauld's first readers already construed his maxims in a Jansenist sense. An unknown correspondent wrote to Madame de Schomberg in 1663 that the book was 'a very powerful and ingenious satire on the corruption of nature by original sin . . . and on the malignity of the human spirit, which corrupts everything when it acts by itself without the Spirit of God. . . . It is a school of Christian humility, where we can see the faults of what people so inappropriately call virtues; it is a perfectly fair commentary on the text of Saint Augustine, who says that all the unbelievers' virtues are vices.' That, or something like it, is probably the majority opinion among present-day French La Rochefoucauld scholars, especially in the wake of Jean Lafond's magisterial book *La Rochefoucauld: Augustinisme et littérature* (Paris, 1977), though within this camp there are significant points of disagreement: Laurence Plazenet, for instance, sees La Rochefoucauld as a much more thoroughgoing Augustinian than does Lafond.

According to the other school, the work expresses a sceptical, *libertin* ('freethinking'—though this English word slightly postdates La Rochefoucauld's time) view of human nature. *Libertinisme* is even harder to define than Jansenism (both labels were devised originally by the movements' opponents). Françoise Charles-Daubert, in *Les*

Libertins érudits en France au XVIIe siècle (Paris, 1998), 113–14, finds among the *libertin* writers a 'decisive break with the theological conception of man, the world, and God', characterized by an intellectual elitism (contempt for the unthinking multitude), an independent morality (typically drawn from nature rather than from religious tradition), and an anti-theological critical stance. Not all scholars would agree with all parts of this summary, but it may perhaps provide a rough framework within which such writers as Gassendi, Bayle, Cyrano de Bergerac, Tristan l'Hermite, and Fontenelle may be viewed.

If some of La Rochefoucauld's 1663 readers saw him as a Jansenist, others construed his work as a contribution to the *libertin* movement: one of Madame de Sablé's correspondents told her that the book 'might be good in good hands, such as yours, which are able to draw good from evil itself', but 'that in the hands of freethinkers (*personnes libertines*) or people inclined to new opinions, this book could confirm them in their error, and make them believe that there is no virtue at all, and that it is folly to claim to become virtuous'. Nowadays *libertin* interpretations of La Rochefoucauld seem to be dominant in the English-speaking world, where, as Derek A. Watts says in *La Rochefoucauld: Maximes et Réflexions diverses* (Glasgow, 1993), 41, 'the idea of the *Maximes* as a "school of Christian humility" . . . no longer carries a great weight of conviction. Accusations of *libertinage*, from mild indifference to full-blown atheism, have rained down on La Rochefoucauld's head in recent times.'

Perhaps it is not necessary to choose between these two interpretations; they have more in common than may be apparent. Jansenists and freethinkers shared a common cultural heritage. Certainly La Rochefoucauld alludes to God, Providence, and the like, but there is nothing uniquely Augustinian about such allusions: most *libertins* also maintained that, in some sense or other, they believed in God, accepted the authority of Scriptures, and so on—as Hélène Ostrowiecki reminds us in 'La Bible des libertins' (*XVIIe siècle*, 194 (1997), 43–55). (Her conclusion, 'What the *libertins* set out to unmask was the usurpation of the divine message by human authority,' might almost as truly be said of the Jansenists.) Conversely La Rochefoucauld's reticence about theological matters is not distinctively *libertin*: disapproval of the public flaunting of religion can be traced back through Augustine to the Scriptures—and was also voiced by

many non-partisan (or not overtly partisan) seventeenth-century French writers, for instance by Molière in *Tartuffe* 1: 5. If there is anything distinctive or unusual in La Rochefoucauld's behaviour on this subject—anything that cannot simply be ascribed to his broad cultural heritage—it is not partisan but individual, even idiosyncratic. Many seventeenth-century writers, religious and irreligious alike, have been suspected of making stronger professions of faith in public than they entertained in private. La Rochefoucauld acted in exactly the opposite way. His private writings of every phase from the 1650s to the end of his life contain religious statements; but, for whatever reason, in nearly all cases he either quickly withdrew them from print or never published them. It is hard to think of a close parallel to this behaviour in any writer from La Rochefoucauld's time and place. No doubt his outlook was coloured by Jansenists, *libertins*, and other people with whom he came in contact; but we must not forget its sheer individuality.

Advocates of an Augustinian La Rochefoucauld have cited strikingly close parallels to many of his maxims in the writings of seventeenth-century and earlier Augustinians; advocates of a *libertin* La Rochefoucauld have cited comparable parallels in the writings of *libertins*. But in most cases there is nothing uniquely Augustinian or uniquely *libertin* about the alleged parallel; it has its roots not only in one or other of those camps, but more generally in the Western cultural heritage—the ultimate source, most often, being the Hebrew or Greek Scriptures. To demonstrate that La Rochefoucauld was distinctively Augustinian, or distinctively *libertin*, we would need to cite his views on some point where the two parties disagreed—and this we cannot do. Where there are few theological statements of any kind, there are likely to be even fewer partisan ones, and La Rochefoucauld never touches on the points where a typical Augustinian and a typical *libertin* would differ from each other—or from Scripture. Only two technical theological terms appear in his works, 'original sin' (L 256) and 'special grace' ('To the Reader'); both were common currency in the seventeenth century and were used by writers of diverse persuasions (nor would a non-theologian necessarily use them in their technical senses).

No one will deny that the book's sources can be traced back very far—as far as the Hebrew Proverbs and the book of Job. Yet it conspicuously refuses to align itself with any particular offshoot of

Introduction

those fundamental sources. Perhaps that is one of the features in which it differs most strikingly from the majority of its contemporaries, such as Pascal's *Pensées* and Puget de La Serre's *L'Esprit de Sénèque*.

NOTE ON THE TEXT AND TRANSLATION

Five authorized editions of La Rochefoucauld's *Maxims* appeared in his lifetime. These are conventionally designated by Roman numerals, as follows:

I   *Réflexions ou Sentences et Maximes morales* (Paris: Claude Barbin, 1664; postdated 1665 on its title page). Some of its maxims exist in two states (designated ¹ and ²), as La Rochefoucauld made textual alterations while the work was passing through the press.

II   *Réflexions ou Sentences et Maximes morales* (Paris: Claude Barbin, 1666).

III *Réflexions ou Sentences et Maximes morales* (Paris: Claude Barbin, 1671).

IV   *Réflexions ou Sentences et Maximes morales* (Paris: Claude Barbin, 1674; postdated 1675 on its title page).

V   *Réflexions ou Sentences et Maximes morales* (Paris: Claude Barbin, 1678). Less than a fortnight later 107 of its maxims were issued separately by the same publisher, in a booklet entitled *Nouvelles Réflexions ou Sentences et Maximes morales*; this corrects a couple of errors in the main volume, and is therefore used as our copytext in cases where the two editions differ.

Pages 2–143 of the present book reprint the complete contents of v (a preliminary address to the reader, an unnumbered epigraph, 504 numbered maxims, and a thematic index). To avoid ambiguity, maxims from this edition are cited with a prefixed v, from V: 1 to V: 504. In the French texts, the punctuation and capitalization of the 1678 edition have been preserved for the first time since the seventeenth century. Recent scholarship has attached increasing importance to such details; they were probably determined by the publisher and compositors rather than by La Rochefoucauld himself, but so diligent a reviser would no doubt have altered anything that did not meet with his approval. Spelling has been modernized where appropriate.

At the end of each English translation, a parenthesis in square

brackets lists the editions in which this particular maxim appeared. '[III–V]', for example, indicates that the maxim was first published in III and was reprinted in IV and V.

Pages 144–175 — 'Maxims Finally Withdrawn by La Rochefoucauld' — contain maxims that had been published in one or more of the four earlier editions (I–IV) but were not reprinted in V. These are numbered according to the last edition in which they appeared. Thus 'I: 259²' is the second state of maxim 259 in La Rochefoucauld's first authorized edition. The punctuation and capitalization of the copytexts have been preserved, and a parenthesis at the end of each English translation lists the editions that contained the maxim in question.

Pages 176–191 — 'Maxims Never Published by La Rochefoucauld' — contain maxims absent from I–V, but preserved in the following sources:

L   A partly autograph manuscript (compiled between about 1659 and 1663) formerly at the Château de Liancourt.

PV124   Portefeuilles Vallant, tome 2, folios 124–5, a small manuscript collection of maxims sent by La Rochefoucauld to Jacques Esprit, probably in 1660.

SL   Bibliothèque Nationale Smith-Lesouëf ms 90, a manuscript copy dated 1663 (several similar copies also survive).

PV158   Portefeuilles Vallant, tome 2, folio 158, a small manuscript collection of maxims sent by La Rochefoucauld to Madame de Sablé in 1667.

VIs   A collection of fifty maxims compiled between 1671 and 1674, and published posthumously as a supplement to the sixth edition, *Réflexions ou Sentences morales* (Paris: Claude Barbin, 1693).

Again, these are numbered according to their source. Thus 'VIs : 2' is maxim 2 in the 1693 supplement. Ten of these maxims (L 113, L 121, L 122, L 210, L 212, PV124: 4, PV158: 1, PV158: 3, PV158: 4, and VIs : 39) have been preserved in La Rochefoucauld's own handwriting: in those cases the original punctuation (or absence of punctuation) has been retained. The other maxims in this section were diversely and heterogeneously punctuated by their early copyists, and there is no reason to believe that La Rochefoucauld authorized

the results; in those cases, therefore, punctuation has been silently standardized or emended where appropriate.

Most editions of La Rochefoucauld contain a section of withdrawn and unpublished maxims, but they disagree markedly as to which items should be included, and they number them in bewilderingly different ways. VIS : 21, presented as a distinct maxim by Gilbert, is regarded by Truchet and Lafond as a mere variant of V: 368; L 207, presented as distinct by Truchet, is treated by Gilbert and Lafond as a variant of V: 504; L 249, presented as distinct by Lafond, is treated by Gilbert and Truchet as a variant of V: 243; I: 101, regarded by all three of those editors as a variant of V: 88, is printed as a distinct maxim by Aimé-Martin and Duplessis. Our own policy has been simple. We have included every item that has been reckoned as a separate maxim by any editor at any time during the past two centuries. A table at the back of the volume (pages 324–7) provides a concordance to the different editors' numbering systems. The reader will therefore be able to find quickly the text and translation of any item that has been cited in any reference work whatsoever—regardless of the specific edition on which that reference work was based.

The following abbreviations are used for the works presented on pages 192–275:

RD   *Réflexions diverses* (*Miscellaneous Reflections*), numbered RD 1 to RD 19.

RDA   Four short prose pieces annexed to the *Réflexions diverses* in one manuscript (325bis); they are numbered RDA 1 to RDA 4.

These works were never published by La Rochefoucauld and survive only in imperfect later copies, which are designated as follows:

A(163) A seventeenth-century manuscript of RD 1–19, now lost, but transcribed partly in *Œuvres inédites de La Rochefoucauld*, ed. Édouard de Barthélemy (Paris: Hachette, 1863), and fully in *Œuvres de La Rochefoucauld*, tome 1, ed. D. L. Gilbert (Paris: Hachette, 1868). Barthélemy's transcript is denoted A(163)^{B}, and Gilbert's A(163)^{G}; A(163)^{BG} denotes the agreement of the two. In three places the manuscript contained corrections reportedly in La Rochefoucauld's own hand; [1] denotes the uncorrected state, [2] the corrected.

325bis A seventeenth-century manuscript of RD 1–5, 7–11, 13–19, and RDA 1–4; it too is now lost, but its variant readings were fully recorded in *Œuvres de La Rochefoucauld*, Appendice du tome 1, ed. Adolphe Regnier (Paris: Hachette, 1883).

Ch   The Morgand, Hanotaux, or Chapet manuscript, an eighteenth-century copy of RD 1–19.

Gr   RD 2–5, 10, 13, and 16, as printed in *Recueil de pièces d'histoire et de littérature*, tome 1, ed. François Granet (Paris: Chaubert, 1731).

Br   RD 2–5, 10, 13, and 16, as printed in *Réflexions ou Sentences et Maximes morales de M. le duc de la Rochefoucauld*, ed. Gabriel Brotier (Paris: J.-G. Mérigot, 1789).

All currently available French editions of the *Réflexions diverses* were prepared forty or more years ago, and do not reflect the findings of recent scholarship. Some (including the Pléiade editions) simply reprint A(163)^G; others (including Lafond and Plazenet) reproduce Jacques Truchet's 1967 reconstruction of the text, based mainly on 325bis. Truchet recognized that 325*bis* represented a later state of the text than A(163), and believed that it was prepared by La Rochefoucauld himself. (The most radical changes were that 325bis omitted RD 6 and 12, and transposed RD 17 to the very end of the series; all three of those alterations had been recommended by an unknown hand—or hands—in the margin of A(163).) However, subsequent research has established that the revisions need not have been made under the author's supervision or even within his lifetime; during the first century after La Rochefoucauld's death there were undoubtedly various attempts to improve the *Réflexions diverses*, principally by reworking phraseology and deleting sections that did not appeal to the revisers. Therefore, the present volume contains a new reconstruction of the text, using A(163)^G as copytext, but correcting it from the other copies where appropriate. For RDA 1–4, which were not included in A(163), the text is based on 325bis. We have preserved the punctuation and capitalization of our copytexts, even though it cannot reflect La Rochefoucauld's own practice in every respect.

Because both Gilbert's and Barthélemy's transcripts of the lost manuscript A(163) were inaccurate, there are places where the text of the *Réflexions diverses* cannot be reconstructed with certainty. Never-

theless, more can perhaps be achieved than previous editors have supposed. To take one small example, in the second-last sentence of RD 1 all currently available French texts follow Gilbert's transcript of A(163), reading *bien qu'il ait infiniment plus*. However, Barthélemy's transcript of the same manuscript reads *bien qu'il y ait infiniment plus*—and this is clearly what the manuscript had, because it is the reading found in both the other textual witnesses to the passage (325bis and Ch), neither of which could have been seen by Barthélemy.

Unfortunately, Truchet's textual apparatus was not as complete as his note on the text suggests (in particular, he selectively under-reported errors of 325bis). Therefore, the Explanatory Notes to the present volume contain a new textual apparatus to RD 1–19, recording the variants of all the above sources at all points where A(163)^{G} and 325bis differ substantively, and at all points where our reconstruction differs substantively from other editions now in print.

Throughout the present volume, our translations aim to imitate the syntax and word-order of the original wherever this can be done without falsifying or obscuring the sense. Each French term is usually rendered by a single English term, though not always. The vocabularies of the two languages do not match precisely; moreover, even the most punctilious of professional philosophers have not been absolutely consistent in their use of words, and we must expect La Rochefoucauld's practice to be at least equally flexible.

The term *honnête* poses particular problems for a translator. In the seventeenth century, as the separate entries in La Rochefoucauld's Index implied, it had one range of meanings when applied to women, and another range of meanings when applied to men. In relation to women it referred principally, though not exclusively, to sexual morality; in relation to men it implied both a social and a moral standing, the latter being concerned more with personal integrity in general than with sexuality in particular. A woman could not possibly be an *honnête femme* without being chaste, but even a very unchaste man—Louis XIV, for instance—could be an *honnête homme*. ('Honest' in seventeenth-century English carried some of the same ambiguities. When Othello wonders whether Desdemona is 'honest' he is concerned primarily—if not solely—with her chastity; when he describes Iago as 'honest' he is not at all considering

whether the man is chaste.) In modern English, very few terms have both the moral and the social resonances of *honnête homme*; we have chosen the rendering 'man of honor', 'honorable man', using the *-or* spelling to distinguish it from *honneur*, which we always render 'honour' with a *u*. (Many seventeenth-century French writers, especially poets, played on the verbal similarity between *honneur* and *honnête*, as if it reflected a kinship in sense.) For *honnête femme* we have chosen the translation 'virtuous woman', which nowadays tends to be used primarily of sexual virtue without being absolutely restricted to that.

We have striven to imitate the distinctive stylistic features of La Rochefoucauld's prose—to the very limited extent that this can be done in modern English. La Rochefoucauld sometimes tended to employ a word in ways that surprised his contemporaries a little, and seemed out of keeping with its accepted meaning. The 1678 preliminary note acknowledged that the book did not generally use the term *intérêt* in its most familiar sense; some of the work's first readers made similar comments about various other words—including some of the most important ones (*amour-propre* and *maxime* itself were among them). Such readers were slightly unsettled by the book's use of language: it gave them a little series of jolts, confronting them now and then with words used in marginally unidiomatic ways, or not quite in any accustomed sense. The present translation occasionally aims to reproduce this characteristic, and significant, trait in modern English—though of course it cannot always 'stretch' the usage of exactly the same words as La Rochefoucauld does. We have also tried to imitate in English some of the important stylistic variations within La Rochefoucauld's output, such as the difference between the crisp, epigrammatic manner of the short maxims and the slightly stiff, ungainly phraseology of the more expansive essays.

The translations (unlike the facing French texts) nearly always use modern punctuation and capitalization; very occasionally, however, we have allowed ourselves a seventeenth-century comma, colon, or capital letter, at points where this might help to clarify the sense.

Explanatory Notes will be found at the back of the volume. In the few cases where a note does not refer to the whole of a maxim or reflection, the section discussed is identified by an asterisk in the English translation.

   Judith Luna of Oxford University Press and the Press's anony-
mous pre-publication readers provided valuable assistance with the
preparation of this volume. To Dr and Mrs H. J. Blackmore and Drs
Warner and Erica Quarles de Quarles we have long and extensive
debts of many kinds, which no acknowledgement could adequately
summarize.

SELECT BIBLIOGRAPHY

Editions

La Rochefoucauld, François de, *Œuvres de La Rochefoucauld*, ed. D. L. Gilbert, Jules Gourdault, and Adolphe Régnier (Paris, 1868–83).

—— *Maximes, suivi des Réflections diverses*, ed. Jacques Truchet (Paris, 1967; 3rd edn., 1983).

—— *Maximes et Réflections diverses; Maximes de Madame de Sablé*, ed. Jean Lafond (Paris, 1976).

—— *Maximes, Réflections diverses, Portraits, Mémoires*, ed. Jacques Truchet, Marc Escola, and Alain Brown (Paris, 2001).

—— *Réflections ou Sentences et Maximes morales et Réflections diverses*, ed. Laurence Plazenet (Paris, 2002).

Biographical Studies

Bishop, Morris, *The Life and Adventures of La Rochefoucauld* (Ithaca, NY, 1951).

Fasquelle, Solange, *Les La Rochefoucauld, une famille dans l'histoire de France* (Paris, 1992).

Magne, Émile, *Le Vrai Visage de La Rochefoucauld* (Paris, 1923).

Critical Studies

Baker, Susan Read, *Collaboration et originalité chez La Rochefoucauld* (Gainesville, Fla., 1981).

Bénichou, Paul, *Morales du grand siècle* (Paris, 1948).

Campion, Pierre, *Lectures de La Rochefoucauld* (Rennes, 1998).

Clark, Henry C., *La Rochefoucauld and the Language of Unmasking in Seventeenth-Century France* (Geneva, 1994).

Culpin, D. J., *La Rochefoucauld: Maxims* (London, 1996).

Hippeau, Louis, *Essai sur la morale de La Rochefoucauld* (Paris, 1967).

Hodgson, Richard G., *Falsehood Disguised: Unmasking the Truth in La Rochefoucauld* (West Lafayette, Ind., 1995).

Horowitz, L. K., *Love and Language: A Study of the Classical French Moralist Writers* (Columbus, Ohio, 1977).

Lafond, Jean, *La Rochefoucauld: Augustinisme et littérature* (2nd edn., Paris, 1986).

—— *La Rochefoucauld: L'Homme et son image* (Paris, 1998).

Lewis, Philip E., *La Rochefoucauld: The Art of Abstraction* (Ithaca, NY, 1977).

Moore, W. G., *La Rochefoucauld: His Mind and Art* (Oxford, 1969).

Mourgues, Odette de, *Two French Moralists: La Rochefoucauld and La Bruyère* (Cambridge, 1978).

Parmentier, Bérengère, *Le Siècle des moralistes* (Paris, 2000).

Thweatt, Vivienne, *La Rochefoucauld and the Seventeenth-Century Concept of the Self* (Geneva, 1980).

van Delft, Louis, *Le Moraliste classique: Essai de définition et de typologie* (Geneva, 1982).

Watts, Derek A., *La Rochefoucauld, Maximes et Réflections diverses* (Glasgow, 1993).

Zeller, Mary F., *New Aspects of Style in the Maximes of La Rochefoucauld* (Washington, DC, 1954).

Further Reading in Oxford World's Classics

Lafayette, Madame de, *The Princesse de Clèves*, trans. Terence Cave.

Molière, *Don Juan and Other Plays*, trans. George Gravely and Ian Maclean.

—— *The Misanthrope, Tartuffe, and Other Plays*, trans. Maya Slater.

Pascal, Blaise, *Pensées and Other Writings*, trans. Honor Levi, ed. Anthony Levi.

Racine, Jean, *Britannicus, Phaedra, Athaliah*, trans. C. H. Sisson.

A CHRONOLOGY OF
FRANÇOIS DE LA ROCHEFOUCAULD

1613   15 September: in Paris, birth of François (VI), Prince de Marcil-lac (the future Duc de La Rochefoucauld; hereafter LR), son of François (V) de La Rochefoucauld and his wife, Gabrielle du Plessis-Liancourt.

1628   20 January: marriage to Andrée de Vivonne.

1629   First military campaign, in Italy.

1634   15 June: birth of his first child, François (VII).

1635   Temporarily banished from Paris for uncertain political reasons.

1637   November: imprisoned for a week in the Bastille and then ban-ished to Verneuil for two years, as a result of his participation in a conspiracy led by the Duchesse de Chevreuse.

1642   4 December: death of Richelieu; Mazarin replaces him as chief minister.

1643   14 May: death of Louis XIII; the boy Louis XIV becomes king.

1646–51 Liaison with the Duchesse de Longueville, sister of the Great Condé.

1649–52 During the civil wars of the Fronde, LR sides with Condé, opposing Mazarin and Louis XIV.

1649   January–February: writes the *Apologie de M. le prince de Marcil-lac*, defending his opposition to Mazarin.

        19 February: seriously wounded at Lagny, during the siege of Paris.

1650   8 February: death of his father.

1652   2 July: severely wounded (and temporarily blinded) at the battle of the Faubourg Saint-Antoine.

        21 October: Louis XIV returns to Paris and pardons the rebels.

1653   LR begins to write his *Mémoires*.

1655   April: birth of his last child, Alexandre.

1657–8 LR, Jacques Esprit, and Madame de Sablé begin to compose maxims.

1659	25 January: publication (anonymously) of his self-portrait.
	13 December: publication (anonymously) of I: 1, the first of his maxims to appear in print.
1662	Two pirate editions of his *Mémoires* are issued in Holland; they provoke some public controversy, and LR disowns them.
1663–4	A pirate edition of his maxims is issued in Holland.
1664	27 October: publication of the first authorized edition (I) of LR's *Réflexions ou Sentences et Maximes morales* (hereafter *Maxims*).
1666	1 September: second authorized edition (II) of the *Maxims*.
1669	December: publication of the first part of *Zayde*, a collaborative novel written by Madame de La Fayette, Jean de Segrais, and LR.
1670	19 April: death of LR's wife.
1671	January: publication of the second and final part of *Zayde*.
	After February: third authorized edition (III) of the *Maxims*.
1673–4	Begins to write the *Réflexions diverses* (*Miscellaneous Reflections*).
1674	17 December: fourth authorized edition (IV) of the *Maxims*.
1675	Early June: composes the portrait of Cardinal de Retz (RDA 3).
1677	12 October: publication of Jacques Esprit's *La Fausseté des vertus humaines* (*The Falsehood of Human Virtues*).
1678	16 January: death of Madame de Sablé; her *Maximes* are first published a few months later.
	8 March: publication of Madame de La Fayette's novel *La Princesse de Clèves*.
	6 July: death of Jacques Esprit.
	26 July: fifth and last authorized edition (V) of the *Maxims*.
1680	17 March: death of LR, in Paris.
1693	3 September: sixth edition (VI) of the *Maxims*.
1731	First publication of the *Miscellaneous Reflections* (in part).

COLLECTED MAXIMS
AND OTHER REFLECTIONS

Réflexions ou Sentences et Maximes morales: fifth edition, 1678 (V)

Le Libraire au Lecteur

Cette cinquième édition des Réflexions Morales est augmentée de plus de Cent nouvelles Maximes, et plus exacte que les quatre premières. L'approbation que le public leur a donnée est au-dessus de ce que je puis dire en leur faveur: Et si elles sont telles que je les crois, comme j'ai sujet d'en être persuadé, on ne pourrait leur faire plus de tort que de s'imaginer qu'elles eussent besoin d'apologie. Je me contenterai de vous avertir de deux choses: L'une, que par le mot d'*Intérêt*, on n'entend pas toujours un intérêt de bien, mais le plus souvent un intérêt d'honneur ou de gloire: Et l'autre (qui est comme le fondement de toutes ces Réflexions) que celui qui les a faites n'a considéré les hommes que dans cet état déplorable de la nature corrompue par le péché; et qu'ainsi la manière dont il parle de ce nombre infini de défauts qui se rencontrent dans leurs vertus apparentes, ne regarde point ceux que Dieu en préserve par une grâce particulière.

Pour ce qui est de l'ordre de ces Réflexions, on n'aura pas de peine à juger, que comme elles sont toutes sur des matières différentes, il était difficile d'y en observer: Et bien qu'il y en ait plusieurs sur un même sujet, on n'a pas cru les devoir toujours mettre de suite, de crainte d'ennuyer le Lecteur: mais on les trouvera dans la Table.

Réflexions morales

Nos vertus ne sont le plus souvent, que des vices déguisés.

V: I

Ce que nous prenons pour des vertus, n'est souvent qu'un assemblage de diverses actions et de divers intérêts, que la fortune ou notre industrie savent arranger; et ce n'est pas toujours par valeur et par chasteté que les hommes sont vaillants, et que les femmes sont chastes.

Moral Reflections or Sententiae and Maxims: fifth edition, 1678 (V)

The Publisher to the Reader

This fifth edition of the *Moral Reflections* has been enlarged by more than a hundred maxims, and is more accurate than the four previous ones. The approval that the public has given them surpasses anything I could say in their favour; if they are as I believe them to be (and I have reason to be convinced that they are), one could do them no greater wrong than to imagine that they need a defence.* I shall be content to inform you about two things. The first is that the word *Intérêt* does not always mean interest in the material sense, but most often an interest in honour or glory. And the other—which is, so to speak, the basis of all these reflections—is that the person who wrote them considered men only in the deplorable state of nature corrupted by sin; therefore, his way of referring to the innumerable faults to be found in their apparent virtues, does not apply at all to those people whom God preserves from such things by special grace.*

As for the order of these reflections, you will easily appreciate that it was difficult to arrange them in any order, because all of them deal with different subjects. And even when there are a number on one and the same subject, we did not think we always had to present them in succession, for fear of boring the reader; you can, however, locate them in the Index.* [II–V]

Moral Reflections

Our virtues are, most often, only vices in disguise. [IV–V]

V: 1

What we take for virtues are often merely an assortment of different deeds and interests, which fortune or our own diligence has managed to order; and it is not always valour or chastity that makes men valiant or women chaste. [I–V]

V: 2

L'amour-propre est le plus grand de tous les flatteurs.

V: 3

Quelque découverte que l'on ait faite dans le pays de l'amour-propre, il y reste encore bien des terres inconnues.

V: 4

L'amour-propre est plus habile que le plus habile homme du monde.

V: 5

La durée de nos passions ne dépend pas plus de nous que la durée de notre vie.

V: 6

La passion fait souvent un fou du plus habile homme; et rend souvent les plus sots habiles.

V: 7

Ces grandes et éclatantes actions qui éblouissent les yeux sont représentées par les politiques comme les effets des grands desseins; au lieu que ce sont d'ordinaire les effets de l'humeur et des passions. Ainsi la guerre d'Auguste et d'Antoine qu'on rapporte à l'ambition qu'ils avaient de se rendre maîtres du monde, n'était peut-être qu'un effet de jalousie.

V: 8

Les passions sont les seuls orateurs qui persuadent toujours. Elles sont comme un art de la nature dont les règles sont infaillibles: et l'homme le plus simple qui a de la passion, persuade mieux que le plus éloquent qui n'en a point.

V: 9

Les passions ont une injustice et un propre intérêt qui fait qu'il est

V: 2

Self-love is the greatest flatterer of all. [I–V]

V: 3

Whatever discoveries have been made in the realm of self-love, many unknown lands remain there still. [I–V]

V: 4

Self-love is cleverer than the cleverest man in the world. [I–V]

V: 5

We have no more control over the duration of our passions than over the duration of our lives. [I–V]

V: 6

Passion often turns the cleverest man into a fool, and often makes the worst fools clever. [I–V]

V: 7

Great and brilliant deeds that dazzle the onlooker are depicted by strategists as the result of great plans, whereas they are usually the result of temperament and passion. So the war between Augustus and Antony, which is ascribed to their ambition to gain mastery of the world, may merely have been due to jealousy.* [I–V]

V: 8

Passions are the only orators who always succeed in persuading. They are, so to speak, a natural art, with infallible rules; and the most artless man who is passionate, is more persuasive than the most eloquent man who is not. [I–V]

V: 9

Passions are unjust and self-interested, which makes it dangerous to

dangereux de les suivre, et qu'on s'en doit défier lors même qu'elles paraissent les plus raisonnables.

V: 10

Il y a dans le cœur humain une génération perpétuelle de passions, en sorte que la ruine de l'une est presque toujours l'établissement d'une autre.

V: 11

Les passions en engendrent souvent qui leur sont contraires. L'avarice produit quelquefois la prodigalité, et la prodigalité l'avarice: on est souvent ferme par faiblesse, et audacieux par timidité.

V: 12

Quelque soin que l'on prenne de couvrir ses passions par des apparences de piété et d'honneur, elles paraissent toujours au travers de ces voiles.

V: 13

Notre amour-propre souffre plus impatiemment la condamnation de nos goûts que de nos opinions.

V: 14

Les hommes ne sont pas seulement sujets à perdre le souvenir des bienfaits et des injures: ils haïssent même ceux qui les ont obligés, et cessent de haïr ceux qui leur ont fait des outrages. L'application à récompenser le bien, et à se venger du mal, leur paraît une servitude à laquelle ils ont peine de se soumettre.

V: 15

La clémence des Princes n'est souvent qu'une politique pour gagner l'affection des peuples.

follow them; so we should mistrust them even when they seem most reasonable. [I–V]

V: 10

In the human heart, passions are perpetually being generated— so that the downfall of one is almost always the rise of another. [I–V]

V: 11

Passions often engender their opposites. Avarice sometimes breeds profligacy, and profligacy avarice: we are often strong out of weakness, and bold out of timidity. [I–V]

V: 12

No matter how carefully we hide our passions with appearances of piety and honour, they can always be seen through the veils. [I–V]

V: 13

Our self-love submits less patiently to disapproval of our tastes than of our opinions. [II–V]

V: 14

Not only are men apt to forget favours and insults; they even hate those to whom they are obliged, and stop hating those who have wronged them. Diligence in rewarding a favour and avenging a wrong seems to them a form of bondage, to which they are reluctant to submit. [I–V]

V: 15

The clemency of rulers is often merely a strategy to win their subjects' affections. [I–V]

V : 16

Cette clémence dont on fait une vertu, se pratique tantôt par vanité, quelquefois par paresse, souvent par crainte, et presque toujours par tous les trois ensemble.

V : 17

La modération des personnes heureuses vient du calme que la bonne fortune donne à leur humeur.

V : 18

La modération est une crainte de tomber dans l'envie et dans le mépris que méritent ceux qui s'enivrent de leur bonheur: c'est une vaine ostentation de la force de notre esprit: et enfin la modération des hommes dans leur plus haute élévation, est un désir de paraître plus grands que leur fortune.

V : 19

Nous avons tous assez de force pour supporter les maux d'autrui.

V : 20

La constance des sages n'est que l'art de renfermer leur agitation dans le cœur.

V : 21

Ceux qu'on condamne au supplice, affectent quelquefois une constance et un mépris de la mort, qui n'est en effet que la crainte de l'envisager. De sorte qu'on peut dire que cette constance et ce mépris sont à leur esprit ce que le bandeau est à leurs yeux.

V : 22

La Philosophie triomphe aisément des maux passés et des maux à venir. Mais les maux présents triomphent d'elle.

v: 16

Such clemency, which is treated as a virtue, is prompted sometimes by vanity, sometimes by laziness, often by fear, and nearly always by all three together. [I–V]

v: 17

The moderation of people who are fortunate comes from the calmness that good fortune gives to their temperament. [I–V]

v: 18

Moderation is a fear of falling prey to the envy and disdain that those who are enraptured by their own good fortune deserve: it is a vain and ostentatious display of our mental strength; and finally, the moderation of men at the height of their eminence is a desire to appear greater than their good fortune. [I–V]

v: 19

We all have enough strength to bear the troubles of other people. [I–V]

v: 20

The constancy of the wise is merely the art of keeping their agitation confined within their heart. [I–V]

v: 21

People who are condemned to death sometimes make a pretence of constancy and disdain for death, which is really only a fear of facing it.* It might be said, therefore, that such constancy and disdain do to their minds what the blindfold does to their eyes. [I–V]

v: 22

Philosophy triumphs easily over past and future ills; but present ills triumph over it. [I–V]

V: 23

Peu de gens connaissent la mort: On ne la souffre pas ordinairement par résolution, mais par stupidité et par coutume; et la plupart des hommes meurent, parce qu'on ne peut s'empêcher de mourir.

V: 24

Lorsque les grands hommes se laissent abattre par la longueur de leurs infortunes, ils font voir qu'ils ne les soutenaient que par la force de leur ambition, et non par celle de leur âme; et qu'à une grande vanité près, les Héros sont faits comme les autres hommes.

V: 25

Il faut de plus grandes vertus pour soutenir la bonne fortune que la mauvaise.

V: 26

Le soleil ni la mort ne se peuvent regarder fixement.

V: 27

On fait souvent vanité des passions même les plus criminelles: mais l'envie est une passion timide et honteuse que l'on n'ose jamais avouer.

V: 28

La jalousie est en quelque manière juste et raisonnable, puisqu'elle ne tend qu'à conserver un bien qui nous appartient, ou que nous croyons nous appartenir: au lieu que l'envie est une fureur qui ne peut souffrir le bien des autres.

V: 29

Le mal que nous faisons ne nous attire pas tant de persécution et de haine que nos bonnes qualités.

V: 23

Few people have any knowledge of death. Ordinarily it is endured
not with resolution, but mindlessly and out of habit; most men die
because they cannot avoid dying. [I–V]

V: 24

When great men allow themselves to be disheartened by prolonged
misfortunes,* they demonstrate that they had borne them only by the
strength of their ambition, not by that of their soul; and that, apart
from the greatness of their vanity, heroes are made like other men.
[I–V]

V: 25

It takes greater virtues to bear good fortune than bad. [I–V]

V: 26

Neither the sun nor death can be looked at steadily. [I–V]

V: 27

We often pride ourselves on our passions, even the most criminal
ones; but envy is a timid, shamefaced passion, which we never dare
to acknowledge. [I–V]

V: 28

Jealousy is, in a way, just and reasonable, because its aim is merely to
retain something that belongs to us, or that we think belongs to us;
whereas envy is a frenzy that cannot endure the fact that other
people possess anything. [I–V]

V: 29

Our evil deeds do not bring on us as much persecution and hatred as
our good qualities. [I–V]

v: 30

Nous avons plus de force que de volonté: et c'est souvent pour nous excuser à nous-mêmes, que nous nous imaginons que les choses sont impossibles.

v: 31

Si nous n'avions point de défauts nous ne prendrions pas tant de plaisir à en remarquer dans les autres.

v: 32

La jalousie se nourrit dans les doutes, et elle devient fureur, ou elle finit, sitôt qu'on passe du doute à la certitude.

v: 33

L'orgueil se dédommage toujours, et ne perd rien lors même qu'il renonce à la vanité.

v: 34

Si nous n'avions point d'orgueil, nous ne nous plaindrions pas de celui des autres.

v: 35

L'orgueil est égal dans tous les hommes, et il n'y a de différence qu'aux moyens et à la manière de le mettre au jour.

v: 36

Il semble que la nature qui a si sagement disposé les organes de notre corps pour nous rendre heureux, nous ait aussi donné l'orgueil pour nous épargner la douleur de connaître nos imperfections.

v: 37

L'orgueil a plus de part que la bonté aux remontrances que nous faisons à ceux qui commettent des fautes: et nous ne les reprenons pas tant pour les en corriger, que pour leur persuader que nous en sommes exempts.

V: 30

We are more able than willing; often we imagine that things are impossible because we want to excuse ourselves in our own eyes. [I–V]

V: 31

If we had no faults, we would not derive so much pleasure from noting those of other people. [I–V]

V: 32

Jealousy is sustained by doubt; and it either becomes a frenzy or comes to an end, as soon as we pass from doubt to certainty. [I–V]

V: 33

Pride always finds some compensation for everything; even when it relinquishes vanity, it does not lose anything. [I–V]

V: 34

If we had no pride, we would not complain of it in other people. [I–V]

V: 35

All men are equal in pride; the only difference is in the ways and means by which it is brought to light. [I–V]

V: 36

It seems that nature, which has so wisely arranged the organs of our body for our happiness, has also given us pride to spare us the pain of knowing our deficiencies. [I–V]

V: 37

There is more pride than kindness* in our reprimands to people who are at fault; and we reprove them not so much to correct them as to convince them that we ourselves are free from such wrongdoing. [I–V]

V: 38

Nous promettons selon nos espérances: et nous tenons selon nos craintes.

V: 39

L'intérêt parle toutes sortes de langues, et joue toutes sortes de personnages, même celui de désintéressé.

V: 40

L'intérêt qui aveugle les uns, fait la lumière des autres.

V: 41

Ceux qui s'appliquent trop aux petites choses, deviennent ordinairement incapables des grandes.

V: 42

Nous n'avons pas assez de force pour suivre toute notre raison.

V: 43

L'homme croit souvent se conduire lorsqu'il est conduit: et pendant que par son esprit il tend à un but, son cœur l'entraîne insensiblement à un autre.

V: 44

La force et la faiblesse de l'esprit sont mal nommées: elles ne sont en effet que la bonne ou la mauvaise disposition des organes du corps.

V: 45

Le caprice de notre humeur est encore plus bizarre que celui de la fortune.

V: 46

L'attachement ou l'indifférence que les Philosophes avaient pour la

V: 38

We make promises in accordance with our hopes, and we keep them in accordance with our fears. [I–V]

V: 39

Self-interest speaks all kinds of languages and plays all kinds of parts—even that of disinterestedness. [I–V]

V: 40

Self-interest, which blinds some people, brings light to others. [I–V]

V: 41

Those who devote too much attention to little things generally become incapable of great ones. [I–V]

V: 42

We do not have enough strength to follow our reason fully. [I–V]

V: 43

Man often thinks he is the leader when he is being led; and while his mind is pointing him in one direction, his heart is imperceptibly drawing him in another. [I–V]

V: 44

Strength and weakness of mind are ill-named: in reality they are only good or bad conditions of the body's organs. [I–V]

V: 45

Our quirks of temper are even more bizarre than the quirks of fortune. [I–V]

V: 46

The attachment or indifference to life shown by the philosophers

vie n'était qu'un goût de leur amour-propre, dont on ne doit non plus disputer que du goût de la langue ou du choix des couleurs.

V: 47
Notre humeur met le prix à tout ce qui nous vient de la fortune.

V: 48
La félicité est dans le goût et non pas dans les choses: et c'est par avoir ce qu'on aime qu'on est heureux, et non par avoir ce que les autres trouvent aimable.

V: 49
On n'est jamais si heureux ni si malheureux qu'on s'imagine.

V: 50
Ceux qui croient avoir du mérite, se font un honneur d'être malheureux, pour persuader aux autres et à eux-mêmes qu'ils sont dignes d'être en butte à la fortune.

V: 51
Rien ne doit tant diminuer la satisfaction que nous avons de nous-mêmes, que de voir que nous désapprouvons dans un temps ce que nous approuvions dans un autre.

V: 52
Quelque différence qui paraisse entre les fortunes, il y a néanmoins une certaine compensation de biens et de maux qui les rend égales.

V: 53
Quelques grands avantages que la nature donne, ce n'est pas elle seule, mais la fortune avec elle qui fait les Héros.

was a mere question of taste on the part of their self-love, and should not be debated any more than the tastes of the tongue or preferences for colours. [I–V]

V: 47

Our temperament decides the value of everything brought to us by fortune. [II–V]

V: 48

Bliss lies in our taste, not in the things themselves; we are happy when we have what we like, not what other people find attractive. [I–V]

V: 49

We are never as fortunate or unfortunate as we imagine. [I–V]

V: 50

Those who think they have some merit treat misfortune as an honour, in order to convince other people and themselves that they are worthy of being victimized by fortune. [I–V]

V: 51

Nothing must reduce our self-satisfaction as much as the observation that we disapprove at one time what we approved at another. [I–V]

V: 52

No matter how different our fortunes may seem to be, there is still a certain balancing of things good and bad, which evens them out. [I–V]

V: 53

Whatever great advantages nature may give, heroes are not made by her alone, but by fortune working with her. [I–V]

V: 54

Le mépris des richesses était dans les Philosophes un désir caché de venger leur mérite de l'injustice de la fortune par le mépris des mêmes biens dont elle les privait: c'était un secret pour se garantir de l'avilissement de la pauvreté: c'était un chemin détourné pour aller à la considération qu'ils ne pouvaient avoir par les richesses.

V: 55

La haine pour les favoris n'est autre chose que l'amour de la faveur. Le dépit de ne la pas posséder se console et s'adoucit par le mépris que l'on témoigne de ceux qui la possèdent; et nous leur refusons nos hommages ne pouvant pas leur ôter ce qui leur attire ceux de tout le monde.

V: 56

Pour s'établir dans le monde on fait tout ce que l'on peut pour y paraître établi.

V: 57

Quoique les hommes se flattent de leurs grandes actions, elles ne sont pas souvent les effets d'un grand dessein, mais des effets du hasard.

V: 58

Il semble que nos actions aient des étoiles heureuses ou malheureuses à qui elles doivent une grande partie de la louange et du blâme qu'on leur donne.

V: 59

Il n'y a point d'accidents si malheureux dont les habiles gens ne tirent quelque avantage; ni de si heureux que les imprudents ne puissent tourner à leur préjudice.

V: 54

The philosophers' disdain for wealth was a hidden desire to compensate their own merit for the injustices of fortune, by showing contempt for the very possessions that she was keeping from them. It was a secret method of protecting themselves against the degradations of poverty; it was an indirect way of attaining the respect that they could not gain by wealth. [I–V]

V: 55

Hatred of favourites is nothing other than love of favour. Our resentment at lacking favour is soothed and appeased by disdain for those who possess it; and we deny them our respect because we cannot strip them of what elicits the respect of other people. [I–V]

V: 56

To gain status in the world, we do all we can to appear as if we had already gained it. [I–V]

V: 57

Though men pride themselves on their great deeds, these are not often the result of great plans, but rather the result of chance. [I–V]

V: 58

It seems that our deeds have lucky or unlucky stars, to which they owe a large part of the praise or blame that is bestowed on them. [I–V]

V: 59

No events are ever so unlucky that clever people cannot draw some advantage from them; nor are any so lucky that imprudent people cannot turn them to their own detriment. [I–V]

V: 60

La fortune tourne tout à l'avantage de ceux qu'elle favorise.

V: 61

Le bonheur et le malheur des hommes ne dépend pas moins de leur humeur que de la fortune.

V: 62

La sincérité est une ouverture de cœur. On la trouve en fort peu de gens: et celle que l'on voit d'ordinaire n'est qu'une fine dissimulation pour attirer la confiance des autres.

V: 63

L'aversion du mensonge est souvent une imperceptible ambition de rendre nos témoignages considérables, et d'attirer à nos paroles un respect de religion.

V: 64

La vérité ne fait pas tant de bien dans le monde que ses apparences y font de mal.

V: 65

Il n'y a point d'éloges qu'on ne donne à la prudence. Cependant elle ne saurait nous assurer du moindre événement.

V: 66

Un habile homme doit régler le rang de ses intérêts et les conduire chacun dans son ordre. Notre avidité le trouble souvent en nous faisant courir à tant de choses à la fois, que pour désirer trop les moins importantes, on manque les plus considérables.

V: 67

La bonne grâce est au corps, ce que le bon sens est à l'esprit.

v: 60

Fortune turns everything to the advantage of those she favours. [I–v]

v: 61

Men's happiness and unhappiness depend on their temperaments, no less than on fortune. [II–v]

v: 62

Sincerity is a form of open-heartedness. It is found in very few people: the kind that is usually seen is merely an astute counterfeit designed to win other people's confidence. [I–v]

v: 63

An aversion to lying is often an unrecognized ambition to make our statements seem more prestigious and gain a kind of religious respect for our words. [I–v]

v: 64

Truth does not do as much good in the world as the appearance of it does evil. [I–v]

v: 65

Prudence is extolled without the slightest reservation. Yet it cannot guarantee us even the smallest occurrence. [I–v]

v: 66

A clever man must arrange his interests in order and carry out each of them in its proper place. Our greed often disturbs this, and makes us run after so many things at the same time that we miss out on the most prestigious ones because we have too great a desire for those of least importance. [I–v]

v: 67

Grace is to the body what good sense is to the mind. [II–v]

v : 68

Il est difficile de définir l'amour. Ce qu'on en peut dire est que dans l'âme c'est une passion de régner; dans les esprits c'est une sympathie; et dans le corps ce n'est qu'une envie cachée et délicate de posséder ce que l'on aime après beaucoup de mystères.

v : 69

S'il y a un amour pur et exempt du mélange de nos autres passions, c'est celui qui est caché au fond du cœur, et que nous ignorons nous-mêmes.

v : 70

Il n'y a point de déguisement qui puisse longtemps cacher l'amour où il est, ni le feindre où il n'est pas.

v : 71

Il n'y a guère de gens qui ne soient honteux de s'être aimés, quand ils ne s'aiment plus.

v : 72

Si on juge de l'amour par la plupart de ses effets, il ressemble plus à la haine qu'à l'amitié.

v : 73

On peut trouver des femmes qui n'ont jamais eu de galanterie; mais il est rare d'en trouver qui n'en aient jamais eu qu'une.

v : 74

Il n'y a que d'une sorte d'amour: mais il y en a mille différentes copies.

v : 75

L'amour aussi bien que le feu ne peut subsister sans un mouvement continuel: et il cesse de vivre dès qu'il cesse d'espérer ou de craindre.

V: 68

It is hard to define love. What can be said about it is that, within the soul, it is a passion to reign; within the mind, it is a kinship of spirit; and within the body, it is merely a hidden subtle wish to possess what we love after going through many mysterious rituals. [I–V]

V: 69

If there is a kind of love that is pure and unmingled with our other passions, it is one that is hidden in the depths of the heart and unknown even to ourselves. [I–V]

V: 70

No disguise can long hide love where it exists, or simulate it where it does not exist. [I–V]

V: 71

There are hardly any people who are not ashamed of having loved, when they no longer love each other. [V]

V: 72

If love is judged by most of its results, it is more like hatred than friendship. [I–V]

V: 73

It is possible to find women who have never had a love affair; but it is rare to find women who have only ever had one. [I–V]

V: 74

There is only one kind of love; but it has thousands of different imitations. [I–V]

V: 75

Love, like fire, is sustained only by constant motion; and it ceases to exist when it ceases to hope or fear. [I–V]

v : 76

Il est du véritable amour comme de l'apparition des esprits: tout le monde en parle, mais peu de gens en ont vu.

v : 77

L'amour prête son nom à un nombre infini de commerces qu'on lui attribue, et où il n'a non plus de part que le Doge à ce qui se fait à Venise.

v : 78

L'amour de la justice n'est en la plupart des hommes que la crainte de souffrir l'injustice.

v : 79

Le silence est le parti le plus sûr de celui qui se défie de soi-même.

v : 80

Ce qui nous rend si changeants dans nos amitiés, c'est qu'il est difficile de connaître les qualités de l'âme, et facile de connaître celles de l'esprit.

v : 81

Nous ne pouvons rien aimer que par rapport à nous, et nous ne faisons que suivre notre goût et notre plaisir quand nous préférons nos amis à nous-mêmes; c'est néanmoins par cette préférence seule que l'amitié peut être vraie et parfaite.

v : 82

La réconciliation avec nos ennemis n'est qu'un désir de rendre notre condition meilleure, une lassitude de la guerre, et une crainte de quelque mauvais événement.

V: 76

True love is like visitations by ghosts: everyone talks about such things, but few people have seen them. [I–V]

V: 77

Love lends its name to innumerable transactions that are ascribed to it, though it has no more relation to them than the Doge has to the things that happen in Venice.* [I–V]

V: 78

With most men, love of justice is merely fear of suffering injustice. [I–V]

V: 79

Silence is the safest policy for someone who does not trust himself. [I–V]

V: 80

What makes us so inconstant in our friendships is the fact that it is hard to know the qualities of the soul, and easy to know those of the mind. [I–V]

V: 81

We cannot love anything except in relation to ourselves, and we are merely following our own taste and pleasure when we prefer our friends to ourselves; yet only by such a preference can friendship be true and perfect. [V]

V: 82

Reconciliation with our enemies is merely desire to improve our position, weariness of conflict, or fear that something bad will happen. [I–V]

v : 83

Ce que les hommes ont nommé amitié, n'est qu'une société, qu'un ménagement réciproque d'intérêts, et qu'un échange de bons offices; ce n'est enfin qu'un commerce où l'amour-propre se propose toujours quelque chose à gagner.

v : 84

Il est plus honteux de se défier de ses amis que d'en être trompé.

v : 85

Nous nous persuadons souvent d'aimer les gens plus puissants que nous: et néanmoins c'est l'intérêt seul qui produit notre amitié. Nous ne nous donnons pas à eux pour le bien que nous leur voulons faire, mais pour celui que nous en voulons recevoir.

v : 86

Notre défiance justifie la tromperie d'autrui.

v : 87

Les hommes ne vivraient pas longtemps en société s'ils n'étaient les dupes les uns des autres.

v : 88

L'amour-propre nous augmente ou nous diminue les bonnes qualités de nos amis à proportion de la satisfaction que nous avons d'eux: et nous jugeons de leur mérite par la manière dont ils vivent avec nous.

v : 89

Tout le monde se plaint de sa mémoire, et personne ne se plaint de son jugement.

v: 83

What men have called friendship is merely social contact, consideration for one another's interests, and exchange of favours; in fact, it is simply a transaction in which self-love always expects to gain something. [I–V]

v: 84

It is more shameful to mistrust our friends than to be deceived by them. [II–V]

v: 85

We often convince ourselves that we are fond of people more powerful than ourselves; yet self-interest is the sole cause of our friendship. We do not devote ourselves to them because we want to do them good, but because we want them to do us good. [I–V]

v: 86

Our own mistrust justifies other people's deceptions. [II–V]

v: 87

Men would not live long in social contact unless they were deceived by one another. [V]

v: 88

Self-love increases or decreases the good qualities that we find in our friends, according to the amount of gratification we are receiving from them; and we judge their merit by the way they behave with us. [I–V]

v: 89

Everyone complains of his memory, and no one complains of his judgement. [II–V]

V : 90

Nous plaisons plus souvent dans le commerce de la vie par nos défauts que par nos bonnes qualités.

V : 91

La plus grande ambition n'en a pas la moindre apparence lorsqu'elle se rencontre dans une impossibilité absolue d'arriver où elle aspire.

V : 92

Détromper un homme préoccupé de son mérite, est lui rendre un aussi mauvais office que celui que l'on rendit à ce fou d'Athènes, qui croyait que tous les vaisseaux qui arrivaient dans le port étaient à lui.

V : 93

Les vieillards aiment à donner de bons préceptes, pour se consoler de n'être plus en état de donner de mauvais exemples.

V : 94

Les grands noms abaissent au lieu d'élever ceux qui ne les savent pas soutenir.

V : 95

La marque d'un mérite extraordinaire est de voir que ceux qui l'envient le plus, sont contraints de le louer.

V : 96

Tel homme est ingrat, qui est moins coupable de son ingratitude, que celui qui lui a fait du bien.

V : 97

On s'est trompé lorsqu'on a cru que l'esprit et le jugement étaient deux choses différentes: Le jugement n'est que la grandeur de la lumière de l'esprit; cette lumière pénètre le fond des choses; elle y

V : 90

In everyday transactions our faults often give more pleasure than our good qualities. [v]

V : 91

The greatest ambition does not seem like anything of the kind, when it finds itself in a situation where it is utterly unable to gain what it wants. [II–v]

V : 92

To disillusion a man who is preoccupied with his own merit, is to do him as bad a turn as was done to the Athenian madman* who believed that every ship entering the harbour was his. [I–v]

V : 93

Old people like to give good advice, as a consolation for the fact that they can no longer set bad examples. [I–v]

V : 94

Great names demean rather than exalt those who cannot live up to them. [II–v]

V : 95

One sign of exceptional merit is that those who envy it most are forced to praise it. [II–v]

V : 96

Some ungrateful men are less guilty of their ingratitude than their benefactors are. [v]

V : 97

We are mistaken if we think that intelligence and judgement are two different things. Judgement is merely the magnitude of the light that resides in the intelligence; its light plumbs the very depths of things,

remarque tout ce qu'il faut remarquer et aperçoit celles qui semblent imperceptibles: Ainsi il faut demeurer d'accord que c'est l'étendue de la lumière de l'esprit qui produit tous les effets qu'on attribue au jugement.

V: 98

Chacun dit du bien de son cœur, et personne n'en ose dire de son esprit.

V: 99

La politesse de l'esprit consiste à penser des choses honnêtes et délicates.

V: 100

La galanterie de l'esprit est de dire des choses flatteuses d'une manière agréable.

V: 101

Il arrive souvent que des choses se présentent plus achevées à notre esprit qu'il ne les pourrait faire avec beaucoup d'art.

V: 102

L'esprit est toujours la dupe du cœur.

V: 103

Tous ceux qui connaissent leur esprit ne connaissent pas leur cœur.

V: 104

Les hommes et les affaires ont leur point de perspective. Il y en a qu'il faut voir de près pour en bien juger; et d'autres dont on ne juge jamais si bien que quand on en est éloigné.

where it draws attention to everything that deserves notice and perceives whatever had seemed imperceptible. We must agree, therefore,
that all the results commonly ascribed to judgement are really produced by the breadth of the light that resides in the intelligence. [I–V]

V: 98

Everyone speaks well of his heart, and no one dares to speak well of
his mind. [I–V]

V: 99

Civility of mind consists of thinking honorable and subtle things.
[I–V]

V: 100

Gallantry of mind is the art of saying flattering things in an attractive
way. [I–V]

V: 101

It often happens that things spring to our minds in a more finished
form than could have been achieved if much art had been lavished on
them. [I–V]

V: 102

The mind is always deceived by the heart. [I–V]

V: 103

Not all those who know their own minds know their own hearts. [I–V]

V: 104

Men and their business affairs all have their proper points of perspective.* Some must be seen close up to be judged rightly; and
others can never be judged so well as when we are far away from
them. [I–V]

V: 105

Celui-là n'est pas raisonnable à qui le hasard fait trouver la raison;
mais celui qui la connaît, qui la discerne, et qui la goûte.

V: 106

Pour bien savoir les choses, il en faut savoir le détail: et comme il est
presque infini, nos connaissances sont toujours superficielles et
imparfaites.

V: 107

C'est une espèce de coquetterie de faire remarquer qu'on n'en fait
jamais.

V: 108

L'esprit ne saurait jouer longtemps le personnage du cœur.

V: 109

La jeunesse change ses goûts par l'ardeur du sang; et la vieillesse
conserve les siens par l'accoutumance.

V: 110

On ne donne rien si libéralement que ses conseils.

V: 111

Plus on aime une maîtresse, et plus on est près de la haïr.

V: 112

Les défauts de l'esprit augmentent en vieillissant comme ceux du
visage.

V: 113

Il y a de bons mariages; mais il n'y en a point de délicieux.

V: 105

A man is reasonable not if he happens by chance on what is reasonable, but if he knows it, appreciates it, and savours its taste. [I–V]

V: 106

To know things well, we must know the details; and as they are almost infinite, our knowledge is always superficial and imperfect.* [I–V]

V: 107

To draw attention to the fact that you never flirt is itself a form of flirtatiousness. [II–V]

V: 108

The mind cannot act the role of the heart for long. [II–V]

V: 109

Passion in the blood changes the tastes of youth, and habit preserves those of old age. [II–V]

V: 110

We give nothing so generously as our advice. [I–V]

V: 111

The more you love your beloved, the closer you are to hating her. [II–V]

V: 112

Faults of the mind, like those of the face, grow worse with age. [II–V]

V: 113

There are good marriages, but there are no rapturous ones. [II–V]

V: 114

On ne se peut consoler d'être trompé par ses ennemis, et trahi par ses amis; et l'on est souvent satisfait de l'être par soi-même.

V: 115

Il est aussi facile de se tromper soi-même sans s'en apercevoir, qu'il est difficile de tromper les autres sans qu'ils s'en aperçoivent.

V: 116

Rien n'est moins sincère que la manière de demander et de donner des conseils. Celui qui en demande paraît avoir une déférence respectueuse pour les sentiments de son ami, bien qu'il ne pense qu'à lui faire approuver les siens; et à le rendre garant de sa conduite. Et celui qui conseille paye la confiance qu'on lui témoigne d'un zèle ardent et désintéressé, quoiqu'il ne cherche le plus souvent dans les conseils qu'il donne que son propre intérêt ou sa gloire.

V: 117

La plus subtile de toutes les finesses est de savoir bien feindre de tomber dans les pièges que l'on nous tend; et on n'est jamais si aisément trompé que quand on songe à tromper les autres.

V: 118

L'intention de ne jamais tromper nous expose à être souvent trompés.

V: 119

Nous sommes si accoutumés à nous déguiser aux autres, qu'enfin nous nous déguisons à nous-mêmes.

V: 120

L'on fait plus souvent des trahisons par faiblesse que par un dessein formé de trahir.

V: 114

Nothing can comfort us when we are deceived by our enemies and betrayed by our friends; yet we are often happy to be deceived and betrayed by ourselves. [I–V]

V: 115

It is as easy to deceive ourselves without noticing it, as it is hard to deceive other people without their noticing it. [I–V]

V: 116

Nothing is less sincere than the procedure of asking for advice and giving it. The asker seems to display a respectful deference for his friend's feelings—though his only thought is to get approval for his own, and to make the other person answerable for his conduct. And the adviser repays the confidence that has been placed in him with a display of fervent and disinterested zeal—though most often he is seeking only his own interest and glory when he gives his advice. [I–V]

V: 117

The most refined form of cunning is the art of pretending to fall into the traps that have been set before us; and we are never so easily deceived as when we are intent on deceiving other people. [I–V]

V: 118

The intention of never deceiving anyone lays us open to being deceived very often. [I–V]

V: 119

We are so accustomed to disguise ourselves from other people, that in the end we disguise ourselves from ourselves. [I–V]

V: 120

We betray people more often from weakness than from a settled plan to betray them. [I–V]

V: 121

On fait souvent du bien pour pouvoir impunément faire du mal.

V: 122

Si nous résistons à nos passions c'est plus par leur faiblesse que par notre force.

V: 123

On n'aurait guère de plaisir si on ne se flattait jamais.

V: 124

Les plus habiles affectent toute leur vie de blâmer les finesses pour s'en servir en quelque grande occasion et pour quelque grand intérêt.

V: 125

L'usage ordinaire de la finesse est la marque d'un petit esprit, et il arrive presque toujours que celui qui s'en sert pour se couvrir en un endroit, se découvre en un autre.

V: 126

Les finesses et les trahisons ne viennent que de manque d'habileté.

V: 127

Le vrai moyen d'être trompé, c'est de se croire plus fin que les autres.

V: 128

La trop grande subtilité est une fausse délicatesse: et la véritable délicatesse est une solide subtilité.

V: 129

Il suffit quelquefois d'être grossier pour n'être pas trompé par un habile homme.

V: 121

We often do good so that we can do evil with impunity. [I–V]

V: 122

If we resist our passions, it is due more to their weakness than to our own strength. [II–V]

V: 123

We would have few pleasures if we never flattered ourselves. [II–V]

V: 124

The cleverest people spend their whole lives pretending to deplore cunning, so that they can make use of it for some great matter of interest to them, when some great circumstance arises. [I–V]

V: 125

Habitual use of cunning is the sign of a small mind; and it nearly always happens that the person who uses it to protect himself at one point, exposes himself at another. [I–V]

V: 126

Betrayals and acts of cunning arise only from lack of cleverness. [I–V]

V: 127

The sure way to be deceived is to think yourself more astute than other people. [I–V]

V: 128

Too much refinement is a false subtlety; and true subtlety is a well-founded refinement. [I–V]

V: 129

Uncouthness is sometimes enough to save you from being deceived by a clever man. [I–V]

v: 130

La faiblesse est le seul défaut que l'on ne saurait corriger.

v: 131

Le moindre défaut des femmes qui se sont abandonnées à faire l'amour, c'est de faire l'amour.

v: 132

Il est plus aisé d'être sage pour les autres, que de l'être pour soi-même.

v: 133

Les seules bonnes copies sont celles qui nous font voir le ridicule des méchants originaux.

v: 134

On n'est jamais si ridicule par les qualités que l'on a, que par celles que l'on affecte d'avoir.

v: 135

On est quelquefois aussi différent de soi-même que des autres.

v: 136

Il y a des gens qui n'auraient jamais été amoureux, s'ils n'avaient jamais entendu parler de l'amour.

v: 137

On parle peu quand la vanité ne fait pas parler.

v: 138

On aime mieux dire du mal de soi-même que de n'en point parler.

V: 130
Weakness is the only fault that we are incapable of correcting. [II–V]

V: 131
When women give themselves up to lovemaking, making love is the least of their faults. [II–V]

V: 132
It is easier to be wise for other people than for yourself. [I–V]

V: 133
The only good copies are those that show us the absurdities of bad originals. [II–V]

V: 134
The qualities we have never make us as absurd as those we pretend to have. [I–V]

V: 135
We are sometimes as different from ourselves as we are from other people. [I–V]

V: 136
There are people who would never have been in love if they had never heard love mentioned. [II–V]

V: 137
We have little to say when vanity is not making us speak. [I–V]

V: 138
We would rather speak ill of ourselves than say nothing about ourselves at all. [I–V]

V: 139

Une des choses qui fait que l'on trouve si peu de gens qui paraissent
raisonnables et agréables dans la conversation, c'est qu'il n'y a
presque personne qui ne pense plutôt à ce qu'il veut dire qu'à répondre précisément à ce qu'on lui dit. Les plus habiles et les plus com-
plaisants se contentent de montrer seulement une mine attentive, au
même temps que l'on voit dans leurs yeux et dans leur esprit un
égarement pour ce qu'on leur dit, et une précipitation pour retourner
à ce qu'ils veulent dire: au lieu de considérer que c'est un mauvais
moyen de plaire aux autres ou de les persuader, que de chercher si fort
à se plaire à soi-même; et que bien écouter et bien répondre est une
des plus grandes perfections qu'on puisse avoir dans la conversation.

V: 140

Un homme d'esprit serait souvent bien embarrassé sans la compagnie des sots.

V: 141

Nous nous vantons souvent de ne nous point ennuyer; et nous sommes si glorieux que nous ne voulons pas nous trouver de mauvaise
compagnie.

V: 142

Comme c'est le caractère des grands esprits de faire entendre en peu
de paroles beaucoup de choses; les petits esprits au contraire ont le
don de beaucoup parler, et de ne rien dire.

V: 143

C'est plutôt par l'estime de nos propres sentiments que nous exagérons les bonnes qualités des autres, que par l'estime de leur mérite:
et nous voulons nous attirer des louanges lorsqu'il semble que nous
leur en donnons.

V: 144

On n'aime point à louer, et on ne loue jamais personne sans intérêt.

V: 139

One of the reasons why so few people seem reasonable and attractive in conversation is that almost everyone thinks more about what he himself wants to say than about answering exactly what is said to him. The cleverest and most polite people are content merely to look attentive—while all the time we see in their eyes and minds a distraction from what is being said to them, and an impatience to get back to what they themselves want to say. Instead, they should reflect that striving so hard to please themselves is a poor way to please or convince other people, and that the ability to listen well and answer well is one of the greatest merits we can have in conversation. [I–V]

V: 140

An intelligent man would often be much at a loss without the company of fools. [I–V]

V: 141

We often boast of never being bored by ourselves; we are so vainglorious that we never want to find our own company tedious. [I–V]

V: 142

As great minds have the ability to say much in few words, so, conversely, small minds have the gift of talking much and not saying anything. [I–V]

V: 143

We exaggerate the good qualities of other people less because we prize their merits than because we prize our own feelings; and we want to attract praise ourselves, when we seem to be bestowing it on them. [I–V]

V: 144

We do not like bestowing praise, and we never praise anyone without

La louange est une flatterie habile, cachée, et délicate, qui satisfait différemment celui qui la donne, et celui qui la reçoit. L'un la prend comme une récompense de son mérite; l'autre la donne pour faire remarquer son équité et son discernement.

V: 145

Nous choisissons souvent des louanges empoisonnées qui font voir par contrecoup en ceux que nous louons des défauts que nous n'osons découvrir d'une autre sorte.

V: 146

On ne loue d'ordinaire que pour être loué.

V: 147

Peu de gens sont assez sages pour préférer le blâme qui leur est utile à la louange qui les trahit.

V: 148

Il y a des reproches qui louent, et des louanges qui médisent.

V: 149

Le refus des louanges est un désir d'être loué deux fois.

V: 150

Le désir de mériter les louanges qu'on nous donne fortifie notre vertu: et celles que l'on donne à l'esprit, à la valeur, et à la beauté, contribuent à les augmenter.

V: 151

Il est plus difficile de s'empêcher d'être gouverné que de gouverner les autres.

some motive of self-interest. Praise is a clever, hidden, subtle form of flattery, which gratifies the giver and the recipient in different ways. The latter accepts it as a reward for his merit; the former bestows it to draw attention to his fair-mindedness and perceptiveness. [I–V]

V: 145
We often choose poisoned forms of praise, which rebound and reveal in the people we are praising faults that we dare not divulge in any other way. [I–V]

V: 146
We usually bestow praise only to receive it. [I–V]

V: 147
Few people are wise enough to prefer useful criticism to treacherous praise. [I–V]

V: 148
Some rebukes are praises, and some praises are slanders. [I–V]

V: 149
A refusal of praise is a desire to be praised twice over. [I–V]

V: 150
Our desire to deserve the praise that is bestowed on us strengthens our virtue; and praise that is bestowed on intelligence, valour, and beauty helps to enhance them. [I–V]

V: 151
It is harder to prevent ourselves from being ruled than to rule other people. [II–V]

V: 152

Si nous ne nous flattions point nous-mêmes, la flatterie des autres ne nous pourrait nuire.

V: 153

La nature fait le mérite; et la fortune le met en œuvre.

V: 154

La fortune nous corrige de plusieurs défauts que la raison ne saurait corriger.

V: 155

Il y a des gens dégoûtants avec du mérite, et d'autres qui plaisent avec des défauts.

V: 156

Il y a des gens dont tout le mérite consiste à dire et à faire des sottises utilement et qui gâteraient tout s'ils changeaient de conduite.

V: 157

La gloire des grands hommes se doit toujours mesurer aux moyens dont ils se sont servis pour l'acquérir.

V: 158

La flatterie est une fausse monnaie qui n'a de cours que par notre vanité.

V: 159

Ce n'est pas assez d'avoir de grandes qualités, il en faut avoir l'économie.

V: 152

If we never flattered ourselves, other people's flattery could not harm us. [I–V]

V: 153

Nature creates merit, and fortune puts it on display. [I–V]

V: 154

Fortune corrects us of some faults that reason could not correct. [III–V]

V: 155

There are people with merits who leave a bad taste in the mouth, and people with faults who are likeable. [I–V]

V: 156

There are people whose sole merit consists of saying and doing stupid but useful things, and who would spoil everything if they changed their conduct. [I–V]

V: 157

The glory of great men should always be measured against the means they used to acquire it. [I–V]

V: 158

Flattery is a false coin given currency only by our vanity. [V]

V: 159

It is not enough to have great merits; you must also know how to employ them. [I–V]

v: 160

Quelque éclatante que soit une action, elle ne doit pas passer pour grande lorsqu'elle n'est pas l'effet d'un grand dessein.

v: 161

Il doit y avoir une certaine proportion entre les actions et les desseins si on en veut tirer tous les effets qu'elles peuvent produire.

v: 162

L'art de savoir bien mettre en œuvre de médiocres qualités dérobe l'estime et donne souvent plus de réputation que le véritable mérite.

v: 163

Il y a une infinité de conduites qui paraissent ridicules, et dont les raisons cachées sont très sages et très solides.

v: 164

Il est plus facile de paraître digne des emplois qu'on n'a pas, que de ceux que l'on exerce.

v: 165

Notre mérite nous attire l'estime des honnêtes gens, et notre étoile celle du public.

v: 166

Le monde récompense plus souvent les apparences du mérite que le mérite même.

v: 167

L'avarice est plus opposée à l'économie que la libéralité.

v: 168

L'espérance toute trompeuse qu'elle est sert au moins à nous mener à la fin de la vie par un chemin agréable.

V: 160

However brilliant a deed may be, it should never be taken for a great one unless it results from great plans. [I–V]

V: 161

Our deeds should be in proportion to our plans, if we want to derive the best possible results from them. [I–V]

V: 162

The ability to make good use of average talents is an art that extorts respect, and often wins more repute than real merit does. [I–V]

V: 163

There are innumerable forms of conduct that seem absurd, though their hidden reasons are very wise and very well founded. [I–V]

V: 164

It is easier to seem worthy of positions you do not hold than of those you do. [I–V]

V: 165

Our merits win us the respect of honorable people, and our stars win us that of the public. [I–V]

V: 166

The world rewards appearances of merit more often than merit itself. [I–V]

V: 167

Avarice is more opposed to thrift than generosity is. [II–V]

V: 168

Hope, utterly deceptive though she is, at least leads us to life's end by an attractive route. [I–V]

V: 169

Pendant que la paresse et la timidité nous retiennent dans notre devoir, notre vertu en a souvent tout l'honneur.

V: 170

Il est difficile de juger si un procédé net, sincère et honnête, est un effet de probité ou d'habileté.

V: 171

Les vertus se perdent dans l'intérêt, comme les fleuves se perdent dans la mer.

V: 172

Si on examine bien les divers effets de l'ennui, on trouvera qu'il fait manquer à plus de devoirs que l'intérêt.

V: 173

Il y a diverses sortes de curiosité: l'une d'intérêt, qui nous porte à désirer d'apprendre ce qui nous peut être utile: et l'autre d'orgueil, qui vient du désir de savoir ce que les autres ignorent.

V: 174

Il vaut mieux employer notre esprit à supporter les infortunes qui nous arrivent, qu'à prévoir celles qui nous peuvent arriver.

V: 175

La constance en amour est une inconstance perpétuelle, qui fait que notre cœur s'attache successivement à toutes les qualités de la personne que nous aimons, donnant tantôt la préférence à l'une, tantôt à l'autre: de sorte que cette constance n'est qu'une inconstance arrêtée et renfermée dans un même sujet.

V: 169

While laziness and timidity keep us to the path of duty, our virtue often gets all the honour. [I–V]

V: 170

It is hard to judge whether* a straightforward, sincere, honorable deed has resulted from integrity or cleverness. [I–V]

V: 171

Virtues lose themselves in self-interest, as rivers do in the sea. [I–V]

V: 172

If we carefully consider the various results of heartache,* we shall find that it causes more failures of duty than self-interest does. [V]

V: 173

There are different forms of curiosity. One is due to self-interest, which gives us a desire to learn what could be useful for us; another is due to pride, and comes from a desire to know what other people do not know. [I–V]

V: 174

Our minds are better employed bearing the misfortunes that do happen to us than anticipating those that could happen. [I–V]

V: 175

Constancy in love is a perpetual inconstancy, which makes our hearts fasten in succession on all the qualities of the person we love, preferring now one, now another—so that such constancy is merely inconstancy contained in and confined to a single object. [I–V]

V: 176

Il y a deux sortes de constance en amour. L'une vient de ce que l'on trouve sans cesse dans la personne que l'on aime de nouveaux sujets d'aimer: et l'autre vient de ce que l'on se fait un honneur d'être constant.

V: 177

La persévérance n'est digne ni de blâme ni de louange, parce qu'elle n'est que la durée des goûts et des sentiments qu'on ne s'ôte et qu'on ne se donne point.

V: 178

Ce qui nous fait aimer les nouvelles connaissances n'est pas tant la lassitude que nous avons des vieilles ou le plaisir de changer, que le dégoût de n'être pas assez admirés de ceux qui nous connaissent trop, et l'espérance de l'être davantage de ceux qui ne nous connaissent pas tant.

V: 179

Nous nous plaignons quelquefois légèrement de nos amis pour justifier par avance notre légèreté.

V: 180

Notre repentir n'est pas tant un regret du mal que nous avons fait, qu'une crainte de celui qui nous en peut arriver.

V: 181

Il y a une inconstance qui vient de la légèreté de l'esprit ou de sa faiblesse qui lui fait recevoir toutes les opinions d'autrui: et il y en a une autre qui est plus excusable, qui vient du dégoût des choses.

V: 182

Les vices entrent dans la composition des vertus comme les poisons entrent dans la composition des remèdes. La prudence les assemble

V: 176

There are two kinds of constancy in love. One is due to the fact that
we are continually finding new things to love in the person we love;
the other is due to the fact that we make it a point of honour to be
constant. [I–V]

V: 177

Perseverance deserves neither blame nor praise, because it is merely
the persistence of tastes and feelings that we can neither discard nor
acquire by any means. [I–V]

V: 178

What makes us like new acquaintances is not so much our weariness
of the old ones, or the pleasure of changing, as frustration that we are
not admired enough by those who know us too well, and the hope of
being admired more by those who are less well acquainted with us.
[I–V]

V: 179

We sometimes make fickle complaints about our friends, in order to
justify in advance our own fickleness. [I–V]

V: 180

Our repentance is not so much a regret for the ill that we have done,
as a fear of the ill that could happen to us as a result. [I–V]

V: 181

There is a kind of inconstancy that comes from the mind's fickleness
or weakness, which makes it accept all the opinions of other people,
and there is another kind that is more excusable, which comes from
loss of taste for something. [I–V]

V: 182

Vices have a place in the composition of virtues, as poisons have a
place in the composition of medicines. Prudence gathers them and

et les tempère, et elle s'en sert utilement contre les maux de la vie.

v: 183

Il faut demeurer d'accord à l'honneur de la vertu que les plus grands malheurs des hommes sont ceux où ils tombent par les crimes.

v: 184

Nous avouons nos défauts pour réparer par notre sincérité le tort qu'ils nous font dans l'esprit des autres.

v: 185

Il y a des Héros en mal comme en bien.

v: 186

On ne méprise pas tous ceux qui ont des vices; mais on méprise tous ceux qui n'ont aucune vertu.

v: 187

Le nom de la vertu sert à l'intérêt aussi utilement que les vices.

v: 188

La santé de l'âme n'est pas plus assurée que celle du corps; et quoique l'on paraisse éloigné des passions on n'est pas moins en danger de s'y laisser emporter, que de tomber malade quand on se porte bien.

v: 189

Il semble que la nature ait prescrit à chaque homme dès sa naissance des bornes pour les vertus et pour les vices.

v: 190

Il n'appartient qu'aux grands hommes d'avoir de grands défauts.

tempers them, and puts them to good use against the ills of life. [I–v]

v: 183

We must admit—and let us honour virtue for it—that men's greatest misfortunes are those that befall them because of their crimes. [v]

v: 184

We acknowledge our faults so that our sincerity may repair the damage they do us in other people's eyes. [I–v]

v: 185

There are heroes in evil, just as there are in good. [I–v]

v: 186

We do not disdain all those who have vices; but we do disdain all those who have no virtues. [I–v]

v: 187

The name 'virtue' is as useful to self-interest as the vices themselves are. [I–v]

v: 188

The soul's health is no more secure than the body's; though we may seem safely aloof from the passions, we are no less in danger of being swept away by them, than we are of falling sick when we feel well. [I–v]

v: 189

It seems that nature has set limits to each man's virtues and vices at his birth. [I–v]

v: 190

Only great men can have great faults. [I–v]

V: 191

On peut dire que les vices nous attendent dans le cours de la vie comme des hôtes chez qui il faut successivement loger; et je doute que l'expérience nous les fît éviter s'il nous était permis de faire deux fois le même chemin.

V: 192

Quand les vices nous quittent, nous nous flattons de la créance que c'est nous qui les quittons.

V: 193

Il y a des rechutes dans les maladies de l'âme comme dans celles du corps: Ce que nous prenons pour notre guérison n'est le plus souvent qu'un relâche ou un changement de mal.

V: 194

Les défauts de l'âme sont comme les blessures du corps: quelque soin qu'on prenne de les guérir, la cicatrice paraît toujours, et elles sont à tout moment en danger de se rouvrir.

V: 195

Ce qui nous empêche souvent de nous abandonner à un seul vice, est que nous en avons plusieurs.

V: 196

Nous oublions aisément nos fautes lorsqu'elles ne sont sues que de nous.

V: 197

Il y a des gens de qui l'on peut ne jamais croire du mal sans l'avoir vu: mais il n'y en a point en qui il nous doive surprendre en le voyant.

V: 191

It may be said that, during the course of our lives, the vices await us like landlords at whose inns we must successively lodge; and I doubt whether experience would lead us to avoid them, if we were allowed to travel the same way a second time. [I–V]

V: 192

When vices leave us, we flatter ourselves that we are the ones who are leaving them. [I–V]

V: 193

There are relapses in the soul's illnesses, just as there are in the body's. What we take to be a cure is most often merely a respite or a change of illness. [I–V]

V: 194

Faults of the soul are like wounds of the body: however careful we may be to cure them, the scars are always visible, and they are in danger of breaking open again at any moment. [I–V]

V: 195

Often what prevents us from giving ourselves up to a particular vice is the fact that we have a number of them. [I–V]

V: 196

We forget our faults easily when they are known only to ourselves. [I–V]

V: 197

There are people of whom we would never believe evil unless we saw it; but there are none in whom we should be surprised to see it. [I–V]

V: 198

Nous élevons la gloire des uns pour abaisser celle des autres: Et quelquefois on louerait moins Monsieur le Prince et Monsieur de Turenne, si on ne les voulait point blâmer tous deux.

V: 199

Le désir de paraître habile empêche souvent de le devenir.

V: 200

La vertu n'irait pas si loin si la vanité ne lui tenait compagnie.

V: 201

Celui qui croit pouvoir trouver en soi-même de quoi se passer de tout le monde se trompe fort: mais celui qui croit qu'on ne peut se passer de lui se trompe encore davantage.

V: 202

Les faux honnêtes gens sont ceux qui déguisent leurs défauts aux autres et à eux-mêmes. Les vrais honnêtes gens sont ceux qui les connaissent parfaitement et les confessent.

V: 203

Le vrai honnête homme est celui qui ne se pique de rien.

V: 204

La sévérité des femmes est un ajustement et un fard qu'elles ajoutent à leur beauté.

V: 205

L'honnêteté des femmes est souvent l'amour de leur réputation et de leur repos.

V: 198

We exalt the glory of some people in order to demean that of others;
the Prince and Monsieur de Turenne* would sometimes receive less
praise, if no one ever wanted to criticize either of them. [I–V]

V: 199

The desire to be seen as clever often prevents us from becoming so.
[I–V]

V: 200

Virtue would not go so far if vanity did not keep her company. [I–V]

V: 201

Someone who thinks he can find enough in himself to do without
everyone else is greatly deceived; but someone who thinks that other
people cannot do without him is still more deceived. [I–V]

V: 202

People are falsely honorable when they disguise their faults* from
other people and from themselves. People are truly honorable when
they know them perfectly well and confess them. [I–V]

V: 203

The truly honorable man is the one who never prides himself on
anything. [I–V]

V: 204

Austerity is a kind of adornment and make-up that women add to
their beauty. [I–V]

V: 205

Virtue,* in women, is often love of their reputation and peace of
mind. [I–V]

V : 206

C'est être véritablement honnête homme que de vouloir être toujours exposé à la vue des honnêtes gens.

V : 207

La folie nous suit dans tous les temps de la vie. Si quelqu'un paraît sage, c'est seulement parce que ses folies sont proportionnées à son âge et à sa fortune.

V : 208

Il y a des gens niais qui se connaissent, et qui emploient habilement leur niaiserie.

V : 209

Qui vit sans folie n'est pas si sage qu'il croit.

V : 210

En vieillissant on devient plus fou, et plus sage.

V : 211

Il y a des gens qui ressemblent aux Vaudevilles, qu'on ne chante qu'un certain temps.

V : 212

La plupart des gens ne jugent des hommes que par la vogue qu'ils ont, ou par leur fortune.

V : 213

L'amour de la gloire, la crainte de la honte, le dessein de faire fortune, le désir de rendre notre vie commode et agréable, et l'envie d'abaisser les autres, sont souvent les causes de cette valeur si célèbre parmi les hommes.

V: 206

A man is truly honorable if he is willing to be perpetually exposed to the scrutiny of honorable people. [I–V]

V: 207

Foolishness keeps following us at every stage of life. If someone seems wise, it is only because his follies are in keeping with his age and circumstances. [I–V]

V: 208

There are silly people who know themselves and make use of their silliness cleverly. [I–V]

V: 209

The person who lives without folly is not as wise as he thinks. [I–V]

V: 210

As we grow old we become more foolish and more wise. [I–V]

V: 211

Some people are like popular songs, which are sung only for a short time. [I–V]

V: 212

Most people judge men only by their popularity or their fortune. [I–V]

V: 213

Love of glory, fear of shame, a plan to make our fortune, a desire to make our lives comfortable and attractive, and a wish to demean other people, are often the causes of the valour that men praise so highly. [I–V]

V: 214

La valeur est dans les simples soldats un métier périlleux qu'ils ont pris pour gagner leur vie.

V: 215

La parfaite valeur et la poltronnerie complète sont deux extrémités où l'on arrive rarement. L'espace qui est entre-deux est vaste, et contient toutes les autres espèces de courage: il n'y a pas moins de différence entre elles qu'entre les visages et les humeurs. Il y a des hommes qui s'exposent volontiers au commencement d'une action, et qui se relâchent et se rebutent aisément par sa durée. Il y en a qui sont contents quand ils ont satisfait à l'honneur du monde, et qui font fort peu de chose au-delà. On en voit qui ne sont pas toujours également maîtres de leur peur. D'autres se laissent quelquefois entraîner à des terreurs générales. D'autres vont à la charge, parce qu'ils n'osent demeurer dans leurs postes. Il s'en trouve à qui l'habitude des moindres périls affermit le courage et les prépare à s'exposer à de plus grands. Il y en a qui sont braves à coups d'épée, et qui craignent les coups de mousquet: d'autres sont assurés aux coups de mousquet, et appréhendent de se battre à coups d'épée. Tous ces courages de différentes espèces conviennent en ce que la nuit augmentant la crainte et cachant les bonnes et les mauvaises actions, elle donne la liberté de se ménager. Il y a encore un autre ménagement plus général: car on ne voit point d'homme qui fasse tout ce qu'il serait capable de faire dans une occasion s'il était assuré d'en revenir. De sorte qu'il est visible que la crainte de la mort ôte quelque chose de la valeur.

V: 216

La parfaite valeur est de faire sans témoins ce qu'on serait capable de faire devant tout le monde.

V: 217

L'intrépidité est une force extraordinaire de l'âme qui l'élève au-dessus des troubles, des désordres et des émotions que la vue des grands périls pourrait exciter en elle: et c'est par cette force que les

V: 214

In common soldiers, valour is the perilous occupation they have chosen in order to earn their living. [I–V]

V: 215

Perfect valour and utter cowardice are two extremes, which people rarely attain. The space between the two is vast, and contains all the other kinds of courage, which differ from one another as much as faces and temperaments do. There are men who willingly expose themselves to danger at the start of a battle, but waver and easily lose heart as it progresses. There are some who are content to satisfy the world's conventional standard of honour, and do very little more than that. We see some who are not always uniformly in control of their fears. Others sometimes allow themselves to be swept away by some general outbreak of panic. Others join in a charge because they dare not stay at their posts. Some are so accustomed to minor perils that the experience strengthens their courage and prepares them to face greater ones. Some are brave in sword fights, but afraid of musket fire; others are confident under musket fire, and fearful of sword fights. All these different kinds of courage have this in common: darkness, which enhances fear and hides good and bad deeds alike, gives everyone the freedom to act cautiously. There is also another, more general, kind of caution—because we never see any man do everything he could possibly do in circumstances where he was sure of coming back alive. Thus fear of death clearly does take something away from valour. [I–V]

V: 216

Perfect valour consists of doing without witnesses what you would be capable of doing in front of the whole world. [I–V]

V: 217

Intrepidity is exceptional strength of soul, which raises it above the agitations, disturbances, and emotions that might otherwise be aroused in it by the sight of great dangers. And this strength is

Héros se maintiennent en un état paisible, et conservent l'usage libre de leur raison dans les accidents les plus surprenants et les plus terribles.

V : 218

L'hypocrisie est un hommage que le vice rend à la vertu.

V : 219

La plupart des hommes s'exposent assez dans la guerre pour sauver leur honneur: Mais peu se veulent toujours exposer autant qu'il est nécessaire pour faire réussir le dessein pour lequel ils s'exposent.

V : 220

La vanité, la honte, et surtout le tempérament, font souvent la valeur des hommes, et la vertu des femmes.

V : 221

On ne veut point perdre la vie, et on veut acquérir de la gloire: ce qui fait que les braves ont plus d'adresse et d'esprit pour éviter la mort, que les gens de chicane n'en ont pour conserver leur bien.

V : 222

Il n'y a guère de personnes qui dans le premier penchant de l'âge ne fassent connaître par où leur corps et leur esprit doivent défaillir.

V : 223

Il est de la reconnaissance comme de la bonne foi des marchands: elle entretient le commerce: et nous ne payons pas parce qu'il est juste de nous acquitter; mais pour trouver plus facilement des gens qui nous prêtent.

V : 224

Tous ceux qui s'acquittent des devoirs de la reconnaissance, ne peuvent pas pour cela se flatter d'être reconnaissants.

what enables heroes to remain calm and maintain the free use of
their reasoning powers amid the most startling and terrible events.
[I–V]

V: 218

Hypocrisy is a form of homage that vice pays to virtue. [II–V]

V: 219

In warfare, most men expose themselves to danger enough to preserve their honour; but few are willing to expose themselves to the
amount of danger necessary to ensure the success of the plan that is
leading them to do such things. [I–V]

V: 220

Vanity, shame, and above all temperament often make up the valour
of men and the virtue of women. [I–V]

V: 221

We do not want to lose our lives, and we do want glory—so that
brave men strive with more skill and intelligence to avoid death than
tricksters do in lawsuits to retain their property. [I–V]

V: 222

There are hardly any people who, at the onset of old age, do not
reveal how their body and mind are bound to decline. [II–V]

V: 223

Gratitude is like good faith in business. It keeps commerce going;
we do not pay up because it is right for us to discharge our debt,
but so that we can more easily find people who will lend to us.
[I–V]

V: 224

Not everyone who discharges the duties of gratitude can flatter himself that he is really being grateful by doing so. [I–V]

V: 225

Ce qui fait le mécompte dans la reconnaissance qu'on attend des grâces que l'on a faites, c'est que l'orgueil de celui qui donne, et l'orgueil de celui qui reçoit, ne peuvent convenir du prix du bienfait.

V: 226

Le trop grand empressement qu'on a de s'acquitter d'une obligation est une espèce d'ingratitude.

V: 227

Les gens heureux ne se corrigent guère; et ils croient toujours avoir raison quand la fortune soutient leur mauvaise conduite.

V: 228

L'orgueil ne veut pas devoir, et l'amour-propre ne veut pas payer.

V: 229

Le bien que nous avons reçu de quelqu'un veut que nous respections le mal qu'il nous fait.

V: 230

Rien n'est si contagieux que l'exemple, et nous ne faisons jamais de grands biens ni de grands maux, qui n'en produisent de semblables. Nous imitons les bonnes actions par émulation, et les mauvaises par la malignité de notre nature que la honte retenait prisonnière, et que l'exemple met en liberté.

V: 231

C'est une grande folie de vouloir être sage tout seul.

V: 232

Quelque prétexte que nous donnions à nos afflictions, ce n'est souvent que l'intérêt et la vanité qui les causent.

V: 225

We receive less gratitude than we expect when we are gracious, because the giver's pride and the recipient's pride cannot agree on the value of the favour. [I–V]

V: 226

Too much eagerness to discharge an obligation is a form of ingratitude. [I–V]

V: 227

Fortunate people rarely correct their faults; they always think they are right while fortune is favouring their evil conduct. [V]

V: 228

Pride is not willing to owe, and self-love is not willing to pay. [I–V]

V: 229

The good that we have received from someone should make us respect the evil he also does us. [I–V]

V: 230

Nothing is so contagious as example, and we never do very good deeds or very evil ones without producing imitations. We copy the good deeds in a spirit of emulation, and the bad ones because of the malignity of our nature—which shame used to hold under lock and key, but an example sets free. [I–V]

V: 231

It is a great folly to want to be wise on your own. [II–V]

V: 232

Whatever excuse we may find for our sorrows, often it is only self-interest and vanity that cause them. [I–V]

V: 233

Il y a dans les afflictions diverses sortes d'hypocrisie. Dans l'une, sous prétexte de pleurer la perte d'une personne qui nous est chère, nous nous pleurons nous-mêmes; nous regrettons la bonne opinion qu'il avait de nous; nous pleurons la diminution de notre bien, de notre plaisir, de notre considération. Ainsi les morts ont l'honneur des larmes qui ne coulent que pour les vivants. Je dis que c'est une espèce d'hypocrisie, à cause que dans ces sortes d'afflictions on se trompe soi-même. Il y a une autre hypocrisie qui n'est pas si innocente, parce qu'elle impose à tout le monde: C'est l'affliction de certaines personnes qui aspirent à la gloire d'une belle et immortelle douleur. Après que le temps qui consume tout a fait cesser celle qu'elles avaient en effet, elles ne laissent pas d'opiniâtrer leurs pleurs, leurs plaintes, et leurs soupirs; elles prennent un personnage lugubre, et travaillent à persuader par toutes leurs actions que leur déplaisir ne finira qu'avec leur vie. Cette triste et fatigante vanité se trouve d'ordinaire dans les femmes ambitieuses. Comme leur sexe leur ferme tous les chemins qui mènent à la gloire, elles s'efforcent de se rendre célèbres par la montre d'une inconsolable affliction. Il y a encore une autre espèce de larmes qui n'ont que de petites sources qui coulent et se tarissent facilement: on pleure pour avoir la réputation d'être tendre: on pleure pour être plaint: on pleure pour être pleuré; enfin on pleure pour éviter la honte de ne pleurer pas.

V: 234

C'est plus souvent par orgueil que par défaut de lumières qu'on s'oppose avec tant d'opiniâtreté aux opinions les plus suivies: on trouve les premières places prises dans le bon parti, et on ne veut point des dernières.

V: 235

Nous nous consolons aisément des disgrâces de nos amis lorsqu'elles servent à signaler notre tendresse pour eux.

V: 236

Il semble que l'amour-propre soit la dupe de la bonté, et qu'il

V: 233

In times of sorrow there are different kinds of hypocrisy. In one, under the pretext of mourning the loss of someone who is dear to us, we mourn for ourselves; we regret the loss of his good opinion; we mourn for the reduction in our well-being, our pleasure, our prestige. So the dead are honoured with tears shed only for the living. I say it is a kind of hypocrisy, because in sorrows of this sort we are deceiving ourselves. There is another form of hypocrisy which is not so innocent, because it strives to impress everyone else. This is the sorrow of certain people who are aspiring to the glory of a beautiful and never-ending show of unhappiness. After time, which devours everything, has put an end to all their real unhappiness, they stubbornly maintain their tears, complaints, and sighs; they play a doleful part and strive to demonstrate by their deeds that their unhappiness will end only with their life. This wretched and wearisome form of vanity is usually found in ambitious women. As their sex bars them from all the roads that lead to glory, they try to become famous by a display of inconsolable sorrow.

There is yet another kind of tears, which come only from little springs, flowing easily and drying up easily: people weep to be regarded as loving; they weep to be pitied; they weep to be wept over; and finally, they weep to escape the shame of not weeping. [I–V]

V: 234

It is more often pride than lack of enlightenment that makes us oppose so stubbornly the generally accepted view of something. We find the front seats already taken on the correct side, and we do not want any of the back ones. [V]

V: 235

We are easily consoled for our friends' misfortunes when such things give us a chance to display our affection for them. [I–V]

V: 236

It may seem that self-love is deceived by kindness, and that it forgets

s'oublie lui-même lorsque nous travaillons pour l'avantage des autres. Cependant c'est prendre le chemin le plus assuré pour arriver à ses fins: c'est prêter à usure sous prétexte de donner: c'est enfin s'acquérir tout le monde par un moyen subtil et délicat.

V: 237
Nul ne mérite d'être loué de bonté s'il n'a pas la force d'être méchant: toute autre bonté n'est le plus souvent qu'une paresse ou une impuissance de la volonté.

V: 238
Il n'est pas si dangereux de faire du mal à la plupart des hommes que de leur faire trop de bien.

V: 239
Rien ne flatte plus notre orgueil que la confiance des grands, parce que nous la regardons comme un effet de notre mérite, sans considérer qu'elle ne vient le plus souvent que de vanité, ou d'impuissance de garder le secret.

V: 240
On peut dire de l'agrément séparé de la beauté, que c'est une symétrie dont on ne sait point les règles, et un rapport secret des traits ensemble, et des traits avec les couleurs et avec l'air de la personne.

V: 241
La coquetterie est le fond de l'humeur des femmes. Mais toutes ne la mettent pas en pratique, parce que la coquetterie de quelques-unes est retenue par la crainte ou par la raison.

V: 242
On incommode souvent les autres quand on croit ne les pouvoir jamais incommoder.

its own interests when we are working for the sake of other people. Yet this is the surest way for it to reach its goals: it is lending at interest, under the pretext of giving; in fact, it is a subtle, refined method of winning over everyone else. [I–V]

V: 237

No one deserves to be praised for kindness if he does not have the strength to be bad; every other form of kindness is most often merely laziness or lack of willpower. [I–V]

V: 238

It is less dangerous to do evil to most men than to do them too much good. [I–V]

V: 239

Nothing flatters our pride more than the fact that great people confide in us, because we regard that as a result of our own merit, without considering that it most often arises only from vanity or inability to keep a secret. [I–V]

V: 240

We may say that attractiveness, as distinct from beauty, is a harmony whose rules are quite unknown, a subtle interrelationship between a person's various features, and also between those features and the colouring and the person's manner. [I–V]

V: 241

Flirting is the basis of the female temperament. But not all women put it into practice, because some are restrained by fear or reason. [I–V]

V: 242

We often annoy other people when we think we could not possibly annoy them. [I–V]

V : 243

Il y a peu de choses impossibles d'elles-mêmes; et l'application pour
les faire réussir nous manque plus que les moyens.

V : 244

La souveraine habileté consiste à bien connaître le prix des choses.

V : 245

C'est une grande habileté que de savoir cacher son habileté.

V : 246

Ce qui paraît générosité n'est souvent qu'une ambition déguisée qui
méprise de petits intérêts, pour aller à de plus grands.

V : 247

La fidélité qui paraît en la plupart des hommes, n'est qu'une inven-
tion de l'amour-propre pour attirer la confiance. C'est un moyen de
nous élever au-dessus des autres, et de nous rendre dépositaires des
choses les plus importantes.

V : 248

La magnanimité méprise tout pour avoir tout.

V : 249

Il n'y a pas moins d'éloquence dans le ton de la voix, dans les yeux et
dans l'air de la personne, que dans le choix des paroles.

V : 250

La véritable éloquence consiste à dire tout ce qu'il faut, et à ne dire
que ce qu'il faut.

V: 243

Few things are impossible in themselves; we lack the diligence to make them succeed, rather than the means. [I–V]

V: 244

Supreme cleverness lies in knowing the exact value of things. [I–V]

V: 245

You are immensely clever if you are able to hide your cleverness. [I–V]

V: 246

What seems to be generosity is often merely a disguised form of ambition, which disdains small interests in order to pursue great ones. [I–V]

V: 247

The loyalty shown by most men is a mere device invented by self-love to gain people's confidence. It is a way of exalting ourselves above other people and making ourselves trustees of the most important things. [I–V]

V: 248

Magnanimity disdains everything to gain everything. [I–V]

V: 249

There is no less eloquence in a person's manner, eyes, and tone of voice, than there is in his choice of words. [I–V]

V: 250

True eloquence consists of saying all that is needed and only what is needed. [I–V]

V: 251

Il y a des personnes à qui les défauts siéent bien, et d'autres qui sont disgraciées avec leurs bonnes qualités.

V: 252

Il est aussi ordinaire de voir changer les goûts, qu'il est extraordinaire de voir changer les inclinations.

V: 253

L'intérêt met en œuvre toutes sortes de vertus et de vices.

V: 254

L'humilité n'est souvent qu'une feinte soumission dont on se sert pour soumettre les autres: c'est un artifice de l'orgueil qui s'abaisse pour s'élever: et bien qu'il se transforme en mille manières, il n'est jamais mieux déguisé et plus capable de tromper, que lorsqu'il se cache sous la figure de l'humilité.

V: 255

Tous les sentiments ont chacun un ton de voix, des gestes et des mines qui leur sont propres: Et ce rapport bon ou mauvais, agréable ou désagréable, est ce qui fait que les personnes plaisent ou déplaisent.

V: 256

Dans toutes les professions chacun affecte une mine et un extérieur pour paraître ce qu'il veut qu'on le croie. Ainsi on peut dire que le monde n'est composé que de mines.

V: 257

La gravité est un mystère du corps inventé pour cacher les défauts de l'esprit.

V: 258

Le bon goût vient plus du jugement que de l'esprit.

V: 251

There are some people whose faults become them well, while other people, with all their good qualities, are lacking in charm. [I–V]

V: 252

It is as usual to see changes of taste as it is unusual to see changes of inclination. [I–V]

V: 253

Self-interest puts on display all kinds of virtues and vices. [I–V]

V: 254

Humility is often merely a pretence of submissiveness, which we use to make other people submit to us. It is an artifice by which pride debases itself in order to exalt itself; and though it can transform itself in thousands of ways, pride is never better disguised and more deceptive than when it is hidden behind the mask of humility. [I–V]

V: 255

Each feeling has its own special look, gesture, and tone of voice; and that interrelationship—good or bad, attractive or unattractive—is what makes people pleasant or unpleasant. [I–V]

V: 256

In any profession each person puts on a pretended look and outward appearance to make him seem what he wants people to think him. So we may say that the world is composed only of appearances. [I–V]

V: 257

Solemnity is an outward mystification devised to hide inner faults. [I–V]

V: 258

Good taste is due more to judgement than to intelligence. [V]

V : 259

Le plaisir de l'amour est d'aimer: et l'on est plus heureux par la
passion que l'on a, que par celle que l'on donne.

V : 260

La civilité est un désir d'en recevoir, et d'être estimé poli.

V : 261

L'éducation que l'on donne d'ordinaire aux jeunes gens est un
second amour-propre qu'on leur inspire.

V : 262

Il n'y a point de passion où l'amour de soi-même règne si puissamment que dans l'amour; et on est toujours plus disposé à sacrifier le
repos de ce qu'on aime, qu'à perdre le sien.

V : 263

Ce qu'on nomme libéralité n'est le plus souvent que la vanité de
donner, que nous aimons mieux que ce que nous donnons.

V : 264

La pitié est souvent un sentiment de nos propres maux dans les
maux d'autrui. C'est une habile prévoyance des malheurs où nous
pouvons tomber: nous donnons du secours aux autres pour les
engager à nous en donner en de semblables occasions; et ces services
que nous leur rendons sont à proprement parler des biens que nous
nous faisons à nous-mêmes par avance.

V : 265

La petitesse de l'esprit fait l'opiniâtreté: et nous ne croyons pas
aisément ce qui est au-delà de ce que nous voyons.

V: 259

The pleasure of love consists of loving; we are happier in the passion we feel than in that we inspire. [II–V]

V: 260

Politeness is a desire to receive it in return, and to be thought civil. [I–V]

V: 261

The education usually bestowed on the young gives them a second dose of self-love. [I–V]

V: 262

There is no passion so powerfully ruled by self-love as love; and we are always more willing to sacrifice the peace of our beloved, than to lose our own. [I–V]

V: 263

What we call generosity is most often merely the vanity of giving, which we like more than the thing we are giving. [I–V]

V: 264

Pity is often a feeling of our own ills, prompted by the ills of other people. It is a clever way of anticipating the misfortunes that could possibly befall us: we help other people so that they will be obliged to help us when comparable circumstances arise; and the services we render them are, strictly speaking, good deeds that we do for ourselves in advance. [I–V]

V: 265

Small-mindedness leads to stubbornness; it is hard for us to believe anything that goes beyond what we see. [I–V]

V: 266

C'est se tromper que de croire qu'il n'y ait que les violentes passions, comme l'ambition et l'amour, qui puissent triompher des autres. La paresse toute languissante qu'elle est ne laisse pas d'en être souvent la maîtresse: elle usurpe sur tous les desseins et sur toutes les actions de la vie: elle y détruit et y consume insensiblement les passions et les vertus.

V: 267

La promptitude à croire le mal sans l'avoir assez examiné est un effet de l'orgueil et de la paresse. On veut trouver des coupables; et on ne veut pas se donner la peine d'examiner les crimes.

V: 268

Nous récusons des Juges pour les plus petits intérêts, et nous voulons bien que notre réputation et notre gloire dépendent du jugement des hommes qui nous sont tous contraires, ou par leur jalousie, ou par leur préoccupation, ou par leur peu de lumière: et ce n'est que pour les faire prononcer en notre faveur que nous exposons en tant de manières notre repos et notre vie.

V: 269

Il n'y a guère d'homme assez habile pour connaître tout le mal qu'il fait.

V: 270

L'honneur acquis est caution de celui qu'on doit acquérir.

V: 271

La jeunesse est une ivresse continuelle: c'est la fièvre de la raison.

V: 272

Rien ne devrait plus humilier les hommes qui ont mérité de grandes louanges, que le soin qu'ils prennent encore de se faire valoir par de petites choses.

V: 266

We are deceiving ourselves if we think that only the violent passions, such as ambition and love, can conquer the others. Laziness, sluggish though it is, often manages to dominate them; it wrests from us all of life's plans and deeds, where it imperceptibly destroys and devours the passions and virtues alike. [I–V]

V: 267

Our readiness to believe evil, without investigating it adequately, results from pride and laziness. We want to find the guilty party, and we do not want to go to the trouble of investigating the crime. [I–V]

V: 268

We take exception to judges for the most trivial of interests, yet we are quite willing to let our reputation and glory depend on the judgement of men who are utterly opposed to us, because of either jealousy or self-absorption or lack of enlightenment; and it is merely to have them decide in our favour that we risk our peace of mind and our very life in so many ways. [I–V]

V: 269

Hardly any man is clever enough to know all the evil he does. [II–V]

V: 270

Honours won are down payments for those still to be won. [I–V]

V: 271

Youth is a continual drunkenness: it is the delirium of reason. [I–V]

V: 272

Nothing should be more humbling to men who have deserved great praise than the care they must still take to advertise themselves in trivial ways. [I–V]

v: 273

Il y a des gens qu'on approuve dans le monde, qui n'ont pour tout mérite que les vices qui servent au commerce de la vie.

v: 274

La grâce de la nouveauté est à l'amour ce que la fleur est sur les fruits, elle y donne un lustre qui s'efface aisément, et qui ne revient jamais.

v: 275

Le bon naturel qui se vante d'être si sensible est souvent étouffé par le moindre intérêt.

v: 276

L'absence diminue les médiocres passions, et augmente les grandes, comme le vent éteint les bougies et allume le feu.

v: 277

Les femmes croient souvent aimer encore qu'elles n'aiment pas. L'occupation d'une intrigue, l'émotion d'esprit que donne la galanterie, la pente naturelle au plaisir d'être aimées, et la peine de refuser, leur persuadent qu'elles ont de la passion lorsqu'elles n'ont que de la coquetterie.

v: 278

Ce qui fait que l'on est souvent mécontent de ceux qui négocient, est qu'ils abandonnent presque toujours l'intérêt de leurs amis pour l'intérêt du succès de la négociation, qui devient le leur par l'honneur d'avoir réussi à ce qu'ils avaient entrepris.

v: 279

Quand nous exagérons la tendresse que nos amis ont pour nous, c'est souvent moins par reconnaissance que par le désir de faire juger de notre mérite.

V: 273

There are people who have the approval of society, though their only merits are the vices useful for the transactions of daily life. [I–V]

V: 274

The charm of novelty is to love what the flower is to the fruits: it gives it a lustre that is easily tarnished and never returns. [V]

V: 275

Innate goodness, which takes pride in being so sensitive, is often stifled by the least self-interest. [I–V]

V: 276

Absence makes average passions decrease and great ones increase, just as wind extinguishes candles and kindles a fire. [I–V]

V: 277

Women often think they are in love though they are not. The business of an intrigue, the excitement produced by a love affair, a natural predilection for the pleasure of being loved, and the difficulty of refusing, convince them that they are being passionate when they are merely being flirtatious. [I–V]

V: 278

What makes us often dissatisfied with those who carry out a negotiation is that they almost always abandon their friends' interests in the interests of successful negotiation. The success becomes their own, because they have the honour of accomplishing what they had undertaken. [I–V]

V: 279

When we overestimate our friends' affection for us, it is often less from gratitude than from a desire to have our own merit approved. [I–V]

v: 280

L'approbation que l'on donne à ceux qui entrent dans le monde, vient souvent de l'envie secrète que l'on porte à ceux qui y sont établis.

v: 281

L'orgueil qui nous inspire tant d'envie nous sert souvent aussi à la modérer.

v: 282

Il y a des faussetés déguisées qui représentent si bien la vérité, que ce serait mal juger que de ne s'y pas laisser tromper.

v: 283

Il n'y a pas quelquefois moins d'habileté à savoir profiter d'un bon conseil, qu'à se bien conseiller soi-même.

v: 284

Il y a des méchants qui seraient moins dangereux s'ils n'avaient aucune bonté.

v: 285

La magnanimité est assez définie par son nom: néanmoins on pourrait dire que c'est le bon sens de l'orgueil, et la voie la plus noble pour recevoir des louanges.

v: 286

Il est impossible d'aimer une seconde fois ce qu'on a véritablement cessé d'aimer.

v: 287

Ce n'est pas tant la fertilité de l'esprit qui nous fait trouver plusieurs expédients sur une même affaire, que c'est le défaut de lumière qui nous fait arrêter à tout ce qui se présente à notre imagination, et qui nous empêche de discerner d'abord ce qui est le meilleur.

V: 280

The approval we give to those who are just entering society often arises from secret envy of those who are already established there. [I–V]

V: 281

Often, the pride that rouses so much envy also helps us to mitigate it. [II–V]

V: 282

Some kinds of disguised falseness imitate truth so well that it would be a misjudgement not to be deceived by them. [I–V]

V: 283

Sometimes it takes as much cleverness to profit from good advice as to give ourselves good advice. [I–V]

V: 284

There are some wicked people who would be less dangerous if they had absolutely no goodness. [I–V]

V: 285

Magnanimity is defined well enough by its name;* yet we could say that it is pride's form of good sense, and the noblest way to win praise. [I–V]

V: 286

It is impossible to love again what you have really ceased to love. [I–V]

V: 287

It is not so much a fertile mind that makes us find various solutions to a single matter; rather, it is lack of enlightenment, which makes us pause over everything that springs to our imagination, and prevents us from immediately recognizing which one is best. [I–V]

v: 288

Il y a des affaires et des maladies que les remèdes aigrissent en certains temps: et la grande habileté consiste à connaître quand il est dangereux d'en user.

v: 289

La simplicité affectée est une imposture délicate.

v: 290

Il y a plus de défauts dans l'humeur que dans l'esprit.

v: 291

Le mérite des hommes a sa saison aussi bien que les fruits.

v: 292

On peut dire de l'humeur des hommes comme de la plupart des bâtiments, qu'elle a diverses faces; les unes agréables, et les autres désagréables.

v: 293

La modération ne peut avoir le mérite de combattre l'ambition et de la soumettre: elles ne se trouvent jamais ensemble. La modération est la langueur et la paresse de l'âme, comme l'ambition en est l'activité et l'ardeur.

v: 294

Nous aimons toujours ceux qui nous admirent: et nous n'aimons pas toujours ceux que nous admirons.

v: 295

Il s'en faut bien que nous ne connaissions toutes nos volontés.

v: 288

Some business matters and some illnesses can be aggravated by remedies, at certain times; the really clever thing is to know when it is dangerous to make use of them. [I–V]

v: 289

A pretence of simplicity is a subtle imposture. [II–V]

v: 290

There are more faults of temperament than of mind. [II–V]

v: 291

Men's virtues have their season, as fruits do. [II–V]

v: 292

It may be said of men's temperaments, as of most buildings, that they have various different sides, some attractive and others unattractive. [II–V]

v: 293

Moderation cannot claim any merit for fighting ambition and subjugating it; the two things are never found together. Moderation is sluggishness and laziness of the soul, as ambition is its activity and passion. [I–V]

v: 294

We always like those who admire us, and we do not always like those whom we admire. [II–V]

v: 295

We are very far from knowing all our wishes. [II–V]

v: 296

Il est difficile d'aimer ceux que nous n'estimons point: mais il ne l'est pas moins d'aimer ceux que nous estimons beaucoup plus que nous.

v: 297

Les humeurs du corps ont un cours ordinaire et réglé, qui meut et qui tourne imperceptiblement notre volonté: elles roulent ensemble et exercent successivement un empire secret en nous: de sorte qu'elles ont une part considérable à toutes nos actions, sans que nous le puissions connaître.

v: 298

La reconnaissance de la plupart des hommes n'est qu'une secrète envie de recevoir de plus grands bienfaits.

v: 299

Presque tout le monde prend plaisir à s'acquitter des petites obligations: beaucoup de gens ont de la reconnaissance pour les médiocres: mais il n'y a quasi personne qui n'ait de l'ingratitude pour les grandes.

v: 300

Il y a des folies qui se prennent comme les maladies contagieuses.

v: 301

Assez de gens méprisent le bien; mais peu savent le donner.

v: 302

Ce n'est d'ordinaire que dans de petits intérêts où nous prenons le hasard de ne pas croire aux apparences.

v: 303

Quelque bien qu'on nous dise de nous on ne nous apprend rien de nouveau.

V: 296

It is hard to like those whom we do not respect at all; but it is no easier to like those whom we respect far more than ourselves. [II–V]

V: 297

The body's humours follow a normal, regular course, which imperceptibly impels and bends our will. They progress together and successively exercise secret dominion over us, so that they play an important part in all our deeds, though we do not know it. [I–V]

V: 298

Most men's gratitude is merely a secret wish to receive greater favours. [II–V]

V: 299

Almost everyone takes pleasure in discharging small obligations; many people are grateful for average-sized ones; but there is hardly anyone who does not lack gratitude for great ones. [II–V]

V: 300

Some follies are catching, like contagious illnesses. [II–V]

V: 301

Plenty of people disdain possessions, but few know how to give them away. [II–V]

V: 302

It is usually only in matters of little interest that we take the risk of not believing in appearances. [III–V]

V: 303

Whatever good is said about us never teaches us anything new. [III–V]

V: 304

Nous pardonnons souvent à ceux qui nous ennuient, mais nous ne pouvons pardonner à ceux que nous ennuyons.

V: 305

L'intérêt que l'on accuse de tous nos crimes mérite souvent d'être loué de nos bonnes actions.

V: 306

On ne trouve guère d'ingrats tant qu'on est en état de faire du bien.

V: 307

Il est aussi honnête d'être glorieux avec soi-même, qu'il est ridicule de l'être avec les autres.

V: 308

On a fait une vertu de la modération pour borner l'ambition des grands hommes, et pour consoler les gens médiocres de leur peu de fortune, et de leur peu de mérite.

V: 309

Il y a des gens destinés à être sots, qui ne font pas seulement des sottises par leur choix, mais que la fortune même contraint d'en faire.

V: 310

Il arrive quelquefois des accidents dans la vie, d'où il faut être un peu fou pour se bien tirer.

V: 311

S'il y a des hommes dont le ridicule n'ait jamais paru, c'est qu'on ne l'a pas bien cherché.

V: 304

We often forgive those who bore us, but we cannot forgive those whom we bore. [III–V]

V: 305

Self-interest, which is accused of all our crimes, often deserves to be praised for our good deeds. [III–V]

V: 306

We find very few ungrateful people as long as we are in a position to do good. [III–V]

V: 307

It is as honorable to glory in our achievements privately, as it is absurd to do so publicly. [III–V]

V: 308

Moderation has been turned into a virtue to limit the ambition of great men, and to comfort average people for their lack of fortune and lack of merit. [III–V]

V: 309

Some people are destined to be fools, and do foolish things not merely by choice, but because fortune itself compels them to do so. [III–V]

V: 310

Sometimes in life there are events that you need to be a little foolish to handle. [III–V]

V: 311

If there are men whose absurd side has never been revealed, it is because no one has looked for it properly. [III–V]

V: 312

Ce qui fait que les amants et les maîtresses ne s'ennuient point d'être ensemble, c'est qu'ils parlent toujours d'eux-mêmes.

V: 313

Pourquoi faut-il que nous ayons assez de mémoire pour retenir jusqu'aux moindres particularités de ce qui nous est arrivé, et que nous n'en ayons pas assez pour nous souvenir combien de fois nous les avons contées à une même personne?

V: 314

L'extrême plaisir que nous prenons à parler de nous-mêmes, nous doit faire craindre de n'en donner guère à ceux qui nous écoutent.

V: 315

Ce qui nous empêche d'ordinaire de faire voir le fond de notre cœur à nos amis, n'est pas tant la défiance que nous avons d'eux, que celle que nous avons de nous-mêmes.

V: 316

Les personnes faibles ne peuvent être sincères.

V: 317

Ce n'est pas un grand malheur d'obliger des ingrats, mais c'en est un insupportable d'être obligé à un malhonnête homme.

V: 318

On trouve des moyens pour guérir de la folie, mais on n'en trouve point pour redresser un esprit de travers.

V: 319

On ne saurait conserver longtemps les sentiments qu'on doit avoir

V: 312

The reason why lovers are never bored with each other's company is because they are always talking about themselves. [III–V]

V: 313

Why is it that we have enough memory to preserve even the slightest details of what has happened to us, but we do not have enough to remind us how many times we have told them to the same person? [III–V]

V: 314

The extreme pleasure we take in talking about ourselves should make us afraid that we may scarcely be giving any to our listeners. [III–V]

V: 315

What usually prevents us from showing the depths of our hearts to our friends is not so much mistrust of them as mistrust of ourselves. [III–V]

V: 316

Weak people cannot be sincere. [III–V]

V: 317

It is no great misfortune to oblige someone who is ungrateful, but it is an unbearable misfortune to be obligated to a dishonorable man. [III–V]

V: 318

We can find ways to cure folly, but we can find none to correct waywardness. [III–V]

V: 319

We cannot long feel as we should toward our friends and benefactors

pour ses amis et pour ses bienfaiteurs, si on se laisse la liberté de parler souvent de leurs défauts.

V: 320

Louer les Princes des vertus qu'ils n'ont pas, c'est leur dire impunément des injures.

V: 321

Nous sommes plus près d'aimer ceux qui nous haïssent que ceux qui nous aiment plus que nous ne voulons.

V: 322

Il n'y a que ceux qui sont méprisables, qui craignent d'être méprisés.

V: 323

Notre sagesse n'est pas moins à la merci de la fortune que nos biens.

V: 324

Il y a dans la jalousie plus d'amour-propre que d'amour.

V: 325

Nous nous consolons souvent par faiblesse des maux dont la raison n'a pas la force de nous consoler.

V: 326

Le ridicule déshonore plus que le déshonneur.

V: 327

Nous n'avouons de petits défauts que pour persuader que nous n'en avons pas de grands.

if we allow ourselves the liberty of talking frequently about their faults. [III–V]

V: 320
To praise princes for virtues they do not have is to insult them with impunity. [III–V]

V: 321
We are closer to loving our enemies than those who love us more than we want. [III–V]

V: 322
Only those who deserve disdain are afraid of being treated with disdain. [III–V]

V: 323
Our wisdom is no less at the mercy of fortune than our possessions are. [III–V]

V: 324
In jealousy there is more self-love than love. [III–V]

V: 325
Weakness often consoles us for ills when reason lacks the strength to do so. [III–V]

V: 326
Ridicule dishonours more than dishonour does. [III–V]

V: 327
We confess small faults only to convince people that we have no greater ones. [III–V]

V: 328

L'envie est plus irréconciliable que la haine.

V: 329

On croit quelquefois haïr la flatterie, mais on ne hait que la manière de flatter.

V: 330

On pardonne tant que l'on aime.

V: 331

Il est plus difficile d'être fidèle à sa maîtresse quand on est heureux, que quand on en est maltraité.

V: 332

Les femmes ne connaissent pas toute leur coquetterie.

V: 333

Les femmes n'ont point de sévérité complète sans aversion.

V: 334

Les femmes peuvent moins surmonter leur coquetterie que leur passion.

V: 335

Dans l'amour la tromperie va presque toujours plus loin que la méfiance.

V: 336

Il y a une certaine sorte d'amour dont l'excès empêche la jalousie.

v: 328

Envy is harder to appease than hatred. [III–V]

v: 329

We sometimes think we hate flattery, but what we hate is merely the way it is done. [III–V]

v: 330

We forgive as long as we love. [III–V]

v: 331

It is harder to be faithful to your beloved when you are happy than when you are ill-treated by her. [III–V]

v: 332

Women do not know just what flirts they are. [III–V]

v: 333

Women never behave with total austerity where they feel no aversion. [III–V]

v: 334

Women are less able to overcome their flirting than their passion. [III–V]

v: 335

In love, deceit nearly always outruns mistrust. [III–V]

v: 336

There is a certain kind of love which is so extreme that it prevents jealousy. [III–V]

V : 337

Il est de certaines bonnes qualités comme des sens, ceux qui en sont entièrement privés ne les peuvent apercevoir ni les comprendre.

V : 338

Lorsque notre haine est trop vive, elle nous met au-dessous de ceux que nous haïssons.

V : 339

Nous ne ressentons nos biens et nos maux qu'à proportion de notre amour-propre.

V : 340

L'esprit de la plupart des femmes sert plus à fortifier leur folie que leur raison.

V : 341

Les passions de la jeunesse ne sont guère plus opposées au salut, que la tiédeur des vieilles gens.

V : 342

L'Accent du Pays où l'on est né, demeure dans l'esprit et dans le cœur comme dans le langage.

V : 343

Pour être un grand homme, il faut savoir profiter de toute sa fortune.

V : 344

La plupart des hommes ont comme les plantes des propriétés cachées, que le hasard fait découvrir.

V: 337

Certain good qualities are like physical senses: people who lack them altogether can neither perceive nor understand them. [III–V]

V: 338

When our hatred is too intense, it puts us on a lower level than those we hate. [III–V]

V: 339

We feel our good and ill fortune only in proportion to our self-love. [III–V]

V: 340

Most women's minds are used more to strengthen their folly than their reason. [III–V]

V: 341

The passions of youth are scarcely more opposed to salvation than the lukewarmness of old age is. [IV–V]

V: 342

The accent of our native land remains in our mind and heart, as it does in our speech. [IV–V]

V: 343

To be a great man, you must know how to take advantage of every turn of fortune. [IV–V]

V: 344

Most men, like plants, have hidden characteristics that are revealed by chance. [IV–V]

V: 345

Les occasions nous font connaître aux autres, et encore plus à nous-mêmes.

V: 346

Il ne peut y avoir de règle dans l'esprit ni dans le cœur des femmes, si le tempérament n'en est d'accord.

V: 347

Nous ne trouvons guère de gens de bon sens, que ceux qui sont de notre avis.

V: 348

Quand on aime, on doute souvent de ce qu'on croit le plus.

V: 349

Le plus grand miracle de l'amour, c'est de guérir de la coquetterie.

V: 350

Ce qui nous donne tant d'aigreur contre ceux qui nous font des finesses, c'est qu'ils croient être plus habiles que nous.

V: 351

On a bien de la peine à rompre, quand on ne s'aime plus.

V: 352

On s'ennuie presque toujours avec les gens avec qui il n'est pas permis de s'ennuyer.

V: 353

Un honnête homme peut être amoureux comme un fou, mais non pas comme un sot.

V: 345

Circumstances reveal our nature to other people, and still more to ourselves. [IV–V]

V: 346

There can be nothing well regulated in a woman's mind or heart, unless it suits her temperament. [IV–V]

V: 347

We find very few sensible people except those who agree with our own opinion. [IV–V]

V: 348

When we are in love, we often doubt what we most believe. [IV–V]

V: 349

Love's greatest miracle is to cure flirting. [IV–V]

V: 350

What makes us so bitter against people who act cunningly is the fact that they think they are cleverer than we are. [IV–V]

V: 351

It is very hard to break with someone, when you no longer love each other. [IV–V]

V: 352

We are nearly always bored with the people whose company should not bore us. [IV–V]

V: 353

In love, a man of honor may be mad, but not foolish. [IV–V]

v: 354

Il y a de certains défauts, qui bien mis en œuvre, brillent plus que la vertu même.

v: 355

On perd quelquefois des personnes qu'on regrette plus qu'on n'en est affligé: et d'autres dont on est affligé, et qu'on ne regrette guère.

v: 356

Nous ne louons d'ordinaire de bon cœur que ceux qui nous admirent.

v: 357

Les petits esprits sont trop blessés des petites choses; les grands esprits les voient toutes, et n'en sont point blessés.

v: 358

L'humilité est la véritable preuve des vertus Chrétiennes: sans elle nous conservons tous nos défauts, et ils sont seulement couverts par l'orgueil qui les cache aux autres, et souvent à nous-mêmes.

v: 359

Les infidélités devraient éteindre l'amour, et il ne faudrait point être jaloux quand on a sujet de l'être: Il n'y a que les personnes qui évitent de donner de la jalousie, qui soient dignes qu'on en ait pour elles.

v: 360

On se décrie beaucoup plus auprès de nous par les moindres infidélités qu'on nous fait, que par les plus grandes qu'on fait aux autres.

v: 361

La jalousie naît toujours avec l'amour, mais elle ne meurt pas toujours avec lui.

V: 354

Some faults, properly displayed, shine more brightly than virtue itself. [IV–V]

V: 355

Some people, when we lose them, are missed more than lamented; and others are lamented but scarcely missed. [IV–V]

V: 356

We usually bestow wholehearted praise only on those who admire us. [IV–V]

V: 357

Little minds are too easily wounded by little things; great minds see all such things without being wounded by them. [IV–V]

V: 358

Humility is the true test of the Christian virtues:* without it, we retain all our faults, and they are merely covered by pride, which hides them from other people and often from ourselves. [IV–V]

V: 359

Infidelities ought to extinguish love, and we should never be jealous when we have good reason to be. Only people who avoid giving any cause for jealousy are worthy to inspire it. [IV–V]

V: 360

People are discredited much more, in our eyes, by the slight infidelities they do to us, than by the greater ones they do to other people. [IV–V]

V: 361

Jealousy is always born with love, but does not always die with it. [IV–V]

v: 362

La plupart des femmes ne pleurent pas tant la mort de leurs amants
pour les avoir aimés, que pour paraître plus dignes d'être aimées.

v: 363

Les violences qu'on nous fait nous font souvent moins de peine que
celles que nous nous faisons à nous-mêmes.

v: 364

On sait assez qu'il ne faut guère parler de sa femme; mais on ne sait
pas assez qu'on devrait encore moins parler de soi.

v: 365

Il y a de bonnes qualités qui dégénèrent en défauts quand elles sont
naturelles, et d'autres qui ne sont jamais parfaites quand elles sont
acquises: Il faut, par exemple, que la raison nous fasse ménagers de
notre bien et de notre confiance; et il faut au contraire que la nature
nous donne la bonté et la valeur.

v: 366

Quelque défiance que nous ayons de la sincérité de ceux qui nous
parlent, nous croyons toujours qu'ils nous disent plus vrai qu'aux
autres.

v: 367

Il y a peu d'honnêtes femmes qui ne soient lasses de leur métier.

v: 368

La plupart des honnêtes femmes sont des trésors cachés, qui ne sont
en sûreté que parce qu'on ne les cherche pas.

V: 362

Most women mourn the death of their lovers less because they loved them than to seem worthy of being loved. [IV–V]

V: 363

Injuries done to us by others often cause us less pain than those that we do to ourselves. [IV–V]

V: 364

We are well aware that it is best to say little about our wives; but we are not sufficiently aware that we should say even less about ourselves. [IV–V]

V: 365

There are some good qualities that degenerate into faults when they are innate, and others that are never perfect when they are acquired. For example, our powers of reason must make us careful of our possessions and our confidence; by contrast, nature must give us kindness and valour. [IV–V]

V: 366

However we may mistrust the sincerity of those who talk to us, we always think they are more truthful with us than with other people. [IV–V]

V: 367

There are few virtuous women who are not weary of their occupation. [IV–V]

V: 368

Most virtuous women are hidden treasures: they are safe only because they are not sought after. [IV–V]

V : 369

Les violences qu'on se fait pour s'empêcher d'aimer, sont souvent plus cruelles que les rigueurs de ce qu'on aime.

V : 370

Il n'y a guère de poltrons qui connaissent toujours toute leur peur.

V : 371

C'est presque toujours la faute de celui qui aime, de ne pas connaître quand on cesse de l'aimer.

V : 372

La plupart des jeunes gens croient être naturels lorsqu'ils ne sont que mal polis et grossiers.

V : 373

Il y a de certaines larmes qui nous trompent souvent nous-mêmes après avoir trompé les autres.

V : 374

Si on croit aimer sa maîtresse pour l'amour d'elle, on est bien trompé.

V : 375

Les esprits médiocres condamnent d'ordinaire tout ce qui passe leur portée.

V : 376

L'envie est détruite par la véritable amitié, et la coquetterie par le véritable amour.

V: 369

The self-inflicted injuries we undergo to prevent ourselves from falling in love are often more brutal than the cruelties of those we love. [IV–V]

V: 370

Very few cowards consistently know the full extent of their fears. [IV–V]

V: 371

An almost universal fault of lovers is failing to realize when they are no longer loved. [IV–V]

V: 372

Most young people think they are being natural when they are merely uncivil and uncouth. [V]

V: 373

There are certain kinds of tears that often deceive us ourselves, after having deceived other people. [IV–V]

V: 374

If you think you love your beloved for her own sake, you are very much deceived. [IV–V]

V: 375

Average minds usually condemn whatever is beyond their grasp. [V]

V: 376

Envy is destroyed by true friendship, and flirting by true love. [IV–V]

V : 377

Le plus grand défaut de la pénétration n'est pas de n'aller point jusqu'au but, c'est de le passer.

V : 378

On donne des conseils, mais on n'inspire point de conduite.

V : 379

Quand notre mérite baisse, notre goût baisse aussi.

V : 380

La fortune fait paraître nos vertus et nos vices, comme la lumière fait paraître les objets.

V : 381

La violence qu'on se fait pour demeurer fidèle à ce qu'on aime, ne vaut guère mieux qu'une infidélité.

V : 382

Nos actions sont comme les bouts-rimés que chacun fait rapporter à ce qu'il lui plaît.

V : 383

L'envie de parler de nous, et de faire voir nos défauts du côté que nous voulons bien les montrer, fait une grande partie de notre sincérité.

V : 384

On ne devrait s'étonner que de pouvoir encore s'étonner.

V: 377

The greatest fault of perceptiveness is not that it falls short of the truth, but that it goes past it. [IV–V]

V: 378

People give advice, but they do not influence anyone's conduct. [IV–V]

V: 379

When our merits sink, our tastes sink too. [IV–V]

V: 380

Fortune reveals our virtues and vices, just as light reveals objects. [IV–V]

V: 381

The self-inflicted injuries we undergo to remain faithful to our love are scarcely better than acts of infidelity. [IV–V]

V: 382

Our deeds are like rhyming words,* which anyone can fit to any subject he likes. [IV–V]

V: 383

The wish to talk about ourselves, and to show our faults from the angles that we ourselves would choose, makes up a large part of our sincerity. [IV–V]

V: 384

Nothing should astonish us except the fact that we are still capable of being astonished. [IV–V]

v: 385

On est presque également difficile à contenter, quand on a beaucoup d'amour, et quand on n'en a plus guère.

v: 386

Il n'y a point de gens qui aient plus souvent tort que ceux qui ne peuvent souffrir d'en avoir.

v: 387

Un sot n'a pas assez d'étoffe pour être bon.

v: 388

Si la vanité ne renverse pas entièrement les vertus, du moins elle les ébranle toutes.

v: 389

Ce qui nous rend la vanité des autres insupportable, c'est qu'elle blesse la nôtre.

v: 390

On renonce plus aisément à son intérêt qu'à son goût.

v: 391

La fortune ne paraît jamais si aveugle, qu'à ceux à qui elle ne fait pas de bien.

v: 392

Il faut gouverner la fortune comme la santé; en jouir quand elle est bonne, prendre patience quand elle est mauvaise, et ne faire jamais de grands remèdes sans un extrême besoin.

v: 393

L'air Bourgeois se perd quelquefois à l'armée; mais il ne se perd jamais à la Cour.

V: 385

We are almost equally hard to please when we are much in love and when we are almost out of it. [IV–V]

V: 386

Nobody is more often wrong than someone who cannot bear being wrong. [IV–V]

V: 387

A fool lacks the substance to be good. [IV–V]

V: 388

Even if vanity does not completely overthrow the virtues, at any rate it shakes them all to the foundations. [IV–V]

V: 389

What makes us unable to bear the vanity of other people is the fact that it wounds our own. [IV–V]

V: 390

We give up our interests more readily than our tastes. [IV–V]

V: 391

Fortune never seems as blind as she does to those whom she never benefits. [IV–V]

V: 392

We ought to treat fortune like health: enjoy it when it is good, be patient when it is bad, and never use drastic remedies except in a case of absolute necessity. [IV–V]

V: 393

A middle-class manner is sometimes shed in the army, but never at court. [IV–V]

V: 394

On peut être plus fin qu'un autre; mais non pas plus fin que tous les autres.

V: 395

On est quelquefois moins malheureux d'être trompé de ce qu'on aime, que d'en être détrompé.

V: 396

On garde longtemps son premier Amant, quand on n'en prend point de second.

V: 397

Nous n'avons pas le courage de dire en général que nous n'avons point de défauts, et que nos ennemis n'ont point de bonnes qualités; mais en détail nous ne sommes pas trop éloignés de le croire.

V: 398

De tous nos défauts, celui dont nous demeurons le plus aisément d'accord, c'est de la paresse; nous nous persuadons qu'elle tient à toutes les vertus paisibles, et que sans détruire entièrement les autres, elle en suspend seulement les fonctions.

V: 399

Il y a une élévation qui ne dépend point de la fortune: C'est un certain air qui nous distingue et qui semble nous destiner aux grandes choses; c'est un prix que nous nous donnons imperceptiblement à nous-mêmes; c'est par cette qualité que nous usurpons les déférences des autres hommes; et c'est elle d'ordinaire qui nous met plus au-dessus d'eux, que la naissance, les dignités, et le mérite même.

V: 400

Il y a du mérite sans élévation, mais il n'y a point d'élévation sans quelque mérite.

V: 394

We may be more astute than the next person—but not than all other people. [IV–V]

V: 395

Sometimes it is less unfortunate to be deceived by your beloved than to be disillusioned by her. [IV–V]

V: 396

A woman keeps her first lover a long time if she does not take a second. [IV–V]

V: 397

We lack the courage to say as a general truth that we have no faults and our enemies have no good qualities; but in points of detail, we are not very far from believing it. [IV–V]

V: 398

Of all our faults, the one that we tolerate most readily is laziness. We convince ourselves that it stems from all the calm virtues, and that far from completely destroying the other virtues, it merely suspends their activity. [IV–V]

V: 399

There is a kind of eminence that is not dependent on fortune. It is a certain manner that gives us distinction and seems to destine us for great things; it is a value that we imperceptibly grant to ourselves. By means of this quality we wrest deference from other men; and this is usually what sets us above them, more than birth, honours, or merit itself. [IV–V]

V: 400

There is merit without eminence, but there is no eminence without some merit. [IV–V]

v: 401

L'élévation est au mérite, ce que la parure est aux belles personnes.

v: 402

Ce qui se trouve le moins dans la galanterie, c'est de l'amour.

v: 403

La fortune se sert quelquefois de nos défauts pour nous élever; et il y a des gens incommodes, dont le mérite serait mal récompensé, si on ne voulait acheter leur absence.

v: 404

Il semble que la Nature ait caché dans le fond de notre esprit des talents et une habileté que nous ne connaissons pas: les passions seules ont le droit de les mettre au jour, et de nous donner quelquefois des vues plus certaines et plus achevées que l'art ne saurait faire.

v: 405

Nous arrivons tout nouveaux aux divers âges de la vie, et nous y manquons souvent d'expérience malgré le nombre des années.

v: 406

Les coquettes se font honneur d'être jalouses de leurs amants, pour cacher qu'elles sont envieuses des autres femmes.

v: 407

Il s'en faut bien que ceux qui s'attrapent à nos finesses, ne nous paraissent aussi ridicules que nous nous le paraissons à nous-mêmes, quand les finesses des autres nous ont attrapés.

v: 408

Le plus dangereux ridicule des vieilles personnes qui ont été aimables, c'est d'oublier qu'elles ne le sont plus.

V: 401

Eminence is to merit what adornment is to beauty. [IV–V]

V: 402

What is least often found in love affairs is love. [IV–V]

V: 403

Fortune sometimes uses our faults to make us more eminent; and there are annoying people whose merits would receive little reward unless we were willing to pay for their absence. [IV–V]

V: 404

In the depths of our minds, it seems, nature has hidden away talents and forms of cleverness unknown to us; only the passions have the power of bringing them to light, sometimes giving us surer and more complete insights than art could possibly do. [IV–V]

V: 405

We come as utter novices to the various different stages of life, and in such situations we often lack experience, in spite of the number of our years. [IV–V]

V: 406

Flirts pride themselves on being jealous of their lovers, to hide the fact that they are envious of other women. [IV–V]

V: 407

Those who are snared by our cunning are very far from seeming as absurd to us as we seem to ourselves when we are snared by the cunning of other people. [IV–V]

V: 408

The most dangerous folly of old people who used to be attractive is to forget that they are no longer so. [IV–V]

V: 409

Nous aurions souvent honte de nos plus belles actions, si le monde voyait tous les motifs qui les produisent.

V: 410

Le plus grand effort de l'amitié n'est pas de montrer nos défauts à un ami, c'est de lui faire voir les siens.

V: 411

On n'a guère de défauts qui ne soient plus pardonnables, que les moyens dont on se sert pour les cacher.

V: 412

Quelque honte que nous ayons méritée, il est presque toujours en notre pouvoir de rétablir notre réputation.

V: 413

On ne plaît pas longtemps quand on n'a que d'une sorte d'esprit.

V: 414

Les fous et les sottes gens ne voient que par leur humeur.

V: 415

L'esprit nous sert quelquefois à faire hardiment des sottises.

V: 416

La vivacité qui augmente en vieillissant, ne va pas loin de la folie.

V: 417

En amour celui qui est guéri le premier est toujours le mieux guéri.

V: 409

We would often be ashamed of our finest deeds, if people could see all the motives that produced them. [IV–V]

V: 410

The hardest task in a friendship is not to disclose our faults to our friend, but to make him see his own. [IV–V]

V: 411

Nearly all of our faults are more forgivable than the means we use to hide them. [IV–V]

V: 412

Whatever shame we may have earned, it is almost always in our power to re-establish our reputation. [IV–V]

V: 413

We do not please for long if our minds have only one way of looking at things. [IV–V]

V: 414

Fools and stupid people see things only in the light of their own temper. [V]

V: 415

Our intelligence sometimes gives us the courage to do foolish things. [V]

V: 416

The liveliness that increases with age is not far from folly. [V]

V: 417

In love, the first cured is always the best cured. [V]

V : 418

Les jeunes femmes qui ne veulent point paraître coquettes, et les hommes d'un âge avancé qui ne veulent pas être ridicules, ne doivent jamais parler de l'amour comme d'une chose où ils puissent avoir part.

V : 419

Nous pouvons paraître grands dans un emploi au-dessous de notre mérite, mais nous paraissons souvent petits dans un emploi plus grand que nous.

V : 420

Nous croyons souvent avoir de la constance dans les malheurs lorsque nous n'avons que de l'abattement, et nous les souffrons sans oser les regarder comme les poltrons se laissent tuer de peur de se défendre.

V : 421

La confiance fournit plus à la conversation que l'esprit.

V : 422

Toutes les passions nous font faire des fautes, mais l'amour nous en fait faire de plus ridicules.

V : 423

Peu de gens savent être vieux.

V : 424

Nous nous faisons honneur des défauts opposés à ceux que nous avons; quand nous sommes faibles nous nous vantons d'être opiniâtres.

V : 425

La pénétration a un air de deviner qui flatte plus notre vanité, que toutes les autres qualités de l'esprit.

V: 418

Young women who do not want to look like flirts, and elderly men who do not want to be foolish, should never speak of love as something in which they might possibly be involved. [v]

V: 419

We may look great in a position that is less than we deserve, but we often look small in a position that is too great for us. [v]

V: 420

We often think we are being constant in a time of misfortune when we are merely downcast and endure it without daring to face it, like cowards who let themselves be killed because they are afraid to defend themselves. [v]

V: 421

Confidence contributes more to conversation than intelligence does. [v]

V: 422

All our passions lead us to make mistakes, but love leads us to make the most absurd ones. [v]

V: 423

Few people know how to be old. [v]

V: 424

We pride ourselves on faults that are opposite to those we really have; when we are weak, we boast that we are being stubborn. [v]

V: 425

Perceptiveness has an air of divination* that flatters our vanity more than any other quality of the mind. [v]

v: 426

La grâce de la nouveauté et la longue habitude quelque opposées qu'elles soient, nous empêchent également de sentir les défauts de nos amis.

v: 427

La plupart des amis dégoûtent de l'amitié, et la plupart des dévots dégoûtent de la dévotion.

v: 428

Nous pardonnons aisément à nos amis les défauts qui ne nous regardent pas.

v: 429

Les femmes qui aiment pardonnent plus aisément les grandes indiscrétions que les petites infidélités.

v: 430

Dans la vieillesse de l'amour comme dans celle de l'âge, on vit encore pour les maux, mais on ne vit plus pour les plaisirs.

v: 431

Rien n'empêche tant d'être naturel, que l'envie de le paraître.

v: 432

C'est en quelque sorte se donner part aux belles actions, que de les louer de bon cœur.

v: 433

La plus véritable marque d'être né avec de grandes qualités, c'est d'être né sans envie.

V: 426

The charm of novelty and long habit, however opposite they may be, alike prevent us from being conscious of our friends' faults. [v]

V: 427

Most friends make us lose our taste for friendship, and most pious people make us lose our taste for piety. [v]

V: 428

We readily forgive our friends for faults that do not affect us. [v]

V: 429

Women in love forgive major indiscretions more readily than minor infidelities. [v]

V: 430

In the final stage of love, as in that of life, we are still living for pains, but no longer for pleasures. [v]

V: 431

Nothing prevents us from being natural as much as the wish to look natural. [v]

V: 432

In a sense we take some credit for fine deeds if we praise them wholeheartedly. [v]

V: 433

The surest sign of being born with great qualities is being born without envy. [v]

V: 434

Quand nos amis nous ont trompés on ne doit que de l'indifférence aux marques de leur amitié, mais on doit toujours de la sensibilité à leurs malheurs.

V: 435

La fortune et l'humeur gouvernent le monde.

V: 436

Il est plus aisé de connaître l'homme en général, que de connaître un homme en particulier.

V: 437

On ne doit pas juger du mérite d'un homme par ses grandes qualités, mais par l'usage qu'il en sait faire.

V: 438

Il y a une certaine reconnaissance vive qui ne nous acquitte pas seulement des bienfaits que nous avons reçus, mais qui fait même que nos amis nous doivent en leur payant ce que nous leur devons.

V: 439

Nous ne désirerions guère de choses avec ardeur, si nous connaissions parfaitement ce que nous désirons.

V: 440

Ce qui fait que la plupart des femmes sont peu touchées de l'amitié, c'est qu'elle est fade quand on a senti de l'amour.

V: 441

Dans l'amitié comme dans l'amour, on est souvent plus heureux par les choses qu'on ignore que par celles que l'on sait.

V: 434

When our friends have deceived us, we should be merely indifferent to their signs of friendship, but we should still be sensitive to their misfortunes. [v]

V: 435

Fortune and temperament rule the world. [v]

V: 436

It is easier to know man in general than to know one man in particular. [v]

V: 437

We should not judge a man's merit by his great qualities, but by the use he makes of them. [v]

V: 438

There is a certain kind of lively gratitude that not only discharges our obligations for the favours we have received, but even puts our friends in our debt by the very act of paying them what we owe them. [v]

V: 439

We would have passionate desires for very few things if we fully understood what we were desiring. [v]

V: 440

The reason why most women are so little affected by friendship is that it tastes insipid when they have felt love. [v]

V: 441

In friendship, as in love, we are often happier in what we do not know than in what we do know. [v]

V : 442

Nous essayons de nous faire honneur des défauts que nous ne voulons pas corriger.

V : 443

Les passions les plus violentes nous laissent quelquefois du relâche, mais la vanité nous agite toujours.

V : 444

Les vieux fous sont plus fous que les jeunes.

V : 445

La faiblesse est plus opposée à la vertu que le vice.

V : 446

Ce qui rend les douleurs de la honte et de la jalousie si aiguës, c'est que la vanité ne peut servir à les supporter.

V : 447

La bienséance est la moindre de toutes les Lois, et la plus suivie.

V : 448

Un esprit droit a moins de peine de se soumettre aux esprits de travers que de les conduire.

V : 449

Lorsque la fortune nous surprend en nous donnant une grande place, sans nous y avoir conduits par degrés, ou sans que nous nous y soyons élevés par nos espérances, il est presque impossible de s'y bien soutenir, et de paraître digne de l'occuper.

V : 450

Notre orgueil s'augmente souvent de ce que nous retranchons de nos autres défauts.

V: 442

We try to pride ourselves on the faults that we do not want to correct. [v]

V: 443

The most violent passions sometimes give us some respite, but vanity is continually stirring us. [v]

V: 444

Old fools are more foolish than young ones. [v]

V: 445

Weakness is more opposed to virtue than vice is. [v]

V: 446

What makes the pangs of shame and jealousy so sharp is the fact that vanity cannot help us to bear them. [v]

V: 447

Propriety is the least of all laws, and the one most often obeyed. [v]

V: 448

A sound mind has less trouble submitting to wayward minds than leading them. [v]

V: 449

When fortune catches us by surprise and gives us a position of greatness without having led us to it step by step, and without our having hoped for it, it is almost impossible to fill it well and seem worthy of holding it. [v]

V: 450

What we take away from our other faults is often added to our pride. [v]

V : 451

Il n'y a point de sots si incommodes que ceux qui ont de l'esprit.

V : 452

Il n'y a point d'homme qui se croie en chacune de ses qualités au-dessous de l'homme du monde qu'il estime le plus.

V : 453

Dans les grandes affaires on doit moins s'appliquer à faire naître des occasions qu'à profiter de celles qui se présentent.

V : 454

Il n'y a guère d'occasion où l'on fît un méchant marché de renoncer au bien qu'on dit de nous, à condition de n'en dire point de mal.

V : 455

Quelque disposition qu'ait le monde à mal juger, il fait encore plus souvent grâce au faux mérite, qu'il ne fait injustice au véritable.

V : 456

On est quelquefois un sot avec de l'esprit, mais on ne l'est jamais avec du jugement.

V : 457

Nous gagnerions plus de nous laisser voir tels que nous sommes, que d'essayer de paraître ce que nous ne sommes pas.

V : 458

Nos ennemis approchent plus de la vérité dans les jugements qu'ils font de nous, que nous n'en approchons nous-mêmes.

V : 459

Il y a plusieurs remèdes qui guérissent de l'Amour; mais il n'y en a point d'infaillibles.

V: 451

No fools are as annoying as intelligent ones. [v]

V: 452

There is no man who thinks all his qualities are inferior to those of the man he admires most of all. [v]

V: 453

In great matters we should strive less to create favourable circumstances than to profit from those that arise. [v]

V: 454

In few circumstances would it be a bad bargain if we renounced the good that was said of us, provided that no evil was said either. [v]

V: 455

However inclined people may be to misjudge, they favour false merit even more often than they are unjust to true merit. [v]

V: 456

There are some fools with intelligence, but none with judgement. [v]

V: 457

We would gain more by showing ourselves as we are than by trying to appear to be what we are not. [v]

V: 458

Our enemies' judgements of us are nearer the truth than our own. [v]

V: 459

There are various cures for love, but none of them is infallible. [v]

v: 460

Il s'en faut bien que nous connaissions tout ce que nos passions nous font faire.

v: 461

La vieillesse est un tyran, qui défend sur peine de la vie tous les plaisirs de la jeunesse.

v: 462

Le même orgueil qui nous fait blâmer les défauts dont nous nous croyons exempts, nous porte à mépriser les bonnes qualités que nous n'avons pas.

v: 463

Il y a souvent plus d'orgueil que de bonté à plaindre les malheurs de nos ennemis; c'est pour leur faire sentir que nous sommes au-dessus d'eux, que nous leur donnons des marques de compassion.

v: 464

Il y a un excès de biens et de maux qui passe notre sensibilité.

v: 465

Il s'en faut bien que l'innocence ne trouve autant de protection que le crime.

v: 466

De toutes les passions violentes, celle qui fait le moins mal aux femmes, c'est l'amour.

v: 467

La vanité nous fait faire plus de choses contre notre goût que la raison.

V: 460

We are very far from knowing all the things that our passions make us do. [v]

V: 461

Old age is a tyrant that forbids all the pleasures of youth on pain of death. [v]

V: 462

The same pride that makes us criticize the faults we think we do not have, also leads us to feel disdain for the good qualities we do not have. [v]

V: 463

There is often more pride than kindness in our pity for our enemies' misfortunes; we show them signs of compassion in order to make them feel how superior to them we are. [v]

V: 464

There are extremes of good and ill fortune to which we are quite insensitive. [v]

V: 465

Innocence is very far from finding as much protection as crime. [v]

V: 466

Of all violent passions, the one that harms women least* is love. [v]

V: 467

Vanity makes us do more things that are distasteful to us than reason does. [v]

V: 468

Il y a de méchantes qualités qui font de grands talents.

V: 469

On ne souhaite jamais ardemment ce qu'on ne souhaite que par raison.

V: 470

Toutes nos qualités sont incertaines et douteuses en bien comme en mal, et elles sont presque toutes à la merci des occasions.

V: 471

Dans les premières passions les femmes aiment l'amant, et dans les autres, elles aiment l'amour.

V: 472

L'orgueil a ses bizarreries comme les autres passions; on a honte d'avouer que l'on ait de la jalousie, et on se fait honneur d'en avoir eu, et d'être capable d'en avoir.

V: 473

Quelque rare que soit le véritable amour, il l'est encore moins que la véritable amitié.

V: 474

Il y a peu de femmes dont le mérite dure plus que la beauté.

V: 475

L'envie d'être plaint ou d'être admiré, fait souvent la plus grande partie de notre confiance.

V: 476

Notre envie dure toujours plus longtemps que le bonheur de ceux que nous envions.

V: 468

There are some bad qualities that make great talents. [v]

V: 469

We never desire passionately what we desire by reason alone. [v]

V: 470

All our qualities, good as well as bad, are doubtful and indeterminate; and almost all of them are at the mercy of circumstances. [v]

V: 471

In her first passion a woman loves her lover; in the others, she loves
love. [v]

V: 472

Pride has its peculiarities, as the other passions do; we are ashamed
to confess that we experience jealousy, yet we pride ourselves on
having experienced it and being capable of it. [v]

V: 473

However rare true love may be, true friendship is even rarer. [v]

V: 474

There are few women whose merit outlasts their beauty. [v]

V: 475

The wish to be pitied or admired is often the main reason that makes
us confide in people. [v]

V: 476

Our envy always lasts longer than the good fortune of those we envy.
[v]

V : 477

La même fermeté qui sert à résister à l'amour, sert aussi à le rendre violent et durable; et les personnes faibles qui sont toujours agitées des passions n'en sont presque jamais véritablement remplies.

V : 478

L'imagination ne saurait inventer tant de diverses contrariétés qu'il y en a naturellement dans le cœur de chaque personne.

V : 479

Il n'y a que les personnes qui ont de la fermeté qui puissent avoir une véritable douceur; celles qui paraissent douces n'ont d'ordinaire que de la faiblesse qui se convertit aisément en aigreur.

V : 480

La timidité est un défaut dont il est dangereux de reprendre les personnes qu'on en veut corriger.

V : 481

Rien n'est plus rare que la véritable bonté; ceux mêmes qui croient en avoir, n'ont d'ordinaire que de la complaisance ou de la faiblesse.

V : 482

L'esprit s'attache par paresse et par constance à ce qui lui est facile ou agréable: cette habitude met toujours des bornes à nos connaissances, et jamais personne ne s'est donné la peine d'étendre et de conduire son esprit aussi loin qu'il pourrait aller.

V : 483

On est d'ordinaire plus médisant par vanité que par malice.

V : 484

Quand on a le cœur encore agité par les restes d'une passion, on est plus près d'en prendre une nouvelle que quand on est entièrement guéri.

V: 477

The very strength of character that helps us resist love also helps that love to become passionate and lasting; weak people who are constantly stirred by passion are almost never really imbued with it. [v]

V: 478

Imagination could never invent the number of different contradictions that exist innately in each person's heart. [v]

V: 479

Only people with some strength of character can be truly gentle: usually, what seems like gentleness is mere weakness, which readily turns to bitterness. [v]

V: 480

Timidity is a fault that is dangerous to rebuke in the people we want to cure of it. [v]

V: 481

Nothing is rarer than true kindness: usually, the very people who think they possess it are merely weak or polite. [v]

V: 482

Through laziness and constancy the mind keeps to what it finds easy and attractive; this habit is constantly limiting our knowledge, and no one ever takes the trouble to extend his mind and lead it as far as it could go. [v]

V: 483

We usually slander out of vanity rather than malice. [v]

V: 484

When our hearts are still stirred by the remnants of a passion, we are more likely to fall into a new one than when we are completely cured. [v]

v: 485

Ceux qui ont eu de grandes passions se trouvent toute leur vie heureux, et malheureux d'en être guéris.

v: 486

Il y a encore plus de gens sans intérêt que sans envie.

v: 487

Nous avons plus de paresse dans l'esprit que dans le corps.

v: 488

Le calme ou l'agitation de notre humeur ne dépend pas tant de ce qui nous arrive de plus considérable dans la vie, que d'un arrangement commode ou désagréable de petites choses qui arrivent tous les jours.

v: 489

Quelque méchants que soient les hommes, ils n'oseraient paraître ennemis de la vertu, et lorsqu'ils la veulent persécuter, ils feignent de croire qu'elle est fausse, ou ils lui supposent des crimes.

v: 490

On passe souvent de l'amour à l'ambition, mais on ne revient guère de l'ambition à l'amour.

v: 491

L'extrême avarice se méprend presque toujours; il n'y a point de passion qui s'éloigne plus souvent de son but, ni sur qui le présent ait tant de pouvoir au préjudice de l'avenir.

v: 492

L'avarice produit souvent des effets contraires, il y a un nombre infini de gens qui sacrifient tout leur bien à des espérances douteuses et éloignées; d'autres méprisent de grands avantages à venir pour de petits intérêts présents.

V: 485

Those who have experienced great passions remain, throughout their lives, both happy and unhappy that they have been cured. [v]

V: 486

There are more people without self-interest than without envy. [v]

V: 487

We are lazier in our minds than in our bodies. [v]

V: 488

Calmness or agitation of temper does not depend on the most important things that happen in our lives as much as on comforting or unpleasant combinations of the little things that happen every day. [v]

V: 489

However bad men may be, they dare not seem to be enemies of virtue; when they want to persecute it, they pretend to believe that it is false, or else they ascribe crimes to it. [v]

V: 490

We often pass from love to ambition, but very seldom return from ambition to love. [v]

V: 491

Extreme avarice almost always goes astray; there is no passion that misses the mark so often, and none that is so powerfully controlled by the present, with detrimental results for the future. [v]

V: 492

Avarice often produces opposite results. There are innumerable people who sacrifice all their possessions to doubtful and distant hopes; others disdain great future advantages for the sake of trivial present interests. [v]

V: 493

Il semble que les hommes ne se trouvent pas assez de défauts, ils en augmentent encore le nombre par de certaines qualités singulières dont ils affectent de se parer; et ils les cultivent avec tant de soin qu'elles deviennent à la fin des défauts naturels, qu'il ne dépend plus d'eux de corriger.

V: 494

Ce qui fait voir que les hommes connaissent mieux leurs fautes qu'on ne pense, c'est qu'ils n'ont jamais tort quand on les entend parler de leur conduite: le même amour-propre qui les aveugle d'ordinaire les éclaire alors, et leur donne des vues si justes, qu'il leur fait supprimer ou déguiser les moindres choses qui peuvent être condamnées.

V: 495

Il faut que les jeunes gens qui entrent dans le monde soient honteux ou étourdis: un air capable et composé se tourne d'ordinaire en impertinence.

V: 496

Les querelles ne dureraient pas longtemps, si le tort n'était que d'un côté.

V: 497

Il ne sert de rien d'être jeune sans être belle, ni d'être belle sans être jeune.

V: 498

Il y a des personnes si légères et si frivoles, qu'elles sont aussi éloignées d'avoir de véritables défauts que des qualités solides.

V: 499

On ne compte d'ordinaire la première galanterie des femmes que lorsqu'elles en ont une seconde.

V: 493

It seems that men do not find enough faults in themselves; they increase the number with certain singular qualities, with which they make a pretence of adorning themselves; and they cultivate them with such care that in the end they become innate faults, which they are no longer capable of correcting. [v]

V: 494

What shows us that men know their own faults better than we might think, is the fact that they are never wrong when we hear them talking about their own conduct. Then, the very self-love that usually blinds them illuminates them, and gives them such accurate insights that they suppress or disguise even the slightest things that might be condemned. [v]

V: 495

Young people just entering society should look shamefaced or half-witted; a confident, assured manner usually turns into insolence. [v]

V: 496

Quarrels would not last long if the fault was only on one side. [v]

V: 497

It is useless for a woman to be young but not beautiful, or beautiful but not young. [v]

V: 498

There are people so fickle and frivolous that they are as far from having any true faults as from having any substantial qualities. [v]

V: 499

We do not usually count a woman's first love affair until she has a second. [v]

V: 500

Il y a des gens si remplis d'eux-mêmes, que lorsqu'ils sont amoureux, ils trouvent moyen d'être occupés de leur passion sans l'être de la personne qu'ils aiment.

V: 501

L'amour tout agréable qu'il est, plaît encore plus par les manières dont il se montre que par lui-même.

V: 502

Peu d'esprit avec de la droiture ennuie moins à la longue, que beaucoup d'esprit avec du travers.

V: 503

La jalousie est le plus grand de tous les maux, et celui qui fait le moins de pitié aux personnes qui le causent.

V: 504

Après avoir parlé de la fausseté de tant de vertus apparentes, il est raisonnable de dire quelque chose de la fausseté du mépris de la mort. J'entends parler de ce mépris de la mort que les païens se vantent de tirer de leurs propres forces, sans l'espérance d'une meilleure vie. Il y a différence entre souffrir la mort constamment, et la mépriser. Le premier est assez ordinaire; mais je crois que l'autre n'est jamais sincère. On a écrit néanmoins tout ce qui peut le plus persuader que la mort n'est point un mal: et les hommes les plus faibles aussi bien que les Héros, ont donné mille exemples célèbres pour établir cette opinion. Cependant je doute que personne de bon sens l'ait jamais cru: et la peine que l'on prend pour le persuader aux autres et à soi-même, fait assez voir que cette entreprise n'est pas aisée. On peut avoir divers sujets de dégoût dans la vie; mais on n'a jamais raison de mépriser la mort: ceux mêmes qui se la donnent volontairement, ne la comptent pas pour si peu de chose; et ils s'en étonnent et la rejettent comme les autres, lorsqu'elle vient à eux par une autre voie que celle qu'ils ont choisie. L'inégalité que l'on remarque dans le courage d'un nombre infini de vaillants hommes, vient de ce que la mort se découvre différemment à leur imagination;

V: 500

There are people so full of themselves that when they are in love, they find a way to be intent on their own passion rather than on the person they love. [v]

V: 501

Love, attractive as it is, gives us pleasure less in itself than in the ways it reveals itself. [v]

V: 502

In the long run, little intelligence combined with sound sense is less tiresome than plenty of intelligence combined with waywardness. [v]

V: 503

Jealousy is the greatest of all ills—and the one that elicits least pity in the people who cause it. [v]

V: 504

After we have discussed the falsity of so many apparent virtues, it is reasonable to say something about the falsity of disdain for death. I want to discuss the kind of disdain for death that pagans claim to derive from their own strength, and not from the hope of a better life hereafter. There is a difference between enduring death with constancy and treating it with disdain. The former is not unusual; but I do not think the latter is ever sincere. Yet writers have done their very best to persuade us that death is not an evil at all; and the weakest men, no less than the heroes, have provided thousands of examples in confirmation of that opinion. But I doubt whether any sensible person ever believed it; and the trouble that people take on the subject, trying to convince others as well as themselves, shows clearly enough that the task is not easy. We may have various motives for finding life distasteful, but we never have any reason to treat death with disdain. Even those who willingly inflict it on themselves do not count it as such a small thing; when it comes to them in some other way than the one they have chosen, they panic and resist it just like other people. The variations that we see in the courage of innumerable valiant men come from the fact that death presents

et y paraît plus présente en un temps qu'en un autre: Ainsi il arrive qu'après avoir méprisé ce qu'ils ne connaissent pas, ils craignent enfin ce qu'ils connaissent. Il faut éviter de l'envisager avec toutes ses circonstances, si on ne veut pas croire qu'elle soit le plus grand de tous les maux. Les plus habiles et les plus braves sont ceux qui prennent de plus honnêtes prétextes pour s'empêcher de la considérer. Mais tout homme qui la sait voir telle qu'elle est, trouve que c'est une chose épouvantable. La nécessité de mourir faisait toute la constance des Philosophes. Ils croyaient qu'il fallait aller de bonne grâce où l'on ne saurait s'empêcher d'aller; et ne pouvant éterniser leur vie, il n'y avait rien qu'ils ne fissent pour éterniser leur réputation, et sauver du naufrage ce qui n'en peut être garanti. Contentons-nous pour faire bonne mine de ne nous pas dire à nous-mêmes tout ce que nous en pensons, et espérons plus de notre tempérament que de ces faibles raisonnements qui nous font croire que nous pouvons approcher de la mort avec indifférence. La gloire de mourir avec fermeté, l'espérance d'être regretté, le désir de laisser une belle réputation, l'assurance d'être affranchi des misères de la vie, et de ne dépendre plus des caprices de la fortune, sont des remèdes qu'on ne doit pas rejeter. Mais on ne doit pas croire aussi qu'ils soient infaillibles. Ils font pour nous assurer ce qu'une simple haie fait souvent à la guerre, pour assurer ceux qui doivent approcher d'un lieu d'où l'on tire. Quand on en est éloigné, on s'imagine qu'elle peut mettre à couvert; mais quand on en est proche, on trouve que c'est un faible secours. C'est nous flatter de croire que la mort nous paraisse de près ce que nous en avons jugé de loin, et que nos sentiments qui ne sont que faiblesse, soient d'une trempe assez forte pour ne point souffrir d'atteinte par la plus rude de toutes les épreuves. C'est aussi mal connaître les effets de l'amour-propre, que de penser qu'il puisse nous aider à compter pour rien ce qui le doit nécessairement détruire; et la raison dans laquelle on croit trouver tant de ressources, est trop faible en cette rencontre pour nous persuader ce que nous voulons. C'est elle au contraire qui nous trahit le plus souvent, et qui au lieu de nous inspirer le mépris de la mort, sert à nous découvrir ce qu'elle a d'affreux et de terrible. Tout ce qu'elle peut faire pour nous, est de nous conseiller d'en détourner les yeux pour les arrêter sur d'autres objets. Caton et Brutus en choisirent d'illustres. Un laquais se contenta il y a quelque temps de danser sur

itself to their imagination in different ways, and appears more vividly there at one time than at another. So it happens that, having
disdained what they did not know, they finally fear what they do
know. We must avoid looking it in the face with all its attendant
circumstances, if we do not want to believe that it is the greatest of
all evils. The cleverest and bravest people are the ones who use the
most honorable pretexts to prevent themselves from thinking about
it. But every man who is able to see it as it really is, finds it a
terrifying thing. The constancy of the philosophers was due entirely
to the inevitability of death. They believed that a journey that could
not be prevented should be undertaken with a good grace; and not
being able to perpetuate their lives for all time, they did their utmost
to perpetuate their reputations and save from the wreck something
that they could not be sure of saving. To look on the bright side of
things, let us be content not to tell ourselves all that we think on the
subject, and let us trust more in our own character than in the weak
arguments that claim we can approach death with indifference. The
glory of dying with strength of character, the hope of being missed,
the desire to leave behind a good reputation, the assurance of being
set free from the sufferings of life and no longer being subject to the
whims of fortune—these things are remedies that should not be
disregarded. Yet neither should we think that they are infallible.
They give us the kind of reassurance that a simple hedge often does
in wartime, when it reassures those who need to approach the
enemy's fire. When you are far away from it,* you imagine that it
could provide cover; but when you are close to it, you find that it
offers little protection. We flatter ourselves if we think that death
will seem the same at close range as we judged it to be from afar, and
that our personal feelings, which are mere weakness, will be strong
enough to be unaffected by this most severe of all trials. We also have
little understanding of the effects of self-love, if we think that it can
help us discount something that must necessarily destroy it; and our
reason, in which we expect to find so many resources, is too weak in
such a crisis to persuade us as we would want. On the contrary, it is
the very thing that most often betrays us, and instead of inspiring us
with disdain for death, shows us how horrific and terrible death is.
All that reason can do for us is advise us to avert our eyes and fix
them on other objects. Cato and Brutus* chose such objects—and
illustrious ones; a lackey,* not long ago, was content merely to dance

l'échafaud où il allait être roué. Ainsi bien que les motifs soient différents, ils produisent les mêmes effets. De sorte qu'il est vrai que, quelque disproportion qu'il y ait entre les grands hommes et les gens du commun, on a vu mille fois les uns et les autres recevoir la mort d'un même visage; mais ç'a toujours été avec cette différence, que dans le mépris que les grands hommes font paraître pour la mort, c'est l'amour de la gloire qui leur en ôte la vue, et dans les gens du commun ce n'est qu'un effet de leur peu de lumière qui les empêche de connaître la grandeur de leur mal, et leur laisse la liberté de penser à autre chose.

on the scaffold where he was about to be broken. Though the motives may be different, they produce the same results. Thus it is true that, whatever difference there may be between great men and common people, on thousands of occasions both kinds have been seen to face death with the same demeanour. But there has always been this difference: when great men treat death with disdain, love of glory is what shields it from their sight, whereas when common people do so, mere lack of enlightenment is what prevents them from recognizing the greatness of the evil ahead of them, and leaves them free to think of other things. [I–V]

Table des matières de ces *Réflexions morales*
Index to these *Moral Reflections*

Le chiffre marque les Maximes, et non pas les Pages
The numbers designate maxims, not pages

Maxims Finally Withdrawn by La Rochefoucauld

Withdrawn after the first edition, 1664 (I)

Avis au Lecteur

Voici un Portrait du cœur de l'homme que je donne au public, sous le Nom de *Réflexions ou Maximes Morales*. Il court fortune de ne plaire pas à tout le monde, parce qu'on trouvera peut-être qu'il ressemble trop, et qu'il ne flatte pas assez: Il y a apparence que l'intention du Peintre n'a jamais été de faire paraître cet ouvrage, et qu'il serait encore renfermé dans son cabinet si une méchante copie qui en a couru, et qui a passé même depuis quelque temps en Hollande, n'avait obligé un de ses Amis de m'en donner une autre, qu'il dit être tout à fait conforme à l'Original; Mais toute correcte qu'elle est, possible n'évitera-t-elle pas la censure de certaines Personnes qui ne peuvent souffrir que l'on se mêle de pénétrer dans le fond de leur cœur, et qui croient être en droit d'empêcher que les autres les connaissent, parce qu'elles ne veulent pas se connaître elles-mêmes. Il est vrai que comme ces *Maximes* sont remplies de ces sortes de vérités dont l'orgueil humain ne se peut accommoder, il est presque impossible qu'il ne se soulève contre elles, et qu'elles ne s'attirent des Censeurs. Aussi est-ce pour eux que je mets ici une *Lettre* que l'on m'a donnée, qui a été faite depuis que le manuscrit a paru, et dans le temps que chacun se mêlait d'en dire son avis, elle m'a semblé assez propre pour répondre aux principales difficultés que l'on peut opposer aux *Réflexions*, et pour expliquer les sentiments de leur Auteur: Elle suffit pour faire voir que ce qu'elles contiennent n'est autre chose que l'abrégé d'une Morale conforme aux pensées de plusieurs Pères de l'Église, et que celui qui les a écrites a eu beaucoup de raison de croire qu'il ne pouvait s'égarer en suivant de si bons guides, et qu'il lui était permis de parler de *l'Homme* comme les Pères en ont parlé; Mais si le respect qui leur est dû n'est pas capable de retenir le chagrin des Critiques, s'ils ne font point de scrupule de condamner l'opinion de ces grands Hommes en condamnant ce

Maxims Finally Withdrawn by La Rochefoucauld

Withdrawn after the first edition, 1664 (I)

Note to the Reader

Here is a portrait of man's heart, which I am presenting to the public
under the title of *Moral Reflections or Maxims*. It is likely to run the
risk of not pleasing everyone, because people may find that it is too
close a likeness, and not flattering enough. The painter, it seems,
never intended to publish this work, and it would still be confined to
his study, but for the fact that a bad copy got into circulation and
even spent some time in Holland,* forcing one of his friends to give
me another copy, which, he says, tallies with the original in all
respects. Yet, accurate as it is, it may not escape the criticism of
certain people who cannot endure anyone daring to probe the depths
of their hearts, and who think they have the right to prevent anyone
else knowing them, because they do not want to know themselves.
Admittedly, as these maxims are full of truths unacceptable to
human pride, it is almost certain that pride will rebel against them
and they will attract critics. So, for the benefit of such people, I am
including a letter* that I have received; it was written after the manuscript appeared, at the time when everyone was rushing in with his
own opinion on the subject. It seems to me an appropriate way to
answer the main difficulties that might be raised against these reflections, and to explain the author's own feelings. It will show well
enough that they contain nothing more than a moral digest in keeping with the thought of various church fathers,* and that their author
had good reason to think that he could not go astray if he followed
such good guides, and that he would be entitled to talk of mankind in
the way that the fathers did. But if the respect that we owe the
fathers cannot keep the critics from feeling uncomfortable, if they do
not scruple to condemn the opinions of those great men by condemning this book, I must beg the reader not to follow their

Livre; Je prie le Lecteur de ne les pas imiter, de ne laisser point
entraîner son esprit au premier mouvement de son cœur, et de donner ordre s'il est possible que *l'Amour-propre* ne se mêle point dans le
jugement qu'il en fera, car s'il le consulte, il ne faut pas s'attendre
qu'il puisse être favorable à ces *Maximes*; comme elles traitent
l'Amour-propre de corrupteur de la raison: Il ne manquera pas de
prévenir l'esprit contre elles. Il faut donc prendre garde que cette
prévention ne les justifie, et se persuader qu'il n'y a rien de plus
propre à établir la vérité de ces *Réflexions* que la chaleur et la subtilité
que l'on témoignera pour les combattre. En effet, il sera difficile de
faire croire à tout homme de bon sens, que l'on les condamne par
d'autre motif que par celui de l'intérêt caché, de l'orgueil et de l'amour-
propre: En un mot, le meilleur parti que le Lecteur ait à prendre, est de
se mettre d'abord dans l'esprit qu'il n'y a aucune de ces Maximes qui le
regarde en particulier, et qu'il en est seul excepté, bien qu'elles paraissent générales. Après cela je lui réponds, qu'il sera le premier à y
souscrire, et qu'il croira qu'elles font encore grâce au cœur humain.
Voilà ce que j'avais à dire sur cet écrit en général, pour ce qui est de la
méthode que l'on y eût pu observer, je crois qu'il eût été à désirer que
chaque *Maxime* eût eu un titre du sujet qu'elle traite, et qu'elles eussent
été mises dans un plus grand ordre, mais je ne l'ai pu faire sans ren-
verser entièrement celui de la copie qu'on m'a donnée, et comme il y a
plusieurs *Maximes* sur une même matière, ceux à qui j'en ai demandé
avis, ont jugé qu'il était plus expédient de faire une table à laquelle on
aura recours pour trouver celles qui traitent d'une même chose.

I: I

L'Amour-propre est l'amour de soi-même, et de toutes choses
pour soi; il rend les hommes idolâtres d'eux-mêmes, et les
rendrait les tyrans des autres, si la fortune leur en donnait les
moyens; il ne se repose jamais hors de soi, et ne s'arrête dans
les sujets étrangers que comme les Abeilles sur les fleurs, pour
en tirer ce qui lui est propre; Rien n'est si impétueux que ses
désirs, rien de si caché que ses desseins, rien de si habile que
ses conduites; ses souplesses ne se peuvent représenter, ses
transformations passent celles des Métamorphoses, et ses raff-
inements ceux de la Chimie: On ne peut sonder la profondeur,
ni percer les ténèbres de ses abîmes. Là, il est à couvert des

example—not to allow his mind to be misled by the first impulse that enters his heart, but to make sure, if possible, that self-love does not contribute to his judgement; because if he listens to self-love, he cannot expect to view these *Maxims* favourably: they present self-love as a corrupter of reason, and that will not fail to prejudice his mind against them. It is necessary, therefore, to avoid justifying one's criticisms by such a prejudice, and to accept that nothing can establish the truth of these *Reflections* more effectively than the warmth and refinement with which they will be attacked. Indeed it will be difficult to persuade any man of good sense that they are being condemned for any other reasons than hidden self-interest, pride, and self-love. In short, the reader's best policy is to start with the premiss that none of these maxims is directed specifically at him, and that he is the sole exception to them, even though they seem to be generally applicable. After that, I guarantee that he will be the first to subscribe to them, and that he will think them only too favourable to the human heart. That is what I have to say about the work in general. As for the method that has been followed in it, I think it might have been desirable to give each maxim a title indicating its subject, and to arrange them in a more orderly way; but I could not have done that without totally overturning the order of the copy that was given to me; and as there are sometimes a number of maxims on one and the same subject, my advisers thought it would be more convenient to prepare an Index that could be consulted to find those that deal with a single topic.

I: I

Self-love is the love of oneself, and of all things for the sake of oneself. It makes men idolize themselves, and it would make them tyrannize other people, if fortune gave them the means to do so. It never finds any rest beyond the self; and it settles on alien things only as bees do on flowers—to draw from them what suits itself. Nothing is as impetuous as its desires, nothing is as secret as its plans, nothing is as clever as its conduct. Its convolutions are beyond imagining; its transformations surpass those of any metamorphosis, and its subtleties those of chemistry.

No one can fathom the depth of its chasms, or penetrate their darkness. There it is hidden from the most perceptive eyes; there it

yeux les plus pénétrants, il y fait mille insensibles tours et retours; Là, il est souvent invisible à lui-même, il y conçoit, il y nourrit, et il y élève sans le savoir, un grand nombre d'affections et de haines; il en forme de si monstrueuses, que lorsqu'il les a mises au jour il les méconnaît, ou il ne peut se résoudre à les avouer: de cette nuit qui le couvre naissent les ridicules persuasions qu'il a de lui-même, de là viennent ses erreurs, ses ignorances, ses grossièretés, et ses niaiseries sur son sujet; de là vient qu'il croit que ses sentiments sont morts lorsqu'ils ne sont qu'endormis, qu'il s'imagine n'avoir plus envie de courir dès qu'il se repose, et qu'il pense avoir perdu tous les goûts qu'il a rassasiés; Mais cette obscurité épaisse qui le cache à lui-même, n'empêche pas qu'il ne voie parfaitement ce qui est hors de lui, en quoi il est semblable à nos yeux qui découvrent tout, et sont aveugles seulement pour eux-mêmes. En effet dans ses plus grands intérêts, et dans ses plus importantes affaires, où la violence de ses souhaits appelle toute son attention, il voit, il sent, il entend, il imagine, il soupçonne, il pénètre, il devine tout; de sorte qu'on est tenté de croire que chacune de ses passions a une espèce de magie qui lui est propre. Rien n'est si intime et si fort que ses attachements, qu'il essaye de rompre inutilement à la vue des malheurs extrêmes qui le menacent. Cependant il fait quelquefois en peu de temps, et sans aucun effort, ce qu'il n'a pu faire avec tous ceux dont il est capable dans le cours de plusieurs années; d'où l'on pourrait conclure assez vraisemblablement, que c'est par lui-même que ses désirs sont allumés, plutôt que par la beauté, et par le mérite de ses objets; que son goût est le prix qui les relève, et le fard qui les embellit; que c'est après lui-même qu'il court, et qu'il suit son gré, lorsqu'il suit les choses qui sont à son gré: il est tous les contraires, il est impérieux et obéissant, sincère et dissimulé, miséricordieux et cruel, timide et audacieux: il a de différentes inclinations selon la diversité des tempéraments qui le tournent, et le dévouent tantôt à la gloire, tantôt aux richesses, et tantôt aux plaisirs; il en change selon le changement de nos âges, de nos fortunes, et de nos expériences: mais il lui est indifférent d'en avoir plusieurs, ou de n'en avoir qu'une, parce qu'il se partage en plusieurs, et se ramasse en une quand il le faut, et comme il lui plaît: il est inconstant,

twists and turns in a thousand imperceptible ways. There it is often invisible even to itself; there, unknowingly, it breeds, nurtures, and raises a vast number of affections and hatreds. Some of them are so monstrous that, when it has given birth to them, it either fails to recognize them or cannot bring itself to acknowledge them.

Its absurd opinions about itself are born from the night that envelops it. From that source come its errors, its ignorances, its uncouth and silly ideas about itself. From that source come its belief that its feelings are dead when they are merely dormant, its fancy that it no longer wishes to progress merely because it has come to a halt, and its idea that it has lost all the tastes that it has merely satiated.

But the thick darkness that hides it from itself does not prevent it from seeing clearly what is outside itself. In that respect it is like our eyes, which discover everything and are blind only to themselves. Indeed where its greatest interests and most important affairs are concerned, when the violence of its desires summons up its full attention, it sees, feels, hears, imagines, suspects, perceives, and deduces everything. As a result, we are tempted to believe that each of its passions has a kind of magic that is distinctively its own.

Nothing is closer or stronger than its bonds of attachment; its attempts to break them are vain, even when it sees the extreme misfortune that threatens it. Yet sometimes, in a very short time and without any effort at all, it manages to do what its utmost powers had been unable to achieve over a period of years. From this we may plausibly conclude that its desires are kindled solely by itself, rather than by the beauty and worth of the things it is desiring; that its own taste is the rouge that embellishes them and the price that makes them valuable; that it is running after its own self, and pursuing its own pleasure, when it pursues something that pleases it.

It is opposites of all kinds: it is domineering and submissive, sincere and deceitful, compassionate and cruel, timid and daring.

Its inclinations vary with the different moods that motivate it, impelling it to seek now glory, now wealth, now pleasures. It rings the changes on these, as our own age, fortune, and experience changes; but it does not care whether it has several such inclinations or only one, because it can divide itself among several or concentrate itself on one, whenever that is necessary or desirable. It is inconstant; and apart from the changes caused by alien factors, infinite numbers arise from itself, from its own reserves: it is inconstant because of

et outre les changements qui viennent des causes étrangères, il y en a une infinité qui naissent de lui, et de son propre fonds; il est inconstant d'inconstance, de légèreté, d'amour de nouveauté, de lassitude, et de dégoût; il est capricieux, et on le voit quelquefois travailler avec le dernier empressement, et avec des travaux incroyables à obtenir des choses qui ne lui sont point avantageuses, et qui même lui sont nuisibles, mais qu'il poursuit parce qu'il les veut. Il est bizarre, et met souvent toute son application dans les emplois les plus frivoles, il trouve tout son plaisir dans les plus fades, et conserve toute sa fierté dans les plus méprisables. Il est dans tous les états de la vie, et dans toutes les conditions, il vit partout, et il vit de tout, il vit de rien; il s'accommode des choses, et de leur privation, il passe même dans le parti des gens qui lui font la guerre, il entre dans leurs desseins; et ce qui est admirable il se hait lui-même avec eux, il conjure sa perte, il travaille même à sa ruine; Enfin il ne se soucie que d'être, et pourvu qu'il soit, il veut bien être son ennemi. Il ne faut donc pas s'étonner s'il se joint quelquefois à la plus rude austérité, et s'il entre si hardiment en société avec elle pour se détruire, parce que dans le même temps qu'il se ruine en un endroit, il se rétablit en un autre; quand on pense qu'il quitte son plaisir, il ne fait que le suspendre, ou le changer, et lors même qu'il est vaincu, et qu'on croit en être défait, on le retrouve qui triomphe dans sa propre défaite. Voilà la peinture de l'amour-propre, dont toute la vie n'est qu'une grande et longue agitation: la mer en est une image sensible, et l'amour-propre trouve dans le flux et le reflux de ses vagues continuelles, une fidèle expression de la succession turbulente de ses pensées, et de ses éternels mouvements.

I: 13

Toutes les passions ne sont autre chose que les divers degrés de la chaleur, et de la froideur du sang.

I: 18

La modération dans la bonne fortune, n'est que l'appréhension de la honte qui suit l'emportement, ou la peur de perdre ce que l'on a.

sheer inconstancy, because of fickleness, because of a love for novelty,* because of weariness, because of distaste.

It is capricious; and sometimes we see it striving with the utmost zeal, and with incredible industry, to gain things that can be of no advantage and may indeed be actually harmful to it—yet it still pursues them, simply because it wants them.

It is extravagant; it often lavishes all its diligence on some task of the most frivolous kind. It finds unmitigated delight in the most insipid tasks, and retains every drop of its pride in the tasks that deserve the most disdain.

It exists at every stage of life and in every walk of life. It lives everywhere; it lives off everything—or nothing; it adapts to anything—or the loss of anything. It even enlists among those who wage war against it;* it participates in their plans; and, most remarkably, it hates itself just as they do, it plots its own downfall, it even toils to bring about its own ruin. In fact, all it cares about is existing; and as long as it can exist, it is quite willing to be its own enemy.

So there is no reason to be surprised if it sometimes joins forces with the harshest austerity,* in whose society it sets out boldly to destroy itself—because while it is crushing itself on one side, it is recovering on another. When we think that it has abandoned one of its pleasures, it has only adjourned it—or exchanged it for something else. And even when it is defeated and we think we are rid of it, it reappears glorying in its own defeat.

That is the portrait of self-love, whose entire life is merely one big long flurry of agitation. The sea is a tangible image of it; and in the perpetual ebb and flow of the waves, it finds a faithful picture of its own eternal restlessness and the turbulent succession of its thoughts. [1]

I: 13

All passions are merely differing degrees of heat or cold in the blood. [1]

I: 18

In a situation of good fortune, moderation is merely dread of the shame that follows excess, or fear of losing what we have. [1]

1: 21

La modération est comme la sobriété, on voudrait bien manger davantage, mais on craint de se faire mal.

1: 33

Tout le monde trouve à redire en autrui, ce qu'on trouve à redire en lui.

1: 37

L'orgueil comme lassé de ses artifices, et de ses différentes Métamorphoses, après avoir joué tout seul tous les personnages de la Comédie humaine, se montre avec un visage naturel, et se découvre par la fierté; de sorte qu'à proprement parler la fierté est l'éclat, et la déclaration de l'orgueil.

1: 51

La complexion qui fait le talent pour les petites choses, est contraire à celle qu'il faut pour le talent des grandes.

1: 53

C'est une espèce de bonheur, de connaître jusques à quel point on doit être malheureux.

1: 59

On n'est jamais si malheureux qu'on croit, ni si heureux qu'on avait espéré.

1: 60

On se console souvent d'être malheureux, par un certain plaisir qu'on trouve à le paraître.

1: 70

Il faudrait pouvoir répondre de sa fortune, pour pouvoir répondre de ce que l'on fera.

I: 21

Moderation is like sobriety: you would dearly love to eat more, but you are afraid of harming yourself. [I]

I: 33

Everyone objects to something in other people that they object to in him. [I]

I: 37

After pride has played every part in the human comedy all by itself, finally, as if weary of its artifices and its various transformations, it shows its natural face and reveals itself as arrogance—so that, properly speaking, arrogance is the affirmation and spontaneous display of pride. [I]

I: 51

The temperament that produces a talent for little things is the opposite of that required for great ones. [I]

I: 53

It is a kind of happiness to know just how unhappy we could be. [I]

I: 59

We are never as unhappy as we think, or as happy as we had hoped. [I]

I: 60

When we really are unhappy, we often comfort ourselves by taking a certain pleasure in appearing to be unhappy. [I]

I: 70

If you cannot predict your future fortunes, you cannot predict what you will do with them. [I]

I: 74

Comment peut-on répondre de ce qu'on voudra à l'avenir, puisque l'on ne sait pas précisément ce que l'on veut dans le temps présent.

I: 77

L'amour est à l'âme de celui qui aime, ce que l'âme est au corps qu'elle anime.

I: 88

La justice n'est qu'une vive appréhension qu'on ne nous ôte ce qui nous appartient; de là vient cette considération, et ce respect pour tous les intérêts du prochain, et cette scrupuleuse application à ne lui faire aucun préjudice; cette crainte retient l'homme dans les bornes des biens que la naissance, ou la fortune lui ont donnés, et sans cette crainte, il ferait des courses continuelles sur les autres.

I: 89

La justice dans les juges qui sont modérés, n'est que l'amour de leur élévation.

I: 90

On blâme l'injustice, non pas par l'aversion que l'on a pour elle, mais, pour le préjudice que l'on en reçoit.

I: 97

Le premier mouvement de joie que nous avons du bonheur de nos Amis, ne vient ni de la bonté de notre naturel, ni de l'amitié que nous avons pour eux, c'est un effet de l'amour-propre qui nous flatte de l'espérance d'être heureux à notre tour, ou de retirer quelque utilité de leur bonne fortune.

I: 99

Dans l'adversité de nos meilleurs amis, nous trouvons toujours quelque chose qui ne nous déplaît pas.

1: 74

How can we predict what we shall want in the future, since we do not know exactly what we want at the moment? [I]

1: 77

Love is to the lover's soul what the soul is to the body it animates. [I]

1: 88

Justice is merely an intense fear that our belongings will be taken away from us. That is what leads us to be considerate and respectful for all our neighbour's interests, and scrupulously diligent never to harm him. This fear keeps man within the limits of the possessions that birth or fortune has given him; and without such fear, he would be constantly making raids on other people. [I]

1: 89

In judges who act with moderation, justice is merely love of their own eminence. [I]

1: 90

We complain of injustice, not because of an aversion to it, but because of the harm it does us. [I]

1: 97

The first impulse of joy that we have when our friends are fortunate, comes neither from the kindness of our nature nor from the friend-ship we feel for them. It is a product of self-love, which flatters us with the hope that we in turn may be fortunate too, or that we may derive something useful from their good fortune. [I]

1: 99

In the adversity of our best friends we always find something that does not displease us. [I]

I: 101

Comme si ce n'était pas assez à l'amour-propre d'avoir la vertu de se transformer lui-même, il a encore celle de transformer les objets; ce qu'il fait d'une manière fort étonnante; car non seulement il les déguise si bien, qu'il y est lui-même trompé, mais il change aussi l'état, et la nature des choses. En effet, lorsqu'une personne nous est contraire, et qu'elle tourne sa haine, et sa persécution contre nous, c'est avec toute la sévérité de la justice que l'amour-propre juge ses actions, il donne à ses défauts une étendue qui les rend énormes, et il met ses bonnes qualités dans un jour si désavantageux, qu'elles deviennent plus dégoûtantes que ses défauts, cependant dès que cette même personne nous devient favorable, ou que quelqu'un de nos intérêts la réconcilie avec nous, notre seule satisfaction rend aussitôt à son mérite, le lustre que notre aversion venait de lui ôter; les mauvaises qualités s'effacent et les bonnes paraissent avec plus d'avantage qu'auparavant, nous rappelons même toute notre indulgence pour la forcer à justifier la guerre qu'elle nous a faite. Quoique toutes les passions montrent cette vérité, l'amour la fait voir plus clairement que les autres; car nous voyons un amoureux agité de la rage où l'a mis l'oubli ou l'infidélité de ce qu'il aime, méditer pour sa vengeance, tout ce que cette passion inspire de plus violent; néanmoins aussitôt que sa vue a calmé la fureur de ses mouvements, son ravissement rend cette beauté innocente, il n'accuse plus que lui-même, il condamne ses condamnations, et par cette vertu miraculeuse de l'amour-propre, il ôte la noirceur aux mauvaises actions de sa maîtresse, et en sépare le crime pour s'en charger lui-même.

I: 102

L'aveuglement des hommes est le plus dangereux effet de leur orgueil: il sert à le nourrir et à l'augmenter, et nous ôte la connaissance des remèdes qui pourraient soulager nos misères et nous guérir de nos défauts.

I: 103

On n'a plus de raison, quand on n'espère plus d'en trouver aux autres.

I: 101

As if it were not enough for self-love to have the power to transform itself, it can also transform its objects, which it does in an utterly astonishing way—for not only does it disguise them so well that it is itself deceived by them, but also it changes the condition and nature of everything. In fact, when somebody opposes and hates and persecutes us, our self-love judges his deeds with all the rigour of justice. It enlarges his faults until they are enormous, and casts such an unfavourable light on his good qualities that they become more distasteful than his faults. Yet when the same person has become favourable to us, or when one of our personal interests has reconciled us to him, the mere fact that we are satisfied restores to his merit the lustre that our aversion had just removed. His bad qualities are overshadowed, and the good ones appear to better advantage than before; we summon back all our indulgence to justify the attack that he had made on us.

Though all the passions display that truth, love shows it more clearly than the others. When a lover is enraged by his beloved's neglect or infidelity, we see him contemplating all the most violent things that this passion can inspire for his revenge; yet when her presence has calmed his fury, his rapture acquits the beautiful creature of wrong, he now blames only himself, he condemns his own condemnations, and by the miraculous power of self-love, he strips his beloved's bad deeds of their blackness, which he transfers from the crime to himself. [I]

I: 102

Blindness is the most dangerous effect of men's pride, which nurtures and increases it and prevents us from recognizing the cures that could relieve our woes and rid us of our faults. [I]

I: 103

When we no longer hope to find sense in other people, we have lost it ourselves. [I]

I: 104

On a autant de sujet de se plaindre de ceux qui nous apprennent à nous connaître nous-mêmes, qu'en eut ce fou d'Athènes, de se plaindre du Médecin qui l'avait guéri de l'opinion d'être riche.

I: 105

Les Philosophes et Sénèque surtout, n'ont point ôté les crimes par leurs préceptes, ils n'ont fait que les employer au bâtiment de l'orgueil.

I: 132

Les plus sages le sont dans les choses indifférentes, mais ils ne le sont presque jamais dans leurs plus sérieuses affaires.

I: 134

La plus subtile folie se fait de la plus subtile sagesse.

I: 135

La sobriété est l'amour de la santé, ou l'impuissance de manger beaucoup.

I: 138

Chaque talent dans les hommes, de même que chaque arbre, a ses propriétés et ses effets, qui lui sont tous particuliers.

I: 144

On n'oublie jamais mieux les choses que quand on s'est lassé d'en parler.

I: 147

La modestie qui semble refuser les louanges, n'est en effet qu'un désir d'en avoir de plus délicates.

I: 104

We have as much cause to complain about those who tell us to know ourselves, as the Athenian madman* had when he complained that his doctor had cured him of thinking he was wealthy. [I]

I: 105

The philosophers—and Seneca above all—did not eradicate crime by the advice they gave; they only used it to build up their own pride. [I]

I: 132

The wisest people are wise in insignificant things, but they are hardly ever wise in the things that matter most to them. [I]

I: 134

The most refined folly is begotten by the most refined wisdom. [I]

I: 135

Temperance is simply a love of one's health, or an inability to eat too much. [I]

I: 138

Every kind of human talent, like every kind of tree, has its own unique characteristics and bears its own unique fruits. [I]

I: 144

We never forget things more readily than when we are tired of talking about them. [I]

I: 147

Modesty, which seems to shun praise, is only a desire to have it in a more subtle form. [I]

I: 151

On ne blâme le vice, et on ne loue la vertu que par intérêt.

I: 155

La louange qu'on nous donne sert au moins à nous fixer dans la pratique des vertus.

I: 156

L'approbation que l'on donne à l'esprit, à la beauté, et à la valeur, les augmente, les perfectionne, et leur fait faire de plus grands effets, qu'ils n'auraient été capables de faire d'eux-mêmes.

I: 157

L'amour-propre empêche bien que celui qui nous flatte ne soit jamais celui qui nous flatte le plus.

I: 159

On ne fait point de distinction dans les espèces de colères, bien qu'il y en ait une légère et quasi innocente, qui vient de l'ardeur de la complexion; et une autre très criminelle, qui est à proprement parler la fureur de l'orgueil.

I: 161

Les grandes âmes ne sont pas celles qui ont moins de passions, et plus de vertu que les âmes communes, mais celles seulement qui ont de plus grands desseins.

I: 174

La férocité naturelle fait moins de cruels que l'amour-propre.

I: 176

On peut dire de toutes nos vertus, ce qu'un Poète Italien a dit de l'honnêteté des femmes, que ce n'est souvent autre chose qu'un art de paraître honnête.

I: 151

We never denounce vice or praise virtue except out of self-interest. [I]

I: 155

At least the praise that is bestowed on us helps to keep us practising virtue. [I]

I: 156

Praise that is bestowed on intelligence, valour, and beauty enhances them, perfects them, and makes them produce greater results than they could have achieved by themselves. [I]

I: 157

Our self-love is sure to prevent the person who flatters us from ever being the one who flatters us most. [I]

I: 159

People make no distinction at all between different kinds of anger, though there is one kind that is slight and almost innocent, which arises from a passionate temperament, and another kind that is very much a crime, which is, properly speaking, pride gone mad. [I]

I: 161

Great souls are not those with fewer passions and more virtues than common souls, but simply those that have greater plans. [I]

I: 174

Fewer people are made cruel by natural ferocity than by self-love. [I]

I: 176

What an Italian poet has said about women's virtue—that it is often merely a talent for seeming virtuous—could be said about all our virtues. [I]

I: 179

Ce que le monde nomme vertu, n'est d'ordinaire qu'un fantôme formé par nos passions, à qui on donne un nom honnête pour faire impunément ce qu'on veut.

I: 200

Nous n'avouons jamais nos défauts que par vanité.

I: 201

On ne trouve point dans l'homme le bien ni le mal dans l'excès.

I: 208

Ceux qui sont incapables de commettre de grands crimes, n'en soupçonnent pas facilement les autres.

I: 213

La pompe des enterrements regarde plus la vanité des vivants que l'honneur des morts.

I: 225

Quelque incertitude et quelque variété qui paraisse dans le monde, on y remarque néanmoins un certain enchaînement secret, et un ordre réglé de tout temps par la Providence, qui fait que chaque chose marche en son rang, et suit le cours de sa destinée.

I: 231

L'intrépidité doit soutenir le cœur dans les conjurations, au lieu que la seule valeur lui fournit toute la fermeté qui lui est nécessaire dans les périls de la guerre.

I: 232

Ceux qui voudraient définir la victoire par sa naissance, seraient tentés comme les Poètes de l'appeler la fille du Ciel, puisqu'on ne trouve point son origine sur la terre; En effet elle est produite par une infinité d'actions, qui au lieu de l'avoir pour but, regardent

1: 179

Usually, what the world calls virtue is a mere phantom created by our passions, to which we give an honorable name so that we can do what we want with impunity. [1]

1: 200

We never admit our faults except out of vanity. [1]

1: 201

Neither extreme good nor extreme evil can be found in man. [1]

1: 208

Those who are incapable of committing great crimes do not readily suspect other people of doing so. [1]

1: 213

The pomp of funerals has more to do with the vanity of the living than with paying honour to the dead. [1]

1: 225

However uncertain and diverse the world may seem, we still see in it a hidden interconnection and an orderliness regulated by Providence from the beginning of time, so that everything proceeds in its due sphere and pursues its destined course. [1]

1: 231

Intrepidity is required to sustain the heart during conspiracies, whereas valour alone can give it all the strength it needs amid the perils of war. [1]

1: 232

Those who would like to define victory in terms of its origin might be tempted (like the poets) to call it the daughter* of Heaven, since we cannot find its source anywhere on earth. In reality it is produced by innumerable deeds which, far from having victory as their goal, arise

seulement les intérêts particuliers de ceux qui les font; puisque tous ceux qui composent une armée allant à leur propre gloire et à leur élévation; procurent un bien si grand et si général.

1: 236

On ne peut répondre de son courage, quand on n'a jamais été dans le péril.

1: 245

L'imitation est toujours malheureuse, et tout ce qui est contrefait, déplaît avec les mêmes choses qui charment lorsqu'elles sont naturelles.

1: 252

Il est bien malaisé de distinguer la bonté générale et répandue sur tout le monde, de la grande habileté.

1: 254

Pour pouvoir être toujours bon, il faut que les autres croient qu'ils ne peuvent jamais nous être impunément méchants.

1: 256

La confiance de plaire, est souvent un moyen de déplaire infailliblement.

1: 257

Nous ne croyons pas aisément ce qui est au-delà de ce que nous voyons.

1: 258

La confiance que l'on a en soi, fait naître la plus grande partie de celle que l'on a aux autres.

solely from the personal interests of their doers—because all the individuals who make up an army are working to promote their own glory and eminence, and yet they produce such a great and general benefit. [I]

I: 236

You cannot answer for your courage when you have never been in danger. [I]

I: 245

Imitation is always unfortunate; and the very things that are delightful when they are natural, are displeasing in any counterfeit. [I]

I: 252

It is very hard to distinguish universal all-embracing kindness from immense cleverness. [I]

I: 254

If we are to be consistently good, other people must believe that they can never do us any harm with impunity. [I]

I: 256

When you feel confident of being liked, you are often sure to be disliked.* [I]

I: 257

It is hard for us to believe anything beyond what we see. [I]

I: 258

A large part of our confidence in other people derives from confidence in ourselves. [I]

1: 259²

Il y a une révolution générale qui change le goût des Esprits, aussi bien que les fortunes du monde.

1: 260

La vérité est le fondement et la raison de la perfection, et de la beauté, une chose, de quelque nature qu'elle soit, ne saurait être belle, et parfaite, si elle n'est véritablement tout ce qu'elle doit être, et si elle n'a tout ce qu'elle doit avoir.

1: 262

Il y a de belles choses qui ont plus d'éclat quand elles demeurent imparfaites, que quand elles sont trop achevées.

1: 271

La magnanimité est un noble effort de l'orgueil, par lequel il rend l'homme maître de lui-même, pour le rendre maître de toutes choses.

1: 282

Le luxe et la trop grande politesse dans les États, sont le présage assuré de leur décadence; parce que tous les particuliers s'attachant à leurs intérêts propres, ils se détournent du bien public.

1: 284¹

L'éducation que l'on donne aux Princes, est un second amour-propre qu'on leur inspire.

1: 285¹

Rien ne prouve tant que les Philosophes ne sont pas si persuadés qu'ils disent que la mort n'est pas un mal, que le tourment qu'ils se donnent pour établir l'immortalité de leur nom par la perte de la vie.

1: 290

De toutes les passions celle qui est la plus inconnue à nous-mêmes, c'est la paresse, elle est la plus ardente et la plus maligne de toutes,

I: 259²

There is a general process of change that alters taste in matters of thought, as well as the fortunes of the world. [1]

I: 260

Truth is the basis of, and the reason for, perfection and beauty. A thing of any kind whatever cannot be beautiful and perfect unless it truly is everything that it should be, and unless it has everything that it should have. [1]

I: 262

Some beautiful things are more dazzling when they are still imperfect than when they have been too perfectly crafted. [1]

I: 271

Magnanimity is a noble effort of pride, which makes a man master of himself so that he can master all things. [1]

I: 282

Luxury and excessive civility are sure predictors of national decadence, because all the private citizens cling to their own interests and lose sight of the public good. [1]

I: 284¹

The education given to princes gives them a second dose of self-love. [1]

I: 285¹

The philosophers are less convinced than they claim that death is not an evil. Nothing proves this as clearly as the trouble they take to secure the immortality of their names through the loss of their lives.*
[1]

I: 290

Of all our passions, laziness is the one least known to ourselves. It is the most intense and malignant of them all, though its violence is

quoique sa violence soit insensible, et que les dommages qu'elle cause soient très cachés; si nous considérons attentivement son pouvoir, nous verrons qu'elle se rend en toutes rencontres maîtresse de nos sentiments, de nos intérêts, et de nos plaisirs; c'est la rémore qui a la force d'arrêter les plus grands vaisseaux, c'est une bonace plus dangereuse aux plus importantes affaires que les écueils, et que les plus grandes tempêtes; le repos de la paresse est un charme secret de l'âme qui suspend soudainement les plus ardentes poursuites, et les plus opiniâtres résolutions; pour donner enfin la véritable idée de cette passion, il faut dire que la paresse est comme une béatitude de l'âme, qui la console de toutes ses pertes, et qui lui tient lieu de tous les biens.

I: 293

De plusieurs actions différentes que la Fortune arrange comme il lui plaît, il s'en fait plusieurs vertus.

I: 300²

Il est plus facile de prendre de l'amour quand on n'en a pas, que de s'en défaire quand on en a.

I: 301²

La plupart des femmes se rendent plutôt par faiblesse, que par passion, de là vient que pour l'ordinaire les hommes entreprenants réussissent mieux que les autres, quoiqu'ils ne soient pas plus aimables.

I: 302

N'aimer guère en amour, est un moyen assuré pour être aimé.

I: 303

La sincérité que se demandent les Amants et les Maîtresses, pour savoir l'un et l'autre, quand ils cesseront de s'aimer, est bien moins pour vouloir être avertis quand on ne les aimera plus, que pour être mieux assurés qu'on les aime, lorsque l'on ne dit point le contraire.

imperceptible and the harm it does is very well hidden. If we carefully consider its power, we shall see that in every situation it dominates our feelings, interests, and pleasures. It is a remora* that is strong enough to stop the greatest ships; it is a doldrum that imperils important business more than any reef or even the fiercest storm. The inertia of laziness casts a secret spell over the soul, which suddenly halts our most zealous pursuits and our most stubbornly held resolutions. Finally, to give a true idea of this passion, it must be said that laziness is like a blissful state of the soul, which comforts it for all its losses, and which acts as a substitute for all good things.* [I]

I: 293

We make various virtues out of various different deeds that fortune orders as it pleases. [I]

I: 300^2

It is easier to fall in love when you are not, than to fall out of love when you are in. [I]

I: 301^2

Most women yield through weakness rather than passion. Usually, therefore, enterprising men are more successful than other men, even though they are no more attractive. [I]

I: 302

When you love very little, you are sure to be loved. [I]

I: 303

Why do pairs of lovers want each other to be absolutely sincere, so that they will know when they no longer love each other? Not so much because they want to be warned when they are no longer loved, as because they want to be reassured that they are still loved when nothing is said to the contrary. [I]

I: 305

La plus juste comparaison qu'on puisse faire de l'amour c'est celle de la fièvre, nous n'avons non plus de pouvoir sur l'un que sur l'autre, soit pour sa violence ou pour sa durée.

I: 309

La plus grande habileté des moins habiles, est de se savoir soumettre à la bonne conduite d'autrui.

Withdrawn after the second edition, 1666 (II)

II: 49

Quand on ne trouve pas son repos en soi-même, il est inutile de le chercher ailleurs.

Withdrawn after the fourth edition, 1674 (IV)

IV: 71

Comme on n'est jamais en liberté d'aimer ou de cesser d'aimer, l'amant ne peut se plaindre avec justice de l'inconstance de sa maîtresse; ni elle de la légèreté de son amant.

IV: 83

Quand nous sommes las d'aimer nous sommes bien aises qu'on nous devienne infidèle pour nous dégager de notre fidélité.

IV: 87

Comment prétendons-nous qu'un autre garde notre Secret si nous ne pouvons le garder nous-mêmes?

IV: 90

Il n'y en a point qui pressent tant les autres que les paresseux lorsqu'ils ont satisfait à leur Paresse, afin de paraître diligents.

I: 305

Love may most aptly be compared to a fever. We have no more power over the one than over the other—either in terms of its intensity or in terms of its duration. [I]

I: 309

For people who are not very clever, the cleverest thing they can do is submit to good leadership. [I]

Withdrawn after the second edition, 1666 (II)

II: 49

When you cannot find peace within yourself, it is useless to look for it elsewhere. [I–II]

Withdrawn after the fourth edition, 1674 (IV)

IV: 71

We are never at liberty either to love or to stop loving; therefore, a lover has no right to complain of his loved one's inconstancy,* nor she of her lover's fickleness. [I–IV]

IV: 83

When we ourselves have grown weary of loving, we are well pleased if our beloved becomes unfaithful: it releases us from having to be faithful. [I–IV]

IV: 87

How can we expect another person to keep our secret, if we cannot keep it ourselves? [I–IV]

IV: 90

Nobody puts as much pressure on others as lazy people who have gratified their own laziness and now want to seem diligent. [II–IV]

IV: 96

C'est une preuve de peu d'Amitié de ne s'apercevoir pas du refroidissement de celle de nos amis.

IV: 158

Les Rois font des hommes comme des pièces de monnaie: ils les font valoir ce qu'ils veulent, et l'on est forcé de les recevoir selon leur cours, et non pas selon leur véritable prix.

IV: 172

Nous sommes si préoccupés en notre faveur que souvent ce que nous prenons pour des vertus n'est que des vices qui leur ressemblent, et que l'amour-propre nous déguise.

IV: 183

Il y a des Crimes qui deviennent innocents et même glorieux par leur éclat, leur nombre, et leur excès. De là vient que les voleries publiques sont des habiletés; et que prendre des provinces injustement s'appelle faire des conquêtes.

IV: 227

On donne plus aisément des bornes à sa Reconnaissance qu'à ses espérances et qu'à ses désirs.

IV: 234

Nous ne regrettons pas toujours la perte de nos amis par la considération de leur mérite; mais par celle de nos besoins et de la bonne opinion qu'ils avaient de nous.

IV: 258

Il y a une éloquence dans les yeux et dans l'air de la personne qui ne persuade pas moins que celle de la parole.

IV: 272

On aime à deviner les autres; mais l'on n'aime pas à être deviné.

IV: 96

If we fail to notice that our friends' affection is cooling, it proves that we have little affection ourselves. [II–IV]

IV: 158

Kings make men as they mint coins: they put their own valuation on them, and we are forced to take them at the standard rate, and not at their true worth. [I–IV]

IV: 172

We are so thoroughly biased in our own favour that, most often, what we take for virtues are really only vices which resemble them, and which self-love has disguised from us. [I–IV]

IV: 183

There are crimes that become innocent, and even glorious, because of their brilliance, number, and enormity. Hence public theft is cleverness, and unjust seizure of provinces is called conquest. [I–IV]

IV: 227

We more readily set limits to our gratitude than to our hopes and desires. [I–IV]

IV: 234

We do not always regret losing a friend because of his worth, but because of our own needs and the good opinion he used to have of us. [I–IV]

IV: 258

There is an eloquence in a person's eyes and manner, which is no less persuasive than that of his words. [I–IV]

IV: 272

We like to see through other people, but we do not like being seen through ourselves. [I–IV]

IV: 274

C'est une ennuyeuse maladie que de conserver sa santé par un trop grand régime.

IV: 372

On craint toujours de voir ce qu'on aime, quand on vient de faire des coquetteries ailleurs.

IV: 375

On doit se consoler de ses fautes, quand on a la force de les avouer.

IV: 274

Keeping your health by means of too strict a diet is itself a tiresome illness. [I–IV]

IV: 372

We are always afraid of seeing our beloved when we have just been flirting with someone else. [IV]

IV: 375

When we have the strength to admit our faults, that in itself should be some compensation for them.* [IV]

Maxims Never Published by
La Rochefoucauld

First recorded 1659–63 (L, PV124, and SL)

L 38

Comme la plus heureuse personne du monde est celle à qui peu de choses suffit, les grands et les ambitieux sont en ce point les plus misérables qu'il leur faut l'assemblage d'une infinité de biens pour les rendre heureux.

L 44

La finesse n'est qu'une pauvre habileté.

L 62

Les philosophes ne condamnent les richesses, que par le mauvais usage que nous en faisons; il dépend de nous de les acquérir et de nous en servir sans crime, et au lieu qu'elles nourrissent et accroissent les vices, comme le bois entretient et augmente le feu, nous pouvons les consacrer à toutes les vertus, et les rendre même par là plus agréables et plus éclatantes.

L 97

La ruine du prochain plaît aux amis et aux ennemis.

L 113

Chacun pense être plus fin que les autres.

L 121

Tout le monde est plein de pelles qui se moquent des fourgons.

L 122

On ne saurait compter toutes les espèces de vanité.

Maxims Never Published by
La Rochefoucauld

First recorded 1659–63 (L, PV124, and SL)

L 38

Just as the happiest person in the world is the one who is satisfied
with few things, the great and the ambitious are the most wretched
in that respect—because they need to accumulate innumerable possessions in order to be happy.

L 44

Cunning is only an impoverished form of cleverness.

L 62

Philosophers condemn wealth only because of the bad use we make
of it. We have a responsibility to acquire and use it without committing any crime, and then it will not nurture and enhance vices, as
wood supports and increases fire; instead, we can dedicate it to all
the virtues and thus make them even more attractive and
remarkable.

L 97

The downfall of a neighbour delights friends and enemies alike.

L 113

Everyone thinks himself more astute than other people.

L 121

The world is full of pots calling kettles black.

L 122

The various kinds of vanity are beyond enumeration.

L 143

Ce qui nous empêche souvent de bien juger des sentences qui prouvent la fausseté des vertus, c'est que nous croyons trop aisément qu'elles sont véritables en nous.

L 160

Nous craignons toutes choses comme mortels, et nous désirons toutes choses comme si nous étions immortels.

L 190

Dieu a mis des talents différents dans l'homme comme il a planté de différents arbres dans la nature, en sorte que chaque talent de même que chaque arbre a ses propriétés et ses effets qui lui sont tous particuliers; de là vient que le poirier le meilleur du monde ne saurait porter les pommes les plus communes, et que le talent le plus excellent ne saurait produire les mêmes effets des talents les plus communs; de là vient encore qu'il est aussi ridicule de vouloir faire des sentences sans en avoir la graine en soi que de vouloir qu'un parterre produise des tulipes quoiqu'on n'y ait point semé les oignons.

L 195

Une preuve convaincante que l'homme n'a pas été créé comme il est, c'est que plus il devient raisonnable et plus il rougit en soi-même de l'extravagance, de la bassesse et de la corruption de ses sentiments et de ses inclinations.

L 206

Il ne faut pas s'offenser que les autres nous cachent la vérité puisque nous nous la cachons si souvent nous-mêmes.

L 207

Rien ne prouve davantage combien la mort est redoutable, que la peine que les philosophes se donnent pour persuader qu'on la doit mépriser.

L 143

What often prevents us from approving the maxims that show virtues to be false, is that we too readily believe our own virtues to be genuine.

L 160

We fear all things as mortals, and we desire all things as if we were immortal.

L 190

God has placed different kinds of talents in man, as he has planted different kinds of trees in nature, with the result that each kind of talent, like each kind of tree, has its own unique characteristics and bears its own unique fruits. Thus the best pear tree in the world would not be capable of bearing the most commonplace apples, and the most excellent talent would not be capable of yielding the same fruits as the most commonplace talents. Thus, also, wanting to compose maxims when you do not have the seed for them within you is as absurd as wanting a flowerbed to produce tulips when no bulbs have been planted there.

L 195

The more reasonable man becomes, the more he blushes inwardly at the extravagance, baseness, and corruption of his feelings and inclinations. This is conclusive evidence that he was not created as he is.

L 206

We should not be offended that other people hide the truth from us, since we so often hide it from ourselves.

L 207

Nothing demonstrates more clearly how dreadful death is, than the trouble philosophers take to show that we ought to disdain it.

L 209

Il semble que c'est le diable qui a tout exprès placé la paresse sur la frontière de plusieurs vertus.

L 210

La fin du bien est un mal, la fin du mal est un bien.

L 212

On blâme aisément les défauts des autres, mais on s'en sert rarement à corriger les siens.

L 228

Les biens et les maux qui nous arrivent ne nous touchent pas selon leur grandeur, mais selon notre sensibilité.

L 237

Ceux qui prisent trop leur noblesse ne prisent d'ordinaire pas assez ce qui en est l'origine.

L 240

Le remède de la jalousie est la certitude de ce qu'on craint, parce qu'elle cause la fin de la vie ou la fin de l'amour; c'est un cruel remède, mais il est plus doux que les doutes et les soupçons.

L 241

Il est difficile de comprendre combien est grande la ressemblance et la différence qu'il y a entre tous les hommes.

L 245

Ce qui fait tant disputer contre les maximes qui découvrent le cœur de l'homme, c'est que l'on craint d'y être découvert.

L 249

On peut toujours ce qu'on veut, pourvu qu'on le veuille bien.

L 209

The devil seems to be the one who has deliberately placed laziness on the threshold of various virtues.

L 210

The end of good is an evil thing; the end of evil is a good thing.

L 212

We readily criticize other people's faults, but we rarely use them to correct our own.

L 228

The good and evil things that happen to us, affect us not according to their extent, but according to our own sensitivity.

L 237

Usually, those who prize their nobility too much do not prize its origin enough.

L 240

Jealousy is cured by definite knowledge of what we fear, because that puts an end to life or love. It is a cruel cure—but gentler than doubts and suspicions.

L 241

It is hard to appreciate how very similar and how very different all men are.

L 245

The reason why we argue so much against the maxims that expose the human heart, is that we ourselves are afraid of being exposed by them.

L 249

You can always do what you want—if you want it enough.

L 255

L'homme est si misérable, que tournant toutes ses conduites à
satisfaire ses passions, il gémit incessamment sous leur tyrannie; il
ne peut supporter ni leur violence ni celle qu'il faut qu'il se fasse
pour s'affranchir de leur joug; il trouve du dégoût non seulement
dans ses vices mais encore dans leurs remèdes, et ne peut s'accommoder ni des chagrins de ses maladies ni du travail de sa
guérison.

L 256

Dieu a permis, pour punir l'homme du péché originel, qu'il se fît un
dieu de son amour-propre pour en être tourmenté dans toutes les
actions de sa vie.

L 261

L'espérance et la crainte sont inséparables, et il n'y a point de crainte
sans espérance ni d'espérance sans crainte.

L 267

Le pouvoir que les personnes que nous aimons ont sur nous est
presque toujours plus grand que celui que nous y avons nous-
mêmes.

L 269

Ce qui nous fait croire si facilement que les autres ont des défauts,
c'est la facilité que l'on a de croire ce qu'on souhaite.

L 270

L'intérêt est l'âme de l'Amour-propre, de sorte que comme le corps
privé de son Âme est sans vue, sans ouïe, sans connaissance, sans
sentiment, et sans mouvement, de même l'amour-propre séparé, s'il
le faut dire ainsi, de son intérêt, ne voit, n'entend, ne sent, et ne se
remue plus; de là vient qu'un même homme qui court la terre et les
mers pour son intérêt devient soudainement paralytique pour l'intérêt des autres; de là vient le soudain assoupissement et cette mort
que nous causons à tous ceux à qui nous contons nos affaires; de là
vient leur prompte résurrection lorsque dans notre narration nous y

L 255

Man is so wretched that, while he shapes all of his conduct to gratify his passions, he keeps groaning incessantly under their tyranny. He can endure neither their violence, nor the violence that he would have to inflict on himself in order to rid himself of their yoke. He is frustrated not only by his vices, but also by the things that would cure them; and he cannot come to terms either with the discomfort of his afflictions or with the task of curing himself.

L 256

To punish man for original sin,* God has allowed him to make a god of his self-love, so that it may torment him in every deed he ever does.

L 261

Hope and fear are inseparable; and there is no fear without hope, or hope without fear.

L 267

Nearly always, the people we love have more power over us than we have over ourselves.

L 269

What makes us believe so easily that other people have failings, is that it is so easy to believe what you want to believe.

L 270

Self-interest is the soul of self-love. Hence, just as the body without its soul has no sight, no hearing, no consciousness, no feelings, and no movements, similarly self-love cut off (so to speak) from its self-interest can no longer see, hear, feel, or move. Thus the very man who travels over land and sea when his own interests are at stake, suddenly becomes paralysed when other people's interests are at stake. Hence the sudden coma and death that we cause to all those whom we tell about our own affairs; hence the promptness of their resurrection when we introduce into our tale something that con-

mêlons quelque chose qui les regarde: de sorte que nous voyons dans nos conversations et dans nos traités que dans un même moment un homme perd connaissance et revient à soi, selon que son propre intérêt s'approche de lui ou qu'il s'en retire.

PV124 : 4

On ne donne des louanges que pour en profiter.

SL 2

Si on avait ôté de ce que l'on appelle force le désir de conserver, et la crainte de perdre, il ne lui resterait pas grand-chose.

First recorded 1667 (PV158)

PV158 : 1

Les passions ne sont que les divers goûts de l'amour-propre.

PV158 : 3

L'extrême ennui sert à nous désennuyer.

PV158 : 4

On loue et on blâme la plupart des choses, parce que c'est la mode de les louer ou de les blâmer.

First recorded 1671–4 (VIs)

VIS : 1

Force gens veulent être dévots, mais personne ne veut être humble.

VIS : 2

Le travail du corps délivre des peines de l'esprit, et c'est ce qui rend les pauvres heureux.

VIS : 3

Les véritables mortifications sont celles qui ne sont point connues; la vanité rend les autres faciles.

cerns them personally. So we see, during our conversations and interactions, that a man instantaneously loses consciousness and regains his faculties, as his own interests come to the fore or recede.

PV124: 4

We bestow praise only to benefit from it.

SL 2

Not much of what we call strength would be left, if we took away from it the desire to retain and the fear of losing.

First recorded 1667 (PV158)

PV158: 1

The passions are merely self-love's variations in taste.

PV158: 3

Extreme heartache rids us of heartache.

PV158: 4

We praise or condemn most things because it is fashionable to praise or condemn them.

First recorded 1671–4 (VIs)

VIS: 1

Many people want to be pious, but nobody wants to be humble.

VIS: 2

Physical labour frees people from mental pain; and that is what makes the poor happy.

VIS: 3

The true acts of self-mortification are those that no one can see; vanity makes the others easy to perform.

VIS: 4

L'humilité est l'autel sur lequel Dieu veut qu'on lui offre des sacrifices.

VIS: 5

Il faut peu de choses pour rendre le sage heureux; rien ne peut rendre un fol content; c'est pourquoi presque tous les hommes sont misérables.

VIS: 6

Nous nous tourmentons moins pour devenir heureux que pour faire croire que nous le sommes.

VIS: 7

Il est bien plus aisé d'éteindre un premier désir que de satisfaire tous ceux qui le suivent.

VIS: 8

La sagesse est à l'âme ce que la santé est pour le corps.

VIS: 9

Les grands de la terre ne pouvant donner la santé du corps ni le repos d'esprit, on achète toujours trop cher tous les biens qu'ils peuvent faire.

VIS: 10

Avant que de désirer fortement une chose, il faut examiner quel est le bonheur de celui qui la possède.

VIS: 11

Un véritable ami est le plus grand de tous les biens et celui de tous qu'on songe le moins à acquérir.

VIS: 12

Les amants ne voient les défauts de leurs maîtresses que lorsque leur enchantement est fini.

VIS: 4

Humility is the altar on which God wants us to sacrifice to him.

VIS: 5

A wise man needs few things to make him happy; nothing can satisfy a fool. That is why nearly all men are wretched.

VIS: 6

We strive less hard to be happy than to make people think we are happy.

VIS: 7

It is much easier to stifle a first desire than to gratify all those that follow it.

VIS: 8

Wisdom is to the soul what health is to the body.

VIS: 9

The great people of this world can never bestow health of body or peace of mind; so we always pay too dearly for any good things they can do.

VIS: 10

Before intensely desiring anything, we should consider how happy is the person who possesses it.

VIS: 11

A true friend is the greatest of all possessions, and the one that we give least thought to acquiring.

VIS: 12

Lovers never see their loved ones' failings until the enchantment is over.

VIS: 13

La prudence et l'amour ne sont pas faits l'un pour l'autre: à mesure que l'amour croît, la prudence diminue.

VIS: 14

Il est quelquefois agréable à un mari d'avoir une femme jalouse: il entend toujours parler de ce qu'il aime.

VIS: 15

Qu'une femme est à plaindre, quand elle a tout ensemble de l'amour et de la vertu.

VIS: 16

Le sage trouve mieux son compte à ne point s'engager qu'à vaincre.

VIS: 17

Il est plus nécessaire d'étudier les hommes que les livres.

VIS: 18

Le bonheur ou le malheur vont d'ordinaire à ceux qui ont le plus de l'un ou de l'autre.

VIS: 21

Une honnête femme est un trésor caché; celui qui l'a trouvé fait fort bien de ne s'en pas vanter.

VIS: 28

Quand nous aimons trop, il est malaisé de reconnaître si l'on cesse de nous aimer.

VIS: 33

On ne se blâme que pour être loué.

VIS: 37

On s'ennuie presque toujours avec ceux que l'on ennuie.

VIS: 13

Prudence and love are not made for each other: as love increases, prudence decreases.

VIS: 14

Sometimes a husband finds it attractive to have a jealous wife: he is constantly hearing about what he loves.

VIS: 15

How a woman is to be pitied, when she has love and virtue together!

VIS: 16

A wise man finds it more advantageous to avoid enlisting than to win the battle.

VIS: 17

It is more vital to study men than books.

VIS: 18

Good or ill fortune usually goes to those who already have most of one or the other.

VIS: 21

A virtuous woman is a hidden treasure: the man who finds her is well advised not to boast about it.

VIS: 28

If we are too much in love, it is hard to recognize when we are no longer loved.

VIS: 33

We criticize ourselves only to be praised.

VIS: 37

We are nearly always bored with those whom we bore.

VIS: 39

Il n'est jamais plus difficile de bien parler que quand on a honte de se taire.

VIS: 46

Il n'est rien de plus naturel ni de plus trompeur que de croire qu'on est aimé.

VIS: 47

Nous aimons mieux voir ceux à qui nous faisons du bien que ceux qui nous en font.

VIS: 48

Il est plus difficile de dissimuler les sentiments que l'on a que de feindre ceux que l'on n'a pas.

VIS: 49

Les amitiés renouées demandent plus de soins que celles qui n'ont jamais été rompues.

VIS: 50

Un homme à qui personne ne plaît est bien plus malheureux que celui qui ne plaît à personne.

VIS: 39

It is never harder to speak well than when we are ashamed of being silent.

VIS: 46

Nothing is more natural or more deceptive than to believe that you are loved.

VIS: 47

We would rather see those to whom we do good, than those who do good to us.

VIS: 48

It is harder to hide feelings that you have, than to counterfeit feelings that you do not have.

VIS: 49

Mended friendships require more care than friendships that have never been broken.

VIS: 50

A man who likes nobody is much more unhappy than a man whom nobody likes.

Réflexions diverses

RD 1. Du Vrai

Le vrai, dans quelque sujet qu'il se trouve, ne peut être effacé par aucune comparaison d'un autre vrai, et quelque différence qui puisse être entre deux sujets, ce qui est vrai dans l'un n'efface point ce qui est vrai dans l'autre: ils peuvent avoir plus ou moins d'étendue et être plus ou moins éclatants, mais ils sont toujours égaux par leur vérité, qui n'est pas plus vérité dans le plus grand que dans le plus petit. L'art de la guerre est plus étendu, plus noble et plus brillant que celui de la poésie; mais le poète et le conquérant sont comparables l'un à l'autre; en tant qu'ils sont véritablement ce qu'ils sont, le législateur et le peintre, etc.

Deux sujets de même nature peuvent être différents, et même opposés, comme le sont Scipion et Annibal, Fabius Maximus et Marcellus; cependant, parce que leurs qualités sont vraies, elles subsistent en présence l'une de l'autre, et ne s'effacent point par la comparaison. Alexandre et César donnent des royaumes; la veuve donne une pite: quelque différents que soient ces présents, la libéralité est vraie et égale en chacun d'eux, et chacun donne à proportion de ce qu'il est.

Un sujet peut avoir plusieurs vérités, et un autre sujet peut n'en avoir qu'une: le sujet qui a plusieurs vérités est d'un plus grand prix, et peut briller par des endroits où l'autre ne brille pas; mais dans l'endroit où l'un et l'autre est vrai, ils brillent également. Épaminondas était grand capitaine, bon citoyen, grand philosophe; il était plus estimable que Virgile, parce qu'il avait plus de vérités que lui; mais comme grand capitaine, Épaminondas n'était pas plus excellent que Virgile comme grand poète, parce que, par cet endroit, il n'était pas plus vrai que lui. La cruauté de cet enfant qu'un consul fit mourir pour avoir crevé les yeux d'une corneille, était moins importante que celle de Philippe second, qui fit mourir son fils, et elle était peut-être mêlée avec moins d'autres vices; mais le degré de cruauté exercée sur un simple animal ne laisse pas de tenir son rang avec la cruauté des princes les plus cruels, parce que leurs différents degrés de cruauté ont une vérité égale.

Miscellaneous Reflections

RD 1. Truth

Truth, wherever it is found, cannot be overshadowed by comparison with any other truth; and whatever differences there may be between two entities, what is true in one can never overshadow what is true in the other. They may be more or less extensive and more or less conspicuous, but they are always equal in truth—which is no truer in the greater entity than in the lesser. The art of war is greater in scope, nobility, and brilliance than the art of poetry, but the poet and the conqueror are comparable to each other (as far as they truly are what they are), the legislator and the painter, etc.

Two entities of the same kind may be different and even opposed, as Scipio and Hannibal, Fabius Maximus and Marcellus* are. Yet their merits, because they are true, continue to exist in each other's presence, and are never overshadowed by the comparison. Alexander and Caesar* bestow kingdoms; the widow* bestows a mite. However different those gifts may be, the generosity is true and equal in each case, and each of them gives in proportion to what he is.

One entity may contain multiple truths, while another may have only one. The entity that contains multiple truths is greater in value, and may shine in contexts where the other does not; but in the context where each one is true, they shine equally. Epaminondas* was a great captain, a good citizen, a great thinker. He contained more truths than Virgil,* and therefore he was more estimable; but Epaminondas was no more excellent as a great captain than Virgil as a great poet—because, from such a perspective, the former was no truer than the latter. The cruelty of the boy* who was sentenced to death by a consul for blinding a crow was less significant than the cruelty of Philip II,* who had his son murdered, and it may not have been combined with so many other vices; but the amount of cruelty inflicted on a mere animal can stand comparison with the cruelty of the cruellest rulers, because their different degrees of cruelty are equal in truth.

Quelque disproportion qu'il y ait entre deux maisons qui ont les beautés qui leur conviennent, elles ne s'effacent point l'une l'autre: ce qui fait que Chantilly n'efface point Liancourt, bien qu'il y ait infiniment plus de diverses beautés, et que Liancourt n'efface pas aussi Chantilly, c'est que Chantilly a les beautés qui conviennent à la grandeur de Monsieur le Prince, et que Liancourt a les beautés qui conviennent à un particulier, et qu'ils ont chacun de vraies beautés. On voit néanmoins des femmes d'une beauté éclatante, mais irrégulière, qui en effacent souvent de plus véritablement belles; mais comme le goût, qui se prévient aisément, est le juge de la beauté, et que la beauté des plus belles personnes n'est pas toujours égale, s'il arrive que les moins belles effacent les autres, ce sera seulement durant quelques moments; ce sera que la différence de la lumière et du jour fera plus ou moins discerner la vérité qui est dans les traits ou dans les couleurs, qu'elle fera paraître ce que la moins belle aura de beau, et empêchera de paraître ce qui est de vrai et de beau dans l'autre.

RD 2. De la Société

Mon dessein n'est pas de parler de l'amitié en parlant de la société; bien qu'elles aient quelque rapport, elles sont néanmoins très différentes: la première a plus d'élévation et de dignité, et le plus grand mérite de l'autre, c'est de lui ressembler. Je ne parlerai donc présentement que du commerce particulier que les honnêtes gens doivent avoir ensemble.

Il serait inutile de dire combien la société est nécessaire aux hommes: tous la désirent et tous la cherchent, mais peu se servent des moyens de la rendre agréable et de la faire durer. Chacun veut trouver son plaisir et ses avantages aux dépens des autres; on se préfère toujours à ceux avec qui on se propose de vivre, et on leur fait presque toujours sentir cette préférence; c'est ce qui trouble et qui détruit la société. Il faudrait du moins savoir cacher ce désir de préférence, puisqu'il est trop naturel en nous pour nous en pouvoir défaire; il faudrait faire son plaisir de celui des autres, ménager leur amour-propre, et ne le blesser jamais.

L'esprit a beaucoup de part à un si grand ouvrage, mais il ne suffit pas seul pour nous conduire dans les divers chemins qu'il faut tenir.

Whatever disproportion there may be between two houses that have appropriate types of beauty, neither of them can ever overshadow the other. Chantilly* can never overshadow Liancourt,* although there may be infinitely more beauties there, and neither can Liancourt overshadow Chantilly, because Chantilly's beauties are appropriate for the greatness of the Prince, and Liancourt's beauties are appropriate for a private individual, and the beauties of each are true. Admittedly, we often see women of dazzling but irregular beauty overshadowing those who are more truly beautiful. Yet taste, which is readily biased, is the judge of beauty, and the most beautiful people are not always equally beautiful; so, if the less beautiful do happen to overshadow the others, it will be only for a few moments: it will be because variations in daylight and illumination display to a greater or lesser extent the truth that is in the features or colours, revealing what is beautiful in the less beautiful person, and concealing what is true and beautiful in the other.

RD 2. Social Contact

In speaking of social contact, my plan is not to speak of friendship. Although they are related, they are very different: the latter has more eminence and dignity, and the greatest merit of the former is to resemble it. At present, therefore, I shall speak only of the particular way in which people of honor ought to deal with each other.

It would be idle to state how much men need social contact. All of them desire it and seek it; but few use methods to make it attractive and make it last. Everyone is seeking his own pleasure and advantage, at the expense of other people. We always prefer ourselves to those with whom we intend to live, and we almost always make them conscious of this preference; that is what disturbs and destroys social intercourse. We should at least learn to hide this desire to put our own preferences first—because they are too innate for us to override. We should find our pleasure in that of other people, showing consideration for their self-love and never wounding it.

The mind plays a great part in so great a work, but it alone is not enough to guide us in the various paths we should follow. Social intercourse would not long be maintained by the understanding that

Le rapport qui se rencontre entre les esprits ne maintiendrait pas longtemps la société, si elle n'était réglée et soutenue par le bon sens, par l'humeur, et par des égards qui doivent être entre les personnes qui veulent vivre ensemble. S'il arrive quelquefois que des gens opposés d'humeur et d'esprit paraissent unis, ils tiennent sans doute par des liaisons étrangères, qui ne durent pas longtemps. On peut être aussi en société avec des personnes sur qui nous avons de la supériorité par la naissance ou par des qualités personnelles; mais ceux qui ont cet avantage n'en doivent pas abuser: ils doivent rarement le faire sentir, et ne s'en servir que pour instruire les autres; ils doivent leur faire apercevoir qu'ils ont besoin d'être conduits, et les mener par raison, en s'accommodant, autant qu'il est possible, à leurs sentiments et à leurs intérêts.

Pour rendre la société commode, il faut que chacun conserve sa liberté: il faut se voir, ou ne se voir point, sans sujétion, se divertir ensemble, et même s'ennuyer ensemble; il faut se pouvoir séparer, sans que cette séparation apporte de changement; il faut se pouvoir passer les uns des autres, si on ne veut pas s'exposer à embarrasser quelquefois, et on doit se souvenir qu'on incommode souvent, quand on croit ne pouvoir jamais incommoder. Il faut contribuer, autant qu'on le peut, au divertissement des personnes avec qui on veut vivre; mais il ne faut pas être toujours chargé du soin d'y contribuer. La complaisance est nécessaire dans la société, mais elle doit avoir des bornes: elle devient une servitude quand elle est excessive; il faut du moins qu'elle paraisse libre, et qu'en suivant le sentiment de nos amis, ils soient persuadés que c'est le nôtre aussi que nous suivons.

Il faut être facile à excuser nos amis, quand leurs défauts sont nés avec eux, et qu'ils sont moindres que leurs bonnes qualités; il faut souvent éviter de leur faire voir qu'on les ait remarqués et qu'on en soit choqué, et on doit essayer de faire en sorte qu'ils puissent s'en apercevoir eux-mêmes, pour leur laisser le mérite de s'en corriger.

Il y a une sorte de politesse qui est nécessaire dans le commerce des honnêtes gens: elle leur fait entendre raillerie, et elle les empêche d'être choqués et de choquer les autres par de certaines façons de parler trop sèches et trop dures, qui échappent souvent sans y penser, quand on soutient son opinion avec chaleur.

Le commerce des honnêtes gens ne peut subsister sans une certaine sorte de confiance; elle doit être commune entre eux; il faut que

exists between minds, unless this was regulated and supported by good sense, temperament, and the tact that ought to exist between people who wish to live together. If people who are opposite in temperament and mind sometimes seem united, no doubt they are held together by alien links, which do not last for long. We may also have social contact with people to whom we are superior, either by birth or in personal qualities; but those who possess such an advantage should not abuse it. Rarely should they let it be felt; they should use it only to teach other people, showing them that they need to be led, and guiding them by reason, while adapting themselves as far as possible to the others' feelings and interests.

For a social group to be comfortable, everyone must retain his personal freedom. We must be allowed to see each other or not to see each other, without any constraint; to entertain each other or even to bore each other. We must be able to part without changing the situation. We must be able to do without each other sometimes, if we do not want to put others in an awkward position; and we must remember that we often annoy people when we think we could not possibly annoy them. We should contribute, as far as we can, to the entertainment of the people with whom we wish to live—but we should not be burdened with the task of contributing to it all the time. Politeness is necessary in any social group, but there should be limits to it; when it goes too far, it becomes a form of slavery. It should at least seem to be free—so that when we follow our friends' feelings, they feel convinced that we are also following our own.

We should readily excuse our friends when their faults are inborn and less significant than their good qualities. We should seldom let them see that we have noticed any such thing or are offended by it; we should try to act so that they may become aware of it themselves, leaving the merit of correcting it to them.

In dealings between honorable people, a kind of civility is needed. This makes them understand how to be jocular; it prevents them from being offended themselves, and offending other people, by the use of excessively dry or harsh expressions, which often slip out thoughtlessly when people are heatedly expounding their own opinions.

Honorable people cannot deal with each other unless there is a certain feeling of confidence, which needs to be mutual; each person

chacun ait un air de sûreté et de discrétion qui ne donne jamais lieu de craindre qu'on puisse rien dire par imprudence.

Il faut de la variété dans l'esprit: ceux qui n'ont que d'une sorte d'esprit ne peuvent pas plaire longtemps. On peut prendre des routes diverses, n'avoir pas les mêmes vues ni les mêmes talents, pourvu qu'on aide au plaisir de la société, et qu'on y observe la même justesse que les différentes voix et les divers instruments doivent observer dans la musique.

Comme il est malaisé que plusieurs personnes puissent avoir les mêmes intérêts, il est nécessaire au moins, pour la douceur de la société, qu'ils n'en aient pas de contraires. On doit aller au-devant de ce qui peut plaire à ses amis, chercher les moyens de leur être utile, leur épargner des chagrins, leur faire voir qu'on les partage avec eux quand on ne peut les détourner, les effacer insensiblement sans prétendre de les arracher tout d'un coup, et mettre en la place des objets agréables, ou du moins qui les occupent. On peut leur parler des choses qui les regardent, mais ce n'est qu'autant qu'ils le permettent, et on y doit garder beaucoup de mesure: il y a de la politesse, et quelquefois même de l'humanité, à ne pas entrer trop avant dans les replis de leur cœur; ils ont souvent de la peine à laisser voir tout ce qu'ils en connaissent, et ils en ont encore davantage quand on pénètre ce qu'ils ne connaissent pas. Bien que le commerce que les honnêtes gens ont ensemble leur donne de la familiarité, et leur fournisse un nombre infini de sujets de se parler sincèrement, personne presque n'a assez de docilité et de bon sens pour bien recevoir plusieurs avis qui sont nécessaires pour maintenir la société: on veut être averti jusqu'à un certain point, mais on ne veut pas l'être en toutes choses, et on craint de savoir toutes sortes de vérités.

Comme on doit garder des distances pour voir les objets, il en faut garder aussi pour la société: chacun a son point de vue, d'où il veut être regardé; on a raison, le plus souvent, de ne vouloir pas être éclairé de trop près, et il n'y a presque point d'homme qui veuille, en toutes choses, se laisser voir tel qu'il est.

RD 3. De l'Air et des Manières

Il y a un air qui convient à la figure et aux talents de chaque personne: on perd toujours quand on le quitte pour en prendre un autre.

should have an air of reassurance and tact, so that there is never any reason to fear that anything imprudent could possibly be said.

There needs to be some variety of thought; those whose minds work in only one way cannot please for long. We can travel along different paths, we need not have the same views or the same talents, as long as we are contributing to the pleasure of the social group, preserving in it the same harmony that different voices and instruments should preserve in music.

It is difficult for different people to have the same interests; to make social contact more agreeable, at least their interests should not be in opposition. We should anticipate what would please our friends, look for ways to be useful to them, spare them from trouble, show them that we are sharing it when it cannot be averted, shroud it imperceptibly without claiming to destroy it all at once, and replace it with something attractive, or at least something that will keep them busy. We should talk about things that concern them—but only as far as they themselves will let us; in such matters we need to avoid going too far. It is an act of civility, sometimes even of humanity, not to penetrate too deeply into the recesses of their hearts. Often it would be painful for them to reveal everything that they themselves know about their own hearts, and still more painful if we were to perceive what they do not know. Though dealings between honorable people make them familiar with each other, and provide them with innumerable subjects that they can discuss sincerely, hardly anyone has enough flexibility and good sense to accept fully the variety of opinion that is necessary for the maintenance of the social group. We want to be informed up to a certain point, but not in every respect; there are all kinds of truths we are afraid of knowing.

Just as we must keep at a distance to see objects clearly, so we must do in a social group; each person has a specific point of view from which he wants to be considered.* We are usually right when we do not want to be too brightly illuminated, and there is hardly any man who would want to be seen as he really is in every respect.

RD 3. Manners and Ways of Behaving

There is a particular manner that suits each person's appearance and talents; when we abandon it in order to adopt another, we are always

Il faut essayer de connaître celui qui nous est naturel, n'en point sortir, et le perfectionner autant qu'il nous est possible.

Ce qui fait que la plupart des petits enfants plaisent, c'est qu'ils sont encore renfermés dans cet air et dans ces manières que la nature leur a données, et qu'ils n'en connaissent point d'autres. Ils les changent et les corrompent quand ils sortent de l'enfance: ils croient qu'il faut imiter ce qu'ils voient faire aux autres, et ils ne le peuvent parfaitement imiter; il y a toujours quelque chose de faux et d'incertain dans cette imitation. Ils n'ont rien de fixe dans leurs manières ni dans leurs sentiments; au lieu d'être en effet ce qu'ils veulent paraître, ils cherchent à paraître ce qu'ils ne sont pas. Chacun veut être un autre, et n'être plus ce qu'il est: ils cherchent une contenance hors d'eux-mêmes, et un autre esprit que le leur; ils prennent des tons et des manières au hasard; ils en font l'expérience sur eux, sans considérer que ce qui convient à quelques-uns ne convient pas à tout le monde, qu'il n'y a point de règle générale pour les tons et pour les manières, et qu'il n'y a point de bonnes copies. Deux hommes néanmoins peuvent avoir du rapport en plusieurs choses sans être copie l'un de l'autre, si chacun suit son naturel; mais personne presque ne le suit entièrement, on aime à imiter; on imite souvent, même sans s'en apercevoir, et on néglige ses propres biens pour des biens étrangers, qui d'ordinaire ne nous conviennent pas.

Je ne prétends pas, par ce que je dis, nous renfermer tellement en nous-mêmes, que nous n'ayons pas la liberté de suivre des exemples, et de joindre à nous des qualités utiles ou nécessaires que la nature ne nous a pas données: les arts et les sciences conviennent à la plupart de ceux qui s'en rendent capables; la bonne grâce et la politesse conviennent à tout le monde; mais ces qualités acquises doivent avoir un certain rapport et une certaine union avec nos propres qualités, qui les étendent et les augmentent imperceptiblement.

Nous sommes quelquefois élevés à un rang et à des dignités au-dessus de nous; nous sommes souvent engagés dans une profession nouvelle où la nature ne nous avait pas destinés: tous ces états ont chacun un air qui leur convient, mais qui ne convient pas toujours avec notre air naturel; ce changement de notre fortune change souvent notre air et nos manières, et y ajoute l'air de la dignité, qui est toujours faux quand il est trop marqué et qu'il n'est pas joint et confondu avec l'air que la nature nous a donné: il faut les unir et les mêler ensemble, et qu'ils ne paraissent jamais séparés.

the losers. We should try to discover the manner that comes naturally to us and not depart from it, perfecting it as much as we can.

What makes the majority of young children so pleasant is the fact that they are still confined to the manner and the ways of behaving that nature gave them; they are ignorant of any others. When they start to leave childhood behind, they change and corrupt their ways. They think they ought to copy what they see other people doing, and yet they cannot copy it perfectly—there is always something false and indeterminate in the copy. There is nothing steady in their feelings and their ways of behaving; instead of really being what they want to seem, they strive to seem what they are not. Each of them wants to be someone else, and not what he is. They are searching for a demeanour that is beyond them, a mind that is different from their own; they adopt manners and ways of behaving at random; they experiment with them, not realizing that what suits some people does not suit everyone, that there are no general rules for manners and ways of behaving, and copies are never good.* Yet two men can be similar in various respects without copying one another, if each of them is simply following his own nature; but hardly anyone follows it altogether—we love to copy; we often copy even without realizing it, and we neglect our own good qualities for alien ones, which usually do not suit us.

In saying this, I am not claiming that we should be so self-confined that we have no freedom to follow examples and supplement ourselves with useful or necessary qualities which nature has not given us. The arts and sciences suit most people who are able to learn them; grace and civility suit everyone; but such acquired qualities should always have a certain relationship and unity with our own qualities, which imperceptibly extend and increase them.

Sometimes we are exalted to a rank and dignity too great for us; often we are obliged to enter a new profession, for which nature has not destined us. Any such position has its own manner—which suits it, but does not necessarily suit the manner that comes naturally to us; the change in our fortune often changes our manner and our ways of behaving, and supplements them with an air of dignity which is always false when it is too marked and fails to combine and merge with the manner that nature has given us. We need to unite and blend them so that they seem inseparable.

On ne parle pas de toutes choses sur un même ton et avec les mêmes manières; on ne marche pas à la tête d'un régiment comme on marche en se promenant; mais il faut qu'un même air nous fasse dire naturellement des choses différentes, et qu'il nous fasse marcher différemment, mais toujours naturellement, et comme il convient de marcher à la tête d'un régiment et à une promenade.

Il y en a qui ne se contentent pas de renoncer à leur air propre et naturel, pour suivre celui du rang et des dignités où ils sont parvenus; il y en a même qui prennent par avance l'air des dignités et du rang où ils aspirent. Combien de lieutenants généraux apprennent à paraître maréchaux de France! Combien de gens de robe répètent inutilement l'air de chancelier, et combien de bourgeoises se donnent l'air de duchesses!

Ce qui fait qu'on déplaît souvent, c'est que personne ne sait accorder son air et ses manières avec sa figure, ni ses tons et ses paroles avec ses pensées et ses sentiments; on trouble leur harmonie par quelque chose de faux et d'étranger; on s'oublie soi-même, et on s'en éloigne insensiblement; tout le monde presque tombe, par quelque endroit, dans ce défaut; personne n'a l'oreille assez juste pour entendre parfaitement cette sorte de cadence. Mille gens déplaisent avec des qualités aimables; mille gens plaisent avec de moindres talents: c'est que les uns veulent paraître ce qu'ils ne sont pas; les autres sont ce qu'ils paraissent; et enfin, quelques avantages ou quelques désavantages que nous ayons reçus de la nature, on plaît à proportion de ce qu'on suit l'air, les tons, les manières et les sentiments qui conviennent à notre état et à notre figure, et on déplaît à proportion de ce qu'on s'en éloigne.

RD 4. De la Conversation

Ce qui fait que si peu de personnes sont agréables dans la conversation, c'est que chacun songe plus à ce qu'il veut dire qu'à ce que les autres disent. Il faut écouter ceux qui parlent, si on en veut être écouté; il faut leur laisser la liberté de se faire entendre, et même de dire des choses inutiles. Au lieu de les contredire ou de les interrompre, comme on fait souvent, on doit, au contraire, entrer dans leur esprit et dans leur goût, montrer qu'on les entend, leur parler de ce qui les touche, louer ce qu'ils disent autant qu'il mérite d'être

Not all things should be discussed in the same tone and style—we do not march at the head of a regiment as we walk during a stroll; but we should say different things in the same natural manner. Though we should walk in different ways, we should always do so naturally and as is suitable, whether at the head of a regiment or during a stroll.

There are some people who are not content merely to abandon their appropriate natural manner and accept that of the rank and dignity they have attained; they even adopt prematurely the manner of a rank and dignity to which they aspire. How many lieutenant-generals are practising to be field marshals! How many lawyers are imitating in vain the manner of a chancellor, and how many middle-class women are assuming the air of a duchess!

What we often dislike is the fact that no one knows how to reconcile his manner and his ways of behaving with his demeanour, or his words and his tones of voice with his thoughts and sentiments. People disturb their harmony with something false and alien; they forget themselves and drift imperceptibly out of harmony. Almost everyone falls into this fault in some respect; nobody has a fine enough ear to recognize the proper cadence on every occasion. Thousands of people with attractive qualities are disliked; thousands of less talented people are liked—because the former want to seem something that they are not, while the latter are exactly what they seem. In short, whatever advantages or disadvantages we may have received from nature, we are pleasing only in so far as we follow the manner, tones, feelings, and ways of behaving that suit our condition and demeanour, and we are displeasing to the extent that we depart from them.

RD 4. Conversation

The reason why so few people are attractive in conversation is that everyone thinks more about what he himself wants to say than about what the other people are saying. We should listen to those who are speaking, if we want them to listen to us; we should give them a hearing, and even let them say things that are pointless. Instead of contradicting or interrupting them, as people often do, we should penetrate their own thought and taste, showing that we understand them, speaking about things that concern them, praising what they

loué, et faire voir que c'est plutôt par choix qu'on le loue que par complaisance. Il faut éviter de contester sur des choses indifférentes, faire rarement des questions, qui sont presque toujours inutiles, ne laisser jamais croire qu'on prétend avoir plus de raison que les autres, et céder aisément l'avantage de décider.

On doit dire des choses naturelles, faciles et plus ou moins sérieuses, selon l'humeur et l'inclination des personnes que l'on entretient, ne les presser pas d'approuver ce qu'on dit, ni même d'y répondre. Quand on a satisfait de cette sorte aux devoirs de la politesse, on peut dire ses sentiments, sans prévention et sans opiniâtreté, en faisant paraître qu'on cherche à les appuyer de l'avis de ceux qui écoutent.

Il faut éviter de parler longtemps de soi-même, et de se donner souvent pour exemple. On ne saurait avoir trop d'application à connaître la pente et la portée de ceux à qui on parle, pour se joindre à l'esprit de celui qui en a le plus, et pour ajouter ses pensées aux siennes, en lui faisant croire, autant qu'il est possible, que c'est de lui qu'on les prend. Il y a de l'habileté à n'épuiser pas les sujets qu'on traite, et à laisser toujours aux autres quelque chose à penser et à dire.

On ne doit jamais parler avec des airs d'autorité, ni se servir de paroles et de termes plus grands que les choses. On peut conserver ses opinions, si elles sont raisonnables; mais en les conservant, il ne faut jamais blesser les sentiments des autres, ni paraître choqué de ce qu'ils ont dit. Il est dangereux de vouloir être toujours le maître de la conversation, et de parler trop souvent d'une même chose; on doit entrer indifféremment sur tous les sujets agréables qui se présentent, et ne faire jamais voir qu'on veut entraîner la conversation sur ce qu'on a envie de dire.

Il est nécessaire d'observer que toute sorte de conversation, quelque honnête et quelque spirituelle qu'elle soit, n'est pas également propre à toute sorte d'honnêtes gens: il faut choisir ce qui convient à chacun, et choisir même le temps de le dire; mais s'il y a beaucoup d'art à savoir parler à propos, il n'y en a pas moins à savoir se taire. Il y a un silence éloquent: il sert quelquefois à approuver et à condamner; il y a un silence moqueur; il y a un silence respectueux; il y a enfin des airs, des tons et des manières qui font souvent ce qu'il y a d'agréable ou de désagréable, de délicat ou de choquant dans la conversation; le secret de s'en bien servir est donné à peu de person-

say when it deserves to be praised, and showing that we are praising them by choice rather than out of mere politeness. We should avoid disputes about insignificant things; we should rarely question what they say (this is almost always useless), we should never let them think we claim to be more reasonable than other people, and we should readily give them the privilege of deciding for themselves.

We should say things that are natural, simple, and more or less serious, depending on the temperaments and inclinations of the people with whom we are speaking—not pressing them to approve what we have said, or even to answer it. When we have thus satisfied the requirements of civility, we can voice our own feelings without any prejudice or stubbornness, while showing that we are trying to base them on the opinions of our listeners.

We should not talk long about ourselves, or often set ourselves up as examples. We cannot be too diligent in learning the inclinations and capacities of those with whom we are speaking, so that we can associate with the most intelligent person and add our thoughts to his, giving him the impression, wherever possible, that we are deriving them from him. We need to be clever enough not to exhaust the subjects under discussion, but always leave something for other people to think and say.

We should never speak with an air of authority or use words and terms that are too lofty. We can hold to our own opinions, if they are reasonable; but when we do so, we should never wound other people's feelings or seem offended by what they have said. It is dangerous to want to lead the conversation all the time, or to talk too often about one thing; we should participate equally in all the attractive subjects that arise, and never show that we want to draw the conversation around to something that we ourselves wish to say.

It must be said that no conversation, however honorable and intelligent, is equally suitable for all kinds of honorable people. We need to choose what is suitable for each person—and even choose the right time to say it; if there is great art in knowing how to speak appropriately, there is no less in knowing how to be silent. There is an eloquent silence, which can sometimes be used to approve or condemn; there is a mocking silence; there is a respectful silence. In fact, there are tones, manners, and ways of behaving that often determine what is attractive or unattractive, subtle or offensive in a

nes; ceux mêmes qui en font des règles s'y méprennent quelquefois; la plus sûre, à mon avis, c'est de n'en point avoir qu'on ne puisse changer, de laisser plutôt voir des négligences dans ce qu'on dit que de l'affectation, d'écouter, de ne parler guère, et de ne se forcer jamais à parler.

RD 5. De la Confiance

Bien que la sincérité et la confiance aient du rapport, elles sont néanmoins différentes en plusieurs choses: la sincérité est une ouverture de cœur, qui nous montre tels que nous sommes; c'est un amour de la vérité, une répugnance à se déguiser, un désir de se dédommager de ses défauts, et de les diminuer même par le mérite de les avouer. La confiance ne nous laisse pas tant de liberté; ses règles sont plus étroites; elle demande plus de prudence et de retenue, et nous ne sommes pas toujours libres d'en disposer; il ne s'agit pas de nous uniquement, et nos intérêts sont mêlés d'ordinaire avec les intérêts des autres. Elle a besoin d'une grande justesse pour ne livrer pas nos amis en nous livrant nous-mêmes, et pour ne faire pas des présents de leur bien, dans la vue d'augmenter le prix de ce que nous donnons.

La confiance plaît toujours à celui qui la reçoit: c'est un tribut que nous payons à son mérite; c'est un dépôt que l'on commet à sa foi; ce sont des gages qui lui donnent un droit sur nous, et une sorte de dépendance où nous nous assujettissons volontairement. Je ne prétends pas détruire par ce que je dis la confiance, si nécessaire entre les hommes, puisqu'elle est le lien de la société et de l'amitié: je prétends seulement y mettre des bornes, et la rendre honnête et fidèle. Je veux qu'elle soit toujours vraie et toujours prudente, et qu'elle n'ait ni faiblesse, ni intérêt; mais je sais bien qu'il est malaisé de donner de justes limites à la manière de recevoir toute sorte de confiance de nos amis, et de leur faire part de la nôtre.

On se confie le plus souvent par vanité, par envie de parler, par le désir de s'attirer la confiance des autres, et pour faire un échange de secrets. Il y a des personnes qui peuvent avoir raison de se fier en nous, vers qui nous n'aurions pas raison d'avoir la même conduite, et on s'acquitte envers ceux-ci en leur gardant le secret, et en les payant de légères confidences. Il y en a d'autres dont la fidélité nous est

conversation. Few people know the secret of using them properly. Even those who lay down rules on the subject go astray from time to time. The safest rule, in my opinion, is to have no rules that cannot be changed, to speak negligently rather than pretentiously, to listen and say very little, never forcing yourself to talk.

RD 5. Confiding

Though confiding and being sincere are related, they differ in various respects. Sincerity is a form of open-heartedness,* and shows us as we really are; it is a love of truth, a dislike of disguising ourselves, a desire to compensate for our faults and even reduce them in a meritorious way by confessing them. When we confide, we have less freedom; the rules are stricter. The act calls for more prudence and more reserve, and is not always under our own control—it does not depend solely on us; other people's interests are usually mingled with our own. We must be meticulously careful not to unmask our friends when we unmask ourselves, and not to enhance the value of our own offerings by doling out anything that our friends possess.

A confidence always gives pleasure to the person who receives it. It is a tribute paid to his merit, a deposit entrusted to his fidelity, a pledge that gives him a claim on us, a kind of dependence to which we submit voluntarily. In saying this, I am not intending to destroy confidence, which is so necessary among men, since it is the bond that maintains social contact and friendship; I am intending merely to set limits to it, so that it is honorable and faithful. I want it to be always true and prudent, without weakness or self-interest; but I know well that it is hard to define the proper extent to which we and our friends should exchange confidences.

Most often we confide out of vanity, out of a wish to speak, out of a desire to draw confidences from other people, and in order to exchange secrets. There are people who may have reason to trust us, though we have no reason to trust them. We discharge our obligations toward them by keeping their secrets and repaying them with slight confidences of our own. There are other people whose fidelity is well known to us, who never act cautiously with us, and in whom we can confide by choice and inclination. We should not hide from

connue, qui ne ménagent rien avec nous, et à qui on peut se confier
par choix et par estime. On doit ne leur cacher rien de ce qui ne
regarde que nous, se montrer à eux toujours vrais, dans nos bonnes
qualités et dans nos défauts même, sans exagérer les unes, et sans
diminuer les autres; se faire une loi de ne leur faire jamais de demi-
confidences, qui embarrassent toujours ceux qui les font, et ne contentent presque jamais ceux qui les reçoivent: on leur donne des
lumières confuses de ce qu'on veut cacher, et on augmente leur
curiosité; on les met en droit d'en vouloir savoir davantage, et ils se
croient en liberté de disposer de ce qu'ils ont pénétré. Il est plus sûr
et plus honnête de ne leur rien dire, que de se taire quand on a
commencé à parler.

Il y a d'autres règles à suivre pour les choses qui nous ont été
confiées: plus elles sont importantes, et plus la prudence et la fidélité
y sont nécessaires. Tout le monde convient que le secret doit être
inviolable; mais on ne convient pas toujours de la nature et de l'importance du secret: nous ne consultons le plus souvent que nous-
mêmes sur ce que nous devons dire et sur ce que nous devons taire; il
y a peu de secrets de tous les temps, et le scrupule de les révéler ne
dure pas toujours.

On a des liaisons étroites avec des amis dont on connaît la fidélité;
ils nous ont toujours parlé sans réserve, et nous avons toujours gardé
les mêmes mesures avec eux; ils savent nos habitudes et nos commerces, et ils nous voient de trop près pour ne s'apercevoir pas du
moindre changement; ils peuvent savoir par ailleurs ce que nous
sommes engagés de ne dire jamais à personne; il n'a pas été en notre
pouvoir de les faire entrer dans ce qu'on nous a confié, et qu'ils ont
peut-être quelque intérêt de savoir; on est assuré d'eux comme de
soi, et on se voit cependant réduit à la cruelle nécessité de perdre leur
amitié, qui nous est précieuse, ou de manquer à la foi du secret. Cet
état est sans doute la plus rude épreuve de la fidélité; mais il ne doit
pas ébranler un honnête homme: c'est alors qu'il lui est permis de se
préférer aux autres; son premier devoir est indispensablement de
conserver le dépôt en son entier, sans en peser les suites: il doit non
seulement ménager ses paroles et ses tons, il doit encore ménager ses
conjectures, et ne laisser jamais rien voir, dans ses discours ni dans
son air, qui puisse tourner l'esprit des autres vers ce qu'il ne veut pas
dire.

On a souvent besoin de force et de prudence pour opposer à la

them anything that concerns us; we should always show ourselves to them as we truly are, with our good qualities and even our faults, neither exaggerating the former nor trying to reduce the latter. With such people, we should make it a rule never to impart half-confidences—which always put the giver in an awkward position and hardly ever satisfy the receiver: they dimly illuminate what we want to keep hidden, and they arouse the curiosity of our hearers, who feel entitled to know more and feel free to discuss what they have perceived. It is safer and more honorable to tell them nothing than to fall silent after we have started to speak.

There are other rules to be followed when something has been confided to us. The more important it is, the more prudence and fidelity it demands. Everyone agrees that a secret should be inviolable; but not everyone agrees on the nature and importance of such secrecy. Most often we consult only our own judgement when deciding what we should say or not say. Few secrets are permanent, and our scruples about revealing them do not last for ever.

We have very close links with friends whom we know to be faithful. They have always spoken to us frankly, and we have dealt with them in the same way; they know our habits and procedures, and they can see us at such close range that they notice the slightest change. From another source they may learn something that we have promised never to tell anyone—it has not been in our power to take them into our confidence, even though they might have some personal interest in the subject; we are as sure of them as we are of ourselves, and yet we find ourselves reduced to the hard fate of either losing their friendship, which is dear to us, or else breaking our pledge of secrecy. This situation is no doubt the most severe test of fidelity, but it should not sway a man of honor. At such a time he may permissibly choose his own interests in preference to other people's; his first duty is necessarily to keep the entrusted secret intact, regardless of the consequences. Not only must his words and tones of voice be cautious; so must his suggestions, and he must never reveal anything, either in his conversation or in his manner, which could lead other people's minds toward the matter that he cannot state.

We often need strength and prudence to resist the demands of our friends, most of whom make claims on our confidence and want

tyrannie de la plupart de nos amis, qui se font un droit sur notre confiance, et qui veulent tout savoir de nous. On ne doit jamais leur laisser établir ce droit sans exception: il y a des rencontres et des circonstances qui ne sont pas de leur juridiction; s'ils s'en plaignent, on doit souffrir leurs plaintes, et s'en justifier avec douceur; mais s'ils demeurent injustes, on doit sacrifier leur amitié à son devoir, et choisir entre deux maux inévitables, dont l'un se peut réparer, et l'autre est sans remède.

RD 6. De l'Amour et de la Mer

Ceux qui ont voulu nous représenter l'amour et ses caprices l'ont comparé en tant de sortes à la mer, qu'il est malaisé de rien ajouter à ce qu'ils en ont dit: ils nous ont fait voir que l'un et l'autre ont une inconstance et une infidélité égales, que leurs biens et leurs maux sont sans nombre, que les navigations les plus heureuses sont exposées à mille dangers, que les tempêtes et les écueils sont toujours à craindre, et que souvent même on fait naufrage dans le port; mais en nous exprimant tant d'espérances et tant de craintes, ils ne nous ont pas assez montré, ce me semble, le rapport qu'il y a d'un amour usé, languissant et sur sa fin, à ces longues bonaces, à ces calmes ennuyeux, que l'on rencontre sous la ligne. On est fatigué d'un grand voyage, on souhaite de l'achever; on voit la terre, mais on manque de vent pour y arriver; on se voit exposé aux injures des saisons; les maladies et les langueurs empêchent d'agir; l'eau et les vivres manquent ou changent de goût; on a recours inutilement aux secours étrangers; on essaie de pêcher, et on prend quelques poissons, sans en tirer de soulagement ni de nourriture; on est las de tout ce qu'on voit, on est toujours avec ses mêmes pensées, et on est toujours ennuyé; on vit encore, et on a regret à vivre; on attend des désirs pour sortir d'un état pénible et languissant, mais on n'en forme que de faibles et d'inutiles.

RD 7. Des Exemples

Quelque différence qu'il y ait entre les bons et les mauvais exemples, on trouvera que les uns et les autres ont presque également produit

us to tell them everything. Never, under any circumstances, must we allow them to establish such claims. There are contexts and circumstances that do not fall within their province; if they complain about that, we must endure their complaints and gently defend our conduct; but if they remain unjust, we must sacrifice their friendship to our duty, and make a choice between two inevitable ills—one of which can be put right, whereas the other has no possible cure.

RD 6. Love and the Sea

Those who have sought to depict love and its whims have compared it to the sea in so many ways that it is hard to add anything to what they have said. They have shown that both are equally inconstant and faithless, doing countless good and evil deeds; that the most fortunate voyages face thousands of dangers, that there are always storms and reefs to be feared, and that we are often shipwrecked even in harbour. But although they have listed so many hopes and fears, it seems to me that they have not sufficiently shown us the link between a worn-out, sluggish love that is reaching its end and the prolonged doldrums, the tiresome calm spells, that we encounter below the equator. We are weary of our long journey, we long to finish it; we can see the land, but we do not have enough wind to reach it; we find ourselves subject to the ravages of time; we are too ill and too sluggish to act; water and provisions fail or lose their taste; we turn in vain to aliens for help; we try to fish, and we do catch some fish, but they give us neither comfort nor nourishment; we are weary of everything we see, we are always thinking the same thoughts, and we are always bored; we continue to live, and we regret that we do; we hope to be rescued from our painful, sluggish state by what we desire—yet the only desires we can form are themselves weak and sluggish.

RD 7. Examples

Whatever difference there may be between good and bad examples, we shall find that both have produced almost equally bad results. I

de méchants effets; je ne sais même si les crimes de Tibère et de Néron ne nous éloignent pas plus du vice, que les exemples estimables des plus grands hommes ne nous approchent de la vertu. Combien la valeur d'Alexandre a-t-elle fait de fanfarons! Combien la gloire de César a-t-elle autorisé d'entreprises contre la patrie! Combien Rome et Sparte ont-elles loué de vertus farouches! Combien Diogène a-t-il fait de philosophes importuns, Cicéron de babillards, Pomponius Atticus de gens neutres et paresseux, Marius et Sylla de vindicatifs, Lucullus de voluptueux, Alcibiade et Antoine de débauchés, Caton d'opiniâtres! Tous ces grands originaux ont produit un nombre infini de mauvaises copies. Les vertus sont frontières des vices; les exemples sont des guides qui nous égarent souvent, et nous sommes si remplis de fausseté, que nous ne nous en servons pas moins pour nous éloigner du chemin de la vertu, que pour le suivre.

RD 8. De l'Incertitude de la Jalousie

Plus on parle de sa jalousie, et plus les endroits qui ont déplu paraissent de différents côtés; les moindres circonstances les changent, et font toujours découvrir quelque chose de nouveau. Ces nouveautés font revoir, sous d'autres apparences, ce qu'on croyait avoir assez vu et assez pesé; on cherche à s'attacher à une opinion, et on ne s'attache à rien; tout ce qui est de plus opposé et de plus effacé se présente en même temps; on veut haïr et on veut aimer, mais on aime encore quand on hait, et on hait encore quand on aime. On croit tout, et on doute de tout; on a de la honte et du dépit d'avoir cru et d'avoir douté; on se travaille incessamment pour arrêter son opinion, et on ne la conduit jamais à un lieu fixe.

Les poètes devraient comparer cette opinion à la peine de Sisyphe, puisqu'on roule aussi inutilement que lui un rocher, par un chemin pénible et périlleux; on voit le sommet de la montagne, on s'efforce d'y arriver; on l'espère quelquefois, mais on n'y arrive jamais. On n'est pas assez heureux pour oser croire ce qu'on souhaite, ni même assez heureux aussi pour être assuré de ce qu'on craint le plus; on est assujetti à une incertitude éternelle, qui nous présente successivement des biens et des maux qui nous échappent toujours.

am not even sure whether the crimes of Tiberius and Nero* do not drive us further away from vice than the admirable examples of the greatest men draw us toward virtue. How many braggarts have been produced by the valour of Alexander! How many plots against one's country have been authorized by the glory of Caesar!* How many cruel virtues have received the praise of Rome and Sparta! How many cadging philosophers have been produced by Diogenes, chatterboxes by Cicero, lazy fence-sitters by Pomponius Atticus, avengers by Marius and Sylla, voluptuaries by Lucullus, debauchees by Alcibiades and Antony, stubborn diehards by Cato!* All those great originals have produced infinite numbers of bad copies. The virtues are bordered by vices; examples are guides that often lead us astray, and we are so full of falsehood that we use them as much to depart from the path of virtue as to follow it.

RD 8. The Uncertainty of Jealousy

The more we say about our jealousy, the more varied its unpleasant aspects seem; the slightest circumstances change them, constantly revealing something new. Such novelties make us look again, with different eyes, at what we thought we had already seen enough and weighed enough. We try to commit ourselves to a definite opinion, and we do not commit ourselves to any; everything that is opposite or overshadowed appears at the same time; we want to hate and we want to love—but we still love when we hate, and we still hate when we love. We believe everything and doubt everything; we feel ashamed and resentful for having believed, and also for having doubted; we labour constantly to reach a definite opinion, and we never manage to settle it.

The poets should have compared such opinions to the torments of Sisyphus,* because we too are rolling a rock in vain on a painful, perilous path; we can see the mountaintop, we strive to reach it, sometimes we are in hope—but we never do reach it. We are never fortunate enough to venture to believe what we wish—nor are we even fortunate enough to be sure of what we fear most. We are subject to a kind of endless uncertainty, showing us successive glimpses of good and evil things that constantly escape us.

RD 9. De l'Amour et de la Vie

L'amour est une image de notre vie: l'un et l'autre sont sujets aux mêmes révolutions et aux mêmes changements. Leur jeunesse est pleine de joie et d'espérance: on se trouve heureux d'être jeune, comme on se trouve heureux d'aimer. Cet état si agréable nous conduit à désirer d'autres biens, et on en veut de plus solides; on ne se contente pas de subsister, on veut faire des progrès, on est occupé des moyens de s'avancer et d'assurer sa fortune; on cherche la protection des ministres, on se rend utile à leurs intérêts; on ne peut souffrir que quelqu'un prétende ce que nous prétendons. Cette émulation est traversée de mille soins et de mille peines, qui s'effacent par le plaisir de se voir établi: toutes les passions sont alors satisfaites, et on ne prévoit pas qu'on puisse cesser d'être heureux.

Cette félicité néanmoins est rarement de longue durée, et elle ne peut conserver longtemps la grâce de la nouveauté; pour avoir ce que nous avons souhaité, nous ne laissons pas de souhaiter encore. Nous nous accoutumons à tout ce qui est à nous; les mêmes biens ne conservent pas leur même prix, et ils ne touchent pas toujours également notre goût; nous changeons imperceptiblement, sans remarquer notre changement; ce que nous avons obtenu devient une partie de nous-mêmes; nous serions cruellement touchés de le perdre, mais nous ne sommes plus sensibles au plaisir de le conserver; la joie n'est plus vive; on en cherche ailleurs que dans ce qu'on a tant désiré. Cette inconstance involontaire est un effet du temps, qui prend, malgré nous, sur l'amour, comme sur notre vie; il en efface insensiblement chaque jour un certain air de jeunesse et de gaieté, et en détruit les plus véritables charmes; on prend des manières plus sérieuses, on joint des affaires à la passion; l'amour ne subsiste plus par lui-même, et il emprunte des secours étrangers. Cet état de l'amour représente le penchant de l'âge, où on commence à voir par où on doit finir; mais on n'a pas la force de finir volontairement, et dans le déclin de l'amour, comme dans le déclin de la vie, personne ne se peut résoudre de prévenir les dégoûts qui restent à éprouver; on vit encore pour les maux, mais on ne vit plus pour les plaisirs. La jalousie, la méfiance, la crainte de lasser, la crainte d'être quitté, sont des peines attachées à la vieillesse de l'amour, comme les maladies sont attachées à la trop longue durée de la vie: on ne sent plus qu'on est vivant que parce qu'on sent qu'on est malade, et on ne sent aussi

RD 9. Love and Life

Love is a picture of our life: both are subject to the same upheavals and the same changes. Their early stages are filled with joy and hope; we believe ourselves fortunate to be young, as we believe ourselves fortunate to be in love. This condition is so attractive that it leads to a desire for other good things—and more substantial ones. We are not content to be; we want to progress; we are intent on advancing and making our fortune; we seek the patronage of ministers, we make ourselves useful by promoting their interests; we cannot endure anyone whose aspirations are the same as ours. This spirit of emulation is criss-crossed with thousands of cares and troubles, which are overshadowed by the pleasure of seeing ourselves secure; then all our passions are satisfied, and we do not foresee that we could ever cease to be happy.

Nevertheless, this state of felicity seldom lasts long, and does not long retain the charm of novelty. When we have what we wish, we do not stop wishing. We grow accustomed to everything that we have; the same possessions do not retain the same value, and no longer affect our taste in the same way. We change imperceptibly, without noticing that we have changed. What we have acquired becomes part of ourselves; we would be deeply affected if we lost it, but we are no longer sensitive to the pleasure of retaining it. Our joy has lost its intensity; we seek it elsewhere, no longer in the things that we used to desire so much. This involuntary inconstancy is the result of time; do what we may, time subtracts from our love, as it does from our life—imperceptibly tarnishing each day some of its youth and gaiety, and destroying its true charms. We behave in more serious ways, we add business to passion; love no longer exists for itself, but borrows help from alien things. This state of love depicts the onset of old age, when we begin to see what our end will be. But we are not strong enough to accept the end willingly; in the decline of love, as in the decline of life, no one can avert the frustrations that await us; though we no longer live for pleasures, we continue to live for ills. Jealousy, mistrust, fear of wearying others, fear of being deserted, are troubles associated with the old age of love, just as illnesses are associated with excessive prolongation of life. We feel that we are alive only because we feel ill, and likewise we feel that we are in love only because we feel all the troubles of love. In

qu'on est amoureux que par sentir toutes les peines de l'amour. On ne sort de l'assoupissement des trop longs attachements que par le dépit et le chagrin de se voir toujours attaché; enfin de toutes les décrépitudes, celle de l'amour est la plus insupportable.

RD 10. Du Goût

Il y a des personnes qui ont plus d'esprit que de goût, et d'autres qui ont plus de goût que d'esprit; mais il y a plus de variété et de caprice dans le goût que dans l'esprit.

Ce terme de *goût* a diverses significations, et il est aisé de s'y méprendre: il y a différence entre le goût qui nous porte vers les choses, et le goût qui nous en fait connaître et discerner les qualités, en s'attachant aux règles. On peut aimer la comédie sans avoir le goût assez fin et assez délicat pour en bien juger, et on peut avoir le goût assez bon pour bien juger de la comédie sans l'aimer. Il y a des goûts qui nous approchent imperceptiblement de ce qui se montre à nous; d'autres nous entraînent par leur force ou par leur durée.

Il y a des gens qui ont le goût faux en tout; d'autres ne l'ont faux qu'en de certaines choses, et ils l'ont droit et juste dans ce qui est de leur portée. D'autres ont des goûts particuliers, qu'ils connaissent mauvais, et ne laissent pas de les suivre. Il y en a qui ont le goût incertain; le hasard en décide: ils changent par légèreté, et sont touchés de plaisir ou d'ennui, sur la parole de leurs amis. D'autres sont toujours prévenus; ils sont esclaves de tous leurs goûts, et les respectent en toutes choses. Il y en a qui sont sensibles à ce qui est bon, et choqués de ce qui ne l'est pas; leurs vues sont nettes et justes, et ils trouvent la raison de leur goût dans leur esprit et dans leur discernement.

Il y en a qui, par une sorte d'instinct, dont ils ignorent la cause, décident de ce qui se présente à eux, et prennent toujours le bon parti. Ceux-ci font paraître plus de goût que d'esprit, parce que leur amour-propre et leur humeur ne prévalent point sur leurs lumières naturelles; tout agit de concert en eux, tout y est sur un même ton. Cet accord les fait juger sainement des objets, et leur en forme une idée véritable; mais, à parler généralement, il y a peu de gens qui aient le goût fixe et indépendant de celui des autres: ils suivent

attachments that are too prolonged, we escape becoming comatose only by the resentment and discomfort of seeing that we are still attached; in short, of all forms of decrepitude, the decrepitude of love is the most unbearable.

RD 10. Taste

Some people have more intelligence than taste, others more taste than intelligence; but there are more quirks and variations in taste than in intelligence.

The term 'taste' has various meanings, and here it is easy to go astray. There is a difference between the taste that attracts us to things, and the taste that leads us to become familiar with them and discern their qualities in accordance with certain rules. We may like a play even if our tastes are not sufficiently astute and subtle to judge it properly, and we may have enough taste to judge it properly even if we do not like it. Some tastes draw us imperceptibly toward what lies ahead; others sweep us away by their strength or duration.

Some people have bad taste in everything; others have bad taste only in certain things—their tastes are correct and true on any subject within their capacity. Still others have unique tastes, which they know to be bad but cannot help following. Some people have indeterminate tastes, which are fixed by chance; they are fickle, so they change their minds, and are affected with either pleasure or heartache, depending on their friends' opinions. Others are always prejudiced; they are enslaved by their own tastes, which they respect in every detail. There are also people who are sensitive to what is good and offended by what is not; their views are clear and correct, and they find that the reason for their taste lies in their intelligence and discernment.

Some people, when faced with a matter of judgement, always choose the right side by a kind of instinct, without knowing why. Such people display more taste than intelligence, because their self-love and their temperament are not overriding their innate enlightenment. All their faculties act in concert and have the same tone. This harmony makes them judge things soundly and form a true idea of them. But generally speaking, there are few people whose tastes are fixed and independent of their friends'; most

l'exemple et la coutume, et ils en empruntent presque tout ce qu'ils ont de goût.

Dans toutes ces différences de goûts que l'on vient de marquer, il est très rare, et presque impossible, de rencontrer cette sorte de bon goût qui sait donner le prix à chaque chose, qui en connaît toute la valeur, et qui se porte généralement sur tout: nos connaissances sont trop bornées, et cette juste disposition des qualités qui font bien juger ne se maintient d'ordinaire que sur ce qui ne nous regarde pas directement. Quand il s'agit de nous, notre goût n'a plus cette justesse si nécessaire; la préoccupation la trouble; tout ce qui a du rapport à nous paraît sous une autre figure; personne ne voit des mêmes yeux ce qui le touche et ce qui ne le touche pas; notre goût est conduit alors par la pente de l'amour-propre et de l'humeur, qui nous fournissent des vues nouvelles, et nous assujettissent à un nombre infini de changements et d'incertitudes; notre goût n'est plus à nous, nous n'en disposons plus: il change sans notre consentement, et les mêmes objets nous paraissent par tant de côtés différents, que nous méconnaissons enfin ce que nous avons vu et ce que nous avons senti.

RD 11. Du Rapport des hommes avec les animaux

Il y a autant de diverses espèces d'hommes qu'il y a de diverses espèces d'animaux, et les hommes sont, à l'égard des autres hommes, ce que les différentes espèces d'animaux sont entre elles et à l'égard les unes des autres. Combien y a-t-il d'hommes qui vivent du sang et de la vie des innocents: les uns comme des tigres, toujours farouches et toujours cruels; d'autres comme des lions, en gardant quelque apparence de générosité; d'autres comme des ours, grossiers et avides; d'autres comme des loups, ravissants et impitoyables; d'autres comme des renards, qui vivent d'industrie, et dont le métier est de tromper!

Combien y a-t-il d'hommes qui ont du rapport aux chiens! Ils détruisent leur espèce; ils chassent pour le plaisir de celui qui les nourrit; les uns suivent toujours leur maître, les autres gardent sa maison. Il y a des lévriers d'attache, qui vivent de leur valeur, qui se destinent à la guerre, et qui ont de la noblesse dans leur courage; il y a des dogues acharnés, qui n'ont de qualités que la fureur; il y a des chiens, plus ou moins inutiles, qui aboient souvent, et qui mordent

people, instead, follow example and fashion, from which almost all their tastes are derived.

Amid all the different forms of taste noted above, it is very rare, indeed almost impossible, to find the sort of good taste that is really capable of evaluating each thing—that appreciates its full value, and is universally applicable. Our background knowledge is too limited; and only on matters of no direct concern to us, in most cases, do we maintain the sound combination of qualities required for good judgement. When we ourselves are concerned, our tastes no longer have the necessary soundness; they are disturbed by distracting influences. Everything takes on a different appearance when it relates to us. No one can see with the same eyes both what affects him and what does not affect him. Then our tastes are led by the bent of our self-love and our temperament, which give us new points of view, and subject us to innumerable changes and uncertainties. Our tastes are no longer our own, they are no longer under our own control; they change without our consent, and we see the same things from such different aspects that at last we no longer recognize what we used to see and feel.

RD 11. The Relationship Between Men and Animals

There are as many different kinds of men as there are of animals, and men are to other men what the different kinds of animals are to themselves and to each other. How many men live on the blood and lives of the innocent—some like tigers, perpetually savage and cruel; others like lions, maintaining some appearance of generosity; others like bears, uncouth and greedy; others like wolves, marauding and pitiless; others like foxes, who live by their diligence, and whose occupation is to deceive!

How many men are like dogs! They destroy their own kind; they hunt to please the person who feeds them; some are always following their master, while others are guarding his house. There are wolf-hounds, who live by their valour, who devote themselves to war, and who have nobility in their hearts; there are fierce watchdogs, whose sole merit is their frenzy; there are relatively useless dogs, who often bark and sometimes bite; there are even lapdogs. There are apes and

quelquefois; il y a même des chiens de jardinier. Il y a des singes et
des guenons qui plaisent par leurs manières, qui ont de l'esprit, et
qui font toujours du mal; il y a des paons qui n'ont que de la beauté,
qui déplaisent par leur chant, et qui détruisent les lieux qu'ils
habitent.

Il y a des oiseaux qui ne sont recommandables que par leur ramage
et par leurs couleurs. Combien de perroquets, qui parlent sans cesse,
et qui n'entendent jamais ce qu'ils disent; combien de pies et de
corneilles, qui ne s'apprivoisent que pour dérober; combien d'oiseaux de proie, qui ne vivent que de rapines; combien d'espèces
d'animaux paisibles et tranquilles, qui ne servent qu'à nourrir d'autres animaux!

Il y a des chats, toujours au guet, malicieux et infidèles, et qui font
patte de velours; il y a des vipères, dont la langue est venimeuse, et
dont le reste est utile; il y a des araignées, des mouches, des punaises
et des puces, qui sont toujours incommodes et insupportables; il y a
des crapauds, qui font horreur et qui n'ont que du venin; il y a des
hiboux, qui craignent la lumière. Combien d'animaux qui vivent
sous terre pour se conserver! Combien de chevaux, qu'on emploie à
tant d'usages, et qu'on abandonne quand ils ne servent plus; combien de bœufs, qui travaillent toute leur vie, pour enrichir celui qui
leur impose le joug; de cigales, qui passent leur vie à chanter; de
lièvres, qui ont peur de tout; de lapins, qui s'épouvantent et
rassurent en un moment; de pourceaux, qui vivent dans la crapule
et dans l'ordure; de canards privés, qui trahissent leurs semblables, et
les attirent dans les filets; de corbeaux et de vautours, qui ne vivent
que de pourriture et de corps morts! Combien d'oiseaux passagers,
qui vont si souvent d'un bout du monde à l'autre, et qui s'exposent à
tant de périls, pour chercher à vivre! combien d'hirondelles, qui
suivent toujours le beau temps; de hannetons, inconsidérés et sans
dessein; de papillons, qui cherchent le feu qui les brûle! Combien
d'abeilles, qui respectent leur chef, et qui se maintiennent avec tant
de règle et d'industrie! combien de frelons, vagabonds et fainéants,
qui cherchent à s'établir aux dépens des abeilles! Combien de four-
mis, dont la prévoyance et l'économie soulagent tous leurs besoins!
combien de crocodiles, qui feignent de se plaindre pour dévorer ceux
qui sont touchés de leurs plaintes! Et combien d'animaux qui sont
assujettis parce qu'ils ignorent leur force!

monkeys with pleasing ways, who are intelligent and always do ill; there are peacocks with nothing but beauty, whose singing is disliked, and who destroy the places where they live.

There are birds whose only recommendation is their plumage and their colouring. So many parrots, who talk incessantly and never understand what they are saying; so many crows and magpies, who become tame only in order to steal; so many birds of prey, who live only by depredation; so many kinds of calm and peaceful animals, whose sole purpose is to be food for other animals!

There are cats, always on the alert, malicious, faithless, keeping their claws hidden; there are vipers, whose tongues are venomous, though their other parts have their uses;* there are spiders, flies, lice, and fleas, always annoying and unbearable; there are toads, who are entirely composed of poison and inspire disgust; there are owls, who fear the daylight. So many animals who live underground for reasons of self-preservation! So many horses, who are put to use in many ways and are abandoned when they are no longer useful; so many oxen, who work all their lives to enrich the man who has placed his yoke on them; grasshoppers, who spend their whole lives in song; hares, who are afraid of everything; rabbits, who panic and calm down in a moment; swine, who live in filth and scum; decoy ducks, who betray their own kind and lure them into the snare; ravens and vultures, who live only on corruption and corpses! So many migrant birds, constantly flying from this world to that, and facing so many perils in search of their livelihood! So many swallows, always going where the weather is fair; beetles, with no thoughts and no plans; moths, seeking the very fire that burns them! So many bees, who respect their leader, observe such order, and act with such diligence! So many drones, idle and vagrant, trying to live off the bees! So many ants, whose foresight and economy relieve all their needs! So many crocodiles, pretending to weep and devouring those who are moved by their grief! And so many animals who are in subjection because they do not know their own strength!

Toutes ces qualités se trouvent dans l'homme, et il exerce, à l'égard des autres hommes, tout ce que les animaux dont on vient de parler exercent entre eux.

RD 12. De l'Origine des maladies

Si on examine la nature des maladies, on trouvera qu'elles tirent leur origine des passions et des peines de l'esprit. L'âge d'or, qui en était exempt, était exempt de maladies; l'âge d'argent, qui le suivit, conserva encore sa pureté; l'âge d'airain donna la naissance aux passions et aux peines de l'esprit: elles commencèrent à se former, et elles avaient encore la faiblesse de l'enfance et sa légèreté. Mais elles parurent avec toute leur force et toute leur malignité dans l'âge de fer, et répandirent dans le monde, par la suite de leur corruption, les diverses maladies qui ont affligé les hommes depuis tant de siècles. L'ambition a produit les fièvres aiguës et frénétiques; l'envie a produit la jaunisse et l'insomnie; c'est de la paresse que viennent les léthargies, les paralysies et les langueurs; la colère a fait les étouffements, les ébullitions de sang, et les inflammations de poitrine; la peur a fait les battements de cœur et les syncopes; la vanité a fait les folies; l'avarice, la teigne et la gale; la tristesse a fait le scorbut; la cruauté, la pierre, la calomnie et les faux rapports ont répandu la rougeole, la petite vérole, et le pourpre, et on doit à la jalousie la gangrène, la peste, et la rage. Les disgrâces imprévues ont fait l'apoplexie; les procès ont fait la migraine et le transport au cerveau; les dettes ont fait les fièvres étiques; l'ennui du mariage a produit la fièvre quarte, et la lassitude des amants qui n'osent se quitter a causé les vapeurs. L'amour, lui seul, a fait plus de maux que tout le reste ensemble, et personne ne doit entreprendre de les exprimer; mais comme il fait aussi les plus grands biens de la vie, au lieu de médire de lui, on doit se taire: on doit le craindre et le respecter toujours.

RD 13. Du Faux

On est faux en différentes manières: il y a des hommes faux qui veulent toujours paraître ce qu'ils ne sont pas; il y en a d'autres, de meilleure foi, qui sont nés faux, qui se trompent eux-mêmes, et qui ne voient jamais les choses comme elles sont. Il y en a dont l'esprit

All these qualities are found in man; and he acts toward other men as the animals we have just discussed act toward each other.

RD 12. The Origin of Illnesses

If we study the nature of illnesses, we find that they originate from mental passions and pains. The Golden Age,* which was free from such passions and pains, was also free from illnesses. The Silver Age, which followed it, still preserved its purity. The Bronze Age gave birth to mental passions and pains; they began to take shape, and they still had the weakness and slightness of youth. But they appeared in their full strength and malignity during the Iron Age, and their corrupting influence spread throughout the world the various illnesses that have afflicted men for so many ages. Ambition causes acute and frenzied fevers; envy causes jaundice and insomnia; laziness is the cause of lethargies, paralyses, and states of sluggishness; anger produces suffocation, bleeding fits, and inflammation of the lungs; fear produces palpitations and fainting spells; vanity produces madness, avarice rashes and itching; sadness produces scurvy, cruelty calculi; calumny and falsehood have spread measles, smallpox, and purpura; and to jealousy we owe gangrene, plague, and rabies. Unexpected disgrace produces apoplexy; lawsuits produce migraine and strokes; debts produce consumption; boredom in marriage causes quartan fever, and when lovers dare not separate, their weariness leads to the vapours. Love alone has produced more ills than all the rest together, and no one could undertake to list them—but as it also produces the best things in life, we should keep silent and not slander it; we should always fear and respect it.

RD 13. Falsehood

People are false in different ways. Some false men always want to seem what they are not; others—more trustworthy—are born false, deceive themselves, and never see things as they really are. There are some whose minds are sound, though their tastes are false; others

est droit, et le goût faux; d'autres ont l'esprit faux, et ont quelque droiture dans le goût; il y en a enfin qui n'ont rien de faux dans le goût, ni dans l'esprit. Ceux-ci sont très rares, puisque, à parler généralement, il n'y a presque personne qui n'ait de la fausseté dans quelque endroit de l'esprit ou du goût.

Ce qui fait cette fausseté si universelle, c'est que nos qualités sont incertaines et confuses, et que nos vues le sont aussi: on ne voit point les choses précisément comme elles sont; on les estime plus ou moins qu'elles ne valent, et on ne les fait point rapporter à nous en la manière qui leur convient, et qui convient à notre état et à nos qualités. Ce mécompte met un nombre infini de faussetés dans le goût et dans l'esprit; notre amour-propre est flatté de tout ce qui se présente à nous sous les apparences du bien: mais comme il y a plusieurs sortes de bien qui touchent notre vanité ou notre tempérament, on les suit souvent par coutume, ou par commodité; on les suit parce que les autres les suivent, sans considérer qu'un même sentiment ne doit pas être également embrassé par toute sorte de personnes, et qu'on s'y doit attacher plus ou moins fortement, selon qu'il convient plus ou moins à ceux qui le suivent.

On craint encore plus de se montrer faux par le goût que par l'esprit. Les honnêtes gens doivent approuver sans prévention ce qui mérite d'être approuvé, suivre ce qui mérite d'être suivi, et ne se piquer de rien; mais il y faut une grande proportion et une grande justesse: il faut savoir discerner ce qui est bon en général, et ce qui nous est propre, et suivre alors avec raison la pente naturelle qui nous porte vers les choses qui nous plaisent. Si les hommes ne voulaient exceller que par leurs propres talents, et en suivant leurs devoirs, il n'y aurait rien de faux dans leur goût et dans leur conduite; ils se montreraient tels qu'ils sont; ils jugeraient des choses par leurs lumières, et s'y attacheraient par leur raison; il y aurait de la proportion dans leurs vues et dans leurs sentiments; leur goût serait vrai, il viendrait d'eux et non pas des autres, et ils le suivraient par choix, et non pas par coutume ou par hasard.

Si on est faux en approuvant ce qui ne doit pas être approuvé, on ne l'est pas moins, le plus souvent, par l'envie de se faire valoir en des qualités qui sont bonnes de soi, mais qui ne nous conviennent pas: un magistrat est faux quand il se pique d'être brave, bien qu'il puisse être hardi dans de certaines rencontres; il doit paraître ferme et assuré dans une sédition qu'il a droit d'apaiser, sans craindre d'être

have false minds and relatively sound tastes. There are also some who have no falsehood either in their tastes or in their minds. Such people are very rare, since, generally speaking, almost everyone has something false somewhere in his mind or tastes.

What makes this falseness so universal is the fact that our qualities are indeterminate* and indistinct, and so are our views. We never see things exactly as they are; we prize them more or less than they are worth, and we never relate them to ourselves in the way that would suit both the thing itself and also our own condition and qualities. Such misjudgements make our tastes and minds false in innumerable ways; our self-love is flattered by every seemingly good thing that comes before us; but as there are various kinds of good things affecting our vanity or temperament, we often accept them out of habit, or out of convenience; we accept them because other people are accepting them—we fail to reflect that not all of us should have the same feelings, and that we should cling to them more or less firmly, depending on what is appropriate for those who feel them.

We are even more afraid to show falseness in our tastes than in our minds. People of honor should, without any prejudice, approve what deserves to be approved, accept what deserves to be accepted, and never take pride in themselves. But this requires a great sense of proportion and precision: we must be able to distinguish between what is good in general and what is appropriate for ourselves, so that we can, with good reason, follow our natural inclination toward the things that please us. If men wanted to excel only by means of their own talents, and only by doing their duty, there would be nothing false in their tastes and conduct; they would show themselves as they really are; they would judge everything by their own light, and cling to it by their own powers of reason; there would be a sense of proportion in their views and feelings; their tastes would be true, derived from themselves and not from other people, and would be accepted by choice, not from habit or by chance.

If we act falsely when we approve what should not be approved, very often we act just as falsely when we wish to draw attention to ourselves for qualities that are good in themselves but do not suit us. A magistrate is acting falsely when he takes pride in his courage, even though he may be brave in certain circumstances; he should seem strong and sure, without any fear of acting falsely, when he has

faux, et il serait faux et ridicule de se battre en duel. Une femme peut aimer les sciences, mais toutes les sciences ne lui conviennent pas toujours, et l'entêtement de certaines sciences ne lui convient jamais, et est toujours faux.

Il faut que la raison et le bon sens mettent le prix aux choses, et déterminent notre goût à leur donner le rang qu'elles méritent et qu'il nous convient de leur donner; mais tous les hommes presque se trompent dans ce prix et dans ce rang, et il y a toujours de la fausseté dans ce mécompte.

Les plus grands rois sont ceux qui s'y méprennent le plus souvent: ils veulent surpasser les autres hommes en valeur, en savoir, en galanterie, et dans mille autres qualités où tout le monde a droit de prétendre; mais ce goût d'y surpasser les autres peut être faux en eux, quand il va trop loin. Leur émulation doit avoir un autre objet: ils doivent imiter Alexandre, qui ne voulut disputer du prix de la course que contre des rois, et se souvenir que ce n'est que des qualités particulières à la royauté qu'ils doivent disputer. Quelque vaillant que puisse être un roi, quelque savant et agréable qu'il puisse être, il trouvera un nombre infini de gens qui auront ces mêmes qualités aussi avantageusement que lui, et le désir de les surpasser paraîtra toujours faux, et souvent même il lui sera impossible d'y réussir; mais s'il s'attache à ses devoirs véritables, s'il est magnanime, s'il est grand capitaine et grand politique, s'il est juste, clément et libéral, s'il soulage ses sujets; s'il aime la gloire et le repos de son État, il ne trouvera que des rois à vaincre dans une si noble carrière; il n'y aura rien que de vrai et de grand dans un si juste dessein. Le désir d'y surpasser les autres n'aura rien de faux. Cette émulation est digne d'un roi, et c'est la véritable gloire où il doit prétendre.

RD 14. Des Modèles de la nature et de la fortune

Il semble que la fortune, toute changeante et capricieuse qu'elle est, renonce à ses changements et à ses caprices pour agir de concert avec la nature, et que l'une et l'autre concourent de temps en temps à faire des hommes extraordinaires et singuliers, pour servir de modèles à la postérité. Le soin de la nature est de fournir les qualités; celui de la fortune est de les mettre en œuvre, et de les faire voir dans le jour et avec les proportions qui conviennent à leur dessein: on dirait alors

the task of calming an insurrection, yet it would be false and absurd for him to fight a duel. A woman may like study, but not all studies invariably suit her, and the persistence required for some studies never suits her: it is always false.

Reason and good sense should fix the value of things, defining our taste so that we rank things as they deserve and as it is fitting for us to do; but nearly all men make mistakes in that process of ranking and valuation, and there is always something false in such misjudgements.

The greatest kings make such mistakes most often. They want to surpass other men in valour, knowledge, gallantry, and thousands of other qualities to which any person at all may aspire; but their desire to surpass other people in such respects can be false, if it goes too far. They should aim to emulate a different model; they should imitate Alexander,* who wanted to compete only against kings, and they must remember that they should compete only for specifically royal qualities. However valiant a king may be, however wise and attractive, he will find innumerable people who are just as well endowed with those qualities as he is. A desire to surpass them will always seem false, and must often be unsuccessful. But if he clings to his true duties, if he is magnanimous, if he is a great general and a great statesman, if he is just, clement, and generous, if he eases his subjects' burdens, if he loves glory and the peace of the realm, then, in so noble a course of action, he will find only kings to defeat; so just a plan will contain only what is true and great, and in such matters there will be nothing false about a desire to surpass the others. Emulation of that kind is worthy of a king, and is the true glory to which he should aspire.

RD 14. Models Produced by Nature and Fortune

It seems that fortune, changeable and whimsical though she is, renounces her changes and whims to cooperate with nature, and that the two of them collaborate now and then to produce extraordinary, singular men, in order to provide models for posterity. Nature's concern is to supply the qualities; fortune's is to exercise them, displaying them in the light and with the proportions that suit their

qu'elles imitent les règles des grands peintres, pour nous donner des tableaux parfaits de ce qu'elles veulent représenter. Elles choisissent un sujet, et s'attachent au plan qu'elles se sont proposé; elles disposent de la naissance, de l'éducation, des qualités naturelles et acquises, des temps, des conjonctures, des amis, des ennemis; elles font remarquer des vertus et des vices, des actions heureuses et malheureuses; elles joignent même de petites circonstances aux plus grandes, et les savent placer avec tant d'art, que les actions des hommes et leurs motifs nous paraissent toujours sous la figure et avec les couleurs qu'il plaît à la nature et à la fortune d'y donner.

Quel concours de qualités éclatantes n'ont-elles pas assemblé dans la personne d'Alexandre, pour le montrer au monde comme un modèle d'élévation d'âme et de grandeur de courage! Si on examine sa naissance illustre, son éducation, sa jeunesse, sa beauté, sa complexion heureuse, l'étendue et la capacité de son esprit pour la guerre et pour les sciences, ses vertus, ses défauts même, le petit nombre de ses troupes, la puissance formidable de ses ennemis, la courte durée d'une si belle vie, sa mort et ses successeurs, ne verra-t-on pas l'industrie et l'application de la fortune et de la nature à renfermer dans un même sujet ce nombre infini de diverses circonstances? Ne verra-t-on pas le soin particulier qu'elles ont pris d'arranger tant d'événements extraordinaires, et de les mettre chacun dans son jour, pour composer un modèle d'un jeune conquérant, plus grand encore par ses qualités personnelles que par l'étendue de ses conquêtes?

Si on considère de quelle sorte la nature et la fortune nous montrent César, ne verra-t-on pas qu'elles ont suivi un autre plan, qu'elles n'ont renfermé dans sa personne tant de valeur, de clémence, de libéralité, tant de qualités militaires, tant de pénétration, tant de facilité d'esprit et de mœurs, tant d'éloquence, tant de grâces du corps, tant de supériorité de génie pour la paix et pour la guerre, ne verra-t-on pas, dis-je, qu'elles ne se sont assujetties si longtemps à arranger et à mettre en œuvre tant de talents extraordinaires, et qu'elles n'ont contraint César de s'en servir contre sa patrie, que pour nous laisser un modèle du plus grand homme du monde, et du plus célèbre usurpateur? Elle le fait naître particulier dans une république maîtresse de l'univers, affermie et soutenue par les plus grands hommes qu'elle eût jamais produits; la fortune choisit parmi eux ce qu'il y avait de plus illustre, de plus puissant, et de plus redoutable, pour les rendre ses ennemis; elle le réconcilie,

plan. Thus fortune and nature seemingly follow the rules that great painters use to give us perfect pictures of what they want to depict. They choose a subject and remain committed to the plan they have selected; they make use of birth, education, innate and acquired qualities, times, incidents, friends, enemies; they draw attention to virtues and vices, deeds fortunate and unfortunate; they even combine little circumstances with greater ones, and manage to place them so artfully, that men's deeds and motives always appear to us with the form and colouring that nature and fortune are pleased to give them.

What a coordinated array of brilliant qualities they gathered together in the person of Alexander,* in order to show him to the world as a model of everything that is eminently lofty in soul and great in heart! If we examine his illustrious birth, his education, his youth, his beauty, his fortunate constitution, his mind's breadth and aptitude for war and knowledge, his virtues, his very faults, the small number of his troops, the formidable strength of his enemies, the brevity of so fair a life, his death, and his successors, can we not see what effort and diligence nature and fortune used to encompass those innumerable and varied circumstances within a single person? Can we not see what care they took to order so many extraordinary events, presenting each of them in its own light, to produce a model of a young conqueror whose personal qualities were even greater than the extent of his conquests?

If we consider how nature and fortune depict Caesar* to us, can we not see that they followed a different plan—that they encompassed within him so much valour, clemency, and generosity, so many military qualities, so much perceptiveness, so much ease in mind and manners, so much eloquence, so much physical grace, such a superior genius for peace and war alike—can we not see, I repeat, that they went to such prolonged pains to order and exercise so many extraordinary talents, and that they forced Caesar to use them against his own homeland, only to leave us a model of the world's greatest man and the most famous usurper? They had him born a private citizen in a republic strengthened and supported by the greatest men it had ever produced, and ruling the whole world. Fortune even chose the most illustrious, powerful, and formidable of those men to be his enemies; for a while she reconciled him with the

pour un temps, avec les plus considérables, pour les faire servir à son élévation; elle les éblouit et les aveugle ensuite, pour lui faire une guerre qui le conduit à la souveraine puissance. Combien d'obstacles ne lui a-t-elle pas fait surmonter! De combien de périls, sur terre et sur mer, ne l'a-t-elle pas garanti, sans jamais avoir été blessé! Avec quelle persévérance la fortune n'a-t-elle pas soutenu les desseins de César, et détruit ceux de Pompée! Par quelle industrie n'a-t-elle pas disposé ce peuple romain, si puissant, si fier, et si jaloux de sa liberté, à la soumettre à la puissance d'un seul homme! Ne s'est-elle pas même servie des circonstances de la mort de César, pour la rendre convenable à sa vie? Tant d'avertissements des devins, tant de prodiges, tant d'avis de sa femme et de ses amis, ne peuvent le garantir, et la fortune choisit le propre jour qu'il doit être couronné dans le Sénat, pour le faire assassiner par ceux mêmes qu'il a sauvés, et par un homme qui lui doit la naissance.

Cet accord de la nature et de la fortune n'a jamais été plus marqué que dans la personne de Caton, et il semble qu'elles se soient efforcées l'une et l'autre de renfermer dans un seul homme non seulement les vertus de l'ancienne Rome, mais encore de l'opposer directement aux vertus de César, pour montrer qu'avec une pareille étendue d'esprit et de courage, le désir de gloire conduit l'un à être usurpateur, et l'autre à servir de modèle d'un parfait citoyen. Mon dessein n'est pas de faire ici le parallèle de ces deux grands hommes, après tout ce qui en est écrit; je dirai seulement que, quelque grands et illustres qu'ils nous paraissent, la nature et la fortune n'auraient pu mettre toutes leurs qualités dans le jour qui convenait pour les faire éclater, si elles n'eussent opposé Caton à César. Il fallait les faire naître en même temps, dans une même république, différents par leurs mœurs et par leurs talents, ennemis par les intérêts de la patrie et par des intérêts domestiques; l'un, vaste dans ses desseins, et sans bornes dans son ambition; l'autre, austère, renfermé dans les lois de Rome, et idolâtre de la liberté; tous deux célèbres par des vertus qui les montraient par de si différents côtés, et plus célèbres encore, si on l'ose dire, par l'opposition que la fortune et la nature ont pris soin de mettre entre eux. Quel arrangement, quelle suite, quelle économie de circonstances dans la vie de Caton, et dans sa mort! La destinée même de la République a servi au tableau que la fortune nous a voulu donner de ce grand homme, et elle finit sa vie avec la liberté de son pays.

most noteworthy of them, so that they might enhance his eminence; after which, she dazzled and blinded them so that they would declare war on him—the war that would lead him to sovereign power. How many obstacles she helped him overcome! Through how many dangers by land and sea she protected him, so that he was never wounded! How steadfastly fortune supported Caesar's plans and destroyed Pompey's! How diligently she led the Roman people, so powerful, so proud, so jealous of their liberty, to submit to the power of one man! Did she not use even the circumstances of Caesar's death, so that it would be in agreement with his life? All the sorcerers' warnings, all the marvels, all the advice from his wife and his friends, could not save him; choosing the very day when he was to be crowned in the Senate, fortune had him assassinated by the very people whom he had saved, and by a man who owed his existence to him.*

This harmony between nature and fortune was never more conspicuous than in the case of Cato;* it seems that they strove, not only to encompass the virtues of ancient Rome in one man, but also to oppose him explicitly against the virtues of Caesar—showing that, though the two were similar in breadth of mind and heart, desire for glory led one to be a usurper, and the other to be a model of a perfect citizen. After all that has been written about these two men, my plan here is not to place them in parallel; I shall say only that, however great and illustrious Cato and Caesar seem to us, their full qualities could not have been seen in the appropriate light unless nature and fortune had set them in opposition. They had to be born at the same time, in the same republic, with different manners and talents, at enmity because of both public and private interests; one with vast plans and boundless ambitions, the other austere, encompassed within the laws of Rome, and idolizing liberty; both famous for virtues—which they displayed in such different ways—and still more famous, if we may be permitted to say so, for the opposition that fortune and nature carefully set between them. What order, what consistency, what economy of detail there was in the life of Cato, and in his death! Fortune chose to give us the very fate of the republic as a backdrop for this great man; she ended his life and his country's liberty at the same time.

Si nous laissons les exemples des siècles passés pour venir aux exemples du siècle présent, on trouvera que la nature et la fortune ont conservé cette même union dont j'ai parlé, pour nous montrer de différents modèles en deux hommes consommés en l'art de commander. Nous verrons Monsieur le Prince et M. de Turenne disputer de la gloire des armes, et mériter, par un nombre infini d'actions éclatantes, la réputation qu'ils ont acquise. Ils paraîtront avec une valeur et une expérience égales; infatigables de corps et d'esprit, on les verra agir ensemble, agir séparément, et quelquefois opposés l'un à l'autre; nous les verrons, heureux et malheureux dans diverses occasions de la guerre, devoir les bons succès à leur conduite et à leur courage, et se montrer même toujours plus grands, par leurs disgrâces; tous deux sauver l'État; tous deux contribuer à le détruire, et se servir des mêmes talents, par des voies différentes: M. de Turenne, suivant ses desseins avec plus de règle et moins de vivacité, d'une valeur plus retenue, et toujours proportionnée au besoin de la faire paraître; Monsieur le Prince, inimitable en la manière de voir et d'exécuter les plus grandes choses, entraîné par la supériorité de son génie, qui semble lui soumettre les événements et les faire servir à sa gloire. La faiblesse des armées qu'ils ont commandées dans les dernières campagnes, et la puissance des ennemis qui leur étaient opposés, ont donné de nouveaux sujets à l'un et à l'autre de montrer toute leur vertu, et de réparer par leur mérite tout ce qui leur manquait pour soutenir la guerre. La mort même de M. de Turenne, si convenable à une si belle vie, accompagnée de tant de circonstances singulières, et arrivée dans un moment si important, ne nous paraît-elle pas comme un effet de la crainte et de l'incertitude de la fortune, qui n'a osé décider de la destinée de la France et de l'Empire? Cette même fortune, qui retire Monsieur le Prince du commandement des armées, sous le prétexte de sa santé, et dans un temps où il devait achever de si grandes choses, ne se joint-elle pas à la nature pour nous montrer présentement ce grand homme dans une vie privée, exerçant des vertus paisibles, soutenu de sa propre gloire? Et brille-t-il moins dans sa retraite qu'au milieu de ses victoires?

If we leave the examples of past ages and come to those of the present age, we find that nature and fortune have maintained the union that I have described. As a result, they have shown us different models in two masters of the art of command. We see the Prince and Monsieur de Turenne* competing for military glory, and, as a result of innumerable brilliant deeds, deserving the reputation they earned. They seem equal in valour and experience; we see them acting now together, now separately, and sometimes in opposition to each other, without wearying in body or mind; we see them fortunate and unfortunate in the varied circumstances of war, owing their successes to their conduct and their courage, and always appearing still greater in times of disgrace; both of them saving the realm; both of them helping to destroy it, and making use of the same talents in different ways—Monsieur de Turenne pursuing his plans in a more orderly, less lively manner, with a valour that was more cautious and never more visible than it needed to be; the Prince, incomparable in his way of envisaging and executing the greatest deeds, drawn along by the superiority of his genius, which seemed to place any occurrence in subjection to him and make it serve his glory. The weakness of the armies that they commanded in their last campaigns, and the power of the enemies opposing them, gave each of them new scope for displaying his full ability and repairing by his own merit everything that he otherwise lacked for war. Even the death of Monsieur de Turenne, so well suited to so fine a life, accompanied by so many singular circumstances, and happening at such a crucial moment, looks to us as if it were due to fortune's timidity and uncertainty: she did not dare to decide the fate of France and the Empire. The same fortune withdrew the Prince from military command on the pretext of ill health, and at a time when he would have accomplished such great things—but has she not united with nature at present, to show us the great man in private life, practising peaceful virtues, and maintained by his own glory? Does he shine any less brightly in his retirement than he did in the midst of his victories?

RD 15. Des Coquettes et des Vieillards

S'il est malaisé de rendre raison des goûts en général, il le doit être
encore davantage de rendre raison du goût des femmes coquettes; on
peut dire néanmoins que l'envie de plaire se répand généralement
sur tout ce qui peut flatter leur vanité, et qu'elles ne trouvent rien
d'indigne de leurs conquêtes; mais le plus incompréhensible de tous
leurs goûts est, à mon sens, celui qu'elles ont pour les vieillards qui
ont été galants. Ce goût paraît trop bizarre, et il y en a trop d'exemples, pour ne chercher pas la cause d'un sentiment tout à la fois si
commun, et si contraire à l'opinion que l'on a des femmes. Je laisse
aux philosophes à décider si c'est un soin charitable de la nature, qui
veut consoler les vieillards dans leur misère, et qui leur fournit le
secours des coquettes, par la même prévoyance qui lui fait donner
des ailes aux chenilles, dans le déclin de leur vie, pour les rendre
papillons; mais sans pénétrer dans les secrets de la physique, on peut,
ce me semble, chercher des causes plus sensibles de ce goût dépravé
des coquettes pour les vieilles gens. Ce qui est plus apparent, c'est
qu'elles aiment les prodiges, et qu'il n'y en a point qui doive plus
toucher leur vanité que de ressusciter un mort. Elles ont le plaisir de
l'attacher à leur char, et d'en parer leur triomphe, sans que leur
réputation en soit blessée: au contraire, un vieillard est un ornement
à la suite d'une coquette, et il est aussi nécessaire dans son train, que
les nains l'étaient autrefois dans *Amadis*. Elles n'ont point d'esclaves
si commodes et si utiles: elles paraissent bonnes et solides, en conservant un ami sans conséquence; il publie leurs louanges, il gagne
croyance vers les maris, et leur répond de la conduite de leurs
femmes. S'il a du crédit, elles en retirent mille secours; il entre dans
tous les intérêts et dans tous les besoins de la maison. S'il sait les
bruits qui courent des véritables galanteries, il n'a garde de les croire;
il les étouffe, et assure que le monde est médisant; il juge, par sa
propre expérience, des difficultés qu'il y a de toucher le cœur d'une
si bonne femme; plus on lui fait acheter des grâces et des faveurs,
plus il est discret et fidèle; son propre intérêt l'engage assez au
silence; il craint toujours d'être quitté, et il se trouve trop heureux
d'être souffert. Il se persuade aisément qu'il est aimé, puisqu'on le
choisit contre tant d'apparences: il croit que c'est un privilège de son
vieux mérite, et remercie l'amour de se souvenir de lui dans tous les
temps.

RD 15. Flirts and Old Men

If it is hard to account for tastes in general, it must be still harder to account for the tastes of women who are flirts. Nevertheless, we may say that they indiscriminately wish to please anyone who may flatter their vanity, and they regard no one as unworthy of being conquered. But of all their tastes, the most incomprehensible, to my mind, is their taste for old men who used to have love affairs. The cause of a feeling that is both so common and so contrary to our opinion of women cannot be left unexplored: the taste seems all too bizarre, and yet there are all too many examples of it. I leave philosophers to decide if it is due to the charity of nature, who wants to comfort old men in their destitution by sending flirts to their rescue—just as, with the same foresight, she gives caterpillars wings in their declining days and makes them butterflies. But without plumbing the secrets of medicine, it seems to me that we can find more tangible causes for the depraved taste that flirts have for old men. What is most evident is that they love marvels, and no marvel could touch their vanity more than a man who is raised from the dead. They enjoy the pleasure of attaching him to their chariot to adorn their triumphal procession, without wounding their reputation; on the contrary, an old man in the retinue of a flirt is an ornament; he is as necessary a part of her train as the dwarfs used to be in *Amadis*.*
No slave is so convenient and so useful to such women; they maintain an appearance of goodness—well-founded goodness—while keeping a lover who does not matter. He sings their praises; he wins the trust of their husbands and assures them of their wives' good conduct. If he is trusted, the women are helped by it in a thousand ways; he participates in all their household interests and obligations. If he hears rumours of true love affairs, he is far from believing them; he stifles them, and insists that the world is full of slander; his own experience tells him how hard it is to touch the heart of so good a woman. The more signs of grace and favour he manages to earn, the more discreet and faithful he is; his own interest sufficiently obliges him to be silent; he is constantly afraid of being deserted, and he considers himself only too fortunate if he is endured. He readily convinces himself that he is loved, since he has been chosen in spite of all likelihood; he believes that it is a privilege of his meritorious old age, and he gives thanks to Love for remembering him in all seasons.

Elle, de son côté, ne voudrait pas manquer à ce qu'elle lui a promis: elle lui fait remarquer qu'il a toujours touché son inclination, et qu'elle n'aurait jamais aimé, si elle ne l'avait jamais connu; elle le prie surtout de n'être pas jaloux et de se fier en elle; elle lui avoue qu'elle aime un peu le monde et le commerce des honnêtes gens, qu'elle a même intérêt d'en ménager plusieurs à la fois, pour ne laisser pas voir qu'elle le traite différemment des autres; que si elle fait quelques railleries de lui avec ceux dont on s'est avisé de parler, c'est seulement pour avoir le plaisir de le nommer souvent, ou pour mieux cacher ses sentiments; qu'après tout, il est le maître de sa conduite, et que, pourvu qu'il en soit content, et qu'il l'aime toujours, elle se met aisément en repos du reste. Quel vieillard ne se rassure pas par des raisons si convaincantes, qui l'ont souvent trompé quand il était jeune et aimable? Mais, pour son malheur, il oublie trop aisément qu'il n'est plus ni l'un ni l'autre, et cette faiblesse est, de toutes, la plus ordinaire aux vieilles gens qui ont été aimés. Je ne sais si cette tromperie ne leur vaut pas mieux encore que de connaître la vérité: on les souffre du moins; on les amuse; ils sont détournés de la vue de leurs propres misères; et le ridicule où ils tombent est souvent un moindre mal pour eux que les ennuis et l'anéantissement d'une vie pénible et languissante.

RD 16. De la Différence des esprits

Bien que toutes les qualités de l'esprit se puissent rencontrer dans un grand esprit, il y en a néanmoins qui lui sont propres et particulières: ses lumières n'ont point de bornes; il agit toujours également, et avec la même activité; il discerne les objets éloignés, comme s'ils étaient présents; il comprend, il imagine les plus grandes choses; il voit et connaît les plus petites; ses pensées sont relevées, étendues, justes et intelligibles; rien n'échappe à sa pénétration, et elle lui fait toujours découvrir la vérité, au travers des obscurités qui la cachent aux autres. Mais toutes ces grandes qualités ne peuvent souvent empêcher que l'esprit ne paraisse petit et faible, quand l'humeur s'en est rendue la maîtresse.

Un bel esprit pense toujours noblement; il produit avec facilité des choses claires, agréables et naturelles; il les fait voir dans leur plus

As for the woman herself, she does not want to break her promises to him; she shows him that he has always touched her inclination, and that she would never have been in love if she had never known him; she begs him above all not to be jealous, and to trust her; she admits to him that she rather likes society and dealings with honorable people, that she even has a personal interest in showing consideration for several such people at the same time, in order to avoid showing that she treats him differently from the others; that if she has joked about him to people who happened to be speaking with her, it was only for the pleasure of saying his name frequently, or in order to hide her feelings more effectively; that, after all, her conduct is guided by him, and as long as he is happy with it and still loves her, nothing else matters to her. What old man would not feel reassured by such convincing reasons, which often deceived him when he was young and attractive? But unfortunately he forgets too easily that he is no longer either young or attractive—and that is the commonest weakness of old people who have been loved. I do not know whether it is better for them to be deceived in this way than to know the truth. At least they are endured; they are entertained; they are distracted from the sight of their own destitution; and the mockery that befalls them is often less bad for them than the heartache and dejection of a painful and sluggish life.

RD 16. Different Types of Mind

Although all the qualities of the human mind can be found in a great mind, there are some that are uniquely and specially its. Its understanding has no limits; it acts consistently, and its activity is always the same; it sees distant things as if they were close at hand; it comprehends and conceives the greatest things, it sees and knows the littlest ones; its thoughts are lofty, wide-ranging, just, and intelligible. Nothing escapes its perception, which always leads it to discern truths in the darkness that hides them from other people. Yet all those great qualities cannot stop a mind from seeming small and weak, when temperamental factors take control of it.

A fine mind always thinks nobly; it easily generates clear, attractive, and natural thoughts; it sets them in their best light, adorns them with all the appropriate ornaments, penetrates other people's

beau jour, et il les pare de tous les ornements qui leur conviennent; il entre dans le goût des autres, et retranche de ses pensées ce qui est inutile, ou ce qui peut déplaire. Un esprit adroit, facile, insinuant, sait éviter et surmonter les difficultés; il se plie aisément à ce qu'il veut; il sait connaître et suivre l'esprit et l'humeur de ceux avec qui il traite; et en ménageant leurs intérêts, il avance et il établit les siens. Un bon esprit voit toutes choses comme elles doivent être vues; il leur donne le prix qu'elles méritent, il les sait tourner du côté qui lui est le plus avantageux, et il s'attache avec fermeté à ses pensées, parce qu'il en connaît toute la force et toute la raison.

Il y a de la différence entre un esprit utile et un esprit d'affaires; on peut entendre les affaires, sans s'appliquer à son intérêt particulier: il y a des gens habiles dans tout ce qui ne les regarde pas, et très malhabiles dans ce qui les regarde; et il y en a d'autres, au contraire, qui ont une habileté bornée à ce qui les touche, et qui savent trouver leur avantage en toutes choses.

On peut avoir, tout ensemble, un air sérieux dans l'esprit, et dire souvent des choses agréables et enjouées; cette sorte d'esprit convient à toutes personnes et à tous les âges de la vie. Les jeunes gens ont d'ordinaire l'esprit enjoué et moqueur, sans l'avoir sérieux, et c'est ce qui les rend souvent incommodes. Rien n'est plus malaisé à soutenir que le dessein d'être toujours plaisant, et les applaudissements qu'on reçoit quelquefois en divertissant les autres ne valent pas que l'on s'expose à la honte de les ennuyer souvent, quand ils sont de méchante humeur. La moquerie est une des plus agréables et des plus dangereuses qualités de l'esprit: elle plaît toujours, quand elle est délicate; mais on craint toujours aussi ceux qui s'en servent trop souvent. La moquerie peut néanmoins être permise, quand elle n'est mêlée d'aucune malignité, et quand on y fait entrer les personnes mêmes dont on parle.

Il est malaisé d'avoir un esprit de raillerie sans affecter d'être plaisant, ou sans aimer à se moquer; il faut une grande justesse pour railler longtemps, sans tomber dans l'une ou l'autre de ces extrémités. La raillerie est un air de gaieté qui remplit l'imagination, et qui lui fait voir en ridicule les objets qui se présentent; l'humeur y mêle plus ou moins de douceur ou d'âpreté: il y a une manière de railler, délicate et flatteuse, qui touche seulement les défauts que les personnes dont on parle veulent bien avouer, qui sait déguiser les louanges qu'on leur donne sous des apparences de blâme, et qui découvre ce qu'elles ont d'aimable, en feignant de le vouloir cacher.

tastes, and rids its thoughts of anything useless or disagreeable. A clever, nimble, ingratiating mind is capable of avoiding and overcoming difficulties; it readily conforms with anything it wants; it is capable of understanding and accepting the minds and temperaments of those with whom it is dealing; and when it shows consideration for their interests, it is promoting and establishing its own. A sound mind sees all things as they should be seen, values all things as they deserve to be valued; it can turn everything to its own advantage, and it clings firmly to its own thoughts, because it knows just how strong and reasonable they are.

There is a difference between being practically minded and being business-minded. We can understand business without turning it to our own personal interest. Some people are clever in everything that does not concern them, and very far from clever in everything that does; whereas other people's cleverness is limited to what affects them personally—in any situation they can discern what is to their own advantage.

A person may have a serious turn of mind in general, yet often utter attractive and playful things; that sort of mind suits people of all kinds and all ages. Young people usually have minds that are playful and mocking but not serious; that is what often makes them so annoying. Nothing is harder to maintain than perpetual clowning; the acclaim we sometimes obtain by entertaining people is not worth the shame we often reap by boring them when they are in a bad temper. Mockery is one of the mind's most attractive and yet most dangerous qualities; when subtle it always gives pleasure, but we always dread those who make too much use of it. Nevertheless, mockery is permissible when there is no malice mingled with it, and when the very people of whom we are speaking can share in it.

It is hard to have a jocular mind without loving mockery or playing the clown; great skill is needed to prevent prolonged joking from falling into one or other of those extremes. Jocularity is a spirit of gaiety,* which fills the imagination and makes it see absurdities in whatever it encounters; depending on our temperament, greater or lesser amounts of gentleness or bitterness are blended with it. There is a subtle, flattering way of joking, which deals only with faults that the people under discussion are willing to acknowledge, which is able to disguise praise under an appearance of blame, and which

Un esprit fin et un esprit de finesse sont très différents. Le premier plaît toujours; il est délié, il pense des choses délicates, et voit les plus imperceptibles. Un esprit de finesse ne va jamais droit: il cherche des biais et des détours pour faire réussir ses desseins; cette conduite est bientôt découverte; elle se fait toujours craindre, et ne mène presque jamais aux grandes choses.

Il y a quelque différence entre un esprit de feu et un esprit brillant: un esprit de feu va plus loin et avec plus de rapidité; un esprit brillant a de la vivacité, de l'agrément et de la justesse.

La douceur de l'esprit, c'est un air facile et accommodant, qui plaît toujours, quand il n'est point fade.

Un esprit de détail s'applique avec de l'ordre et de la règle à toutes les particularités des sujets qu'on lui présente: cette application le renferme d'ordinaire à de petites choses; elle n'est pas néanmoins toujours incompatible avec de grandes vues; et quand ces deux qualités se trouvent ensemble dans un même esprit, elles l'élèvent infiniment au-dessus des autres.

On a abusé du terme de *bel esprit*, et bien que tout ce qu'on vient de dire des différentes qualités de l'esprit puisse convenir à un bel esprit, néanmoins comme ce titre a été donné à un nombre infini de mauvais poètes et d'auteurs ennuyeux, on s'en sert plus souvent pour tourner les gens en ridicule, que pour les louer.

Bien qu'il y ait plusieurs épithètes pour l'esprit qui paraissent une même chose, le ton et la manière de les prononcer y mettent de la différence; mais comme les tons et les manières de dire ne se peuvent écrire, je n'entrerai point dans un détail qu'il serait impossible de bien expliquer. L'usage ordinaire le fait assez entendre; et en disant qu'un homme a *de l'esprit*, qu'il a *bien de l'esprit*, qu'il a *beaucoup d'esprit*, et qu'il a *bon esprit*, il n'y a que les tons et les manières qui puissent mettre de la différence entre ces expressions, qui paraissent semblables sur le papier, et qui expriment néanmoins de très différentes sortes d'esprit.

On dit encore qu'un homme n'a que d'*une sorte* d'esprit, qu'il a de *plusieurs sortes* d'esprit, et qu'il a de *toutes sortes* d'esprit. On peut être sot avec beaucoup d'esprit, et on peut n'être pas sot avec peu d'esprit.

Avoir beaucoup d'esprit est un terme équivoque: il peut comprendre toutes les sortes d'esprit dont on vient de parler, mais il peut aussi n'en marquer aucune distinctement. On peut quelquefois faire

reveals people's attractive qualities while pretending that it wishes to hide them.

An astute mind is very different from a cunning mind. The former is always pleasing; it is supple, it thinks subtle thoughts and sees the most imperceptible points. A cunning mind is never quite straightforward; it strives to accomplish its plans by devious and roundabout means. Conduct of that kind is soon detected; it always provokes mistrust and almost never leads to anything great.

There is some difference between an ardent mind and a brilliant mind. An ardent mind goes further and faster; a brilliant mind is lively, attractive, and accurate.

Gentleness of mind is an easy, accommodating manner, which is always attractive when it is not insipid.

A meticulous mind deals systematically and methodically with every detail of the subjects that it encounters. This diligence usually confines it to small matters; but it is not always incompatible with breadth of vision, and when those two qualities are found together in a single mind, they raise it infinitely above the others.

The term 'wit' is often misused. All the different types of mind described above may contribute to a wit; yet, as that title has been bestowed on innumerable bad poets and tiresome writers, it is used more often to ridicule people than to praise them.

Although there are various epithets for wit that seem the same, they are distinguished by the tone of voice and the way they are said. But as tones of voice and ways of speaking cannot be expressed in writing, I shall not go into details that could not be properly elucidated. Common usage makes it clear enough; and when we say that a man has 'wit', 'a good deal of wit', 'a great deal of wit', 'a fine sort of wit', only the tone and the way of speaking can distinguish between those expressions—which look alike on paper, but which express very different kinds of wit.

Again, we say that a man has only one kind of wit, that he has various kinds of wit, or that he has wit of every kind. You can be foolish with a great deal of wit,* and you can be not at all foolish with very little wit.

The term 'a great deal of wit' is ambiguous. It may include all the types of mind described above, but it may also mean no specific type. You can sometimes display wit in your speech without having

paraître de l'esprit dans ce qu'on dit, sans en avoir dans sa conduite; on peut avoir de l'esprit, et l'avoir borné; un esprit peut être propre à de certaines choses, et ne l'être pas à d'autres; on peut avoir beaucoup d'esprit et n'être propre à rien, et avec beaucoup d'esprit, on est souvent fort incommode. Il semble néanmoins que le plus grand mérite de cette sorte d'esprit est de plaire quelquefois dans la conversation.

Bien que les productions d'esprit soient infinies, on peut, ce me semble, les distinguer de cette sorte: il y a des choses si belles, que tout le monde est capable d'en voir et d'en sentir la beauté; il y en a qui ont de la beauté et qui ennuient; il y en a qui sont belles, que tout le monde sent et admire, bien que tous n'en sachent pas la raison; il y en a qui sont si fines et si délicates, que peu de gens sont capables d'en remarquer toutes les beautés; enfin il y en a d'autres qui ne sont pas parfaites, mais qui sont dites avec tant d'art, et qui sont soutenues et conduites avec tant de raison et tant de grâce, qu'elles méritent d'être admirées.

RD 17. Des Événements de ce siècle

L'histoire, qui nous apprend ce qui arrive dans le monde, nous montre également les grands événements et les médiocres: cette confusion d'objets nous empêche souvent de discerner avec assez d'attention les choses extraordinaires qui sont renfermées dans le cours de chaque siècle. Celui où nous vivons en a produit, à mon sens, de plus singuliers que les précédents: j'ai voulu en écrire quelques-uns, pour les rendre plus remarquables aux personnes qui voudront y faire réflexion.

Marie de Médicis, reine de France, femme de Henri le Grand, fut mère du roi Louis XIII, de Gaston, fils de France, de la reine d'Espagne, de la duchesse de Savoie, et de la reine d'Angleterre; elle fut régente en France, et gouverna le Roi, son fils, et son royaume, plusieurs années. Elle éleva Armand de Richelieu à la dignité de cardinal; elle le fit premier ministre, maître de l'État et de l'esprit du Roi. Elle avait peu de vertus et peu de défauts qui la dussent faire craindre, et néanmoins, après tant d'éclat et de grandeurs, cette princesse, veuve de Henri IV et mère de tant de rois, a été arrêtée prisonnière par le Roi, son fils, et par la troupe du cardinal de Richelieu,

any in your conduct; you can have wit and be narrow-minded. Wit can be good for some things and not for others; you can have a great deal of wit and be good for nothing; people with a great deal of wit are often very annoying. Nevertheless, the greatest merit of such wit seems to be the fact that it is sometimes pleasant in conversation.

Although the mind's products are infinite, it seems to me that we can distinguish them as follows: some are so beautiful that everyone is able to see and feel their beauty; some are beautiful but tiresome; some have a beauty that everyone feels and admires, though not everyone knows why; some are so astute and subtle that few people are able to discern all their beauties; finally, others are imperfect, but are spoken with such art and are developed and handled so reasonably and gracefully that they deserve to be admired.

RD 17. Occurrences of the Present Age

History, which teaches us what happens in the world, shows us great occurrences and average ones alike. By presenting its material in disorder, it often prevents us from seeing clearly the extraordinary things that are encompassed within the course of any age. The age in which we are living has produced, in my opinion, more singular events than its predecessors; I want to write about some of them, in order to draw them more fully to the notice of anyone who wishes to ponder on them.

Marie de Médicis,* Queen of France, wife of Henri the Great, was the mother of King Louis XIII, Prince Gaston, the Queen of Spain, the Duchess of Savoy, and the Queen of England; she was regent in France, and ruled her son the King and his kingdom for some years. She raised Armand de Richelieu to the status of cardinal; she made him Prime Minister, controlling both the realm and the King's mind. She had few virtues and few faults to make her feared, yet after so much pomp and eminence, this Queen, the widow of Henri IV, the mother and mother-in-law of so many kings, was taken prisoner by her son the King and by the soldiers of Cardinal Richelieu,

qui lui devait sa fortune. Elle a été délaissée des autres rois, ses enfants, qui n'ont osé même la recevoir dans leurs États, et elle est morte de misère, et presque de faim, à Cologne, après une persécution de dix années.

Ange de Joyeuse, duc et pair, maréchal de France et amiral, jeune, riche, galant et heureux, abandonna tant d'avantages pour se faire capucin. Après quelques années, les besoins de l'État le rappelèrent au monde; le Pape le dispensa de ses vœux, et lui ordonna d'accepter le commandement des armées du Roi contre les huguenots; il demeura quatre ans dans cet emploi, et se laissa entraîner, pendant ce temps, aux mêmes passions qui l'avaient agité pendant sa jeunesse. La guerre étant finie, il renonça une seconde fois au monde, et reprit l'habit de capucin; il vécut longtemps dans une vie sainte et religieuse; mais la vanité, dont il avait triomphé dans le milieu des grandeurs, triompha de lui dans le cloître; il fut élu gardien du couvent de Paris, et son élection étant contestée par quelques religieux, il s'exposa, non seulement à aller à Rome, dans un âge avancé, à pied, et malgré les autres incommodités d'un si pénible voyage; mais la même opposition des religieux s'étant renouvelée à son retour, il partit une seconde fois pour retourner à Rome soutenir un intérêt si peu digne de lui, et il mourut en chemin, de fatigue, de chagrin, et de vieillesse.

Trois hommes de qualité, Portugais, suivis de dix-sept de leurs amis, entreprirent la révolte de Portugal et des Indes qui en dépendent, sans concert avec les peuples ni avec les étrangers, et sans intelligence dans les places. Ce petit nombre de conjurés se rendit maître du palais de Lisbonne, en chassa la douairière de Mantoue, régente pour le roi d'Espagne, et fit soulever tout le royaume; il ne périt dans ce désordre que Vasconcellos, ministre d'Espagne, et deux de ses domestiques. Un si grand changement se fit en faveur du duc de Bragance, et sans sa participation; il fut déclaré roi contre sa propre volonté, et se trouva le seul homme de Portugal qui résistât à son élection; il a possédé ensuite cette couronne pendant quatorze années, n'ayant ni élévation, ni mérite; il est mort dans son lit, et a laissé son royaume paisible à ses enfants.

Le cardinal de Richelieu a été maître absolu du royaume de France pendant le règne d'un roi qui lui laissait le gouvernement de son État, lorsqu'il n'osait lui confier sa propre personne; le Cardinal avait aussi les mêmes défiances du Roi, et il évitait d'aller chez lui,

who owed his good fortune to her. She was deserted by her other royal children, who did not dare even to receive her in their own realms; and she died of poverty—almost of hunger—at Cologne, after ten years of persecution.

Ange de Joyeuse,* Duke and Peer, field marshal and admiral, young, wealthy, elegant, and fortunate, gave up all those advantages to become a Capuchin. After some years, political necessity summoned him back into the world; the Pope absolved him of his vows and ordered him to take command of the King's armies against the Huguenots. For four years he remained in that position, during which time he allowed himself to be led astray by the very passions that had disturbed him in his youth. When the war was over, he renounced the world again and resumed the Capuchin's habit. For a long time he lived a holy and religious life; but vanity, over which he had triumphed in the midst of his eminence, easily triumphed over him in the cloister. He was elected Father Superior of the Paris monastery, and when his election was disputed by some of the clergy, he not only endured a journey to Rome—at an advanced age, on foot, and despite the other discomforts of so painful an expedition— but when the same clerical opposition revived on his return, he set out for Rome again in pursuit of an interest that was far from worthy of him, and on the way he died of fatigue, disappointment, and old age.

Three Portuguese noblemen, supported by seventeen of their friends, led the revolt of Portugal* and its Indian dependencies, with no cooperation from the people of their own country or any other, and without any collusion in high places. That little band of conspirators gained control of the palace at Lisbon, drove out the Dowager Duchess of Mantua (the King of Spain's regent), and roused the whole kingdom to rebel. In the disturbance only the Spanish minister Vasconcelos and two of his servants perished. This great transformation took place on behalf of the Duke of Braganza, yet he himself played no part in it; he was proclaimed king against his will, and found that he was the only man in Portugal opposed to his election. He then held the crown for fourteen years, with neither eminence nor merit; he died in his bed, and left the kingdom in peace to his children.

Cardinal Richelieu* was absolute ruler of the kingdom of France during the reign of a king who left him to govern his realm, even though he dared not entrust him with his own person. The Cardinal was equally mistrustful of the King, and avoided visiting him, for

craignant d'exposer sa vie ou sa liberté; le Roi néanmoins sacrifie Cinq-Mars, son favori, à la vengeance du Cardinal, et consent qu'il périsse sur un échafaud. Ensuite le Cardinal meurt dans son lit; il dispose par son testament des charges et des dignités de l'État, et oblige le Roi, dans le plus fort de ses soupçons et de sa haine, à suivre aussi aveuglément ses volontés après sa mort, qu'il avait fait pendant sa vie.

[On doit sans doute trouver extraordinaire que Anne-Marie-Louise d'Orléans, petite-fille de France, la plus riche sujette de l'Europe, destinée pour les plus grands rois, avare, rude et orgueilleuse, ait pu former le dessein, à quarante-cinq ans, d'épouser Puyguilhem, cadet de la maison de Lauzun, assez mal fait de sa personne, d'un esprit médiocre, et qui n'a, pour toute bonne qualité, que d'être hardi et insinuant. Mais on doit être encore plus surpris que Mademoiselle ait pris cette chimérique résolution par un esprit de servitude et parce que Puyguilhem était bien auprès du Roi; l'envie d'être femme d'un favori lui tint lieu de passion, elle oublia son âge et sa naissance, et, sans avoir d'amour, elle fit des avances à Puyguilhem qu'un amour véritable ferait à peine excuser dans une jeune personne et d'une moindre condition. Elle lui dit un jour qu'il n'y avait qu'un seul homme qu'elle pût choisir pour épouser. Il la pressa de lui apprendre son choix; mais n'ayant pas la force de prononcer son nom, elle voulut l'écrire avec un diamant sur les vitres d'une fenêtre. Puyguilhem jugea sans doute ce qu'elle allait faire, et espérant peut-être qu'elle lui donnerait cette déclaration par écrit, dont il pourrait faire quelque usage, il feignit une délicatesse de passion qui pût plaire à Mademoiselle, et il lui fit un scrupule d'écrire sur du verre un sentiment qui devait durer éternellement. Son dessein réussit comme il désirait, et Mademoiselle écrivit le soir dans du papier: « C'est vous. » Elle le cacheta elle-même; mais, comme cette aventure se passait un jeudi et que minuit sonna avant que Mademoiselle pût donner son billet à Puyguilhem, elle ne voulut pas paraître moins scrupuleuse que lui, et craignant que le vendredi ne fût un jour malheureux, elle lui fit promettre d'attendre au samedi à ouvrir le billet qui lui devait apprendre cette grande nouvelle. L'excessive fortune que cette déclaration faisait envisager à Puyguilhem ne lui parut point au-dessus de son ambition. Il songea à profiter du caprice de Mademoiselle, et il eut la hardiesse d'en rendre compte au Roi. Personne n'ignore qu'avec si grandes et éclatantes qualités nul

fear of risking his own life or liberty. Nevertheless, the King sacrificed his favourite Cinq-Mars to the Cardinal's vengeance, and agreed to his death on the scaffold. Afterwards the Cardinal died in his bed; he bequeathed government offices and titles in his will, and forced the King, in spite of the most intense suspicion and hatred, to follow his wishes as blindly after his death as he had done during his life.

[Surely we must find it extraordinary that Anne-Marie-Louise d'Orléans,* the wealthiest subject in Europe, avaricious, severe, and proud, granddaughter of a King of France, and destined for the greatest kings, should have planned at the age of forty-five to marry Puyguilhem, a younger son of the house of Lauzun, who was not good-looking, who had a rather average mind, and whose sole good quality was the fact that he was bold and ingratiating. But we must be still more surprised that Mademoiselle should have made this fantastic resolution in a servile spirit and because Puyguilhem was in the King's good graces. The wish to be a favourite's wife was her substitute for passion; she forgot her age and her birth, and, without being in love, she made advances to Puyguilhem which true love would scarcely have excused even in a young woman of lower social position. One day she told him that there was only one man whom she could possibly choose to marry. He urged her to tell him her choice; not having the strength to utter his name, she tried to write it with a diamond on a windowpane. No doubt Puyguilhem discerned what she was going to do, and (perhaps because he hoped that she might put her declaration on paper, of which he could make some use) he pretended a passionate delicacy that might please Mademoiselle, and scrupled to see her inscribe her feelings on glass, where they would last for ever. His plan succeeded just as he had desired, and that evening Mademoiselle wrote on paper 'You'. She sealed it herself; but, as this adventure took place on a Thursday, and the clock struck midnight before she could give her note to Puyguilhem, Mademoiselle did not want to seem less scrupulous than he; fearing that Friday was an unlucky day, she made him promise to wait until Saturday before opening the note that would tell him the great news. The prospects of extreme good fortune that this declaration revealed to Puyguilhem did not strike him as too great for his ambition. He thought how he could profit from Mademoiselle's little whim, and he had the boldness to inform the King of it. With all his great and brilliant qualities, no ruler in the world was prouder and more

prince au monde n'a jamais eu plus de hauteur, ni plus de fierté. Cependant, au lieu de perdre Puyguilhem d'avoir osé lui découvrir ses espérances, il lui permit non seulement de les conserver, mais il consentit que quatre officiers de la couronne lui vinssent demander son approbation pour un mariage si surprenant, et sans que Monsieur, ni Monsieur le Prince en eussent entendu parler. Cette nouvelle se répandit dans le monde, et le remplit d'étonnement et d'indignation. Le Roi ne sentit pas alors ce qu'il venait de faire contre sa gloire et contre sa dignité. Il trouva seulement qu'il était de sa grandeur d'élever en un jour Puyguilhem au-dessus des plus grands du Royaume, et, malgré tant de disproportion, il le jugea digne d'être son cousin germain, le premier pair de France, et maître de cinq cent mille livres de rente; mais ce qui le flatta le plus encore, dans un si extraordinaire dessein, ce fut le plaisir secret de surprendre le monde, et de faire, pour un homme qu'il aimait, ce que personne n'avait encore imaginé. Il fut au pouvoir de Puyguilhem de profiter, durant trois jours, de tant de prodiges que la fortune avait faits en sa faveur, et d'épouser Mademoiselle; mais, par un prodige plus grand encore, sa vanité ne put être satisfaite s'il ne l'épousait avec les mêmes cérémonies que s'il eût été de sa qualité: il voulut que le Roi et la Reine fussent témoins de ses noces, et qu'elles eussent tout l'éclat que leur présence y pouvait donner. Cette présomption sans exemple lui fit employer à de vains préparatifs et à passer son contrat tout le temps qui pouvait assurer son bonheur. Mme de Montespan, qui le haïssait, avait suivi néanmoins le penchant du Roi et ne s'était point opposée à ce mariage. Mais le bruit du monde la réveilla; elle fit voir au Roi ce que lui seul ne voyait pas encore; elle lui fit écouter la voix publique; il connut l'étonnement des ambassadeurs, il reçut les plaintes et les remontrances respectueuses de Madame douairière et de toute la maison royale. Tant de raisons firent longtemps balancer le Roi, et ce fut avec une extrême peine qu'il déclara à Puyguilhem qu'il ne pouvait consentir ouvertement à son mariage. Il l'assura néanmoins que ce changement en apparence ne changerait rien en effet; qu'il était forcé, malgré lui, de céder à l'opinion générale, et de lui défendre d'épouser Mademoiselle, mais qu'il ne prétendait pas que cette défense empêchât son bonheur. Il le pressa de se marier en secret, et il lui promit que la disgrâce qui devait suivre une telle faute ne durerait que huit jours. Quelque sentiment que ce discours pût donner à Puyguilhem, il dit au Roi

haughty—as everyone knows. Yet, instead of disgracing Puyguilhem for having dared to reveal his hopes, the King not only permitted him to harbour them, but allowed four officers of the crown to come and ask his consent to this most surprising marriage, before either Monsieur or the Prince had heard any mention of it. The news spread among the people, filling everyone with astonishment and indignation. Even then the King did not feel that he had done something out of keeping with his glory and dignity; he thought only that his rank entitled him to raise Puyguilhem above the greatest men of the kingdom in a single day. In spite of their immense inequality, he judged the man worthy to be his cousin german, the first peer of France, and the possessor of five hundred thousand pounds a year. But what flattered the King most in this extraordinary plan was the secret pleasure of surprising the world and doing for his favourite what no one could have anticipated. For three days it was in Puyguilhem's power to marry Mademoiselle and profit from all the marvels that fortune had worked on his behalf. But, by a still greater marvel, his vanity could not be satisfied unless he married her with the same ceremonies as if he had been of her own rank. He wanted the King and Queen to witness his wedding; he wanted it to have all the pomp that their presence could give it. This unparalleled presumption made him lavish as much time on vain preparations and final settlements as would secure his happiness. Madame de Montespan, though she hated him, had deferred to the King's inclinations and not opposed the marriage. But the world's gossip opened her eyes; she showed the King what he alone had still been unable to see; she made him listen to the people's voice; he recognized the ambassadors' astonishment, he received the respectful complaints and protests of the Dowager Duchess and the entire royal family. All these arguments made the King waver for a long time, and it gave him the greatest pain to tell Puyguilhem that he could not openly consent to the marriage. He reassured him, however, that this apparent change would not really change anything; that he was forced, in spite of himself, to defer to public opinion and forbid him to marry Mademoiselle, but that he did not expect this apology to spoil his happiness. He urged him to marry secretly, and promised him that the disgrace inevitably resulting from such a transgression would last only a week. Whatever Puyguilhem may have felt about this speech, he replied that he gladly renounced

qu'il renonçait avec joie à tout ce qui lui avait permis d'espérer, puisque sa gloire en pouvait être blessée, et qu'il n'y avait point de fortune qui le pût consoler d'être huit jours séparé de lui. Le Roi fut véritablement touché de cette soumission; il n'oublia rien pour obliger Puyguilhem à profiter de la faiblesse de Mademoiselle, et Puyguilhem n'oublia rien aussi, de son côté, pour faire voir au Roi qu'il lui sacrifiait toutes choses. Le désintéressement seul ne fit pas prendre néanmoins cette conduite à Puyguilhem: il crut qu'elle l'assurait pour toujours de l'esprit du Roi, et que rien ne pourrait à l'avenir diminuer sa faveur. Son caprice et sa vanité le portèrent même si loin, que ce mariage si grand et si disproportionné lui parut insupportable, parce qu'il ne lui était plus permis de le faire avec tout le faste et tout l'éclat qu'il s'était proposé. Mais ce qui le détermina le plus puissamment à le rompre, ce fut l'aversion insurmontable qu'il avait pour la personne de Mademoiselle, et le dégoût d'être son mari. Il espéra même de tirer des avantages solides de l'emportement de Mademoiselle, et que, sans l'épouser, elle lui donnerait la souveraineté de Dombes et le duché de Montpensier. Ce fut dans cette vue qu'il refusa d'abord toutes les grâces dont le Roi voulut le combler; mais l'humeur avare et inégale de Mademoiselle, et les difficultés qui se rencontrèrent à assurer de si grands biens à Puyguilhem, rendirent ce dessein inutile, et l'obligèrent à recevoir les bienfaits du Roi. Il lui donna le gouvernement de Berry et cinq cent mille livres. Des avantages si considérables ne répondirent pas toutefois aux espérances que Puyguilhem avait formées. Son chagrin fournit bientôt à ses ennemis, et particulièrement à Mme de Montespan, tous les prétextes qu'ils souhaitaient pour le ruiner. Il connut son état et sa décadence, et, au lieu de se ménager auprès du Roi avec de la douceur, de la patience et de l'habileté, rien ne fut plus capable de retenir son esprit âpre et fier. Il fit enfin des reproches au Roi; il lui dit même des choses rudes et piquantes, jusqu'à casser son épée en sa présence, en disant qu'il ne la tirerait plus pour son service; il lui parla avec mépris de Mme de Montespan, et s'emporta contre elle avec tant de violence qu'elle douta de sa sûreté, et n'en trouva plus qu'à le perdre. Il fut arrêté bientôt après, et on le mena à Pignerol, où il éprouva par une longue et dure prison la douleur d'avoir perdu les bonnes grâces du Roi, et d'avoir laissé échapper par une fausse vanité tant de grandeurs et tant d'avantages que la condescendance de son maître et la bassesse de Mademoiselle lui avaient présentés.]

everything that the King had permitted him to hope, since his honour might be wounded by it; and that no good fortune could console
him for a week's separation from him. The King was genuinely
touched by this deference. He did everything he could to force Puyguilhem to profit from Mademoiselle's weakness; and Puyguilhem,
conversely, did everything he could to show the King how much he
was sacrificing for him. However, Puyguilhem did not adopt this
conduct solely for reasons of disinterest; he thought that it would
permanently secure him the King's affection, and that nothing
would be able to reduce his favour in future. His vanity and his
whims even led him to regard so great and so unequal a marriage as
intolerable, because he was not allowed to celebrate it with all the
pomp and brilliance that he had planned. But what made him most
determined to break it off was his unshakeable aversion for Mademoiselle's person, and his distaste for being her husband. He even
hoped to obtain substantial advantages from Mademoiselle's rage;
and he hoped that, without marrying him, she would give him the
dominion of Dombes and the duchy of Montpensier. That prospect
led him at first to refuse all the marks of grace that the King wanted
to heap on him; but Mademoiselle's avaricious, changeable temper,
and the difficulty of assigning such great possessions to Puyguilhem,
made this plan futile, and forced him to accept the King's favours.
The King made him governor of Berry and gave him five hundred
thousand pounds. Those advantages, notable as they were, still did
not match the hopes that Puyguilhem had formed. His disappointment soon gave his enemies—especially Madame de Montespan—
all the pretexts they sought to disgrace him. He recognized his
decline in status; but he did not take care of his position with the
King in a gentle, patient, and clever way; instead, nothing could
restrain his proud and bitter spirit any longer. Finally he began to
rebuke the King; he even said severe, biting things to him, and went
as far as to break his sword in his presence, saying that he would no
longer draw it to serve him; he spoke disdainfully of Madame de
Montespan, and raged so violently against her that she feared for her
own safety, and henceforth sought only to ruin him. He was arrested
soon afterwards and taken to Pignerol, where, during a long and
harsh imprisonment, he felt the grief of having lost the King's
good graces, and of having let slip through his own false vanity all
the splendours and advantages that his master's indulgence and
Mademoiselle's baseness had offered him.]

Alphonse, roi de Portugal, fils du duc de Bragance dont je viens de parler, s'est marié, en France, à la fille du duc de Nemours, jeune, sans biens et sans protection. Peu de temps après, cette princesse a formé le dessein de quitter le Roi, son mari; elle l'a fait arrêter dans Lisbonne, et les mêmes troupes qui, un jour auparavant, le gardaient comme leur roi, l'ont gardé le lendemain comme prisonnier; il a été confiné dans une île de ses propres États, et on lui a laissé la vie et le titre de roi. Le prince de Portugal, son frère, a épousé la Reine; elle conserve sa dignité, et elle a revêtu le prince, son mari, de toute l'autorité du gouvernement, sans lui donner le nom de roi; elle jouit tranquillement du succès d'une entreprise si extraordinaire, en paix avec les Espagnols, et sans guerre civile dans le royaume.

Un vendeur d'herbes, nommé Masaniel, fit soulever le menu peuple de Naples, et malgré la puissance des Espagnols, il usurpa l'autorité royale; il disposa souverainement de la vie, de la liberté, et des biens de tout ce qui lui fut suspect; il se rendit maître des douanes; il dépouilla les partisans de tout leur argent et de leurs meubles, et fit brûler publiquement toutes ces richesses immenses dans le milieu de la ville, sans qu'un seul de cette foule confuse de révoltés voulût profiter d'un bien qu'on croyait mal acquis. Ce prodige ne dura que quinze jours, et finit par un autre prodige: ce même Masaniel, qui achevait de si grandes choses avec tant de bonheur, de gloire, et de conduite, perdit subitement l'esprit, et mourut frénétique, en vingt-quatre heures.

La reine de Suède, en paix dans ses États et avec ses voisins, aimée de ses sujets, respectée des étrangers, jeune et sans dévotion, a quitté volontairement son royaume, et s'est réduite à une vie privée. Le roi de Pologne, de la même maison que la reine de Suède, s'est démis aussi de la royauté, par la seule lassitude d'être roi.

Un lieutenant d'infanterie sans nom et sans crédit, a commencé, à l'âge de quarante-cinq ans, de se faire connaître dans les désordres d'Angleterre. Il a dépossédé son roi légitime, bon, juste, doux, vaillant et libéral; il lui a fait trancher la tête, par un arrêt de son parlement; il a changé la royauté en république; il a été dix ans maître de l'Angleterre, plus craint de ses voisins, et plus absolu dans son pays que tous les rois qui y ont régné. Il est mort paisible, et en pleine possession de toute la puissance du royaume.

Les Hollandais ont secoué le joug de la domination d'Espagne; ils

Afonso VI,* King of Portugal, son of the Duke of Braganza whom I have just mentioned, was married in France to the young, fortune-less, unprotected daughter of the Duke of Nemours. Not long after-wards, the Queen formed a plan to leave her husband the King; she had him arrested at Lisbon, and the very troops who had guarded him one day as their king, guarded him next day as their prisoner. He was confined on an island in his own realm, and allowed to keep his life and the title of king. His brother the Prince of Portugal married the Queen; she retained her rank, and she endowed her husband the prince with full governing authority, without giving him the name of king; at peace with the Spaniards, and without any civil war in the kingdom, she coolly enjoyed the fruits of so extraordinary a plot.

A vegetable seller named Masaniello* caused the tiny population of Naples to rebel, and despite the power of the Spaniards, he usurped royal authority. He disposed as a sovereign of the life, liberty, and possessions of everyone whom he suspected. He took control of the Customs; he despoiled the partisans of all their money and chattels, and publicly burnt the whole of that immense wealth in the midst of the city, without a single man in the disorderly crowd of rebels trying to profit from possessions that they believed to be ill-gotten. This marvel lasted only a fortnight, and ended with another marvel: the same Masaniello, who had accomplished such great things with so much good fortune, glory, and leadership, suddenly lost his mind and died in a frenzy within twenty-four hours.

The Queen of Sweden,* who was young and not pious, at peace both in her own realms and with her neighbours, loved by her sub-jects and respected by foreigners, voluntarily left her kingdom and retired to private life. The King of Poland,* who belonged to the same dynasty as the Queen of Sweden, also abdicated simply because he was weary of being king.

An infantry lieutenant,* with no name and no reputation, began to draw attention to himself at the age of forty-five during the disturb-ances in England. He overthrew his lawful king, who was good, just, gentle, brave, and generous; he had him beheaded by act of parlia-ment; he turned the kingdom into a republic; for ten years he was the ruler of England, and was more feared by the neighbouring lands, and held more absolute power within his own country, than any king who had ruled it. He died peacefully, in full possession of the author-ity of the kingdom.

ont formé une puissante république, et ils ont soutenu cent ans la guerre contre leur roi légitime, pour conserver leur liberté. Ils doivent tant de grandes choses à la conduite et à la valeur des princes d'Orange, dont ils ont néanmoins toujours redouté l'ambition, et limité le pouvoir. Présentement cette république, si jalouse de sa puissance, accorde au prince d'Orange d'aujourd'hui, malgré son peu d'expérience et ses malheureux succès dans la guerre, ce qu'elle a refusé à ses pères; elle ne se contente pas de relever sa fortune abattue: elle le met en état de se faire souverain de Hollande, et elle a souffert qu'il ait fait déchirer par le peuple un homme qui maintenait seul la liberté publique.

Cette puissance d'Espagne, si étendue et si formidable à tous les rois du monde, trouve aujourd'hui son principal appui dans ses sujets rebelles, et se soutient par la protection des Hollandais.

Un empereur, jeune, faible, simple, gouverné par des ministres incapables, et pendant le plus grand abaissement de la maison d'Autriche, se trouve, en un moment, chef de tous les princes d'Allemagne, qui craignent son autorité et méprisent sa personne, et il est plus absolu que n'a jamais été Charles-Quint.

Le roi d'Angleterre, faible, paresseux, et plongé dans les plaisirs, oubliant les intérêts de son royaume et ses exemples domestiques, s'est exposé avec fermeté, depuis six ans, à la fureur de ses peuples et à la haine de son parlement, pour conserver une liaison étroite avec le roi de France; au lieu d'arrêter les conquêtes de ce prince dans les Pays-Bas, il y a même contribué, en lui fournissant des troupes. Cet attachement l'a empêché d'être maître absolu de l'Angleterre, et d'en étendre les frontières en Flandre et en Hollande, par des places et par des ports qu'il a toujours refusés; mais dans le temps qu'il reçoit des sommes considérables du Roi, et qu'il a le plus de besoin d'en être soutenu contre ses propres sujets, il renonce, sans prétexte, à tant d'engagements, et il se déclare contre la France, précisément quand il lui est utile et honnête d'y être attaché; par une mauvaise politique précipitée, il perd, en un moment, le seul avantage qu'il pouvait retirer d'une mauvaise politique de six années, et ayant pu donner la paix comme médiateur, il est réduit à la demander comme suppliant, quand le Roi l'accorde à l'Espagne, à l'Allemagne et à la Hollande.

Les propositions qui avaient été faites au roi d'Angleterre de marier sa nièce, la princesse d'York, au prince d'Orange, ne lui étaient

The Dutch shook off the yoke of Spanish domination;* they formed a powerful republic, and for a hundred years, to preserve their liberty, they continued to wage war against their lawful king. They owed all these great achievements to the leadership and valour of the Princes of Orange, whose ambition they nonetheless always mistrusted, and whose power they always limited. At present this republic, so jealous of its power, is granting the current Prince of Orange,* in spite of his inexperience and his lack of success on the battlefield, what it refused to his forefathers. The republic, not satisfied with repairing his downcast fortune, is setting about making him king of Holland, and has let him incite the populace to tear in pieces a man who was single-handedly defending the liberty of the people.

The power of Spain, so vast and so dreaded by every king in the world, is nowadays supported primarily by its rebel subjects, and is maintained by Dutch protection.*

An Emperor,* young, weak, simple-minded, governed by incompetent ministers, while the fortunes of the Austrian royal family are at their lowest, now finds himself supreme over all the princes of Germany, who fear his authority and treat his person with disdain; and he wields more absolute power than Charles V ever did.

The King of England,* weak, lazy, and wallowing in pleasures, forgetting the interests of his kingdom and the precedents in his own household, staunchly endured his peoples' frenzy and his parliament's hatred for six years, in order to maintain close links with the King of France; instead of halting that ruler's conquests in the Netherlands, he even contributed to them by supplying him with troops. This commitment prevented him from holding absolute power in England and extending its frontiers in Flanders and Holland by means of towns and ports that he always refused; but at the very time when he was receiving considerable sums of money from the King, and when he most needed the King's support against his own subjects, he renounced all those obligations, without any excuse, and declared his opposition to France precisely when it would have been useful and honorable for him to maintain his commitment. His hasty, ill-judged strategy instantly lost him the sole advantage he could have drawn from six years of similarly ill-judged strategy; and though he had been in a position to make peace as a mediator, he was reduced to suing for it as a beggar, when the King was granting it to Spain, Germany, and Holland.

pas agréables; le duc d'York en paraissait aussi éloigné que le Roi son frère, et le prince d'Orange même, rebuté par les difficultés de ce dessein, ne pensait plus à le faire réussir. Le roi d'Angleterre, étroitement lié au roi de France, consentait à ses conquêtes, lorsque les intérêts du grand trésorier d'Angleterre, et la crainte d'être attaqué par le Parlement, lui ont fait chercher sa sûreté particulière, en disposant le Roi, son maître, à s'unir avec le prince d'Orange, par le mariage de la princesse d'York, et à faire déclarer l'Angleterre contre la France, pour la protection des Pays-Bas. Ce changement du roi d'Angleterre a été si prompt et si secret, que le duc d'York l'ignorait encore deux jours devant le mariage de sa fille, et personne ne se pouvait persuader que le roi d'Angleterre, qui avait hasardé dix ans sa vie et sa couronne pour demeurer attaché à la France, pût renoncer, en un moment, à tout ce qu'il en espérait, pour suivre le sentiment de son ministre. Le prince d'Orange, de son côté, qui avait tant d'intérêt de se faire un chemin pour être un jour roi d'Angleterre, négligeait ce mariage, qui le rendait héritier présomptif du royaume; il bornait ses desseins à affermir son autorité en Hollande, malgré les mauvais succès de ses dernières campagnes, et il s'appliquait à se rendre aussi absolu dans les autres provinces de cet État qu'il le croyait être dans la Zélande; mais il s'aperçut bientôt qu'il devait prendre d'autres mesures, et une aventure ridicule lui fit mieux connaître l'état où il était dans son pays, qu'il ne le voyait par ses propres lumières. Un crieur public vendait des meubles à un encan où beaucoup de monde s'assembla; il mit en vente un atlas, et voyant que personne ne l'enchérissait, il dit au peuple que ce livre était néanmoins plus rare qu'on ne pensait, et que les cartes en étaient si exactes, que la rivière dont M. le prince d'Orange n'avait eu aucune connaissance, lorsqu'il perdit la bataille de Cassel, y était fidèlement marquée. Cette raillerie, qui fut reçue avec un applaudissement universel, a été un des plus puissants motifs qui ont obligé le prince d'Orange à rechercher de nouveau l'alliance de l'Angleterre, pour contenir la Hollande, et pour joindre tant de puissances contre nous. Il semble néanmoins que ceux qui ont désiré ce mariage, et ceux qui y ont été contraires, n'ont pas connu leurs intérêts: le grand trésorier d'Angleterre a voulu adoucir le Parlement et se garantir d'en être attaqué en portant le Roi, son maître, à donner sa nièce au prince d'Orange, et à se déclarer contre la France; le roi d'Angleterre a

The King of England was not attracted by the proposal to marry his niece,* the Duke of York's daughter, to the Prince of Orange. The Duke seemed to receive the idea as coldly as the King his brother; and even the Prince of Orange, deterred by the difficulties of the plan, no longer thought of accomplishing it successfully. The King of England had close ties with the King of France and approved of his conquests, but the Lord Treasurer's personal interests and fear of parliamentary opposition made him strive to strengthen his own position by encouraging his master the King to form an alliance with the Prince of Orange by marriage with the Duke of York's daughter, and to declare England's opposition to France, in order to protect the Netherlands. This change in the King of England's attitude was so prompt and so secret that the Duke of York was still unaware of it two days before his daughter's wedding, and no one felt sure that the King of England, who had been risking his life and crown for ten years to remain committed to France, could renounce all his hopes in a single moment and follow his minister's feelings. As for the Prince of Orange, who had so much personal interest in clearing a path that might one day make him King of England, he treated the marriage with neglect, even though it made him heir presumptive to the kingdom. He limited his plans to strengthening his authority in Holland, in spite of his lack of success during his last campaigns; and he strove to gain as much absolute power in the other provinces of his realm as he thought he possessed in Zeeland. But he soon saw that he would need to take other steps, and an absurd adventure gave him more insight into his position in his own country than he had been able to gain for himself. A town crier was selling goods at an auction in front of a large crowd. He put an atlas up for sale; and, seeing that no one was taking any interest in it, he told the crowd that the book was more precious than they imagined: its maps were so precise that they faithfully marked the stream which the Prince of Orange had not known about when he lost the battle of Cassel. This little joke, which was received with universal applause, was one of the strongest motives that forced the Prince of Orange to seek an alliance with England again—thus keeping Holland under control, and uniting so many foreign powers against us. It seems, however, that neither the people who desired this marriage, nor the people who opposed it, knew what was in their own interests. The Lord Treasurer of England wanted to appease parliament and protect himself from its

cru affermir son autorité dans son royaume par l'appui du prince d'Orange, et il a prétendu engager ses peuples à lui fournir de l'argent pour ses plaisirs, sous prétexte de faire la guerre au roi de France, et de le contraindre à recevoir la paix; le prince d'Orange a eu dessein de soumettre la Hollande par la protection d'Angleterre; la France a appréhendé qu'un mariage si opposé à ses intérêts n'emportât la balance, en joignant l'Angleterre à tous nos ennemis. L'événement a fait voir, en six semaines, la fausseté de tant de raisonnements: ce mariage met une défiance éternelle entre l'Angleterre et la Hollande, et toutes deux le regardent comme un dessein d'opprimer leur liberté; le parlement d'Angleterre attaque les ministres du Roi, pour attaquer ensuite sa propre personne; les états de Hollande, lassés de la guerre et jaloux de leur liberté, se repentent d'avoir mis leur autorité entre les mains d'un jeune homme ambitieux, et héritier présomptif de la couronne d'Angleterre; le roi de France, qui a d'abord regardé ce mariage comme une nouvelle ligue qui se formait contre lui, a su s'en servir pour diviser ses ennemis, et pour se mettre en état de prendre la Flandre, s'il n'avait préféré la gloire de faire la paix à la gloire de faire de nouvelles conquêtes.

Si le siècle présent n'a pas moins produit d'événements extraordinaires que les siècles passés, on conviendra sans doute qu'il a le malheureux avantage de les surpasser dans l'excès des crimes. La France même, qui les a toujours détestés, qui y est opposée par l'humeur de la nation, par la religion, et qui est soutenue par les exemples du prince qui règne, se trouve néanmoins aujourd'hui le théâtre où l'on voit paraître tout ce que l'histoire et la fable nous ont dit des crimes de l'antiquité. Les vices sont de tous les temps; les hommes sont nés avec de l'intérêt, de la cruauté et de la débauche; mais si des personnes que tout le monde connaît avaient paru dans les premiers siècles, parlerait-on présentement des prostitutions d'Héliogabale, de la foi des Grecs, et des poisons et des parricides de Médée?

RD 18. De l'Inconstance

Je ne prétends pas justifier ici l'inconstance en général, et moins encore celle qui vient de la seule légèreté; mais il n'est pas juste aussi

opposition, by prompting his master the King to give his niece to the Prince of Orange and declare his opposition to France. The King of England thought he was strengthening his authority in the kingdom by gaining the support of the Prince of Orange, and he tried to obtain money for his pleasures from his subjects, under the pretext that he was making war against the King of France and trying to force him to make peace. The Prince of Orange planned to use English protection to make Holland submissive. France was apprehensive that a marriage so opposed to her interests might tip the balance of power by uniting England with all our enemies. Within six weeks, the outcome showed how false all those reasonings were. The marriage aroused lasting mistrust between England and Holland, and both countries saw it as a plan to suppress their liberty; the parliament of England attacked the King's ministers, paving the way for an attack on the King himself; the provinces of Holland, weary of war and jealous of their liberty, regretted that they had given their authority to an ambitious young man, the heir presumptive to the English crown; the King of France, who at first saw this marriage as a new league against him, was able to use it to sow division among his enemies and place himself in a position to seize Flanders—but for the fact that he preferred the glory of making peace to the glory of new conquests.

If the present age has produced no fewer extraordinary occurrences than past ages, surely we must also admit that it has the unfortunate advantage of surpassing them in its exceptional crimes. France herself has always detested such crimes, is opposed to them by both national temperament and religion, and is supported by her king's example; yet today she finds herself a stage on which are being played all the crimes of the ancient world as reported to us by history and legend. Vices belong to every age; men are born with self-interest, cruelty, and debauchery; but if people known to all of us had appeared in previous ages, would we speak today of Heliogabalian licentiousness, Greek dishonesty, and Medea's poisonings and parricides?*

RD 18. Inconstancy

I do not claim that I am here trying to justify inconstancy in general, let alone the kind of inconstancy that comes only from fickleness;

de lui imputer tous les autres changements de l'amour. Il y a une première fleur d'agrément et de vivacité dans l'amour, qui passe insensiblement, comme celle des fruits; ce n'est la faute de personne; c'est seulement la faute du temps. Dans les commencements, la figure est aimable; les sentiments ont du rapport: on cherche de la douceur et du plaisir; on veut plaire, parce qu'on nous plaît, et on cherche à faire voir qu'on sait donner un prix infini à ce qu'on aime; mais, dans la suite, on ne sent plus ce qu'on croyait sentir toujours: le feu n'y est plus; le mérite de la nouveauté s'efface; la beauté, qui a tant de part à l'amour, ou diminue, ou ne fait plus la même impression; le nom d'amour se conserve, mais on ne se retrouve plus les mêmes personnes, ni les mêmes sentiments; on suit encore ses engagements, par honneur, par accoutumance, et pour n'être pas assez assuré de son propre changement.

Quelles personnes auraient commencé de s'aimer, si elles s'étaient vues d'abord comme on se voit dans la suite des années? Mais quelles personnes aussi se pourraient séparer, si elles se revoyaient comme on s'est vu la première fois? L'orgueil, qui est presque toujours le maître de nos goûts, et qui ne se rassasie jamais, serait flatté sans cesse par quelque nouveau plaisir. La constance perdrait son mérite, elle n'aurait plus de part à une si agréable liaison; les faveurs présentes auraient la même grâce que les faveurs premières, et le souvenir n'y mettrait point de différence; l'inconstance serait même inconnue, et on s'aimerait toujours avec le même plaisir, parce qu'on aurait toujours les mêmes sujets de s'aimer. Les changements qui arrivent dans l'amitié ont à peu près des causes pareilles à ceux qui arrivent dans l'amour; leurs règles ont beaucoup de rapport: si l'un a plus d'enjouement et de plaisir, l'autre doit être plus égale et plus sévère, elle ne pardonne rien; mais le temps, qui change l'humeur et les intérêts, les détruit presque également tous deux. Les hommes sont trop faibles et trop changeants pour soutenir longtemps le poids de l'amitié: l'antiquité en a fourni des exemples; mais dans le temps où nous vivons, on peut dire qu'il est encore moins impossible de trouver un véritable amour qu'une véritable amitié.

but it is equally unjust to blame it for all the other changes of love. There is an attractive, lively first bloom in love, which passes away imperceptibly, like that of fruit. That is no one's fault; it is merely time's fault. In the early stages, the other person's appearance is attractive; our feelings are akin; we seek what is pleasant and agreeable; we want to please, because we ourselves are pleased, and we try to show that we are capable of setting the highest possible value on what we love. Later, however, we no longer feel what we thought we would always feel; the fire goes out; the charm of novelty is tarnished; beauty, which plays such a great part in love, either decreases or no longer makes the same impression; the name of love remains, but neither the people nor the feelings are still the same; we keep observing our obligations, out of honour, out of habit, and in order to avoid being too aware of our own change.

What couples would have fallen in love, if they had seen each other at first as people see each other with the passage of the years? And yet what couples could separate, if they could again see each other as they did at first? Then our pride, which is nearly always in control of our tastes, and which is never sated, would incessantly be flattered with new pleasures; but constancy would lose its merit—in so attractive a relationship, it would no longer play any part; the present favours would have the same charm as the very first favours, and memory would draw no distinction between them; inconstancy would even be unknown, and couples would continue to love each other with the same pleasure, because they would always have the same reasons to love each other.

The changes that happen in friendship have almost the same causes as those that happen in love; they are regulated in very similar ways. If one yields more enjoyment and pleasure, the other should be more even and more austere, and forgive nothing; but time, which changes our temperaments and interests, destroys them both in almost the same way. Men are too weak and too changeable to bear the burden of friendship for long. Ancient history does provide some examples of that,* but in our own age we may say that even true love is less impossible to find than true friendship.

RD 19. De la Retraite

Je m'engagerais à un trop long discours si je rapportais ici, en particulier, toutes les raisons naturelles qui portent les vieilles gens à se
retirer du commerce du monde: le changement de leur humeur, de
leur figure, et l'affaiblissement des organes, les conduisent insensiblement, comme la plupart des autres animaux, à s'éloigner de la
fréquentation de leurs semblables. L'orgueil, qui est inséparable de
l'amour-propre, leur tient alors lieu de raison: il ne peut plus être
flatté de plusieurs choses qui flattent les autres; l'expérience leur a
fait connaître le prix de ce que tous les hommes désirent dans la
jeunesse, et l'impossibilité d'en jouir plus longtemps; les diverses
voies qui paraissent ouvertes aux jeunes gens pour parvenir aux
grandeurs, aux plaisirs, à la réputation et à tout ce qui élève les
hommes, leur sont fermées, ou par la fortune, ou par leur conduite,
ou par l'envie et l'injustice des autres; le chemin pour y rentrer est
trop long et trop pénible, quand on s'est une fois égaré; les difficultés
leur en paraissent insurmontables, et l'âge ne leur permet plus d'y
prétendre. Ils deviennent insensibles à l'amitié, non seulement parce
qu'ils n'en ont peut-être jamais trouvé de véritables, mais parce
qu'ils ont vu mourir un grand nombre de leurs amis qui n'avaient
pas encore eu le temps ni les occasions de manquer à l'amitié, et ils se
persuadent aisément qu'ils auraient été plus fidèles que ceux qui leur
restent. Ils n'ont plus de part aux premiers biens qui ont d'abord
rempli leur imagination; ils n'ont même presque plus de part à la
gloire: celle qu'ils ont acquise est déjà flétrie par le temps, et souvent
les hommes en perdent plus en vieillissant qu'ils n'en acquièrent.
Chaque jour leur ôte une portion d'eux-mêmes; ils n'ont plus assez
de vie pour jouir de ce qu'ils ont, et bien moins encore pour arriver à
ce qu'ils désirent; ils ne voient plus devant eux que des chagrins, des
maladies et de l'abaissement; tout est vu, et rien ne peut avoir pour
eux la grâce de la nouveauté; le temps les éloigne imperceptiblement
du point de vue d'où il leur convient de voir les objets, et d'où ils
doivent être vus. Les plus heureux sont encore soufferts, les autres
sont méprisés; le seul bon parti qu'il leur reste, c'est de cacher au
monde ce qu'ils ne lui ont peut-être que trop montré. Leur goût,
détrompé des désirs inutiles, se tourne alors vers des objets muets et
insensibles; les bâtiments, l'agriculture, l'économie, l'étude, toutes
ces choses sont soumises à leurs volontés; ils s'en approchent ou s'en

RD 19. Retirement

I would be obliged to write too long an essay if I here gave a full and detailed account of the reasons that naturally cause old people to withdraw from dealing with the world. The changes in their temperament and appearance, and the weakening of their bodies, imperceptibly lead them, like most other animals, to draw back from the company of their own kind. Pride, which is inseparable from self-love, then becomes their substitute for reason. It can no longer be flattered by various things that flatter other people's pride; experience has taught them the value of the things that all men desire in their youth, and the impossibility of enjoying them much longer. The different ways of attaining greatness, pleasure, reputation, and every source of human eminence, which seem open to young people, are closed to them by fortune, or by their own conduct, or by the envy and injustice of other people. The path in that direction is too long and too painful, when they have once gone astray from it; they find its difficulties insurmountable, and they are now too old for such aspirations. They become insensitive to friendship, not only because they may never have found any true friends, but also because they have seen the death of many friends who had not yet had time or opportunity to be bad friends—and they easily convince themselves that those people would have been more faithful than the ones who remain. They no longer have any share of the good things that formerly filled their imagination; they no longer have much share even of glory; the glory that they gained is already withered by time, and often, as men grow old, they lose more of it than they gain. Every day takes away some part of themselves; they now have too little life to enjoy what they still have, and even less to gain what they still desire. They see before them only discomforts, afflictions, and debasement; everything is familiar, and nothing can have the charm of novelty for them; time is imperceptibly removing them from the most suitable viewpoint for contemplating objects—the viewpoint from which objects ought to be contemplated. The most fortunate of them are still endured, the others are disdained. The only good course still open for them is to hide from the world what they may have shown it only too clearly. Their taste, disillusioned with futile desires, turns then to silent, insensible objects—buildings, agriculture, economics, study—all of which are forced to suit their

éloignent comme il leur plaît; ils sont maîtres de leurs desseins et de leurs occupations; tout ce qu'ils désirent est en leur pouvoir, et s'étant affranchis de la dépendance du monde, ils font tout dépendre d'eux. Les plus sages savent employer à leur salut le temps qu'il leur reste, et n'ayant qu'une si petite part à cette vie, ils se rendent dignes d'une meilleure. Les autres n'ont au moins qu'eux-mêmes pour témoins de leur misère; leurs propres infirmités les amusent; le moindre relâche leur tient lieu de bonheur; la nature, défaillante, et plus sage qu'eux, leur ôte souvent la peine de désirer; enfin ils oublient le monde, qui est si disposé à les oublier; leur vanité même est consolée par leur retraite, et avec beaucoup d'ennuis, d'incertitudes et de faiblesses, tantôt par piété, tantôt par raison, et le plus souvent par accoutumance, ils soutiennent le poids d'une vie insipide et languissante.

wishes; they approach them or recede from them as they please.
They are in control of their plans and activities; whatever they desire
is in their power, and now that they are free from dependence on the
world, they make it depend on them. The wisest of them are able to
use their remaining time for their own salvation; having so little
share in this life, they make themselves worthy of a better one. The
others, at least, have no one to witness their degradation but themselves. Their own infirmities keep them entertained; for them, the
smallest respite is a substitute for happiness. Nature, failing, is wiser
than they are, and often takes from them the pangs of desire. At last
they forget the world, which is so ready to forget them; their vanity
itself is comforted by their retirement, and with many troubles,
uncertainties, and weaknesses, sometimes out of piety, sometimes
out of reason, and most often out of habit, they bear the weight of an
insipid, sluggish life.

Addenda to the Réflexions diverses

RDA 1. Portrait de Mme de Montespan

Diane de Rochechouart est fille du duc de Mortemart et femme du marquis de Montespan. Sa beauté est surprenante; son esprit et sa conversation ont encore plus de charme que sa beauté. Elle fit dessein de plaire au Roi et de l'ôter à la Vallière dont il était amoureux. Il négligea longtemps cette conquête, et il en fit même des railleries. Deux ou trois années se passèrent sans qu'elle fît d'autres progrès que d'être dame du palais attachée particulièrement à la Reine, et dans une étroite familiarité avec le Roi et la Vallière. Elle ne se rebuta pas néanmoins, et se confiant à sa beauté, à son esprit, et aux offices de Mme de Montausier, dame d'honneur de la Reine, elle suivit son projet sans douter de l'événement. Elle ne s'y est pas trompée: ses charmes et le temps détachèrent le Roi de la Vallière, et elle se vit maîtresse déclarée. Le marquis de Montespan sentit son malheur avec toute la violence d'un homme jaloux. Il s'emporta contre sa femme; il reprocha publiquement à Mme de Montausier qu'elle l'avait entraînée dans la honte où elle était plongée. Sa douleur et son désespoir firent tant d'éclat qu'il fut contraint de sortir du Royaume pour conserver sa liberté. Mme de Montespan eut alors toute la facilité qu'elle désirait, et son crédit n'eut plus de bornes. Elle eut un logement particulier dans toutes les maisons du Roi; les conseils secrets se tenaient chez elle. La Reine céda à sa faveur comme tout le reste de la cour, et non seulement il ne lui fut plus permis d'ignorer un amour si public, mais elle fut obligée d'en voir toutes les suites sans oser se plaindre, et elle dut à Mme de Montespan les marques d'amitié et de douceur qu'elle recevait du Roi. Mme de Montespan voulut encore que la Vallière fût témoin de son triomphe, qu'elle fût présente et auprès d'elle à tous les divertissements publics et particuliers; elle la fit entrer dans le secret de la naissance de ses enfants dans les temps où elle cachait son état à ses propres domestiques. Elle se lassa enfin de la présence de la Vallière, malgré ses soumissions et ses souffrances, et cette fille simple et crédule fut réduite à prendre l'habit de carmélite, moins

Addenda to the Miscellaneous Reflections

RDA 1. Portrait of Madame de Montespan

Diane* de Rochechouart is the Duc de Mortemart's daughter and the Marquis de Montespan's wife. Her beauty is startling; her intelligence and conversation are even more charming than her beauty. She formed the plan of pleasing the King and taking him away from La Vallière, with whom he was in love. For a long time he paid no attention to this conquest, and even joked about it. Two or three years passed, and her only progress was to gain a secure position at court, attached to the Queen* in particular, and on very familiar terms with the King and La Vallière. Nevertheless she was not discouraged. Having full confidence in her beauty, her intelligence, and the aid of the Queen's maid of honour Madame de Montausier,* she pursued her scheme without doubting the outcome. She was not mistaken. Time and her charms separated the King from La Vallière, and she found herself his acknowledged mistress. The Marquis de Montespan felt his misfortune with all the violence of a jealous man. He raged at his wife; he publicly rebuked Madame de Montausier for having brought her to the shame in which she was now wallowing. His grief and despair caused such commotion that he was forced to leave the kingdom in order to retain his liberty. Then Madame de Montespan had all the freedom she desired, and there was no limit to her influence. She had private rooms in all the King's apartments; secret councils were held in her presence. Like the rest of the court, the Queen deferred to her favour; not only could she no longer overlook so public a love affair, but she was forced to witness all its consequences without venturing to complain; whenever the King showed her any sign of friendship or gentleness, she owed it to Madame de Montespan. Madame de Montespan wanted more; she wanted La Vallière to witness her triumph, to be present and at her side during all the public and private entertainments; she told her the secret of her pregnancies* when she was still hiding her condition from her own servants. At last she wearied of the presence of La Vallière, despite the latter's deference and suffering; and that simple, credulous girl was reduced to taking the habit of a Carmelite nun*—

par dévotion que par faiblesse, et on peut dire qu'elle ne quitta le monde que pour faire sa cour.

RDA 2. Portrait du cardinal de Retz

Paul de Gondi, cardinal de Retz, a beaucoup d'élévation, d'étendue d'esprit, et plus d'ostentation que de vraie grandeur de courage. Il a une mémoire extraordinaire; plus de force que de politesse dans ses paroles; l'humeur facile, de la docilité et de la faiblesse à souffrir les plaintes et les reproches de ses amis; peu de piété, quelques apparences de religion. Il paraît ambitieux sans l'être; la vanité, et ceux qui l'ont conduit lui ont fait entreprendre de grandes choses, presque toutes opposées à sa profession; il a suscité les plus grands désordres de l'État, sans avoir un dessein formé de s'en prévaloir, et bien loin de se déclarer ennemi du cardinal Mazarin pour occuper sa place, il n'a pensé qu'à lui paraître redoutable, et à se flatter de la fausse vanité de lui être opposé. Il a su profiter néanmoins avec habileté des malheurs publics pour se faire cardinal; il a souffert la prison avec fermeté, et n'a dû sa liberté qu'à sa hardiesse. La paresse l'a soutenu avec gloire, durant plusieurs années, dans l'obscurité d'une vie errante et cachée. Il a conservé l'archevêché de Paris, contre la puissance du cardinal Mazarin; mais après la mort de ce ministre, il s'en est démis, sans connaître ce qu'il faisait, et sans prendre cette conjoncture pour ménager les intérêts de ses amis et les siens propres. Il est entré dans divers conclaves, et sa conduite a toujours augmenté sa réputation. Sa pente naturelle est l'oisiveté; il travaille néanmoins avec activité dans les affaires qui le pressent, et il se repose avec nonchalance quand elles sont finies. Il a une présence d'esprit, et il sait tellement tourner à son avantage les occasions que la fortune lui offre, qu'il semble qu'il les ait prévues et désirées. Il aime à raconter; il veut éblouir indifféremment tous ceux qui l'écoutent par des aventures extraordinaires, et souvent son imagination lui fournit plus que sa mémoire. Il est faux dans la plupart de ses qualités, et ce qui a le plus contribué à sa réputation, c'est de savoir donner un beau jour à ses défauts. Il est insensible à la haine et à l'amitié,

out of weakness rather than piety; we may say that she left the world only in order to pay court.

RDA 2. Portrait of Cardinal de Retz

Paul de Gondi, Cardinal de Retz, has considerable eminence and breadth of mind, with more ostentation than true greatness of heart. He has an extraordinary memory; there is more strength than civility in his speech; his temperament is easygoing; he is flexible enough and weak enough to endure his friends' complaints and rebukes; he has little piety, though some appearances of religion. He seems ambitious, without being so; vanity, and those who have led him, have made him undertake great things, almost all of which have been contrary to his profession; he has stirred up the greatest disturbances in the realm without having any settled plan to take advantage of them, and instead of declaring his enmity to Cardinal Mazarin* in order to take his place, he thought only of making himself seem formidable to Mazarin and flattering himself with the illusory vanity of being his opponent. Nevertheless, he managed to profit cleverly from public misfortunes and become a cardinal. He endured prison with great strength of character, and owed his freedom only to his own boldness.* For several years his laziness kept him with some glory in the obscurity of private life, wandering and hidden from publicity. He continued to retain the archbishopric of Paris* despite the power of Cardinal Mazarin; but after that minister's death he resigned from it, without knowing what he was doing, and without making use of the incident to care for his friends' interests or his own. He has participated in various conclaves,* and his conduct has always enhanced his reputation. He is naturally inclined to be idle; he works actively when business is pressing, but rests nonchalantly when it is completed. He has a certain presence of mind, and he is so capable of turning to his own advantage whatever opportunities fortune presents, that he seems to have foreseen and desired them. He loves storytelling; he wants to impress all his listeners indiscriminately with extraordinary adventures, and often his imagination provides more of these than his memory. Most of his qualities are false, and what has contributed most to his reputation is the fact that he can present his faults in a good light. He is insensitive to either

quelque soin qu'il ait pris de paraître occupé de l'une ou de l'autre; il est incapable d'envie ni d'avarice, soit par vertu, ou par inapplication. Il a plus emprunté de ses amis qu'un particulier ne devait espérer de leur pouvoir rendre; il a senti de la vanité à trouver tant de crédit, et à entreprendre de s'acquitter. Il n'a point de goût, ni de délicatesse; il s'amuse à tout, et ne se plaît à rien; il évite avec adresse de laisser pénétrer qu'il n'a qu'une légère connaissance de toutes choses. La retraite qu'il vient de faire est la plus éclatante et la plus fausse action de sa vie; c'est un sacrifice qu'il fait à son orgueil, sous prétexte de dévotion: il quitte la cour, où il ne peut s'attacher, et il s'éloigne du monde, qui s'éloigne de lui.

RDA 3. Remarques sur les commencements de la vie du cardinal de Richelieu

Monsieur de Luçon, qui depuis a été cardinal de Richelieu, s'étant attaché entièrement aux intérêts du maréchal d'Ancre, lui conseilla de faire la guerre; mais après lui avoir donné cette pensée et que la proposition en fut faite au Conseil, Monsieur de Luçon témoigna de la désapprouver et s'y opposa pour ce que M. de Nevers, qui croyait que la paix fût avantageuse pour ses desseins, lui avait fait offrir le prieuré de la Charité par le P. Joseph, pourvu qu'il la fît résoudre au Conseil. Ce changement d'opinion de Monsieur de Luçon surprit le maréchal d'Ancre, et l'obligea de lui dire avec quelque aigreur qu'il s'étonnait de le voir passer si promptement d'un sentiment à un autre tout contraire: à quoi Monsieur de Luçon répondit ces propres paroles, que les nouvelles rencontres demandent de nouveaux conseils. Mais jugeant bien par là qu'il avait déplu au maréchal, il résolut de chercher les moyens de le perdre; et un jour que Déageant l'était allé trouver pour lui faire signer quelques expéditions, il lui dit qu'il avait une affaire importante à communiquer à M. de Luynes, et qu'il souhaitait de l'entretenir. Le lendemain, M. de Luynes et lui se virent, où Monsieur de Luçon lui dit que le maréchal d'Ancre était résolu de le perdre, et que le seul moyen de se garantir d'être opprimé par un si puissant ennemi était de le prévenir. Ce discours surprit beaucoup M. de Luynes, qui avait déjà pris cette résolution,

hatred or friendship, however carefully he has tried to seem intent on one or the other. He is incapable of envy or avarice—either because of virtue, or because he has not applied himself diligently to them. He has borrowed more from his friends than a private citizen could hope to repay; but his own vanity has made him undertake to find the requisite credit and discharge his obligations. He has no taste and no delicacy; he is entertained by everything and pleased by nothing; he has the skill to prevent people from perceiving that he has only a slight knowledge of every subject. His recent retirement* has been the most brilliant deed he has done, and the falsest; it has been a sacrifice offered to his own pride under the pretext of piety: he is leaving the court, where he cannot find any security, and he is turning his back on the world, which is turning its back on him.

RDA 3. Remarks on the Early Stages of Cardinal Richelieu's Life

The Bishop of Luçon, who later became Cardinal Richelieu, was completely devoted to the Maréchal d'Ancre's interests, and therefore advised him to declare war. But after he had given him that idea and the proposal had been submitted to the Council, the Bishop showed that he disapproved of it and was opposed to it, because the Bishop of Nevers,* who thought that peace would aid his own plans, had promised that if the Bishop of Luçon induced the Council to decide in favour of peace, Father Joseph* would offer him the priory of La Charité. This change of opinion surprised the Maréchal d'Ancre, and forced him to say with some bitterness that he was astonished to find the Bishop of Luçon's feelings shifting so quickly from one position to its exact opposite; to which the Bishop replied (in these very words) that new contexts require new advice. He discerned, however, that he had displeased the Maréchal, and therefore he decided to look for a way to ruin him. One day, when Déageant* came to ask him to sign some letters, he told Déageant that he had an important matter to pass on to Monsieur de Luynes, and asked him to talk to him. Next day Monsieur de Luynes met him. The Bishop told him that the Maréchal d'Ancre was determined to ruin him, and that the only way to avoid being crushed by so powerful an enemy was to forestall him. This speech greatly surprised Monsieur de

ne sachant si ce conseil qui lui était donné par une créature du maréchal n'était point un piège pour le surprendre et pour lui faire découvrir ses sentiments. Néanmoins Monsieur de Luçon lui fit paraître tant de zèle pour le service du Roi et un si grand attachement à la ruine du maréchal, qu'il disait être le plus grand ennemi de l'État, que M. de Luynes, persuadé de sa sincérité, fut sur le point de lui découvrir son dessein, et de lui communiquer le projet qu'il avait fait de tuer le maréchal; mais, s'étant retenu alors de lui en parler, il dit à Déageant la conversation qu'ils avaient eue ensemble et l'envie qu'il avait de lui faire part de son secret: ce que Déageant désapprouva entièrement, et lui fit voir que ce serait donner un moyen infaillible à Monsieur de Luçon de se réconcilier, à ses dépens, avec le maréchal, et de se joindre plus étroitement que jamais avec lui, en lui découvrant une affaire de cette conséquence: de sorte que la chose s'exécuta, et le maréchal d'Ancre fut tué, sans que Monsieur de Luçon en eût connaissance. Mais les conseils qu'il avait donnés à M. de Luynes, et l'animosité qu'il lui avait témoigné d'avoir contre le maréchal le conservèrent, et firent que le Roi lui commanda de continuer d'assister au Conseil, et d'exercer sa charge de secrétaire d'État, comme il avait accoutumé: si bien qu'il demeura encore quelque temps à la cour, sans que la chute du maréchal qui l'avait avancé nuisît à sa fortune. Mais, comme il n'avait pas pris les mêmes précautions envers les vieux ministres qu'il avait fait auprès de M. de Luynes, M. de Villeroy et M. le président Jeannin, qui virent par quel biais il entrait dans les affaires, firent connaître à M. de Luynes qu'il ne devait pas attendre plus de fidélité de lui qu'il en avait témoigné pour le maréchal d'Ancre, et qu'il était nécessaire de l'éloigner, comme une personne dangereuse et qui voulait s'établir par quelques voies que ce pût être: ce qui fit résoudre M. de Luynes à lui commander de se retirer à Avignon. Cependant la Reine, mère du Roi, alla à Blois, et Monsieur de Luçon, qui ne pouvait souffrir de se voir privé de toutes ses espérances, essaya de renouer avec M. de Luynes, et lui fit offrir que, s'il lui permettait de retourner auprès de la Reine, qu'il se servirait du pouvoir qu'il avait sur son esprit pour lui faire chasser tous ceux qui lui étaient désagréables, et pour lui faire faire toutes les choses que M. de Luynes lui prescrirait. Cette proposition fut reçue, et Monsieur de Luçon, retournant, produisit l'affaire du Pont-de-Cé, en suite de quoi il fut fait cardinal, et commença d'établir les fondements de la grandeur où il est parvenu.

Luynes, who had already resolved to do just that; and he did not know whether this advice, coming from one of the Maréchal's minions, might be a trap to surprise him and make him reveal his own feelings. Nevertheless, the Bishop seemed to him so zealous on behalf of the King, and so committed to ruining the Maréchal—whom he called the greatest enemy of the realm—that Monsieur de Luynes was convinced of his sincerity, and came close to revealing his own plan and describing his scheme to kill the Maréchal. However, he refrained from telling him about it at that time; instead, he told Déageant about the conversation, saying that he wished to share the secret with the Bishop—of which Déageant totally disapproved, pointing out that this would give the Bishop a sure way of making peace with the Maréchal and being more united with him than ever at Monsieur de Luynes's expense, by revealing to the Cardinal a matter of such importance. As a result, the deed was done, and the Maréchal d'Ancre was killed, without the Bishop's knowledge. But the advice he had given Monsieur de Luynes, and the hatred for the Maréchal that he had displayed, kept him in favour, so that the King commanded him to continue attending the Council and exercising his customary duties as Secretary of State. Consequently, he remained some further time at court, without his fortunes being harmed by the fall of the Maréchal who had advanced him. But he had not taken the same steps toward the old ministers as he had toward Monsieur de Luynes. Therefore, Monsieur de Villeroy and President Jeannin,* who could see how deviously he was doing business, advised Monsieur de Luynes not to expect more fidelity from him than he had displayed for the Maréchal d'Ancre, but to keep him at arm's length as a dangerous person who was willing to gain status in any way whatever. As a result, Monsieur de Luynes commanded him to retire to Avignon. However, the Queen Mother went to Blois, and the Bishop, who could not endure the loss of all his hopes, tried to renew his relationship with Monsieur de Luynes, saying that, if he were allowed to attend the Queen once more, he would make use of his influence with her, so that she would dismiss everyone whom Monsieur de Luynes disliked and arrange for all his instructions to be carried out. The proposal was accepted; the Bishop returned to favour and arranged the Pont-de-Cé* business, following which he was made cardinal and began to lay the foundations of his ensuing greatness.

RDA 4. Le Comte d'Harcourt

Le soin que la fortune a pris d'élever et d'abattre le mérite des hommes, est connu dans tous les temps, et il y a mille exemples du droit qu'elle s'est donné de mettre le prix à leurs qualités, comme les souverains mettent le prix à la monnaie, pour faire voir que sa marque leur donne le cours qu'il lui plaît. Si elle s'est servie des talents extraordinaires de Monsieur le Prince et de M. de Turenne pour les faire admirer, il paraît qu'elle a respecté leur vertu, et que, tout injuste qu'elle est, elle n'a pu se dispenser de leur faire justice. Mais on peut dire qu'elle veut montrer toute l'étendue de son pouvoir, lorsqu'elle choisit des sujets médiocres pour les égaler aux plus grands hommes. Ceux qui ont connu le comte d'Harcourt conviendront de ce que je dis, et ils le regarderont comme un chef-d'œuvre de la fortune, qui a voulu que la postérité le jugeât digne d'être comparé dans la gloire des armes aux plus célèbres capitaines. Ils lui verront exécuter heureusement les plus difficiles et les plus glorieuses entreprises. Les succès des îles Sainte-Marguerite, de Casal, le combat de la Route, le siège de Turin, les batailles gagnées en Catalogne, une si longue suite de victoires étonneront les siècles à venir. La gloire du comte d'Harcourt sera en balance avec celle de Monsieur le Prince et de M. de Turenne, malgré les distances que la nature a mises entre eux; elle aura un même rang dans l'histoire, et on n'osera refuser à son mérite ce que l'on sait présentement qui n'est dû qu'à sa seule fortune.

RDA 4. Comte d'Harcourt

The care with which fortune raises and casts down men's merits has been familiar in every age; and there are thousands of examples of her self-appointed right to set the value of their qualities, just as rulers set the value of money, to show that her stamp gives them whatever currency she pleases.* If she made use of the extraordinary talents of the Prince and Monsieur de Turenne* so that they would be admired, she seems to have treated their virtue with respect; totally unjust though she is, she was not able to avoid doing them justice. But we may say that she wants to show the full extent of her power when she chooses average people and makes them equal to the greatest men. Those who knew the Comte d'Harcourt will agree with what I say, and will see him as a masterpiece painted by fortune, who wants posterity to judge him worthy of comparison in military glory with the most famous army leaders. Posterity will behold his good fortune in carrying out the most difficult and glorious enterprises. The successes at the Lérins Islands, Casale, the battle of the Chieri Road, the siege of Turin, the battles won in Catalonia—such a long succession of victories will impress the ages to come. Comte d'Harcourt's glory will match the Prince's and Monsieur de Turenne's, despite the distance that nature set between them; his glory will have the same standing in history as theirs, and no one will refrain from assigning to his merit what we today know was due only to his good fortune.

Portrait de M. R. D. fait par lui-même

Je suis d'une taille médiocre, libre et bien proportionnée. J'ai le teint brun mais assez uni, le front élevé et d'une raisonnable grandeur, les yeux noirs, petits et enfoncés, et les sourcils noirs et épais, mais bien tournés. Je serais fort empêché à dire de quelle sorte j'ai le nez fait, car il n'est ni camus ni aquilin, ni gros ni pointu, au moins à ce que je crois. Tout ce que je sais, c'est qu'il est plutôt grand que petit, et qu'il descend un peu trop en bas. J'ai la bouche grande, et les lèvres assez rouges d'ordinaire, et ni bien ni mal taillées. J'ai les dents blanches, et passablement bien rangées. On m'a dit autrefois que j'avais un peu trop de menton: je viens de me tâter et de me regarder dans le miroir pour savoir ce qui en est, et je ne sais pas trop bien qu'en juger. Pour le tour du visage, je l'ai ou carré ou en ovale; lequel des deux, il me serait fort difficile de le dire. J'ai les cheveux noirs, naturellement frisés, et avec cela assez épais et assez longs pour pouvoir prétendre en belle tête. J'ai quelque chose de chagrin et de fier dans la mine; cela fait croire à la plupart des gens que je suis méprisant, quoique je ne le sois point du tout. J'ai l'action fort aisée, et même un peu trop, et jusques à faire beaucoup de gestes en parlant. Voilà naïvement comme je pense que je suis fait au-dehors, et l'on trouvera, je crois, que ce que je pense de moi là-dessus n'est pas fort éloigné de ce qui en est. J'en userai avec la même fidélité dans ce qui me reste à faire de mon portrait; car je me suis assez étudié pour me bien connaître, et je ne manque ni d'assurance pour dire librement ce que je puis avoir de bonnes qualités, ni de sincérité pour avouer franchement ce que j'ai de défauts. Premièrement, pour parler de mon humeur, je suis mélancolique, et je le suis à un point que depuis trois ou quatre ans à peine m'a-t-on vu rire trois ou quatre fois. J'aurais pourtant, ce me semble, une mélancolie assez supportable et assez douce, si je n'en avais point d'autre que celle qui me vient de mon tempérament; mais il m'en vient tant d'ailleurs, et ce qui m'en vient me remplit de telle sorte l'imagination, et m'occupe si fort l'esprit, que la plupart du temps ou je rêve sans dire mot ou je n'ai presque point d'attache à ce que je dis. Je suis fort resserré

Portrait of Monsieur R———d, by Himself

I am of average height, well-built and well-proportioned. My complexion is dark, but fairly uniform; my forehead is high and reasonably broad; my eyes are dark, small, and deep-set, and my eyebrows black and thick, but well-shaped. I would be hard-pressed to say what kind of nose I have; for it is neither snub, nor aquiline, nor thick, nor pointed, at least I do not think so; all I know is that it is on the large rather than the small side, and that it comes down a little too low. My mouth is large, and my lips usually rather red, neither well- nor ill-shaped. My teeth are white and passably regular. I have been told that my chin was somewhat too prominent; I have just examined myself and looked in the mirror to see if this is so, and I am not quite sure what to think. As for the shape of my face, it is either square or oval—but which of the two, I would find it very hard to say. My hair is black, naturally curled, thick enough and long enough for me to claim that I have a fine head of hair. I look somewhat gloomy and proud; this makes most people think me disdainful, although I am nothing of the kind. I move with ease, even with too much ease, to the extent that I gesticulate a great deal while talking. That, without any pretence, is how I think I look from the outside, and people will find, I believe, that my thoughts on the subject are not far from the truth. I shall deal just as faithfully with the rest of my portrait, because I have studied myself enough to know myself well, and I shall lack neither the assurance to state openly any good qualities I may have, nor the sincerity to acknowledge frankly whatever faults I have. To speak first of my temperament, I am melancholy—to such a degree that, in the last three or four years, I have hardly been seen to laugh three or four times. Nevertheless, I think my melancholy would be fairly tolerable and fairly gentle if it came only from my temperament; but so much of it comes from other sources, and it fills my imagination and busies my mind to such an extent, that most of the time I am either daydreaming without uttering a word or else giving very little attention to what I am saying. I am very reserved with people I do not know, and

avec ceux que je ne connais pas, et je ne suis pas même extrêmement
ouvert avec la plupart de ceux que je connais. C'est un défaut, je le
sais bien, et je ne négligerai rien pour m'en corriger; mais comme un
certain air sombre que j'ai dans le visage contribue à me faire paraître
encore plus réservé que je ne le suis, et qu'il n'est pas en notre
pouvoir de nous défaire d'un méchant air qui nous vient de la disposition naturelle des traits, je pense qu'après m'être corrigé au-
dedans, il ne laissera pas de me demeurer toujours de mauvaises
marques au-dehors. J'ai de l'esprit et je ne fais point difficulté de le
dire; car à quoi bon façonner là-dessus? Tant biaiser et tant apporter
d'adoucissement pour dire les avantages que l'on a, c'est, ce me
semble, cacher un peu de vanité sous une modestie apparente et se
servir d'une manière bien adroite pour faire croire de soi beaucoup
plus de bien que l'on n'en dit. Pour moi, je suis content qu'on ne me
croie ni plus beau que je me fais, ni de meilleure humeur que je me
dépeins, ni plus spirituel et plus raisonnable que je dirai que je le
suis. J'ai donc de l'esprit, encore une fois, mais un esprit que la
mélancolie gâte; car, encore que je possède assez bien ma langue, que
j'aie la mémoire heureuse, et que je ne pense pas les choses fort
confusément, j'ai pourtant une si forte application à mon chagrin
que souvent j'exprime assez mal ce que je veux dire. La conversation
des honnêtes gens est un des plaisirs qui me touchent le plus. J'aime
qu'elle soit sérieuse et que la morale en fasse la plus grande partie;
cependant je sais la goûter aussi quand elle est enjouée, et si je n'y dis
pas beaucoup de petites choses pour rire, ce n'est pas du moins que
je ne connaisse bien ce que valent les bagatelles bien dites, et que je
ne trouve fort divertissante cette manière de badiner où il y a certains
esprits prompts et aisés qui réussissent si bien. J'écris bien en prose,
je fais bien en vers, et si j'étais sensible à la gloire qui vient de ce côté-
là, je pense qu'avec peu de travail je pourrais m'acquérir assez de
réputation. J'aime la lecture en général; celle où il se trouve quelque
chose qui peut façonner l'esprit et fortifier l'âme est celle que j'aime
le plus. Surtout, j'ai une extrême satisfaction à lire avec une personne d'esprit; car de cette sorte on réfléchit à tous moments sur ce
qu'on lit, et des réflexions que l'on fait il se forme une conversation
la plus agréable du monde, et la plus utile. Je juge assez bien des
ouvrages de vers et de prose que l'on me montre; mais j'en dis
peut-être mon sentiment avec un peu trop de liberté. Ce qu'il y a
encore de mal en moi, c'est que j'ai quelquefois une délicatesse trop

I am not particularly open even with most of the people I do know. This is a fault, I know that, and I shall leave no stone unturned to correct it; but since a certain air of gloom on my face tends to make me look even more reserved than I really am, and since it is not in our power to rid ourselves of a bad expression caused by the innate arrangement of our features, I think that when I have corrected myself inwardly, I shall still be left with unpleasant signs outwardly. I am intelligent, and I have no trouble saying so; what is the good of being coy about it? To state your advantages too evasively and too gently is, in my opinion, to hide a bit of vanity under a show of modesty; it is a skilful way to make people think much better of you than you say. For my part, I am content to be thought no finer than I make myself out to be, no better-tempered than I portray myself as being, no more intelligent and no more reasonable than I am. I repeat then that I am intelligent, but my intelligence is spoiled by melancholy, because, although I have a fairly good command of words, a fortunate memory, and I can think without too much confusion, still I am so concerned with my own discomfort that I often express rather badly what I am trying to say. The conversation of honorable people is one of the pleasures that affects me most deeply. I like it to be serious and mainly devoted to moral subjects. However, I also have a taste for it when it is playful; and if I do not utter many little jokes, that is not because I underrate the value of well-phrased trifles or because I fail to get much amusement from that kind of banter, at which certain quick, fluent minds succeed so well. I write good prose, I compose good verse; and if I were sensitive to the glory that comes from such things, I think I could, with a little work, gain rather a reputation. I like reading in general; I like best the kind that contains something to shape the mind and strengthen the soul. Above all, I derive the greatest pleasure from reading in the company of an intelligent person, because in such a situation you are constantly reflecting on what you are reading; and your reflections can form conversation of the most attractive and useful kind. I am a fairly good judge of works in verse and prose, when they are shown me; but I may express my feelings a little too freely. Another of my bad points is the fact that I am sometimes too scrupulous and too

scrupuleuse, et une critique trop sévère. Je ne hais pas à entendre disputer, et souvent aussi je me mêle assez volontiers dans la dispute: mais je soutiens d'ordinaire mon opinion avec trop de chaleur et lorsqu'on défend un parti injuste contre moi, quelquefois, à force de me passionner pour celui de la raison, je deviens moi-même fort peu raisonnable. J'ai les sentiments vertueux, les inclinations belles, et une si forte envie d'être tout à fait honnête homme que mes amis ne me sauraient faire un plus grand plaisir que de m'avertir sincèrement de mes défauts. Ceux qui me connaissent un peu particulièrement et qui ont eu la bonté de me donner quelquefois des avis là-dessus savent que je les ai toujours reçus avec toute la joie imaginable, et toute la soumission d'esprit que l'on saurait désirer. J'ai toutes les passions assez douces et assez réglées: on ne m'a presque jamais vu en colère et je n'ai jamais eu de haine pour personne. Je ne suis pas pourtant incapable de me venger, si l'on m'avait offensé, et qu'il y allât de mon honneur à me ressentir de l'injure qu'on m'aurait faite. Au contraire je suis assuré que le devoir ferait si bien en moi l'office de la haine que je poursuivrais ma vengeance avec encore plus de vigueur qu'un autre. L'ambition ne me travaille point. Je ne crains guère de choses, et ne crains aucunement la mort. Je suis peu sensible à la pitié, et je voudrais ne l'y être point du tout. Cependant il n'est rien que je ne fisse pour le soulagement d'une personne affligée, et je crois effectivement que l'on doit tout faire, jusques à lui témoigner même beaucoup de compassion de son mal, car les misérables sont si sots que cela leur fait le plus grand bien du monde; mais je tiens aussi qu'il faut se contenter d'en témoigner, et se garder soigneusement d'en avoir. C'est une passion qui n'est bonne à rien au-dedans d'une âme bien faite, qui ne sert qu'à affaiblir le cœur et qu'on doit laisser au peuple qui, n'exécutant jamais rien par raison, a besoin de passions pour le porter à faire les choses. J'aime mes amis, et je les aime d'une façon que je ne balancerais pas un moment à sacrifier mes intérêts aux leurs; j'ai de la condescendance pour eux, je souffre patiemment leurs mauvaises humeurs et j'en excuse facilement toutes choses; seulement je ne leur fais pas beaucoup de caresses, et je n'ai pas non plus de grandes inquiétudes en leur absence. J'ai naturellement fort peu de curiosité pour la plus grande partie de tout ce qui en donne aux autres gens. Je suis fort secret, et j'ai moins de difficulté que personne à taire ce qu'on m'a dit en confidence. Je suis extrêmement régulier à ma parole; je n'y manque

severely critical. I do not dislike listening to arguments, indeed, quite often I take part in the argument willingly enough; but I usually expound my opinion too heatedly; and when someone is defending an unjust cause against me, I sometimes become so passionate for the cause of reason that I grow quite unreasonable myself. My feelings are virtuous, and I am naturally inclined to what is good; so strongly do I wish to be in all respects a man of honor that my friends could give me no greater pleasure than by sincerely showing me my faults. People who know me at all intimately, and who have been kind enough to give me such advice from time to time, will recognize that I have always accepted it with the greatest possible joy and in the most submissive spirit that anyone could desire. All my passions are fairly gentle and fairly well regulated; I have hardly ever displayed a fit of anger, and I have never hated anyone. However, I would not be incapable of taking revenge if I were offended and if it were a point of honour to show resentment for the insult. On the contrary, I feel sure that my sense of duty would take the place of hatred so effectively that I would pursue my revenge even more vigorously than another person might do. I am not troubled by ambition at all. I am not afraid of many things, and I have absolutely no fear of death. I have very little sensitivity to pity, and I wish I had none at all. However, there is nothing I would not do to comfort people in distress; and in fact I believe we should do everything possible, even to the extent of showing great compassion for their sufferings—for unhappy people are so foolish that this can do them all the good in the world. But I also hold that we should be content to show pity, and be careful not to harbour it ourselves. It is a passion that serves no good purpose in a healthy soul; it tends only to weaken the heart, and it should be left to the common people, who never do anything on the basis of reason and therefore need the help of the passions to prompt them to action. I am fond of my friends—so fond of them that I would not for a moment hesitate to sacrifice my own interests to theirs. I am indulgent toward them; I endure their spells of bad temper patiently, and I readily excuse everything they do; yet I do not make many displays of affection, and I am not very anxious when they are absent. By nature I have very little curiosity about most of the things that make other people curious. I am very secretive, and no one has less difficulty keeping silent about anything that he has been told in confidence. I am very particular about keeping my word;

jamais, de quelque conséquence que puisse être ce que j'ai promis et je m'en suis fait toute ma vie une loi indispensable. J'ai une civilité fort exacte parmi les femmes, et je ne crois pas avoir jamais rien dit devant elles qui leur ait pu faire de la peine. Quand elles ont l'esprit bien fait, j'aime mieux leur conversation que celle des hommes: on y trouve une certaine douceur qui ne se rencontre point parmi nous, et il me semble outre cela qu'elles s'expliquent avec plus de netteté et qu'elles donnent un tour plus agréable aux choses qu'elles disent. Pour galant, je l'ai été un peu autrefois; présentement je ne le suis plus, quelque jeune que je sois. J'ai renoncé aux fleurettes et je m'étonne seulement de ce qu'il y a encore tant d'honnêtes gens qui s'occupent à en débiter. J'approuve extrêmement les belles passions: elles marquent la grandeur de l'âme, et quoique dans les inquiétudes qu'elles donnent il y ait quelque chose de contraire à la sévère sagesse, elles s'accommodent si bien d'ailleurs avec la plus austère vertu que je crois qu'on ne les saurait condamner avec justice. Moi qui connais tout ce qu'il y a de délicat et de fort dans les grands sentiments de l'amour, si jamais je viens à aimer, ce sera assurément de cette sorte; mais, de la façon dont je suis, je ne crois pas que cette connaissance que j'ai me passe jamais de l'esprit au cœur.

I never break it, whatever the importance of the promise—I have made that an unshakeable rule all my life. I am meticulously polite with women, and I do not think I have ever said anything in a woman's presence that could have caused her pain. When women are intelligent I like their conversation better than men's; it has a certain gentleness that is not found in ours; besides, it seems to me that they express themselves more clearly and give a more attractive turn to their remarks. As for love affairs, I have had a few in the past; but I no longer do so, even though I am still young. I have given up flirting, and I can only wonder that so many people of honor still spend their time indulging in it. I wholeheartedly approve of the noble passions; they are the sign of true greatness of soul; and though the anxiety they cause is contrary to austere wisdom in some respects, they are otherwise so much in keeping with the strictest virtue that I do not think they could justly be condemned. I myself, knowing just how strong and delicate the most intense feelings of love are, would surely fall in love like that, if I ever fell in love at all; but, being made the way I am, I do not think this knowledge of mine will ever pass from my mind to my heart.

APPENDIX

Maxims of Doubtful Authenticity

The following maxims are of doubtful authenticity, but have often been attributed to La Rochefoucauld by recent editors. They fall into three distinct groups.

The first two items come from the pirated Dutch edition of the maxims, *Sentences et Maximes de morale* (The Hague: Jean and Daniel Steucker, 1663 or 1664). Nearly everything in this edition can be found in well-authenticated manuscripts of La Rochefoucauld's maxims and/or in the first authorized edition, but these two sections (paragraphs 108–10a and 152–5) cannot. They read as follows:

> *La familiarité est un relâchement presque de toutes les règles de la vie civile, que le libertinage a introduit dans la société pour nous faire parvenir à celle qu'on appelle commode.*
>
> *C'est un effet de l'amour-propre qui, voulant tout accommoder à notre faiblesse, nous soustrait à l'honnête sujétion que nous imposent les bonnes mœurs et, pour chercher trop les moyens de nous les rendre commodes, les fait dégénérer en vices.*
>
> *Les femmes, ayant naturellement plus de mollesse que les hommes, tombent plutôt dans ce relâchement, et y perdent davantage: l'autorité du sexe ne se maintient pas, le respect qu'on lui doit diminue, et l'on peut dire que l'honnête y perd la plus grande partie de ses droits.*

(Familiarity is a weakening of almost every rule of polite life; it has been introduced into society by licentiousness, so that we might attain the kind of life that is called 'comfortable'.

This results from self-love, which wants to reconcile everything to our own frailty; it releases us from the virtuous state of submissiveness imposed on us by good moral values, and it tries so hard to make them comfortable for us, that it allows them to degenerate into vices.

Women, being inherently softer than men, fall more easily into this weakness and lose more by doing so; the authority of their sex is weakened, the respect it deserves is diminished, and we may say that virtue has lost the largest part of its rights in this way.)

> *La raillerie est une gaieté agréable de l'esprit, qui enjoue la conversation, et qui lie la société si elle est obligeante, ou qui la trouble si elle ne l'est pas.*
>
> *Elle est plus pour celui qui la fait que pour celui qui la souffre.*
>
> *C'est toujours un combat de bel esprit, que produit la vanité; d'où vient*

que ceux qui en manquent pour la soutenir, et ceux qu'un défaut reproché fait rougir, s'en offensent également, comme d'une défaite injurieuse qu'ils ne sauraient pardonner.

C'est un poison qui tout pur éteint l'amitié et excite la haine, mais qui corrigé par l'agrément de l'esprit, et la flatterie de la louange, l'acquiert ou la conserve; et il en faut user sobrement avec ses amis et avec les faibles.

(Jocularity is an attractive gaiety of the mind, which makes conversation playful; if it is helpful, it unites the social group, and if it is not, it perturbs it.

It does more for the joker than for his victim.

It is always a battle of wits produced by vanity. As a result, those who lack the wit to sustain it, and those who blush when rebuked for a fault, are equally offended by it—as if by an insulting defeat that they are unable to forgive.

It is a poison which, in its pure form, extinguishes friendship and arouses hatred, but when corrected by the attraction of wit and the flattery of praise, it wins friends or retains them; and it should be used sparingly with one's friends, or with the weak.)

The discussion of jocularity may be compared with RD 16.

The next two items come from a seventeenth-century manuscript (Arsenal ms 6041) containing copies of fourteen maxims. The manuscript does not indicate their author(s), but twelve of them are certainly by La Rochefoucauld; they are V: 154 and 302–12, all of which first appeared in the third authorized edition (1671). However, the manuscript's maxims 8 and 9 (placed between V: 307 and 308) are otherwise unknown. They are:

Nos actions paraissent moins par ce qu'elles sont que par le jour qu'il plaît à la fortune de leur donner.

(The appearance of our deeds depends less on what they are than on the light that fortune is pleased to shed on them.)

On se venge quelquefois mieux de ses ennemis en leur faisant du bien qu'en leur faisant du mal.

(We sometimes take better vengeance on our enemies by doing good to them than by doing evil to them.)

Finally, three alleged sayings of La Rochefoucauld are recorded in early eighteenth-century memoirs. The first of them comes from Pierre Desmaiseaux (or Desmaizeaux), *La Vie de ... Saint-Évremont* (publisher unspecified, 1705), the others from Jean de Segrais, *Segraisiana* (Paris: Compagnie des libraires associés, 1721), 81 and 89. Of course, even if they were indeed uttered by La Rochefoucauld, they need not be reckoned

among his maxims. As Jean Lafond has pointed out, the first is more a witticism than a maxim—though the two categories are not mutually exclusive.

L'enfer des femmes, c'est la vieillesse.

(For women, hell is old age.)

Monsieur de La Rochefoucauld disait que les soumissions et les bassesses que les Seigneurs de la Cour font auprès des Ministres qui ne sont pas de leur rang, sont des lâchetés de gens de cœur.

(Monsieur de La Rochefoucauld said that acts of deference and self-abasement done by noblemen in the presence of socially inferior ministers are acts of cowardice done by brave men.)

Monsieur de La Rochefoucauld disait que l'honnêteté n'était d'aucun état en particulier, mais de tous les états en général.

(Monsieur de La Rochefoucauld said that honor was of no estate in particular, but of all estates in general.)

EXPLANATORY NOTES

Wherever possible, obscure (or deceptively simple) passages are elucidated by comparison or contrast (*a*) with other texts by La Rochefoucauld (including other drafts of the same passage), cited according to the system of abbreviations described on pp. xxxiii–xxxvi; (*b*) with the works of his collaborators Jacques Esprit, *La Fausseté des vertus humaines* (cited by volume and chapter number, as 'Esprit, *Fausseté*'), and Madame de Sablé, *Maximes*, and (*c*) with works that there is particular reason to believe La Rochefoucauld may have known first-hand, such as the Bible (citations follow the Latin Vulgate, using its conventional book names), Seneca, Plutarch (citations follow Jacques Amyot's sixteenth-century French translation), and Montaigne—these should be construed not as sources (see pp. xv–xix) but as reminders of certain aspects of the broad context within which La Rochefoucauld was working. In some cases, the differences between the compared passages may be as instructive as the similarities. All translations are by the present editors.

The Publisher to the Reader

Internal evidence shows that this preface and the much longer version appended to the first edition (pp. 145–6) were prepared by La Rochefoucauld himself, in keeping with a common seventeenth-century practice.

3   *a defence*: the October 1664 edition had contained such a defence, by Henri de La Chapelle-Bessé (see p. xiii–xiv); this sentence first appeared in the 1666 edition, when La Chapelle-Bessé's essay was omitted.

    whom God preserves . . . by special grace: 'everyone who is born of God does not sin, but his birth from God preserves him, and the evil one does not touch him' (1 John 5: 18); this grace is 'special' because it is provided for some people, not for all. The phrasing evokes the great seventeenth-century debate between Jansenists and Jesuits about the grace of God (see e.g. Pascal, *Les Provinciales*), but does not commit the writer to any particular position in that debate.

    the Index: pp. 141–3.

V: epigraph ('Our virtues are, most often, only vices . . .')
The thought is explored further in IV: 172.

V: 1
Compare V: 220; I: 293.

V: 7
After Julius Caesar's death (44 BCE), his supporter Mark Antony and his heir Octavian (the future Augustus) gained effective control of the Roman world; war ultimately broke out between them, ending with Antony's defeat and death in 31 BCE.

v: 7

5 *jealousy*: perhaps 'because they were sharing world dominion' (so Vauve-
nargues—who notes, however, that such jealousy would hardly be distinct
from ambition—and all subsequent commentators); but La Rochefoucauld may also be thinking of Plutarch, *Antony* 54: Octavian's sister
Octavia, whom Antony had deserted for Cleopatra, feared it might be
said 'that the two greatest leaders in the world had gone to war because
one was infatuated with, and the other wanted to avenge, a woman'.
Compare Guez de Balzac, *Aristippe* (1658): 'great events are not always
caused by great things; . . . a private love jealousy has been the reason for
a general war'.

v: 9

The earliest known drafts add, at the end of the maxim, 'Charity alone has the
privilege of saying almost anything it likes and never wounding anyone.'

v: 10

The earliest known drafts clarify the underlying comparison: 'As in nature
things are eternally being generated, and the death of one thing is always the
creation of another, so in the human heart . . .'

v: 11

Again the comparison is made explicit in the earliest known drafts: 'I am not
sure whether the maxim "Everything breeds its like" is true in the physical
realm; but I am quite sure that it is false in the moral realm, and that passions
often engender their opposites . . .' Compare v: 492.

v: 14

Compare Esprit, *Fausseté* 1: 28: 'the person who has received great favours . . .
begins to regard his benefactor as a creditor who presses hard both on him and
on what he owes, like so many burdening chains'; Sablé, *Maximes* 12: 'our
good deeds often make enemies for us, and the ungrateful person's ingratitude
is seldom half-hearted; not only does he fail to be thankful as he should be, but
he even wants his ingratitude to pass unnoticed by his benefactor'.

v: 15–16

Compare Plutarch, *Alexander* 13: after the sack of Thebes, Alexander may
have 'wished to offset so brutal and barbarous a deed with one of outstanding
clemency'; Esprit, *Fausseté* 1: 10: the clemency of such kings as Alexander,
Julius Caesar, and Augustus is 'merely a strategy', since the very kings who are
clement on some occasions are extremely cruel on others; sometimes such
clemency is 'a means of winning their subjects' hearts' in order to reduce the
risk of factions and conspiracies; sometimes 'merely a vain and ostentatious
display of their sovereign power' to show that they 'are above the law, and have
the power not only to take away life, but also to grant it'; sometimes 'a secret
fear . . . of being destroyed by factions of grandees or murdered by the common people'; sometimes due to the fact that they 'want to be at ease and enjoy

a repose undisturbed by anything'. See also La Rochefoucauld's letter dated 6 February 1664 to Thomas Esprit: 'in Augustus' clemency to Cinna there was a desire to try a new remedy, a weariness of so much useless bloodshed, and a fear of consequences'.

V: 17–18

In the earliest known drafts, these are two parts of a single maxim (the second part begins '. . . it is also a fear . . .'). Compare 1: 18; Esprit, *Fausseté* 2: 4: people act with moderation 'to arouse less of the envy that is directed against all those who are in favour' and 'so that everyone will believe that, however great their eminence may be, their souls are even greater than their fortune'.

V: 20

Compare Esprit, *Fausseté* 2: 1: although 'pride appears to prevent passionate impulses from arising in great men . . . in reality it merely restrains them and confines them within the soul'.

V: 21

9   *which is really only a fear of facing it*: the earliest known drafts read: 'in order not to think about it, and to numb themselves'. Compare V: 504.

V: 23

Contrast Seneca, *Epistles* 30: 'when death is imminent, it gives even untrained people the courage not to avoid the unavoidable'.

V: 24

Compare Montaigne, *Essais* 2: 12: 'the souls of emperors and cobblers are cast in the same mould'; Esprit, *Fausseté* 2: 12: 'however wearily heroes toil all their lives to establish their position and set themselves above other men, they have the same fears and frailties as those who are called faint-hearted; and, apart from the vanity that inflates and strengthens their hearts, they are made like other men' (citing the example of Alexander the Great, whose heart seemed firm while 'ambition' and 'glory' filled his sight, but 'was seriously shaken' by the terrors of impending death, according to Plutarch, *Alexander* 75).

11   *by prolonged misfortunes*: the earliest known draft (L 201) adds: 'this means, not that they were strong when they bore them, but only that they took pains to convey that impression, and that they bore their misfortunes by the strength of their ambition'.

V: 25

Compare V: 227; Deuteronomy 8: 11–14: 'beware . . . lest, when you have eaten and are full . . . and have plenty of everything, your heart should be lifted up and you forget the Lord'; Seneca, *Epistles* 39: 'the soul . . . is ruined by unrestricted prosperity'; Esprit, *Fausseté* 2: 4: 'fortune's hatred is far less to be feared than her favour'.

V: 30

The earliest known drafts are substantially different: 'Nothing is impossible in itself. There are paths that lead to all things; if we had the willpower, we would always have the means.'

V: 37

13   *kindness*: the earliest known drafts read 'charity'.

V: 39

Compare Esprit, *Fausseté* 1: 20: 'those excellent performers who appear disinterested . . . are assuming a role and playing a part'.

V: 41

The earliest known draft (L 85) adds the explanation 'because they expend all their attention on the little things'; in his *Mémoires* 1, La Rochefoucauld depicts Louis XIII as such a person. Compare 1: 51; RD 16; Matthew 23: 23: 'you tithe mint and anise and cumin, and you have abandoned the weightier things of the law, justice and mercy and faith; those things you ought to have done, without neglecting the others'; Montaigne, *Essais* 3: 5: our 'diligence in slight things takes us away from just ones'.

V: 44

Compare Cicero, *Tusculan Disputations* 1: 33: 'it is of great importance in what body the soul is lodged; there are many bodily matters that sharpen the mind, and many that blunt it'; Montaigne, *Essais* 2: 12: 'our understanding, our judgement, and our soul's faculties in general, suffer according to the body's movements and changes'.

V: 49

The earliest known drafts preface this with the statement: 'Good and ill are greater in our imagination than they are in reality.' Compare Ovid, *Ex Ponto* 4: 4: 5–6: 'fortune has made nothing so wretched that there are no joys to reduce its evil somewhat'.

V: 56

Compare RD 3: people 'adopt prematurely the manner of a rank and dignity to which they aspire. How many lieutenant-generals are practising to be field marshals!'

V: 62

RD 5 repeats and develops this description of sincerity. Compare also Esprit, *Fausseté* 1: 3: 'sincerity is a form of open-heartedness designed to open our friends' hearts to us', in contrast to 'Christian and virtuous sincerity', which 'results from no self-interest or passion, not even a desire to be thought sincere; and those who practise it aim only to please God, who forbids dissimulation and duplicity'.

v: 63

Compare Esprit, *Fausseté* 1: 2: some people's truthfulness is 'a secret ambition for everyone to have faith in everything they say, thus putting themselves on a footing that is not only virtuous but valuable'; 1: 3: 'we make a profession of sincerity so that people may trust us and have faith in our words, because nothing flatters our vanity as much as the authority that our words gain from people's belief that we are sincere'.

v: 65

The earliest known drafts pursue the subject much further: 'Prudence is extolled to the skies, and no kind of praise is withheld from it. It is the guiding rule of our deeds and our conduct, it is the mistress of fortune, it decides the fate of empires; without it, we have ills of all kinds; with it, we have good things of all kinds. As a poet of old once said, when we have prudence, we lack nothing divine—meaning that we find in prudence all the help that we seek from the gods. Yet the most consummate prudence could not guarantee us the smallest result in the world, because it is acting through something as inconstant and incomprehensible as man, and therefore cannot carry out any of its plans with certainty. God alone, who holds all men's hearts in his hands and moves them when he pleases, successfully accomplishes the things that depend on them—from which it must be concluded that all the praises lavished on our prudence by our own ignorance and vanity are insults offered by us to Providence.' Compare Job 5: 13 (and 1 Corinthians 3: 19): God 'catches the wise in their cleverness, and frustrates the plans of the crafty'; Esprit, *Fausseté* 1: 1: 'prudence cannot guarantee anything, because man . . . never remains in one stable position; he adopts different positions within a short time, for infinite numbers of inward and external reasons'.

v: 70

Compare Sablé, *Maximes* 80: 'love is so distinctive in character that we cannot hide it when it exists, or simulate it when it does not'.

v: 77

25   *the Doge . . . in Venice*: in La Rochefoucauld's day the Doge of Venice had far less power than most European rulers; Truchet quotes Moreri, *Grand Dictionnaire historique* (1674): 'the Doge . . . can neither undertake nor accomplish any of the important business of the Republic without the counsel of the senators'.

v: 78

Compare 1: 88; Esprit, *Fausseté* 2: 24: 'in private individuals, fair-mindedness . . . is a fear that injustices may be done to them, for the man who finds himself in the society of men exists there with greater fear and trembling than if he were in the midst of a forest full of wild animals, because he is afraid not only for his life, but also for his possessions, his comfort, and his reputation'.

v: 83

Compare Aristotle, *Eudemian Ethics* 7: 1236ª: 'most people's friendship is based on usefulness: they treat each other as friends because—and in so far as—they are useful to them'; Esprit, *Fausseté* 1: 4: 'what seems to us the purest form of friendship is a search for various good things which we want, and which we hope to obtain by the good we do for other people'; Sablé, *Maximes* 77: 'most people's friendship is merely a transaction that lasts only as long as it is needed'.

v: 86

Compare Seneca, *Epistles* 3: 'some people who are afraid of being deceived have taught other people to deceive; by their suspicions they have given their friends the right to do wrong'.

v: 88

Compare 1: 101.

v: 92

29 *the Athenian madman*: Thrasyllos, who 'complained that his doctor had cured him of thinking he was wealthy' (1: 104). The story (from Athenaeus, *Deipnosophistae* 12: 81; Aelian, *Historia varia* 4: 25) is told by Montaigne, *Essais* 2: 12.

v: 96

Compare v: 317.

v: 97

The earliest known drafts are substantially different: 'The judgement is merely a great light of the intelligence; the same may be said about its breadth, its depth, its discernment, its accuracy, its integrity, and its perceptiveness. The breadth of the intelligence is the measure of its light. Its depth is what reveals the very depths of things. Its discernment compares them and distinguishes them. Its accuracy sees only what ought to be seen. Its integrity always looks at things from the best viewpoint. Its perceptiveness perceives the things that are imperceptible. And its judgement declares what they are. If we consider the matter well, we shall find that all these qualities are nothing but the magnitude of the intelligence, which sees everything and, in the fullness of its light, encompasses all the advantages that we have just mentioned.'

v: 98

Contrast La Rochefoucauld's self-portrait: 'I am intelligent, and I have no trouble saying so.'

v: 99

Compare Esprit, *Fausseté* 1: 19: civility is a matter not only of speech (as most people think) but of the soul, which 'makes thoughts, tastes, and feelings honorable and subtle'.

V: 101

Compare (and contrast) the earliest known drafts: 'There are some fine things, which the mind is not seeking at all, but which it discovers, absolutely finished, within itself—so that they seem to be hidden there, as gold and diamonds are in the depths of the earth.'

V: 104

31   *have their proper points of perspective*: the earliest known drafts make the analogy explicit: 'as statues do'. Compare RD 2.

V: 106

33   *our knowledge is always superficial and imperfect*: radically abridged from the extended statement in the earliest known draft (L 123): 'it follows that very few people are knowledgeable, that our knowledge is superficial and imperfect, and that we describe things instead of defining them. In fact we know them, and make them known, only in broad terms and by common signs—just as if someone said that the human body is upright and composed of different parts, without stating the number, position, functions, relationships, and different characteristics of its parts.'

V: 118

Compare Seneca, *Oedipus* 686: 'loyalty enables a treacherous person to do harm'.

V: 126

Compare Psalm 35. 4 (36: 3): 'the words of his mouth are iniquity and deceit: he has ceased to understand, and to do good'.

V: 127

Compare L 113.

V: 135

Compare Montaigne, *Essais* 2: 2: 'there is sometimes as much difference between us and ourselves as there is between us and other people'.

V: 139

Compare RD 4; Sablé, *Maximes* 3: 'instead of striving to know other people, we think only of making ourselves known to them'; 29: 'everyone is so preoccupied with his own passions and interests that he wants to talk about them constantly, without ever entering into the passions and interests of his listeners—though they themselves have the same need to be heard and attended to'. Her maxim 31 is virtually identical with La Rochefoucauld's V: 139.

V: 142

Compare Proverbs 10: 19: 'in a multitude of words, sin will not be lacking; but the one who restrains his lips is most wise'.

V: 145

The earliest known drafts add V: 198 to this maxim.

V: 146

Compare PV124: 4.

V: 147

Compare Proverbs 27: 6: 'better are the wounds of a friend than the deceitful kisses of an enemy'; Isaiah 30: 10: people say to the prophets, 'Do not prophesy right things to us; speak pleasant things to us, prophesy false things for us.'

V: 149

Compare Esprit, *Fausseté* 2: 5: 'the modesty that seems unable to endure praise is a secret quest for it and a skilful type of pride, which rids its possessors of the vanity of boasting'.

V: 150

Compare I: 155–6; Sablé, *Maximes* 70: 'the shame of seeing ourselves praised for no reason often leads us to do things that we should never have done without it'.

V: 153

The subject is studied further in RD 14.

V: 155

RD 3 provides an explanation: 'because the former want to seem something that they are not, while the latter are exactly what they seem'. Compare also V: 251; Mark 9: 49 (50): 'Salt is good; but if the salt loses its saltiness, with what will you season it? Have salt in yourselves.' The earliest known drafts develop the analogy more fully: 'As there are good foods that sicken us, so there is an insipid kind of merit, and there are people who leave a bad taste in the mouth in spite of good and estimable qualities.' In his *Lettres* (1682) Antoine Gombaud, Chevalier de Méré, quotes La Rochefoucauld as saying: 'I think one could make a maxim that misguided virtue is hardly less annoying than well-ordered vice. . . . I've used these words only to fit in with the language of certain people, who often name vice virtue and virtue vice. . . . I love true virtue and I hate true vice,' he adds; but there are many 'false virtuous people' (he gives the example of Seneca) who 'are seeking only appearances'.

V: 166

The earliest known drafts are more expansive: 'Having no knowledge of true merit, the world is far from able to reward it; so it raises to its positions of greatness and dignity only those people who seem to have fine qualities, and it generally crowns all that glitters—though all that glitters is not gold.' Compare James 2: 2–4: 'If there comes into your assembly a man with a gold ring, in fine clothing, and there also comes in a poor man, in dirty clothes, and you

favour the one who is wearing fine clothing . . . have you not become judges who think unjustly?'

v: 170

49   *It is hard to judge whether*: the earliest known drafts read: 'Only God knows whether . . .'. Compare 1 Samuel 16: 7: 'man sees the appearances, but the Lord looks at the heart'.

v: 172

49   *heartache*: French *ennui*—here used primarily in its older, more intense sense ('anguish'), though with a further suggestion of the modern meaning 'boredom'.

v: 174

Compare Matthew 6: 34: 'do not be anxious for tomorrow, because tomorrow will be anxious for itself; sufficient for the day is its evil'.

v: 182

Compare La Rochefoucauld's letter dated 6 February 1664 to Thomas Esprit: 'I think that there was pride, injustice, and thousands of other ingredients in the magnanimity and generosity of Alexander and many other people; that in Cato's virtue there was harshness—and much envy and hatred toward Caesar; that in Augustus' clemency to Cinna there was a desire to try a new remedy, a weariness of so much useless bloodshed, and a fear of consequences, to which people have preferred to give the name of virtue instead of dissecting all the crannies of the heart.'

v: 184

Compare Sablé, *Maximes* 16: 'often, people who blame themselves excessively do it to avoid being blamed by other people—or else out of vanity, by giving the impression that they are apt to confess their failings'.

v: 185

Compare Esprit, *Fausseté* 2: 4: 'there are heroes in evil, just as there are in good, because we see people intending to make their crimes and misdeeds illustrious, devising sustained, organized plans—great revenges that they want to accomplish, dark outrages that they want to commit—and executing these things resolutely, brilliantly, and firmly'.

v: 191–3

The earliest known draft (L 218) presents v: 193, 192, and 191 (in that order) as parts of a single maxim, the image of a change of illness leading to that of a change of inn. Compare Montaigne, *Essais* 3: 3: 'we do not leave our vices as much as change them'; Esprit, *Fausseté* 1: 10: it is an 'error' to think 'that inclinations that have been set aside or suspended or discarded are destroyed'.

v: 198

In La Rochefoucauld's index, this maxim is listed under 'Flattery'. In the earliest known drafts, it is the conclusion of v: 145.

57 *the Prince and Monsieur de Turenne*: Louis II de Bourbon, Prince de Condé (1621–86), and Henri de La Tour d'Auvergne, Vicomte de Turenne (1611–75), the most famous French military leaders of the century; opponents in the latter stages of the Fronde (1651–9), but allies for most of their careers. Their characters and abilities were already a favourite topic of comparison in their own age.

v: 199

The earliest known drafts add the explanation 'because we are more concerned with how we seem to other people than with actually being what we ought to be'. Compare Proverbs 26: 12: 'have you seen a man who is wise in his own eyes? there is more hope for a fool than for him'; Sablé, *Maximes* 40: 'the desire to appear capable often prevents us from becoming so, because we are more eager to display what we know than to learn what we do not know'.

v: 200

Compare Sablé, *Maximes* 71: 'it is almost better when great people seek glory—even vanity—by doing good, than when they remain indifferent to it; because although they are not doing it for virtuous reasons, at least there is the benefit that vanity has made them do what they would not have done otherwise'.

v: 202

57 *their faults*: the earliest known drafts read 'the corruption of their hearts'. Compare Proverbs 28: 13: 'the one who hides his sins will not prosper; the one who confesses and abandons them will find mercy'.

v: 203

Compare Luke 17: 10: 'when you have done all the things that you were commanded, say: "We are unworthy slaves; we have done what we were obliged to do" '.

v: 204

The earliest known drafts add: 'it is a sort of value that enhances their own; it is, in fact, a refined, subtle attraction, a sweetness in disguise'.

v: 205

57 *Virtue*: the earliest known drafts read 'Chastity'.

v: 206

Compare Seneca, *Epistles* 25: 'it is much nobler to live as if you were living under the eyes of some good man who was always beside you'.

V: 211

In La Rochefoucauld's index, this maxim is listed under 'Distaste'.

V: 220

Compare Esprit, *Fausseté* 2: 6: 'whereas men's passionate temperament makes them daring, and makes it very easy for them to wage war, women's coolness of temper and natural timidity help them wonderfully in practising virtue and modesty'.

V: 224

The word 'really' (*effectivement*) occurs in the earliest known drafts; it has been added to the translation because it helps to clarify the sense in English. Compare Esprit, *Fausseté* 1: 28: gratitude often arises from 'hope of some greater favour' and/or 'fear of seeing one's honour tarnished'.

V: 227

Compare Ecclesiastes 8: 11: 'Because sentence is not pronounced quickly against evil, the children of humanity commit evils fearlessly.'

V: 231

Probably suggested by Baltasar Gracián, *Oráculo manual* 47: 'it is better to be foolish with everyone else than to be wise on your own'.

V: 233

The paragraphing of the English translation is that of the earliest known drafts; the French text adopts the single-paragraph format of the final authorized edition.

V: 234

Compare Plutarch, *Caesar* 11: 'he would rather be first here [in a poor village] than second at Rome'.

V: 236

The earliest known drafts are substantially different: 'Someone who considers superficially all the results of the kindness that draws us out of ourselves, and constantly sacrifices us for the sake of everyone else, would be tempted to think that when it is doing so, self-love is forgetting and abandoning its own interests, and even that it is unwittingly allowing itself to be plundered and impoverished—so that kindness seems to be a silly and innocent state of self-love. Yet kindness is actually the quickest possible way for self-love to reach its goals: it is a secret pathway that brings it home with greater wealth and prosperity; it is a kind of disinterestedness from which it earns a flurry of interest; in fact, it is an ingenious strategy by which it moves, moulds, and turns every man in its own favour.' Compare Esprit, *Fausseté* 1: 17: 'kindness is a kind of magic that a man uses to appear to be elsewhere, though he remains still at home'.

V: 239

The earliest known drafts expand considerably: 'Nothing pleases our pride more than the fact that great people, and those who are respected for their position, intelligence, or merit, confide in us. This gives us a feeling of exquisite delight and marvellously exalts our pride, because we regard it as a result of our own reliability. Yet we will be confounded if we consider its base and imperfect origin, for it arises from vanity, desire to speak, and inability to keep secrets—so that confidential communication is, we may say, a sort of temporary weakness of the soul, caused by the number and weight of things that fill it.'

V: 243

Compare L 249.

V: 246

The earliest known drafts are substantially different: 'Generosity is a desire to shine by doing extraordinary deeds; it is a clever and diligent method of using disinterestedness, firm friendship, and magnanimity to gain a noble reputation quickly.' Esprit, *Fausseté* 1: 18, lists some of the great interests pursued by generosity: greed, self-love, a desire for glory, a desire 'to confound those who have done us evil and make them guilty if they keep doing so'.

V: 247

The earliest known drafts expand considerably: 'Loyalty is a rare device invented by self-love so that man, elevating himself into a trustee of precious things, can make himself infinitely precious. Of all the transactions of self-love, this is the one that involves least outlay and greatest profit. It is a subtle strategy of self-love, obliging men by means of their possessions, honour, freedom, and life—which they are forced to entrust on some occasions—to exalt the loyal man above everyone else.'

V: 249

Originally this maxim was concerned only with the tone of voice; the phrase 'eyes and manner' was added in v from IV: 258, which was then withdrawn.

V: 251

See the note on V: 155 (p. 294).

V: 252

Compare RD 10: 'our tastes are led by the bent of our self-love and our temperament, which . . . subject us to innumerable changes and uncertainties'.

V: 254

The earliest known draft (L 53) expands considerably: 'Humility is a pretence of submissiveness, which we use to make other people effectively submit to us.

It is an impulse by which pride debases itself before men in order to exalt itself above them; it is pride's greatest disguise and foremost stratagem. Indeed, just as there is no doubt that the Proteus of the legends never existed, so it is certain that pride is a real Proteus in the natural world, because it takes every shape it pleases. But though it may be marvellous and attractive to see its appearance behind them all and its diligence within them all, nevertheless we must admit that it is never so rare and pleasant as when we see it in the form and under the cloak of humility, because then we see it with its eyes lowered; its face is modest and tranquil, its words gentle and respectful, full of esteem for other people and disdain for itself. It is unworthy of any honour, it is unfit for any position, and it receives its elevation to positions of responsibility as merely the results of men's kindness and fortune's blind favour.' In Classical mythology, the elusive sea-god Proteus was able to disguise himself by assuming different shapes. Compare Colossians 2: 18: 'let no one seduce you by a willing humility . . . worthlessly puffed up by his fleshly sense'.

v: 261

Compare 1: 284[1].

v: 264

Compare Esprit, *Fausseté* 1: 15: when people show compassion for their neighbours, 'they take pity only on themselves'; they 'take as much care as possible of the unfortunate, so that the same care may be taken of them if they lack possessions, if they fall sick, and if their fortune changes'.

v: 265

Compare 1: 257; John 20: 29: 'blessed are those who have not seen, and yet have believed'; Montaigne, *Essais* 3: 13: 'assertiveness and stubbornness are manifest signs of stupidity'; Sablé, *Maximes* 7: 'average but ill-developed intellects, especially the half-educated, are the most subject to stubbornness; only strong minds are capable of retracting their words and abandoning a bad position'; 41: 'small-mindedness, ignorance, and presumption lead to stubbornness, because stubborn people want to believe only what they can envisage—and they cannot envisage very much'.

v: 266

Compare Esprit, *Fausseté* 2: 19: 'laziness, sluggish though it is, conquers ambition, which is a burning passion, because laziness is to the soul what opium is to the body, which it puts to sleep and makes it find such a sleep much more delightful than anything that could satisfy it when alert'. This passion is so strong that it has the power 'to make men disdain sceptres and crowns'.

v: 271

Compare Plato, *Laws* 2: 664e: 'by nature all the young are fiery and restless'.

V: 282

Compare Pierre Charron, *De la sagesse* 2: 10: 'some kinds of falseness are more probable and more self-evident than truths'.

V: 285

81   *its name*: 'greatness of soul' (Latin).

V: 291

Contrast Sablé, *Maximes* 2: 'True merit never depends on time or fashion. . . . Good sense, knowledge, and wisdom make people clever and pleasant at any time and in any place.'

V: 293

The earliest known drafts end: 'moderation debases the soul, as ambition exalts it'.

V: 297

The earliest known drafts preface this with the statement: 'We notice only the extreme and exceptional impulses of our humours, such as violent anger etc. But hardly anyone notices that these humours . . .' Classical (and Renaissance) physiology ascribed individual differences in temperament to differences in the balance of the major body fluids (humours). An excess of bile was thought to produce a choleric temperament, an excess of blood a sanguine one, and so on.

V: 299

Compare Seneca, *Epistles* 19: 'a very small debt makes someone your debtor; a large debt makes him your enemy'.

V: 301

In La Rochefoucauld's index, this maxim is listed under 'Favours'.

V: 306

Compare Proverbs 19: 6: there are 'many . . . friends of a person who gives gifts'.

V: 307

Compare Matthew 6: 2–4: 'When you do deeds of charity, do not sound a trumpet before you, as the hypocrites do in the synagogues and in the streets, to be honoured by men. . . . Do not let your left hand know what your right hand is doing, so that your charity may be in secret; and your Father, who sees in secret, will repay you.'

V: 315

Compare Seneca, *Epistles* 43: 'Hardly anyone can live with his doors open; it is our conscience, not our pride, that has placed doorkeepers at our doors.'

V: 327

Compare Esprit, *Fausseté* 1: 21: falsely humble people never 'accuse themselves of essential [faults], such as a lack of honour and integrity, and being a liar and a cheat; they accuse themselves only of being hasty, careless, lazy, and similar faults that do not stain their reputation at all'.

V: 329

One draft (Gilbert ms) reads: 'We think we hate flatterers, but we hate only the bad ones.'

V: 341

Compare Revelation 3: 16: 'because you are lukewarm, and neither cold nor hot, I will vomit you out of my mouth'.

V: 352

Compare VIS: 37.

V: 354

One draft (VIS: 35) reads: 'Some faults, when seen in the proper light, are more pleasing than perfection itself.' See the note on V: 155 (p. 294).

V: 358

99   *the Christian virtues*: in contrast to the (false) 'human virtues' (the distinction is drawn repeatedly by Esprit, *Fausseté*). One draft (Gilbert ms) adds: 'and the thing most often lacking in those who devote themselves to piety'.

V: 368

Compare VIS: 21.

V: 371

Compare VIS: 28.

V: 375

Compare Jude 10: 'they blaspheme whatever they do not know'.

V: 378

One draft (Gilbert ms) reads: 'People give advice, but not the wisdom to profit from it.' Compare Ezekiel 33: 32: 'to them you are like a harmonious song sung by a sweet and pleasant voice: they hear your words and do not do them'.

V: 380

Compare 1 Corinthians 3: 13: 'everyone's work will be manifest; for the day will reveal it, because it will be revealed by fire, and the fire will test everyone's work'.

V: 382

105 *rhyming words*: La Rochefoucauld is alluding to the game of *bouts-rimés*, in which the players had to invent verses ending with certain specified rhyme-words.

V: 387

One draft (Gilbert ms) reads: 'A fool lacks the strength to be either bad or good.' Compare Jeremiah 4: 22: 'they are foolish and senseless children; they are wise to do evil, but they do not have the knowledge to do good'.

V: 392

Compare Esprit, *Fausseté* 2: 13: 'if the wise man is fortunate, he has no reason to abandon his life; and if his life is unfortunate, he is obliged to bear it'.

V: 398

Compare L 209.

V: 410

Compare James 5: 20: 'the one who turns a sinner from the error of his way . . . will cover a multitude of sins'; Pierre Charron, *De la sagesse* 3: 9: 'frank and stimulating admonition . . . is the best office of friendship'.

V: 413

The thought is developed further in RD 2.

V: 414

One draft (Gilbert ms) reads: 'A stupid man sees things only in the light of his own temper, because he cannot see them with his intellect.'

V: 423

Compare La Rochefoucauld's letter dated 2 August 1675 to Madame de Sablé: 'Good sense and intelligence are fitting at any age, but that does not always apply to tastes; what is suitable at one time is unsuitable at another. That is what makes me think that few people know how to be old.'

V: 425

115 *divination*: one draft (Gilbert ms) reads 'prophecy'.

V: 430

The thought is developed further in RD 9.

V: 444

One draft (Gilbert ms) reads: 'There are more old fools than young ones.'

V: 451

'People with a great deal of wit are often very annoying' (RD 16).

v: 457

See the note on v: 199 (p. 296).

v: 466

125 *that harms women least*: the text and translation follow the *Nouvelles Réflexions*; v reads *qui sied le moins mal aux femmes* ('that is least unbecoming to women').

v: 473

RD 18 discusses the reasons, and says that 'ancient history does provide some examples' to the contrary.

v: 478

Compare Jeremiah 17: 9: 'The heart is more corrupt than all things, and is unsearchable; who can know it?'

v: 489

Compare John 16: 2: 'whoever kills you will think he is offering service to God'.

v: 502

Compare 1 Corinthians 1: 18–29: 'the world, by means of wisdom, did not know God . . . but God has chosen the foolish things of the world to confound the wise'.

v: 504

Compare 1: 285^1; L 207. Contrast Seneca, *Epistles* 30: 'philosophy . . . makes us joyful at the very sight of death'.

137 *When you are far away from it*: La Rochefoucauld applies even to the philosopher what Seneca, *Epistles* 82, says only of the unphilosophical man: that he cannot face the actual arrival of death, though he may have 'uttered many a brave boast' against it beforehand ('it was easy enough for [him] to defy evils that were not nearby').

Cato and Brutus: Marcus Porcius Cato the Younger (died 46 BCE) and Marcus Junius Brutus (died 42 BCE), Roman statesmen who committed suicide rather than submit to their conquerors. Compare Esprit, *Fausseté* 2: 13: Cato's suicide, imitated by Brutus, was due (among other things) to 'a desire to make his name famous; . . . those who kill themselves are dazzled by the greatness of their resolution, and . . . think that everyone will admire their strength of character'. La Rochefoucauld wrote to Esprit in an undated (1660?) letter: 'Send me the condemnation of Brutus; I must admit that until now I have sided with him against you.' Thus the point derives from Esprit and was initially resisted by La Rochefoucauld.

v: 504

137 *a lackey*: the incident was reported by Esprit to La Rochefoucauld, who
commented in a letter dated 17 August (year unspecified; 1660?) to Madame de Sablé: 'I think any gaiety in such a situation must strike you as
very suspect.'

Index to these *Moral Reflections*

The Index appeared in all five authorized editions. It was radically remodelled
for II, and further revisions were made for each subsequent edition; nevertheless, it was much less carefully proofread than any other part of the book, and
even its final state contained about twenty-five errors (many of which had been
carried over from previous editions).

   The following entries have been restored to their correct alphabetical position: *Accidents* (placed before *Accents du pays* in v), *Bonté* (placed before *Bon
sens* in v), *Imitation* and *Incommoder* (both placed after *Ingratitude* in v), *Maux*
(placed after *Médisance* in v), *Négociations* (placed after *Niais* in v), *Sentiments*
(placed after *Sagesse* in v). The positions of *Âges de la vie*, *Faiblesse*, and
Hypocrisie are not errors, but are due to the seventeenth-century spelling of
those words. Similarly, the treatment of I and J as one letter, and the listing of
Mépris de la mort after its principal word (*Mort*), follow common seventeenth-
century customs. In the entry for *Jalousie*, 32 (placed after 361 in v) has been
restored to its correct numerical position. We have made the following sub-
stantive emendations: *Amitié*, IV: 96 for 96 (i.e. v: 96); *Amour*, IV: 83 for 83;
Amour-propre, 417 and 418 transferred to *Amour*; *Déguisement*, 119 for 129;
Éloquence, IV: 258 for 258; *Fortune*, 25 for 15; *Fortune*, 323 for 329; *Jeunesse*,
109 for 110; *Inconstance*, 306 and 317 transferred to *Ingratitude*; *Mérite*, IV:
158 for 158; *Mort*, 504 for 302; *Naturel*, 431 for 413; *Persévérance*, 177 for 377;
Repos, II: 49 for 48; *Rois*, IV: 158 for 258; *Vieillesse*, 341 for 241. The citation of
410 under *Vertus* is presumably also an error, but the correct reading cannot
now be reconstructed (and of course v: 410, like almost all of the maxims, does
have *something* to say about virtues). Finally, 33 should perhaps be listed under
Orgueil; it was present in the Index to the first edition, and its subsequent
omission could easily have happened by accidentally deleting one item too
many when the Index was revised for II.

Note to the Reader

Compare 'The Publisher to the Reader', which stands in the analogous place
in the 1678 edition.

145 *in Holland*: a pirated edition of the maxims had been published in The
Hague by Jean and Daniel Steucker, late in 1663 or early in January 1664;
it contained many (no doubt unauthorized) editorial alterations.

   a letter: by the lawyer Henri de La Chapelle-Bessé (1625–94); it was
entitled 'Discours sur les *Réflexions ou Sentences et Maximes morales*'
('Essay on the *Moral Reflections or Sententiae and Maxims*'). A letter
dated 12 July 1664 shows that La Rochefoucauld was not entirely happy

with La Chapelle-Bessé's essay, but does not specify the particular points that made him uneasy.

various church fathers: La Chapelle-Bessé's essay states: 'Even church fathers . . . thought that the soul of the pagans' fine deeds consisted of self-love and pride. . . . The same church fathers . . . declared *that without the help of faith, all our virtues were imperfections, that our will was born blind, that its desires were blind, its conduct still more blind, and that we should not marvel if, amid so much blindness, man was continually going astray.* They spoke of this even more strongly, for they said that, in such a state, *human prudence could not penetrate the future or make any arrangements except in relation to pride, that its temperance moderated only the excesses that pride had condemned, that its constancy was maintained in times of misfortune only insofar as it was maintained by pride, and finally, that all its virtues, with the outward display of merit that earned admiration, had no other goal than such admiration, love of vainglory, and self-interested pride.* On this theme you would find almost infinite numbers of authorities.' The italicized passages do indeed paraphrase the teaching of many patristic and later theologians, but nothing in them is identifiable as a quotation from any one source, and no specific theologian is named anywhere in the essay (this is striking, because the essay does name—in some cases repeatedly—the non-theologians whose testimony it cites: Horace, Seneca, Tacitus, Tasso, Guarini, Montaigne, and Brébeuf).

I: I

First published in a *Recueil de pieces en prose les plus agréables de ce temps* (*Collection of the Most Enjoyable Contemporary Prose Pieces*, 1659), where it bore the title 'Portrait de l'amour-propre' ('Portrait of Self-Love') and the following dedication 'to Mademoiselle ***' (Anne d'Épernon, 1624–1701, a granddaughter of Henri IV with whom La Rochefoucauld had long been acquainted; she entered a Carmelite convent in 1648 despite vehement opposition from her family): 'Dear Mademoiselle, though you have treated me with the utmost contempt, and publicly declared yourself to be my enemy in the sight of all France, I shall not fail to offer you my portrait. I am driven to this by the memory of the tender friendship you once had for me. I cannot see that friendship extinguished without feeling the most intense grief, and my confusion is not reduced by the thought of all the pains I have unavailingly taken to rekindle it. Nevertheless, Mademoiselle, I am resolved never to grow weary, and to keep exerting all my arts; even if they are not capable of softening your obstinacy, I shall never lose heart; I shall never desert you, and I shall remain, until the very last moment of your life, Mademoiselle, your most humble obedient servant, SELF-LOVE.' The paragraphing of the English translation is that of the earliest known draft (L 94), which is partly in La Rochefoucauld's handwriting; the French text adopts the single-paragraph format of I: I. (So that French and English may run parallel despite the difference in paragraphing, in this edition the French text of this maxim is printed to a narrower measure than the English.)

The pervasiveness of self-love, and its blindness regarding itself, had been common themes since antiquity; compare, for example, Plato, *Laws* 731d–e: 'The worst of all evils, implanted in most people's souls, is one that they all excuse in themselves and make no effort to avoid. This is the evil expressed in the saying that everyone is naturally a lover of self, and that it is only right he should be so. In truth, however, this violent love of self causes all kinds of sins in every one of us. For love is blind when it looks at what it loves, so that a person is a bad judge of justice and goodness and honour, because he feels obliged always to value what matters to himself more highly than what is true.'

151   *because of a love for novelty*: Jean Lafond's emendation; all seventeenth-century texts read 'because of love, because of novelty' (*d'amour, de nouveauté*).

      those who wage war against it: the earliest known drafts read 'the pious folk who wage war against it'. Compare Esprit, *Fausseté* 2: 24: 'self-love . . . enters cunningly into the resolutions taken by its self-styled enemies, who fight against it daily and strive to destroy it; . . . the very person who crushes self-love is, at the same time, reviving it, because of the satisfaction he feels when he crushes it'.

      the harshest austerity: the earliest known drafts read 'the strictest piety'.

I: 13

Compare V: 44, 297; I: 305.

I: 33

In the earliest drafts, this maxim stands in the place previously occupied by a metaphorical presentation of the same idea (L 121). Compare Romans 2: 1, 21: 'You have no excuse, O every man who judges, because in judging someone else, you are condemning yourself, for you do the very things that you are judging. . . . You therefore who teach someone else, do you not teach yourself?'

I: 37

The earliest known draft (L 67) adds the word *enfin* ('finally'); this has been incorporated in the translation, as it helps to clarify the syntax in English.

I: 51

RD 16, written much later, takes the view that these two qualities are 'not always incompatible'—and indeed that the combination of them raises a mind 'infinitely above the others'. Compare V: 41.

I: 59

See the note on V: 49 (p. 290).

I: 60

The earliest known draft (L 184) adds the phrase *en effet* ('really'); this has been incorporated in the translation, as it helps to clarify the sense in English.

1: 70

Compare James 4: 13–15: 'you who say "Today or tomorrow we will go to such-and-such a city, and there we will spend a year and trade and make a profit", . . . you do not know what will happen tomorrow; . . . you should say, "If the Lord wills, and if we live, we shall do this or that" '; Seneca, *De providentia* 4: 3–5: 'no one knows his own capacities except by being tested; . . . how do I know how you would face poverty, if you are wallowing in wealth?'

1: 77

Virtually identical with Sablé, *Maximes* 79 (which ends '. . . to the body of the person it animates'). A well-known Latin epigram (fourth century CE or earlier) states: 'The soul is more fully present where it loves (*amat*) than where it lives (*animat*).'

1: 88

See the note on V: 78 (p. 291).

1: 89

The earliest known draft (L 110) reads: 'In judges who are good and act with moderation, justice is merely love of acclaim; in those who are ambitious, it is love of their own eminence.'

1: 99

Compare Montaigne, *Essais* 3: 1 (who cites Lucretius, *De rerum natura* 2: 1–2): 'even in the midst of our compassion we feel, deep within, an indescribable bittersweet speck of malign pleasure when we see someone else suffering'.

1: 101

Compare V: 88. The paragraphing of the English translation is that of the earliest known draft (L 107–8), which is in La Rochefoucauld's handwriting; the French text adopts the single-paragraph format of I: 101.

1: 103

In La Rochefoucauld's index, this maxim is listed under 'Perseverance in Wanting to Persuade'.

1: 104

159 *the Athenian madman*: Thrasyllos, who, until he was cured, 'believed that every ship entering the harbour was his' (V: 92; see p. 292).

1: 105

Compare Matthew 23: 5: those who are teaching the law of Moses 'do all their deeds to be seen by men'. For Seneca, see pp. xvi–xvii.

1: 134

Compare Montaigne, *Essais* 2: 12: 'Of what is the most refined folly composed, if not the most refined wisdom?'

1: 135

Compare Montaigne, *Essais* 2: 11: 'various virtues, such as chastity, sobriety, and temperance, may come to us by way of some physical failing'; Esprit, *Fausseté* 2: 3: temperance may be caused by 'inability to eat too much—which some people present as sobriety, thanks to the ingenuity with which man sometimes turns the failings of his mind and character into virtues'.

1: 138

Compare L 190.

1: 155–6

Subsequently combined and condensed as V: 150.

1: 159

The distinction between two kinds of anger, one more acceptable than the other, may be traced back to Ephesians 4: 26: 'be angry, and do not sin'. Compare Descartes, *Les Passions de l'âme* 3: 201–2: 'We can distinguish two kinds of anger: one that is very hasty and superficially obvious, though it has little result and may readily be appeased, and another that is not so immediately apparent, though it ravages the heart more severely and has more dangerous results. People who are very kind and loving are more subject to the former. . . . The people who allow themselves to be swept away by the latter kind of anger are those who are prouder, baser, and weaker.'

1: 174

The earliest known draft (L 176) reads: 'Few people are cruel simply out of cruelty, but all men are cruel and inhuman out of self-love.'

1: 176

The earliest known draft (L 45) reads: 'God alone makes people good; and what an Italian poet has said about women's virtue—"What is virtue but a talent for seeming virtuous?"—could be said about all our virtues.' The quotation is taken (inexactly) from Battista Guarini's famous play *Il pastor fido* (1590), 3: 5.

1: 201

Compare V: 189; Ecclesiastes 7: 21 (20): 'there is not a righteous man on earth who does good and never sins'.

1: 213

Compare V: 233; Montaigne, *Essais* 1: 3 (citing Augustine, *De civitate dei* 1: 12): 'the care over the funeral arrangements, the selection of the burial site,

and the pomp of the obsequies, are rather a comfort to the living than any benefit to the dead'.

I: 231

In the earliest known draft (L 67), this is the final sentence of the maxim that ultimately became V: 217.

I: 232

Compare Cicero, *Pro Marcello* 2: 6: 'bravery on the part of the soldiers, advantageous positions, support from allies, fleets, convoys, contribute greatly to a victory; above all, fortune claims the greatest share of the honour'.

163 *daughter*: the word has its Classical meaning, 'female descendant'; in Greek mythology (Hesiod, *Theogony* 384) the goddess Nike (Victory) was the great-granddaughter of Ouranos (Heaven).

I: 256

165 *disliked*: the earliest known drafts read 'liked' (a slip of the pen, or a remarkable instance of La Rochefoucauld reversing the sense of a maxim?).

I: 257

In I this sentence also appeared as the second half of I: 288, which became V: 265.

I: 259²

The first state of I: 259 had been an inadvertent duplicate of I: 135.

I: 260

The idea that 'truth is the basis of, and the reason for, beauty' derives from Esprit, to whom La Rochefoucauld initially confessed (in a letter dated 24 October 1660) that he found it hard to understand. Some of the implications are explored more fully in RD 1.

I: 284¹

Compare V: 261; these two maxims were listed separately in the Gilbert ms.

I: 285¹

The thought is developed further in V: 504.

167 *to secure the immortality of their names through the loss of their lives*: the earliest known draft (L 208) reads 'to perpetuate their reputations for all time'.

I: 290

Compare Proverbs 19: 15: 'laziness casts into a deep sleep'.

169 *remora*: echeneid fish, which attaches itself to sharks or other large fishes by means of a sucking disc on the top of its head; an ancient legend

(repeated by Montaigne, *Essais* 2: 12) maintained that if a remora attached itself to a ship, it could slow or even stop the ship's motion.

169 *which acts as a substitute for all good things*: the earliest known draft (L 253) reads 'which induces it to renounce all its pretensions'.

I: 293

Compare V: 1.

II: 49

Compare Seneca, *Epistles* 2: 'in my view, the first sign of a stable mind is the ability to stay in one place and remain in your own company'; 17: 'it matters little whether you lay a sick man on a wooden bed or a gold one, for wherever he goes, he takes his sickness with him'.

IV: 71

171 *inconstancy*: the earliest known draft (L 225) reads 'hard-heartedness'.

IV: 172

Compare V: epigraph.

IV: 183

La Rochefoucauld's contemporaries could hardly have read this without thinking of Louis XIV's conquests in the Netherlands. Compare Esprit, *Fausseté* 2: 14: 'an individual crime is punished, and a multitude of crimes is crowned with honour'; Augustine, *De civitate dei* 4: 4: 'when justice is taken away, what are kingdoms but immense thefts?'

IV: 234

Compare Esprit, *Fausseté* 1: 16: when our friends die 'we weep not because we have lost them, but because we have lost our own pleasures and advantages'.

IV: 258

See the note on V: 249 (p. 298).

IV: 272

Compare Sablé, *Maximes* 35: 'the ability to discern someone else's interior and hide one's own is a great mark of a superior mind'; 37: 'we nearly always become masters of those we know well, because someone who is fully known is, in a sense, subject to the person who knows him'.

IV: 375

175 *that in itself should be some compensation for them*: one draft (VIS: 40) reads 'they can always be forgiven'.

L 38

The last known drafts (e.g. SL 43) are more succinct: 'The great and the ambitious are more wretched than the lowly: it takes fewer things to please the

latter than the former.' Compare VIS: 4; 1 Timothy 6: 8–9: 'when we have food
and covering, with these we are content; for those who want to become rich
fall into temptation and the devil's snare and many worthless and harmful
desires, which drown people in destruction and perdition'; Philippians 4: 11–
12: 'I have learned to be content in whatever state I am; I know both how to be
brought low and how to have an abundance . . . both how to be full and how to
be hungry.'

L 62

Compare Seneca, *Epistles* 17: 'the fault is not in the wealth, but in the mind
itself'.

L 113

Compare V: 127.

L 121

Literally 'The world is full of coal shovels mocking fire pokers.' The expression 'a coal shovel mocking a fire poker' had become proverbial for 'a man
mocking another who would have equal reason to mock at him' (as the 1694
Académie *Dictionnaire* defined it). The maxim was later replaced by a non-
metaphorical presentation of the same idea, I: 33.

L 122

In some drafts this is the first sentence of the maxim that ultimately became V:
106; in others it stands on its own.

L 190

Part of the thought later appears in I: 138.

L 207

The theme was later elaborated in V: 504.

L 209

Compare V: 398.

L 212

Compare Sablé, *Maximes* 47: 'it is very vain and useless to study everything
that happens in the world if our study does not help us to improve ourselves';
73: 'self-love makes us . . . criticize the very failings that we never correct'.

L 245

Compare John 3: 20–1: 'everyone who does evil hates the light, and does not
come to the light, lest his deeds should be rebuked; but the person who does
the truth comes to the light, so that his deeds may be exposed'.

L 249

Compare V: 243.

L 256

183 *original sin*: the sin committed by Adam and Eve in the garden of Eden (Genesis 3: 1–24).

PVI24: 4

Compare V: 146.

VI S: 3

Compare I: 1: self-love 'sometimes joins forces with the harshest austerity' (in early drafts 'the severest piety'), 'in whose society it sets out boldly to destroy itself'; Matthew 6: 16–18: 'the hypocrites disfigure their faces, so that they may be seen by men to be fasting; . . . but when you fast, anoint your head and wash your face, so that you may not be seen by men to be fasting'.

VI S: 5

Compare Seneca, *De constantia* 5: 5: 'the wise man can lose nothing that he can regard as a loss, for his only possession is virtue, and he can never be robbed of that'.

VI S: 15

Compare the protagonist of Madame de La Fayette's *La Princesse de Clèves* (no doubt known to La Rochefoucauld at the time when this maxim was written), whose 'strict virtue' (*austère vertu*) conflicts irreconcilably with her love for the Duc de Nemours. If she had the virtue without the love, or the love without the virtue, there would be less to pity in her condition.

VI S: 18

Compare Matthew 13: 12: 'the person who has, to him shall more be given, and he shall have an abundance; but the person who does not have, from him shall be taken away even what he has'.

VI S: 21

Compare V: 368. The image is drawn from Proverbs 31: 10: 'Who can find a virtuous woman? She is more precious than what comes from the ends of the earth.'

VI S: 28

Compare V: 371.

VI S: 37

Compare V: 352.

RD 1. Truth

See the note on 1: 260 (p. 309).

Textual variants: ¶1 *en tant* 325*bis* Ch *et tant* A(163)*B comme aussi, tant* A(163)*G* | *et le peintre, etc.* 325*bis* Ch *et le peintre.* A(163)*B le peintre, etc., etc.* A(163)*G* | ¶3 *le degré de cruauté exercée* A(163)*BG le degré de cruauté exercé* 325*bis* Ch ¶4 *l'une l'autre:* 325*bis* Ch *l'une par l'autre:* A(163)*BG* | *bien qu'il y ait* A(163)*B* 325*bis* Ch *bien qu'il ait* A(163)*G* |

193 *Scipio and Hannibal, Fabius Maximus and Marcellus*: famous military leaders during the Second Punic War. Scipio Africanus the Elder (died 183 BCE), Fabius Maximus Cunctator (died 203 BCE), and Marcus Claudius Marcellus (died 208 BCE) were rival generals on the Roman side, Hannibal (died 182 BCE) on the Carthaginian side.

Alexander and Caesar: the Macedonian emperor Alexander the Great (died 323 BCE) and the Roman dictator Julius Caesar (died 44 BCE), conquerors and empire builders.

the widow: praised by Jesus for giving a tiny amount of money to the temple treasury: 'this poor widow contributed more than all those who contributed to the treasury; for they all contributed out of their abundance, but she, out of her deprivation, contributed all that she had, her whole living' (Mark 12: 41–4).

Epaminondas: Greek general (died 362 BCE), admired in ancient times for his military strategies, for his services to his native city (Thebes), and for his personal integrity; Esprit, *Fausseté* 2: 4, describes him as 'the pupil of [the Pythagorean philosopher] Lysis, the intimate friend of Plato, and the imitator of Socrates'.

Virgil: the Roman poet Publius Vergilius Maro (died 19 BCE), author of the *Aeneid*.

the boy: Quintilian, *Institutio oratoria* 5: 9: 13, states that he was sentenced to death by the Areopagus for his cruelty in blinding quail.

Philip II: Philip II of Spain (1527–98) ordered the imprisonment of his son Don Carlos in 1568, and was widely held responsible when the prince died in prison a few months later; 'many other vices' alludes to his general reputation for extreme despotism, inflexibility, religious intolerance, and sexual licentiousness.

195 *Chantilly*: château 42 km north of Paris, the residence of La Rochefoucauld's leader Louis II de Bourbon, Prince de Condé (1621–86); it was last visited by La Rochefoucauld in 1673.

Liancourt: château 65 km north of Paris; in 1659 its heiress, Jeanne-Charlotte du Plessis, married La Rochefoucauld's eldest son, François (VII).

RD 2. Social Contact

Textual variants: ¶2 *de celui des autres,* A(163)*G* Gr Br *et celui des autres,* 325*bis* Ch | ¶3 *leur faire apercevoir* A(163)*G* Gr Br *les faire apercevoir* 325*bis* Ch | ¶4 *se divertir ensemble,* A(163)*B* 325*bis* Ch *pour se divertir ensemble,* A(163)*G* *et pour se divertir ensemble,* Gr Br | ¶5 *il faut souvent* 325*bis* Ch Gr Br *il faut surtout*

A(163)^G | *et on doit* 325bis Ch *on doit* Gr Br *et l'on doit* A(163)^G | ¶8 *ne peuvent pas plaire* A(163)^G Gr Br *ne peuvent plaire* 325bis Ch | ¶9 *beaucoup de mesure:* A(163)^G Gr Br *beaucoup de mesures:* 325bis Ch |

199 *a specific point of view from which he wants to be considered:* see V: 104.

RD 3. Manners and Ways of Behaving

Textual variants: ¶2 *leur a données,* 325bis Ch *leur a donnés,* A(163)^G Gr Br | *cette imitation* 325bis Ch Gr Br *toute imitation* A(163)^G | ¶3 *nos propres qualités* 325bis Ch Gr Br *nos qualités naturelles* A(163)^G | ¶4 *au-dessus de nous* 325bis Ch Gr Br *qui sont au-dessus de nous* A(163)^G | ¶6 *Combien de lieutenants généraux apprennent à paraître maréchaux de France! Combien de gens de robe répètent inutilement l'air de chancelier, et combien de bourgeoises se donnent l'air de duchesses!* A(163)^G [these sentences are omitted by 325bis and Ch; A(163)^B, Gr, and Br include them, but read *être* for *paraître*] |

201 *copies are never good:* see V: 133.

RD 4. Conversation

Compare V: 139. 'One who restricts his words is learned . . . even a fool, if he keeps silent, is considered wise' (Proverbs 17: 27–8); 'let every person be swift to hear, but slow to speak and slow to anger' (James 1: 19). Most of this reflection has parallels in many previous writers, e.g. Pierre Charron, *De la sagesse* 2: 9, who gives the general advice 'to see and hear much, to say little, to judge everything'.

In RD 4 only, Br prints a substantially different text of uncertain origin; in the following list its readings are cited only at points where A(163) and 325bis differ. Textual variants: ¶1 *c'est plutôt par choix qu'on le loue* A(163)^G Br *c'est plus par choix qu'on le loue* 325bis *c'est plus par choix qu'on les loue* Ch Gr | *des questions, qui sont presque toujours inutiles,* A(163)^G *des questions,* Br *des questions inutiles,* 325bis Ch Gr | ¶5 *à savoir parler à propos, il n'y en a pas moins à savoir se taire.* A(163)^G Br *à parler, il n'y en a pas moins à se taire.* 325bis Ch Gr | *il y a enfin des airs, des tons* A(163)^G *il y a enfin des tons, des airs* Br *il y a des airs, des tours* 325bis Ch Gr |

RD 5. Confiding

Textual variants: ¶2 *mais je sais bien* A(163)^G *je sais bien* 325bis Ch Gr Br | ¶3 *on s'acquitte envers ceux-ci* A(163)^G *on s'acquitte avec ceux-ci* 325bis Ch Gr Br | *confidences.* A(163)^G Gr Br *confiances.* 325bis Ch | *ne leur cacher rien* A(163)^G *ne leur rien cacher* 325bis Ch Gr Br | *toujours vrais,* A(163)^G Gr Br *toujours vrai,* 325bis Ch | *demi-confidences,* A(163)^G Gr Br *demies confiances;* 325bis Ch | *qui embarrassent* A(163)^G *elles embarrassent* 325bis Ch Gr Br | *et on augmente* A(163)^G *on augmente* 325bis Ch Gr Br | *commencé à parler.* A(163)^G Gr Br *commencé de parler.* 325bis Ch | ¶4 *que nous-mêmes* A(163)^G Gr Br *que nous-même* 325bis Ch | *de les révéler* A(163)^G *de le révéler* 325bis Gr Br *de révéler* Ch | ¶5 *et qu'ils ont peut-être quelque intérêt de* A(163)^G *ils ont peut-être même quelque intérêt de la* 325bis Ch Gr Br | *on se voit cependant* A(163)^G *on se voit* 325bis Ch Gr Br |

est indispensablement de conserver le dépôt A(163)^G *est de conserver indispensablement ce dépôt* 325bis Ch Gr Br |

207 *a form of open-heartedness*: see V: 62.

RD 6. Love and the Sea

'The sea is a tangible image of' self-love (1: 1).

RD 7. Examples

Compare Esprit, *Fausseté* 2: 14, speaking of Caesar: 'if the oppression of Rome, the ruin of his homeland Italy, and the fire with which he burned the whole world, were the results of his magnanimity, we should exhort men to flee virtue just as diligently as we inspire them with a horror of vice'.

Textual variants: *philosophes importuns,* A(163)^{BG} Ch *philosophes importans,* 325bis | *neutres et paresseux* A(163)^{2BG} 325bis Ch *neutres et ennuyeux* A(163)^{1BG} |

213 *Tiberius and Nero*: Roman emperors (died 37 CE and 68 CE respectively); in citing them as examples of exorbitant vice, La Rochefoucauld is following a tradition that goes back at least as far as Tacitus.

   Alexander . . . Caesar: Alexander the Great (died 323 BCE), Macedonian conqueror of the Persian empire and ruler of the civilized world; Julius Caesar (died 44 BCE), Roman general who seized supreme power and ruled as dictator.

   Diogenes . . . Cato: Diogenes of Sinope (died 323 BCE), Cynic philosopher; Marcus Tullius Cicero (died 43 BCE), Roman orator; Titus Pomponius Atticus (died 32 BCE), Roman Epicurean who refused to align himself with any political faction; Gaius Marius (died 86 BCE) and Lucius Cornelius Sylla (died 78 BCE), opposed Roman generals during the civil war of 88–86 BCE (both were regarded at the time as exceptionally brutal in taking revenge); Lucius Licinius Lucullus (died 56 BCE), Roman general famous for his love of luxury and extravagance; the Athenian Alcibiades (died 404 BCE) and the Roman Mark Antony (died 30 BCE), dissipated and intemperate generals. As in RD 14, 'Cato' is no doubt Marcus Porcius Cato the Younger (died 46 BCE), noted for his integrity and his intransigent commitment to the ancient Roman mores.

RD 8. The Uncertainty of Jealousy

Textual variants: ¶1 *et on ne la conduit* A(163)^{BG} Ch *et ne la conduit* 325bis | ¶2 *on s'efforce* A(163)^{BG} Ch *et on s'efforce* 325bis | *On n'est pas assez heureux* A(163)^{BG} Ch *On est pas assez heureux* 325bis | *ce qu'on souhaite,* A(163)^B 325bis Ch *ce que l'on souhaite,* A(163)^G |

213 *Sisyphus*: in Classical mythology, Sisyphus was condemned to roll perpetually up a mountain a rock that perpetually rolled down again.

RD 9. Love and Life

Textual variants: ¶2 *une partie de nous-mêmes;* A(163)^{BG} Ch *une partie de nous-même;* 325bis | *nous ne sommes plus sensibles* A(163)^{BG} Ch *nous ne sommes plus sensible* 325bis |

RD 10. Taste

Textual variants: TITLE *Du Goût* A(163)^G *Des Goûts* 325bis Ch Gr Br | ¶1 *mais il y a* A(163)^G *il y a* 325bis Ch Gr Br | ¶3 *par légèreté* A(163)^G Ch Gr Br *par la légèreté* 325bis | ¶5 *qui sait donner* A(163)^G Ch Gr Br *qui fait donner* 325bis | *la trouble* 325bis Ch Gr Br *le trouble* A(163)^G | *à nous paraît* A(163)^G Gr Br *à nous nous paraît* 325bis Ch |

RD 11. The Relationship Between Men and Animals

Many of La Rochefoucauld's comparisons go back as far as the Scriptures (lions and bears, Proverbs 28: 15; wolves and sheep, John 10: 12; dogs and swine, Proverbs 26: 11; foxes, Ezekiel 13: 4; eagles, Jeremiah 49: 16; doves, Hosea 7: 11; snakes, Psalms 57: 5 (58: 4)); many of them are developed in the *Fables* of La Rochefoucauld's admirer La Fontaine (see especially 10: 15, published in 1678 and dedicated to La Rochefoucauld: 'man . . . behaves, on thousands of occasions, like animals').

Textual variants: ¶1 *quelque apparence* A(163)^{BG} Ch *quelques apparences* 325bis | ¶2 *qui n'ont de qualités* A(163)^{BG} *qui n'ont de qualité* 325bis Ch | *il y a même des chiens de jardinier.* A(163)^{BG} *et il y a même des chiens de jardinier.* 325bis Ch | ¶3 *et par leurs couleurs.* A(163)^{BG} *ou par leurs couleurs.* 325bis *ou par leur couleur.* Ch | *que de rapines;* A(163)^{BG} *que de rapine;* 325bis Ch | ¶4 *et rassurent* A(163)^B 325bis Ch *et se rassurent* A(163)^G | *d'un bout du monde à l'autre,* A(163)^B 325bis Ch *d'un monde à l'autre,* A(163)^G | *le feu qui les brûle!* A(163)^{BG} Ch *le feu qui les brûlent!* 325bis | *de leurs plaintes!* A(163)^{BG} Ch *de leur plainte!* 325bis |

221 *their other parts have their uses*: in La Rochefoucauld's circle they were widely used for medicinal purposes, notably by Madame de Sablé and Madame de La Fayette. La Rochefoucauld refers to the practice in two undated letters to Madame de Sablé.

RD 12. The Origin of Illnesses

'If you do not keep and perform all the words of this law . . . the Lord will increase your plagues: . . . great and lasting plagues, grievous and perpetual illnesses' (Deuteronomy 28: 58–9). The idea that all bodily ills had spiritual or psychological causes was promoted in the Renaissance by such works as Miguel or Oliva Sabuco, *Nueva filosofía de la naturaleza del hombre* (1587); La Rochefoucauld's essay can also be read as a reply to the Stoic doctrine that 'ill health injures your body, but not your soul' (Seneca, *Epistles* 78).

223 *The Golden Age*: Classical mythology (Ovid, *Metamorphoses* 1: 89–150) distinguished four successive ages, declining in moral character.

RD 13. Falsehood

Textual variants: ¶1 *il y en a enfin* A(163)^G *et il y en a* 325bis Ch Gr Br | ¶2 *notre amour-propre est flatté* A(163)^G Ch Gr Br *notre amour-propre est flattée* 325bis | *plusieurs sortes de bien* A(163)^G *plusieurs sortes de biens* 325bis Ch Gr Br | ¶3 *par leur raison;* A(163)^G *par raison;* 325bis Ch Gr Br | ¶4 *en des qualités* A(163)^G *par des qualités* 325bis Ch Gr Br | *certaines sciences ne lui convient* A(163)^G Ch Gr Br *certaines sciences ne lui conviennent* 325bis | ¶5 *et déterminent* A(163)^G *et qu'elles*

déterminent 325bis Ch Gr Br | *et qu'il nous convient* A(163)^G Gr Br *et qui nous convient* 325bis Ch | *mais tous les hommes presque* A(163)^G Ch *mais presque tous les hommes* 325bis Gr Br | ¶6 *qui ne voulut disputer du prix* 325bis Ch *qui ne voulait disputer le prix* A(163)^B [A(163)^G prints *voulait* and cites ^{B} as reading *voulut*— evidently an accidental transposition, since ^{G} could have found *voulut* only in its own copytext; this paragraph is omitted by Gr Br] | *dessein. Le désir* A(163)^B 325bis Ch *dessein, et le désir* A(163)^G |

225   *our qualities are indeterminate*: see V: 470.

227   *Alexander*: Alexander the Great (died 323 BCE); the story that he was willing to compete in the Olympic footrace only 'if I could have kings as my competitors' derives from Plutarch, *Alexander* 4.

RD 14. Models Produced by Nature and Fortune

Compare V: 153. The accounts of Alexander the Great, Julius Caesar, and Cato the Younger are drawn, directly or indirectly, from Plutarch's parallel *Lives*, though La Rochefoucauld stresses carefully that he is not adopting Plutarch's procedure: 'my plan here is not to place them in parallel'.

Textual variants: ¶3 *Elle le fait naître* A(163)^B 325bis Ch *Elles le font naître* A(163)^G | *qu'elle eût jamais produits;* A(163)^G *qu'elle eût jamais produit;* 325bis Ch *qu'elle ait jamais produits;* A(163)^B | *la fortune choisit parmi eux* A(163)^B 325bis Ch *la fortune même choisit parmi eux* A(163)^G | ¶4 *si on l'ose dire* 325bis Ch *si l'on ose dire même* A(163)^{BG} | ¶5 *se montrer même toujours plus grands* A(163)^B Ch *se montrer toujours plus grands* 325bis *se montrer toujours plus grands, même* A(163)^G | *soutenu de sa propre gloire? Et brille-t-il* A(163)^B 325bis Ch *et soutenu de sa propre gloire? Brille-t-il* A(163)^G |

229   *Alexander*: Alexander the Great (died 323 BCE) was educated by Aristotle and inherited a powerful kingdom from his father, Philip II of Macedon; within ten years he conquered the vastly superior forces of the Persian empire. At his death, his lands were divided among his generals. His physical appearance was used as a model by many later Hellenistic and Roman sculptors.

Caesar: Julius Caesar (died 44 BCE), Roman general, rose to a position of supreme power, at first in association with Pompey, and later by opposition to him; after Pompey's death (48 BCE) Caesar ruled as dictator in Rome, until he was assassinated at a time when Antony and others were proposing to have him crowned king.

231   *a man who owed his existence to him*: Marcus Junius Brutus (died 42 BCE), whom Caesar believed to be his son (Plutarch, *Brutus* 5).

Cato: Marcus Porcius Cato the Younger (died 46 BCE), a staunch opponent of Caesar. He was famous for the austerity of his life and for his commitment to the ancient Roman virtues; when the republican cause was finally lost, he committed suicide.

233   *the Prince and Monsieur de Turenne*: Louis II de Bourbon, Prince de Condé (1621–86), and Henri de La Tour d'Auvergne, Vicomte de Turenne (1611–75), the most famous French military leaders of the cen-

tury. On 27 July 1675 Turenne was killed abruptly at Sasbach, in battle against the Holy Roman Empire, and the French troops withdrew inconclusively at the news of his death; Condé, who suffered severely from gout, retired later that year.

RD 15. Flirts and Old Men

Textual variants: ¶1 *dans leur misère*, A(163)^B 325^*bis* Ch *dans leurs misères*, A(163)^G | *il gagne croyance* A(163)^B 325^*bis* Ch *il gagne créance* A(163)^G | *des faveurs, plus il est* A(163)^G *de faveurs, plus il est* A(163)^B *des faveurs, et plus il est* 325^*bis* Ch | ¶2 *Je ne sais si* A(163)^BG *Je ne sais même si* 325^*bis* Ch |

235 *Amadis*: the popular Spanish romance of medieval chivalry *Amadis de Gaule* (published 1508).

RD 16. Different Types of Mind

Textual variants: ¶2 *sait éviter* A(163)^G Ch Gr Br *fait éviter* 325^*bis* | *et il établit* A(163)^G *et établit* 325^*bis* Ch Gr Br | ¶11 *les manières de dire ne se peuvent* A(163)^G *les manières ne se peuvent* 325^*bis* Ch Gr Br | ¶13 *n'en marquer aucune* A(163)^G Gr Br *n'en marquer aucunes* 325^*bis* Ch | ¶14 *enfin il y en a d'autres* A(163)^G *il y en a d'autres* 325^*bis* Ch Gr Br | *et tant de grâce,* A(163)^G Gr Br *et tant de grâces,* 325^*bis* Ch |

239 *Jocularity is a spirit of gaiety*: the thought is developed further in the pirated Dutch edition of the *Maxims* (paragraphs 152–5, pp. 284–5).

241 *You can be foolish with a great deal of wit*: 'with intelligence, but not with judgement' (V: 456).

RD 17. Occurrences of the Present Age

Extraordinary reversals of fortune have always been a favourite subject of moral reflection. Compare Ecclesiastes 9: 11: 'the race is not to the swift, nor the battle to the strong, ... but time and chance are in everything'; Seneca, *Thyestes* 613–14: 'whom the sunrise saw exalted in pride, the sunset has seen laid low'; Sirach 11: 5–6: 'the unexpected man has worn a crown; many mighty men have been brought very low, and those who were glorious have been delivered into the hand of others'.

Textual variants: ¶2 *plusieurs années.* A(163)^B 325^*bis* Ch *pendant plusieurs années.* A(163)^G | *Henri IV* A(163)^BG *Henri IVe* 325^*bis* Ch | *par la troupe* A(163)^BG *par la haine* 325^*bis* Ch | ¶3 *tant d'avantages* A(163)^BG Ch *tant d'avantage* 325^*bis* | ¶5 *le plus fort de ses soupçons* A(163)^2BG 325^*bis* Ch *le plus fort de ses défiances* A(163)^1BG | ¶6 *On doit sans doute ... lui avaient présentés.* 325^*bis* [the paragraph is omitted by A(163)^BG and Ch] | ¶7 *jeune, sans biens* A(163)^BG Ch *jeune, sans bien* 325^*bis* | ¶9 *son royaume* A(163)^2BG 325^*bis* Ch *ses États* A(163)^1BG | ¶11 *leur roi légitime,* A(163)^B 325^*bis* Ch *leurs rois légitimes,* A(163)^G | ¶14 *depuis six ans* A(163)^B 325^*bis* Ch *pendant six ans* A(163)^G | *absolu de l'Angleterre* A(163)^BG *absolu d'Angleterre* 325^*bis* Ch | *dans le temps* A(163)^B 325^*bis* Ch *dans le temps même* A(163)^G | ¶15 *l'alliance de l'Angleterre,* A(163)^BG *l'alliance d'Angleterre,* 325^*bis* Ch | *tant de puissances* A(163)^BG Ch *tant de puissance* 325^*bis* | *la protection d'Angleterre;* A(163)^B 325^*bis* Ch *la protection de l'Angleterre;* A(163)^G |

The long paragraph on Mademoiselle (¶6), found only in 325*bis*, is stylistic-ally and thematically distinct from the rest of the essay, and is clearly a later interpolation. Perhaps La Rochefoucauld added it himself; perhaps he com-posed it as a separate prose piece (like RDA 1–4), but a subsequent copyist felt that it could suitably be inserted here. In the present volume, it is therefore enclosed in square brackets.

In 325*bis* (following a manuscript suggestion written in A(163) by an unknown hand) this essay stands at the end of the *Réflexions diverses*. Editions based on 325*bis* therefore number it RD 19.

243 *Marie de Médicis*: (1573–1642), second wife of Henri IV of France; their four children were Louis XIII, Gaston, Duke of Orléans, Elisabeth, the wife of Philip IV of Spain, and Henrietta Maria, the wife of Charles I of England. After the assassination of Henri IV in 1610, Marie was effect-ively the ruler of France, but her son Louis XIII gradually gained power; Cardinal Richelieu, previously her chief adviser, became Louis's chief minister in 1624 and supported his struggle against her. Marie fled to Brussels in 1631 and remained in exile for the rest of her life.

245 *Ange de Joyeuse*: Henri de Joyeuse (1567–1608), who became a Capuchin in 1587, adopting the name of Father Ange, but left the monastery when he inherited a dukedom in 1592. He fought against Henri IV until 1596 (La Rochefoucauld may be partly confusing him with his brother Anne, the previous duke, who had fought for Henri III against the Huguenots), resumed monastic life in 1599, and died on a barefoot pilgrimage to Rome.

the revolt of Portugal: in 1640, establishing its independence from Spain; the 'Indian dependencies' included territory in the New World (Brazil) as well as the Old. The Spanish regent, Margaret of Savoy, Duchess of Mantua (1589–1655), was overthrown, and her secretary of state, Miguel de Vasconcelos (1600–40), was killed. João IV (1603–56), previously Duke of Braganza, was appointed king; the rebellion is said to have been led primarily by his wife Luiza de Guzman, her adviser João Pinto Ribeiro, and the Archbishop of Lisbon, Rodrigo da Cunha.

Richelieu: Armand Jean du Plessis, Cardinal Richelieu (1583–1642), the most powerful man in France; chief minister under Louis XIII from 1624 until his death. His protégé Henri Coiffier de Ruzé, Marquis de Cinq-Mars (1620–42), became the royal favourite in 1639, but was exe-cuted after leading an unsuccessful conspiracy against Richelieu three years later.

247 *Anne-Marie-Louise d'Orléans*: the Duchesse de Montpensier (1627–93), known as La Grande Mademoiselle; a granddaughter of Henri IV. Her wedding with Antonin, Marquis de Puyguilhem and Comte (later Duc) de Lauzun (1633–1723), was fixed for 20 December 1670, but it was opposed by Monsieur (the King's brother), Condé ('the Prince'), the King's mistress Madame de Montespan, the intending bride's step-mother Marguerite de Lorraine ('the Dowager Duchess'), and many

others; on 18 December it was forbidden by Louis XIV. In November 1671 Lauzun was imprisoned at Pignerol near Turin, a fortress then used for important political prisoners (including the so-called Man in the Iron Mask). He was not released until April 1681, after La Rochefoucauld's death.

253 *Afonso VI*: (1643–83), son of João IV; he married Marie-Françoise of Savoy (1646–83) in 1666. A year later he was banished to the Azores, the marriage was annulled on the grounds of impotence, and his wife married his brother Pedro (1648–1706, the future Pedro II), who then acted as regent.

Masaniello: the fisherman Tomaso Aniello (died 1647), who led an insurrection against a new fruit tax in Naples. The rebellion was successful, but Masaniello soon became mentally disturbed (possibly as a result of poison) and was assassinated.

The Queen of Sweden: Christina (1626–89), who abdicated in 1654 and thereafter lived in exile. La Rochefoucauld was personally acquainted with her; during the early 1670s, she read and annotated his *Maxims*.

The King of Poland: Jan Kazimierz (1609–72), who abdicated in 1668 after the death of his wife and entered a monastery in France.

An infantry lieutenant: Oliver Cromwell (1599–1658), who led the forces of parliament against Charles I (1600–49) and effectively ruled England from 1646 until his death.

255 *The Dutch shook off . . . Spanish domination*: a process essentially completed by the Union of Utrecht in 1579.

the current Prince of Orange: Willem III (1650–1702, subsequently William III of England), who was appointed stadtholder and captain-general, with greater powers than any of his predecessors, in 1672; in the same year the grand pensionary Jan de Witt (1625–72), who had endeavoured to limit the power of the princes of Orange, was murdered by a rioting mob of William's supporters. During the next few years, forces under William's leadership were defeated several times by the French, notably at Seneffe (1673), Saint-Omer (January 1677), and Cassel (April 1677).

maintained by Dutch protection: between 1672 and 1678 French forces were fighting against an alliance of Spanish, Dutch, and other troops; the Dutch were France's strongest opponents during these wars.

An Emperor: the Holy Roman Emperor Leopold I (1640–1705), a long-term opponent of Louis XIV (Leopold's forces were prominent allies of the Dutch during the wars of 1672–8), is here compared with his most illustrious predecessor, Charles V (1500–58).

The King of England: Charles II (1630–85), who formed a secret alliance with Louis XIV in 1670 and attempted to assist him in the Netherlands, but was forced by Parliament to make peace with the Dutch in 1674; he finally abandoned his alliance with Louis in 1677. Thus England did not take part in the Treaties of Nijmegen (1678).

257 *his niece*: Mary (the future Mary II of England; 1662–94), who married William of Orange in 1677. The union was initially opposed both by her father (the future James II) and by her uncle Charles II, but was negotiated by the Lord Treasurer, Thomas Osborne, Earl of Danby (the future Duke of Leeds; 1631–1712), in the vain hope that it might stop parliament from attacking him because of his equivocal French policies.

259 *Heliogabalian licentiousness . . . parricides?*: the profligacy of the Roman emperor Heliogabalus (died 222 CE) became proverbial in his own century; the Greeks' reputation for dishonesty derives from Roman sources, such as Virgil, *Aeneid* 2. 49 (a warning to 'beware of Greeks even when they bear gifts'); in tragedies by Euripides, Seneca, and Corneille, the sorceress Medea kills her children and (by means of a poisoned robe) her lover's new bride. La Rochefoucauld's wording would have reminded his contemporaries of the Marquise de Brinvilliers, executed in 1676 for poisoning her father and brothers.

RD 18. Inconstancy

Textual variants: ¶1 *fleur d'agrément* A(163)^BG *fleur d'agréments* 325bis Ch | *ses engagements* A(163)^BG Ch *les engagements* 325bis | ¶2 *La constance perdrait* A(163)^B 325bis Ch *mais la constance perdrait* A(163)^G | *les faveurs premières* A(163)^BG *les premières faveurs* 325bis Ch | *elle ne pardonne rien;* A(163)^B 325bis Ch *et ne pardonner rien;* A(163)^G |
Editions based on 325bis number this piece RD 17.

261 *some examples of that*: Plutarch, *De amicorum multitudine*, lists Orestes and Pylades, Pythias and Damon, Theseus and Pirithous, Achilles and Patroclus, Epaminondas and Pelopidas; contrast Esprit, *Fausseté* 1: 4, who critically examines the first two pairs in particular.

RD 19. Retirement

Textual variants: *il ne peut plus être flatté* A(163)^B 325bis Ch *ils ne peuvent plus être flattés* A(163)^G | *trouvé de véritables,* A(163)^B 325bis Ch *trouvé de véritable,* A(163)^G | *aux premiers biens qui ont* A(163)^G Ch *au premier bien qui ont* A(163)^B 325bis | *et de faiblesses, tantôt par piété,* A(163)^G Ch *et de faiblesse, tantôt par piété,* A(163)^B *et de faiblesse, tantôt par pitié,* 325bis |
Editions based on 325bis number this piece RD 18.

RDA 1. Portrait of Madame de Montespan

Françoise-Athénaïs de Rochechouart-Mortemart (1640–1707) married the Marquis de Montespan in 1663 and became the mistress of Louis XIV in 1667, gradually displacing Louise de La Vallière (1644–1710) in his affections.

267 *Diane*: a slip of the pen natural in this context; Diane was the first name of Madame de Montespan's mother, the Duchesse de Mortemart.

the Queen: Maria Theresa of Spain (1638–83), who had married Louis in 1660.

RDA 1.

267 *Madame de Montausier*: Julie d'Angennes (1607–71), who became maid of honour in 1664.

her pregnancies: Madame de Montespan had at least seven children by Louis between 1669 and 1678.

a Carmelite nun: Louise de La Vallière became a Carmelite in 1675.

RDA 2. Portrait of Cardinal de Retz

Written early in June 1675 (the date is established both by internal evidence and by the testimony of La Rochefoucauld's contemporaries). Jean-François-Paul de Gondi (1614–79) became Cardinal de Retz in 1651; he played an active role in the civil wars of the Fronde, opposing both Mazarin and Condé. La Rochefoucauld was 'not his most intimate friend' (as Madame de Sévigné put it in a letter of 16 June 1675) and had nearly killed him during a confrontation on 21 August 1651. Retz was shown this portrait (probably in a diluted form) in 1675, and retaliated by composing a hostile portrait of La Rochefoucauld.

269 *Mazarin*: Jules, Cardinal Mazarin (1602–61), chief minister under Louis XIV from 1642 to his death.

his own boldness: Retz was imprisoned at Vincennes in 1652 because of his opposition to Mazarin; he escaped two years later.

the archbishopric of Paris: Retz became Archbishop of Paris in 1654, but resigned the position in 1662.

various conclaves: Retz participated in four papal conclaves between 1655 and 1676 (in the last, he even received eight votes himself).

271 *His recent retirement*: at the time when La Rochefoucauld wrote, Retz was attempting to resign his cardinalship and enter a monastery; however, the Pope opposed this plan. Compare RD 19: old people 'forget the world, which is so ready to forget them'.

RDA 3. Remarks on the Early Stages of Cardinal Richelieu's Life

Armand Jean du Plessis (1585–1642) became Bishop of Luçon in 1607 and Cardinal Richelieu in 1622. He allied himself closely with Louis XIII's chief minister Concino Concini (the Maréchal d'Ancre) and the queen mother Marie de Médicis. In April 1617, with the King's approval, Charles, Duc de Luynes (1578–1621), arranged for Concini to be assassinated; the Queen Mother was exiled to Blois, where Richelieu joined her. During the next few years he gradually gained favour with the king, becoming chief minister in 1624.

271 *the Bishop of Nevers*: Eustache du Lys (died 1643).

Father Joseph: the Capuchin friar François Leclerc du Tremblay (1577–1638), who became Richelieu's principal confidant.

Déageant: Guichard Déageant de Saint-Marcellin (1574–1645), a counsellor of the Queen Mother and confidant of the Duc de Luynes.

273 *Monsieur de Villeroy and President Jeannin*: two senior politicians: the secretary of state Nicolas de Neufville, Seigneur de Villeroy (1542–1617),

and Pierre Jeannin (1540–1622), formerly president of the Parliament of Dijon.

Pont-de-Cé: the forces of Louis XIII defeated those of the Queen Mother at Pont-de-Cé on 7 August 1620; Richelieu's role in this episode remains unclear.

RDA 4. Comte d'Harcourt

Henri de Lorraine, Comte d'Harcourt (1601–66), fought against Spain and Savoy between 1637 and 1645, gaining the victories listed by La Rochefoucauld. During the Fronde he supported Louis XIV, fighting against Condé and La Rochefoucauld.

The manuscript was untitled. The current title was supplied by Adolphe Régnier when the piece was first published in 1883.

275 *whatever currency she pleases*: compare IV: 158.

the Prince and Monsieur de Turenne: Louis II de Bourbon, Prince de Condé (1621–86), and Henri de La Tour d'Auvergne, Vicomte de Turenne (1611–75), the most famous French military leaders of the century.

Portrait of Monsieur R——d, by Himself

Written 1656–8; first published in a *Recueil des portraits et éloges en vers et en prose* (*Collection of Prose and Verse Portraits and Eulogies*, 1659).

TABLE OF ALTERNATIVE
MAXIM NUMBERS

Maxims published in the final (1678) authorized edition are always cited by La Rochefoucauld's own numbers (from 1 to 504).

For the other maxims, three alternative numbering systems are now in common use. In the following table, these three systems are identified by the following abbreviations:

GEF   *Œuvres de La Rochefoucauld*, tome 1, ed. D. L. Gilbert, Collection des Grands Écrivains de la France (Paris: Hachette, 1868). In this system, maxims never published by La Rochefoucauld are numbered 505 to 562; those published by him but subsequently withdrawn are numbered 563 to 641.

Truchet   François de La Rochefoucauld, *Maximes suivi des Réflexions diverses*, ed. Jacques Truchet, Classiques Garnier (Paris: Garnier, 1967). In this system, maxims never published by La Rochefoucauld are numbered MP 1 to MP 61; those published by him but later withdrawn are numbered MS 1 to MS 74. (Marc Escola's 2002 revision of Truchet uses the abbreviation ME instead of MP.)

Lafond   François de La Rochefoucauld, *Maximes et Réflexions diverses*, ed. Jean Lafond, Folio (Paris: Gallimard, 1976). In this system, maxims never published by La Rochefoucauld are numbered ME 1 to ME 57; those published by him but later withdrawn are numbered MS 1 to MS 74.

Truchet criticized the GEF system for combining items from disparate sources into a single numerical sequence. However, both his own system and Lafond's do the same thing on a more limited scale. Moreover, the use of the abbreviation MS for *maxime supprimée* ('withdrawn maxim') as well as for 'manuscript' is unfortunate. All three systems also fail to distinguish maxims of doubtful authenticity from those known to be by La Rochefoucauld. For these reasons, none of the three systems has been used in the present volume.

The following table lists the GEF, Truchet, and Lafond numbers for all maxims other than 1 to 504. The source of each maxim is identified according to the system used in the present volume (the terms Hague, Arsenal, Desmaiseaux, and Segrais designate the items of dubious authenticity on pages 284–6). Each column can be read in numerical sequence by following the entries in **bold** print.

GEF	Truchet	Lafond	Source

Maxims never published by La Rochefoucauld

GEF	Truchet	Lafond	Source
522	MP 1	ME 1	L 38
529	MP 2	ME 2	L 44
520	MP 3	ME 3	L 62
521	MP 4	ME 4	L 97
—	MP 5	—	L 113
507	—	—	L 121
505	MP 9	—	L 190
506	MP 6	ME 5	L 122
507	—	—	L 121
508	MP 17	ME 14	L 237
509	MP 22	ME 20	L 256
510	MP 26	ME 24	L 270
517	MP 7	ME 6	L 143
511	MP 8	ME 7	L 160
505	MP 9	—	L 190
523	MP 10	ME 8	L 195
516	MP 11	ME 9	L 206
—	MP 12	—	L 207
512	MP 13	ME 10	L 209
519	MP 14	ME 11	L 210
526	MP 15	ME 12	L 212
528	MP 16	ME 13	L 228
508	MP 17	ME 14	L 237
513	MP 25	ME 23	L 269
514	MP 18	ME 15	L 240
515	MP 23	ME 21	L 261
516	MP 11	ME 9	L 206
517	MP 7	ME 6	L 143
518	—	—	1: 284[1]
519	MP 14	ME 11	L 210
520	MP 3	ME 3	L 62
521	MP 4	ME 4	L 97
522	MP 1	ME 1	L 38
523	MP 10	ME 8	L 195
—	MP 19	ME 16	L 241
524	MP 20	ME 17	L 245
525	MP 24	ME 22	L 267
526	MP 15	ME 12	L 212
—	—	ME 18	L 249
527	MP 21	ME 19	L 255

GEF	Truchet	Lafond	Source
528	MP 16	ME 13	L 228
529	MP 2	ME 2	L 41
509	MP 22	ME 20	L 256
515	MP 23	ME 21	L 261
525	MP 24	ME 22	L 267
513	MP 25	ME 23	L 269
510	MP 26	ME 24	L 270
530	MP 27	—	PVI24: 4
—	MP 32	ME 25	SL 2
—	MP 33	ME 26	Hague 108–10a
—	MP 34	ME 27	Hague 152–5
531	MP 28	ME 28	PVI58: 1
532	MP 29	ME 29	PVI58: 3
533	MP 30	ME 30	PVI58: 4
—	—	ME 31	Arsenal 8
—	—	ME 32	Arsenal 9
556	MP 31	ME 33	VIS: 39
—	MP 32	ME 25	SL 2
—	MP 33	ME 26	Hague 108–10a
—	MP 34	ME 27	Hague 152–5
534	MP 35	ME 34	VIS: 1
535	MP 36	ME 35	VIS: 2
536	MP 37	ME 36	VIS: 3
537	MP 38	ME 37	VIS: 4
538	MP 39	ME 38	VIS: 5
539	MP 40	ME 39	VIS: 6
540	MP 41	ME 40	VIS: 7
541	MP 42	ME 41	VIS: 8
542	MP 43	ME 42	VIS: 9
543	MP 44	ME 43	VIS: 10
544	MP 45	ME 44	VIS: 11
545	MP 46	ME 45	VIS: 12
546	MP 47	ME 46	VIS: 13
547	MP 48	ME 47	VIS: 14
548	MP 49	ME 48	VIS: 15
549	MP 50	ME 49	VIS: 16
550	MP 51	ME 50	VIS: 17
551	MP 52	ME 51	VIS: 18
552	—	—	VIS: 21
553	—	—	VIS: 28
554	MP 53	ME 52	VIS: 33
555	—	—	VIS: 37
556	MP 31	ME 33	VIS: 39

GEF	Truchet	Lafond	Source	GEF	Truchet	Lafond	Source
557	MP 54	ME 53	VIS: 46	593	MS 24	MS 24	I: 135
558	MP 55	ME 54	VIS: 47	594	MS 25	MS 25	I: 138
559	MP 56	ME 55	VIS: 48	595	MS 26	MS 26	I: 144
560	MP 57	ME 56	VIS: 49	596	MS 27	MS 27	I: 147
561	MP 58	ME 57	VIS: 50	597	MS 28	MS 28	I: 151
562	MP 59	—	Desmaiseaux	598	—	—	I: 155
—	MP 60	—	Segrais 81	599	—	—	I: 156
—	MP 61	—	Segrais 89	600	MS 29	MS 29	I: 157
				601	MS 30	MS 30	I: 159
				602	MS 31	MS 31	I: 161

Maxims finally withdrawn by
La Rochefoucauld

GEF	Truchet	Lafond	Source	GEF	Truchet	Lafond	Source
				603	MS 67	MS 66	IV: 158
				604	MS 32	MS 32	I: 174
563	MS 1	MS 1	I: 1	605	MS 33	MS 33	I: 176
564	MS 2	MS 2	I: 13	606	MS 34	MS 34	I: 179
565	MS 3	MS 3	I: 18	607	—	MS 67	IV: 172
566	MS 4	MS 4	I: 21	608	MS 68	MS 68	IV: 183
567	MS 5	MS 5	I: 33	609	MS 35	MS 35	I: 200
568	MS 6	MS 6	I: 37	610	MS 36	MS 36	I: 201
569	MS 7	MS 7	I: 51	611	MS 37	MS 37	I: 208
570	MS 8	MS 8	I: 53	612	MS 38	MS 38	I: 213
571	MS 61	MS 60	II: 49	613	MS 39	MS 39	I: 225
572	MS 9	MS 9	I: 59	614	MS 40	MS 40	I: 231
573	MS 10	MS 10	I: 60	615	MS 41	MS 41	I: 232
574	MS 11	MS 11	I: 70	616	MS 42	MS 42	I: 236
575	MS 12	MS 12	I: 74	617	MS 69	MS 69	IV: 227
576	MS 13	MS 13	I: 77	618	MS 43	MS 43	I: 245
577	MS 62	MS 61	IV: 71	619	MS 70	MS 70	IV: 234
578	MS 14	MS 14	I: 88	620	MS 44	MS 44	I: 252
579	MS 15	MS 15	I: 89	621	MS 45	MS 45	I: 254
580	MS 16	MS 16	I: 90	622	MS 46	MS 46	I: 256
581	MS 63	MS 62	IV: 83	623	—		I: 257
582	MS 17	MS 17	I: 97	624	MS 47	MS 47	I: 258
583	MS 18	MS 18	I: 99	625	MS 48	MS 48	I: 259[2]
584	MS 64	MS 63	IV: 87	626	MS 49	MS 49	I: 260
—	—	—	I: 101	627	MS 50	MS 50	I: 262
585	MS 19	MS 19	I: 102	628	MS 51	MS 51	I: 271
586	MS 20	MS 20	I: 103	629	MS 52	MS 52	I: 282
587	MS 65	MS 64	IV: 90	518	—	—	I: 284[1]
588	—	—	I: 104	—	MS 53	—	I: 285[1]
589	MS 21	MS 21	I: 105	630	MS 54	MS 53	I: 290
590	MS 66	MS 65	IV: 96	631	—	—	I: 293
591	MS 22	MS 22	I: 132	632	MS 71	MS 71	IV: 272
592	MS 23	MS 23	I: 134	633	MS 72	MS 72	IV: 274

GEF	Truchet	Lafond	Source		GEF	Truchet	Lafond	Source
634	MS 55	MS 54	I: 300[2]		590	MS 66	MS 65	IV: 96
635	MS 56	MS 55	I: 301[2]		603	MS 67	MS 66	IV: 158
636	MS 57	MS 56	I: 302		607	—	MS 67	IV: 172
637	MS 58	MS 57	I: 303		608	MS 68	MS 68	IV: 183
638	MS 59	MS 58	I: 305		617	MS 69	MS 69	IV: 227
639	MS 60	MS 59	I: 309		619	MS 70	MS 70	IV: 234
571	MS 61	MS 60	II: 49		—	—	—	IV: 258
577	MS 62	MS 61	IV: 71		632	MS 71	MS 71	IV: 272
581	MS 63	MS 62	IV: 83		633	MS 72	MS 72	IV: 274
584	MS 64	MS 63	IV: 87		640	MS 73	MS 73	IV: 372
587	MS 65	MS 64	IV: 90		641	MS 74	MS 74	IV: 375

INDEX OF TOPICS

The following pages contain, both in French and in English translation, every index entry that was included in any edition of the *Maxims* authorized by La Rochefoucauld himself. French keywords are printed in SMALL CAPITALS, English keywords in *italics*. Entries are arranged in modern alphabetical order, a separate entry being provided for every English keyword that is not alphabetically adjacent to its French equivalent. Every entry that was withdrawn by La Rochefoucauld before the final authorized edition (v) is printed in square brackets. Obvious errors in the seventeenth-century editions have been silently corrected.

Each entry is accompanied by a partial English résumé of the maxim in question. These English résumés are the work of the present editors; they are not derived from La Rochefoucauld's own indexes, and are offered merely as aids for the reader.

La Rochefoucauld's index to v is printed on pp. 141–3 above.

[ABSENCE, *absence*: absence decreases average passions, increases great ones, v: 276.]

ACCENTS DU PAYS, *accents of our native land*: accent of native land remains in heart, v: 342.

ACCIDENTS, *events*: no events so unlucky that no advantage can be drawn, v: 59.

[*acquaintances, desire for new*, DÉSIR DES CONNAISSANCES NOUVELLES: we hope to be admired more by those less acquainted with us, v: 178.]

ACTIONS, *deeds*: brilliant deeds the result of temperament, v: 7; great deeds the result of chance, v: 57; deeds have lucky or unlucky stars, v: 58; great deeds result from great plans, v: 160; deeds should be in proportion to plans, v: 161; deeds are like rhyming words, v: 382; often ashamed of deeds if people could see motives, v: 409.

advice, CONSEILS: give nothing so generously as advice, v: 110; asker for advice and giver seek their own interests, v: 116; as clever to profit from advice as to give it, v: 283; advice does not influence conduct, v: 378.

[*advice*, PRÉCEPTES: good advice consoles for inability to set bad examples, v: 93; philosophers' advice built up their pride, I: 105.]

AFFAIRES, *matters (of business)*: in great matters we should strive to profit from circumstances, v: 453.

AFFECTATION, *pretence*: qualities we have never make us as absurd as those we pretend to have, v: 134.

AFFLICTIONS, *sorrows*: self-interest and vanity cause sorrows, v: 232; different kinds of hypocrisy in sorrow, v: 233; [consoled for friends' misfortunes when we can display affection, v: 235]; some people missed more than lamented, others vice versa, v: 355; women mourn lovers to seem worthy of being loved, v: 362; [regret losing friend because of our own needs, IV: 234].

Doge has to Venice, v: 77; the more you love, the closer to hating, v: 111; making love is the least fault of lovemaking women, v: 131; people never in love if never heard love mentioned, v: 136; constancy in love is perpetual inconstancy, v: 175; constancy in love either due to finding new things, or a point of honour, v: 176; happier feeling love than inspiring it, v: 259; sacrifice beloved's peace more willingly than ours, v: 262; beloved not loved for her own sake, v: 374; hard to please when much in love or almost out, v: 385; first lover kept long if no second taken, v: 396; in love, first cured best cured, v: 417; young women look like flirts and elderly men foolish when they speak of love, v: 418; to women, friendship tastes insipid after love, v: 440; in love, happier in what we do not know, v: 441; true friendship even rarer than true love, v: 473; often pass from love to ambition, seldom return, v: 490; love less pleasurable than the ways it reveals itself, v: 501; [love is to lover's soul what soul is to body, 1: 77; easier to fall in love than out, 1: 300; sure to be loved when you love little, 1: 302; never at liberty to love or stop, IV: 71]; when weary of loving, pleased if beloved unfaithful, IV: 83.

AMOUR-PROPRE, *self-love*: [virtues only vices in disguise, v: epigraph]; self-love the greatest flatterer, v: 2; many unknown lands in self-love, v: 3; self-love cleverer than cleverest man, v: 4; philosophers' attitude to life a question of taste on the part of their self-love, v: 46; happy when we have what we like, v: 48; [self-love makes us judge friends' merit by the way they behave with us, v: 88]; praise other people to attract praise ourselves, v: 143; self-love not willing to pay, v: 228; kindness is self-love's method of winning over other people, v: 236; loyalty invented by self-love to gain people's confidence, v: 247; education is a second self-love, v: 261; no passion so ruled by self-love as love, v: 262; self-love gives the insight to disguise what might be condemned, v: 494; people in love intent on their passion rather than their beloved, v: 500; [portrait of self-love, 1: 1; self-love transforms its objects, 1: 101].

[*anger*, COLÈRE: different kinds of anger, 1: 159.]

annoy, INCOMMODER: often annoy others when we think we could not, v: 242.

[*appearance, outward*, EXTÉRIEUR: looks, gestures, tones make people pleasant or not, v: 255; outward appearance to make person seem what he wants to be thought, v: 256; solemnity is outward mystification, v: 257.]

APPLICATION, *diligence*: incapable of great things if too attentive to little, v: 41; lack diligence to succeed, not means, v: 243.

astuteness, cunning, FINESSE: pretending to fall into traps is cunning, v: 117; clever people deplore cunning, but use it, v: 124; habitual cunning is sign of small mind, v: 125; cunning arises from lack of cleverness, v: 126; deceived if think yourself more astute than others, v: 127; [too much refinement is false subtlety, v: 128]; bitter against cunning people because they think themselves cleverer, v: 350; may be more astute than some, but not all, v: 394; more absurd when snared by others' cunning than when others snared by ours, v: 407.

attractiveness, AGRÉMENT: attractiveness is a harmony whose rules are unknown, V: 240; attractive interrelationship of looks, gestures, tones makes people pleasant, V: 255.

[*austerity in women*, SÉVÉRITÉ DES FEMMES: women adorn beauty with austerity, V: 204.]

[AVARICE, *avarice*: avarice, not generosity, opposed to thrift, V: 167.]

[AVENIR: RÉSOLUTIONS POUR L'AVENIR, *resolutions for the future*: how can we predict our future wants, I: 74.]

[AVEUGLEMENT DANS SES DÉFAUTS, *blindness to our faults*: happy to be deceived by ourselves, V: 114; everyone objects to something in others that they object to in him, I: 33; too blind to recognize cures for our faults, I: 102.]

[AVIDITÉ, *greed*: greed makes us run after least important things, V: 66.]

BEAUTÉ, *beauty*: attractiveness distinct from beauty, V: 240; useless to be young but not beautiful or vice versa, V: 497; [some beautiful things most dazzling when imperfect, I: 262].

betrayal, TRAHISON: betray from weakness more than plan, V: 120; betrayals arise from lack of cleverness, V: 126.

BIENFAITS, *favours*: men reluctant to reward favours, V: 14; ungrateful for great obligations, V: 299; few know how to give away possessions, V: 301.

BIENSÉANCE, *propriety*: propriety the least law and the most obeyed, V: 447.

[*blindness to our faults*, AVEUGLEMENT DANS SES DÉFAUTS: happy to be deceived by ourselves, V: 114; everyone objects to something in others that they object to in him, I: 33; too blind to recognize cures for our faults, I: 102.]

bliss, FÉLICITÉ: bliss lies in taste, not in thing itself, V: 48.

BONHEUR, *good fortune, happiness*: never as fortunate or unfortunate as we think, V: 49.

BONNE GRÂCE, *grace*: grace is to body what good sense is to mind, V: 67.

BON SENS, *good sense*: grace is to body what good sense is to mind, V: 67; few sensible people except those who agree with us, V: 347.

BONTÉ, *kindness, goodness*: [kindness is self-love's method of winning over other people, V: 236]; kindness often laziness or lack of willpower, V: 237; [dangerous to do too much good, V: 238; some wicked people less dangerous if they had no goodness, V: 284]; fool lacks substance to be good, V: 387; kindness merely weakness or politeness, V: 481; [kindness hard to tell from cleverness, I: 252; cannot be good if people think they can do us harm with impunity, I: 254].

boredom, heartache, ENNUI: too vainglorious to be bored by ourselves, V: 141; heartache causes failures of duty, V: 172; cannot forgive those we bore, V: 304; bored with those who should not bore us, V: 352.

[*cadging*, IMPORTUNITÉ: often annoy others when think we could not, V: 242.]

chance, HASARD: great deeds the result of chance, V: 57.

constancy in love is perpetual inconstancy, V: 175; constancy in love due to finding new things, or a point of honour, V: 176; think we are constant when merely downcast, V: 420.

CONVERSATION, *conversation*: ability to listen and answer a great merit in conversation, V: 139; [intelligent man at a loss without company of fools, V: 140]; confidence contributes more to conversation than intelligence, V: 421.

COQUETTERIE, *flirting*: flirtatious if draw attention to fact that you never flirt, V: 107; flirting restrained by fear or reason, V: 241; love's greatest miracle to cure flirting, V: 349; flirting destroyed by love, V: 376; flirts envious of other women, V: 406.

[*counterfeit*, DISSIMULATION: do not like being seen through, IV: 272.]

CRIMES, *crimes*: greatest misfortunes due to crimes, V: 183; forget faults known only to ourselves, V: 196; never surprised to see evil in people, V: 197; innocence protected less than crime, V: 465; [those incapable of great crimes do not suspect them in others, I: 208; crimes glorified by brilliance and number, IV: 183].

cunning, astuteness, FINESSE: pretending to fall into traps is cunning, V: 117; clever people deplore cunning, but use it, V: 124; habitual cunning is sign of small mind, V: 125; cunning arises from lack of cleverness, V: 126; deceived if think yourself more astute than others, V: 127; [too much refinement is false subtlety, V: 128]; bitter against cunning people because they think themselves cleverer, V: 350; may be more astute than some, but not all, V: 394; more absurd when snared by others' cunning than when others snared by ours, V: 407.

cures for love, REMÈDES DE L'AMOUR: no infallible cures for love, V: 459.

CURIOSITÉ, *curiosity*: curiosity due to self-interest or pride, V: 173; [mind better employed bearing misfortunes than anticipating them, V: 174].

death, MORT: disdain for death is fear of facing it, V: 21; death endured mindlessly, V: 23; neither sun nor death can be looked at, V: 26; falsity of disdain for death, V: 504.

death, disdain for, MÉPRIS DE LA MORT: falsity of disdain for death, V: 504.

deception, TROMPERIE: no comfort when deceived by friends, yet happy to be deceived by ourselves, V: 114; easy to deceive ourselves without noticing, V: 115; often deceived if intend never to deceive, V: 118; deceived if think yourself more astute than others, V: 127; uncouthness may save from deception, V: 129; one who thinks he can do without others or vice versa is deceived, V: 201; less unfortunate to be deceived than disillusioned, V: 395.

deed, PROCÉDÉ: honorable deed may result from integrity or cleverness, V: 170.

deeds, ACTIONS: brilliant deeds the result of temperament, V: 7; great deeds the result of chance, V: 57; deeds have lucky or unlucky stars, V: 58; great deeds result from great plans, V: 160; deeds should be in proportion to plans, V: 161; deeds are like rhyming words, V: 382; often ashamed of deeds if people could see motives, V: 409.

DÉFAUTS, *faults*: if we had no faults, we would not be pleased by others', V: 31;

faults please more than good qualities, V: 90; faults of mind grow worse, V: 112; likeable people with faults, V: 155; acknowledge faults to repair damage they do us, V: 184; great men have great faults, V: 190; soul's faults always in danger of breaking open again, V: 194; falsely honorable when disguise faults, V: 202; some people's faults become them, V: 251; confess small faults to show we have no greater, V: 327; some faults outshine virtue, V: 354; believe we have no faults, our enemies no good, V: 397; faults more forgivable than means to hide them, V: 411; pride ourselves on faults opposite to those we have, V: 424; forgive faults that do not affect us, V: 428; pride ourselves on faults we do not want to correct, V: 442; men increase number of their faults, V: 493; fickle people lack true faults, V: 498; [admit faults only out of vanity, I: 200].

DÉFIANCE, *mistrust*: mistrust justifies deceptions, V: 86; we do not show our hearts because we mistrust ourselves, V: 315; mistrust those who talk to us, but think they are more truthful with us, V: 366.

DÉGOÛT, *distaste*: meritorious people who leave bad taste, V: 155; some people popular only for short time, V: 211.

DÉGUISEMENT, *disguise*: disguise ourselves even from ourselves, V: 119; generosity is disguised ambition, V: 246; disguised falseness imitates truth too well not to deceive, V: 282.

DÉSIR, *desire*: desire few things if we understood them, V: 439; never desire passionately by reason alone, V: 469.

DESSEINS, *plans*: great deeds result from great plans, V: 160; deeds should be in proportion to plans, V: 161.

DÉVOTION, *piety*: pious people make us lose taste for piety, V: 427.

diligence, APPLICATION: incapable of great things if too attentive to little, V: 41; lack diligence to succeed, not means, V: 243.

disguise, DÉGUISEMENT: disguise ourselves even from ourselves, V: 119; generosity is disguised ambition, V: 246; disguised falseness imitates truth too well not to deceive, V: 282.

[DISSIMULATION, *counterfeit*: do not like being seen through, IV: 272.]

distaste, DÉGOÛT: meritorious people who leave bad taste, V: 155; some people popular only for short time, V: 211.

DOUCEUR, *gentleness*: seeming gentleness is weakness, V: 479.

DROITURE, *sound sense*: little intelligence with sound sense less tiresome, V: 502.

ÉDUCATION, *education*: education a second self-love, V: 261.

ÉLÉVATION, *eminence*: eminence is a manner that sets us above others, V: 399; no eminence without merit, V: 400; eminence is to merit what adornment is to beauty, V: 401; fortune uses our faults to make us eminent, V: 403.

ÉLOQUENCE, *eloquence*: eloquence in tone of voice, no less than in words, V: 249; eloquence says all that is needed and only that, V: 250; eloquence in eyes and manner, no less than in words, IV: 258.

eminence, ÉLÉVATION: eminence is a manner that sets us above others, V: 399;

no eminence without merit, V: 400; eminence is to merit what adornment is to beauty, V: 401; fortune uses our faults to make us eminent, V: 403.

EMPLOIS, *positions*: easy to seem worthy of positions you do not hold, V: 164; look small in too great positions, V: 419; hard to seem worthy of great positions gained by surprise, V: 449.

ENNUI, *boredom, heartache*: too vainglorious to be bored by ourselves, V: 141; heartache causes failures of duty, V: 172; cannot forgive those we bore, V: 304; bored with those who should not bore us, V: 352.

[ENTERREMENTS, *funerals*: pomp of funerals has to do with vanity of the living, I: 213.]

ENVIE, *envy*: we never acknowledge envy, V: 27; [envy is a frenzy that cannot endure others' possessions, V: 28; hated for good qualities, V: 29]; secret envy of those in society, V: 280; pride mitigates the envy it rouses, V: 281; envy destroyed by friendship, V: 376; envy lasts longer than fortune of those envied, V: 476; more people lack self-interest than envy, V: 486.

ESPÉRANCE, *hope*: hope, though deceptive, leads on an attractive route, V: 168.

ESPRIT, *mind, intelligence*: strength and weakness of mind are conditions of body, V: 44; judgement is magnitude of light within intelligence, V: 97; no one speaks well of his mind, V: 98; civility of mind thinks honorable things, V: 99; gallantry of mind flatters attractively, V: 100; things spring to mind absolutely finished, V: 101; mind always deceived by heart, V: 102; not all who know their minds know their hearts, V: 103; mind cannot act heart's role for long, V: 108; faults of mind grow worse, V: 112; intelligent man at loss without fools, V: 140; small minds talk much, say nothing, V: 142; mind better employed bearing misfortunes than anticipating them, V: 174; small-mindedness leads to stubbornness, V: 265; not fertile mind but lack of enlightenment makes us find various solutions, V: 287; do not long please if minds look only one way, V: 413; intelligence gives courage to do foolish things, V: 415.

ESPRITS MÉDIOCRES, *average minds*: average minds condemn what is beyond their grasp, V: 375.

[ESTIME, *respect*: merit wins respect from honorable people, stars win respect from public, V: 165; some people approved for useful vices, V: 273.]

[ÉTABLI: FRUIT QUE L'ON PEUT TIRER DE L'OPINION D'ÊTRE ÉTABLI, *benefits derived from reputed status*: gain status by appearing to have gained it, V: 56.]

events, ACCIDENTS: no events so unlucky that no advantage can be drawn, V: 59.

evils, ills, MAUX: philosophy triumphs over past and future ills, V: 22; never surprised to see evil in people, V: 197; should respect evil from those who have done us good, V: 229; less dangerous to do men evil than too much good, V: 238; pity is feeling of our ills prompted by ills of others, V: 264; pride and laziness make us ready to believe evil, V: 267.

EXEMPLE, *example*: nothing so contagious as good or bad example, V: 230.

[EXTÉRIEUR, *outward appearance*: looks, gestures, tones make people pleasant or not, V: 255; outward appearance to make person seem what he wants to be thought, V: 256; solemnity is outward mystification, V: 257.]

FAIBLESSE, *weakness*: betray from weakness more than plan, V: 120; weakness is the only fault incapable of correction, V: 130; weak people cannot be sincere, V: 316; weakness more opposed to virtue than vice, V: 445; kindness is merely weakness, V: 481.

[FAIBLESSES: AVANTAGE D'IGNORER LES FAIBLESSES, *advantage of ignoring weaknesses*: like Athenian madman, complain of those who cure us, I: 104.]

faults, DÉFAUTS: if we had no faults, we would not be pleased by others', V: 31; faults please more than good qualities, V: 90; faults of mind grow worse, V: 112; likeable people with faults, V: 155; acknowledge faults to repair damage they do us, V: 184; great men have great faults, V: 190; soul's faults always in danger of breaking open again, V: 194; falsely honorable when disguise faults, V: 202; some people's faults become them, V: 251; confess small faults to show we have no greater, V: 327; some faults outshine virtue, V: 354; believe we have no faults, our enemies no good, V: 397; faults more forgivable than means to hide them, V: 411; pride ourselves on faults opposite to those we have, V: 424; forgive faults that do not affect us, V: 428; pride ourselves on faults we do not want to correct, V: 442; men increase number of their faults, V: 493; fickle people lack true faults, V: 498; [admit faults only out of vanity, I: 200].

[FAVEUR, *favour*: kings make men as they mint coins, IV: 158.]

FAVORIS, *favourites*: hatred of favourites is love of favour, V: 55.

favours, BIENFAITS: men reluctant to reward favours, V: 14; ungrateful for great obligations, V: 299; few know how to give away possessions, V: 301.

fear, PEUR: few cowards know extent of fears, V: 370.

feelings, SENTIMENTS: each feeling has its look, gesture, tone, V: 255.

FÉLICITÉ, *bliss*: bliss lies in taste, not in thing itself, V: 48.

FEMMES, *women*: women adorn beauty with austerity, V: 204; women's virtue is love of reputation, V: 205; vanity, shame, temperament make women's virtue, V: 220; female temperament based on flirting, V: 241; women think they are in love when not, V: 277; woman's mind and heart well regulated only when it suits her temperament, V: 346; women mourn lovers to seem worthy of love, V: 362; to women, friendship tastes insipid after love, V: 440.

FERMETÉ, *strength of character*: strength of character resists love and makes love passionate, V: 477; only strength of character can be gentle, V: 479.

FIDÉLITÉ, *loyalty*: loyalty invented by self-love to gain people's confidence, V: 247.

FINESSE, *cunning*, *astuteness*: pretending to fall into traps is cunning, V: 117; clever people deplore cunning, but use it, V: 124; habitual cunning is sign of small mind, V: 125; cunning arises from lack of cleverness, V: 126; deceived if think yourself more astute than others, V: 127; [too much refinement is false subtlety, V: 128]; bitter against cunning people because they think themselves cleverer, V: 350; may be more astute than some, but not all, V: 394; more absurd when snared by others' cunning than when others snared by ours, V: 407.

FLATTERIE, *flattery*: few pleasures if never flattered ourselves, V: 123; praise is subtle flattery, V: 144; others' flattery could not harm if we never flattered

ourselves, V: 152; some people's glory exalted to demean others', V: 198; we hate not flattery but the way it is done, V: 329; [self-love determines who flatters us most, I: 157].

flirting, COQUETTERIE: flirtatious if draw attention to fact that you never flirt, V: 107; flirting restrained by fear or reason, V: 241; love's greatest miracle to cure flirting, V: 349; flirting destroyed by love, V: 376; flirts envious of other women, V: 406.

FOLIE, *foolishness*: seeming wisdom is folly in keeping with age, V: 207; without folly not as wise as we think, V: 209; more foolish as we age, V: 210; wanting to be wise on own is great folly, V: 231; contagious follies, V: 300; cures for folly but not waywardness, V: 318.

fools, SOTS: no fools as annoying as intelligent ones, V: 451.

FORCE, *strength*: not strong enough to follow reason, V: 42; strength of mind a condition of body, V: 44; no kindness if no strength to be bad, V: 237.

FORTUNE, *fortune*: virtues merely deeds ordered by fortune, V: 1; greater virtues to bear good fortune than bad, V: 25; balance of good and bad evens out fortunes, V: 52; heroes made by fortune with nature, V: 53; [great deeds often result of chance, V: 57; deeds have lucky or unlucky stars, V: 58]; fortune always advantages those she favours, V: 60; happiness depends on temperament and fortune, V: 61; [fortune displays merit, V: 153]; fortune corrects faults that reason could not, V: 154; men judged by their fortune, V: 212; wisdom at the mercy of fortune, V: 323; great man takes advantage of fortune, V: 343; fortune reveals virtues and vices, V: 380; fortune seems blind to those she never benefits, V: 391; treat fortune like health, V: 392; fortune and temperament rule world, V: 435; [cannot predict future fortunes, I: 70; virtues made out of deeds ordered by fortune, I: 293; kings make men as they mint coins, IV: 158].

[FORTUNE: BONNE FORTUNE, *good fortune*: greater virtues to bear good fortune than bad, V: 25.]

friendship, AMITIÉ: inconstant in friendships because hard to know soul's qualities, V: 80; following our own taste when we prefer friends to ourselves, V: 81; friendship a transaction in which self-love expects to gain, V: 83; more shameful to mistrust friends than to be deceived by them, V: 84; self-interest the sole cause of friendship, V: 85; judge friends' merit by the way they behave with us, V: 88; no comfort when betrayed by friends, yet happy to be betrayed by ourselves, V: 114; fickle complaints about friends to justify our fickleness, V: 179; easily consoled for friends' misfortunes, V: 235; overestimate friends' affection from a desire to have our merit approved, V: 279; cannot love what you have ceased to love, V: 286; we like those who admire us, not always those whom we admire, V: 294; hard to like those we respect more than ourselves or not at all, V: 296; dislike those who love us more than we want, V: 321; hard to make a friend see his faults, V: 410; still sensitive to misfortunes of friends who have deceived us, V: 434; to women, friendship tastes insipid after love, V: 440; in friendship, happier in what we do not know, V: 441; true friendship even rarer than true love, V: 473; [when friends fortunate, our joy comes from self-love, I: 97; in adversity of friends

something does not displease us, I: 99; when weary of loving, pleased if beloved unfaithful, IV: 83;] little affection if fail to notice cooling of friends' affection, IV: 96; [regret losing a friend because of our needs, IV: 234].

[*funerals*, ENTERREMENTS: pomp of funerals has to do with vanity of the living, I: 213.]

[*future, resolutions for the*, RÉSOLUTIONS POUR L'AVENIR: how can we predict our future wants, I: 74.]

GALANTERIE, *love affairs, gallantry*: few women have only one love affair, V: 73; gallantry of mind flatters attractively, V: 100; love rarely found in love affairs, V: 402; first love affair not counted until second, V: 499.

GÉNÉROSITÉ, *generosity*: generosity often disguised ambition, V: 246.

generosity, LIBÉRALITÉ: generosity is the vanity of giving, V: 263.

gentleness, DOUCEUR: seeming gentleness is weakness, V: 479.

GLOIRE, *glory*: measure glory against means used to acquire it, V: 157; some people's glory exalted to demean others', V: 198; [honours won are down payments, V: 270]; to glory in achievements privately is honorable, publicly absurd, V: 307.

good fortune, happiness, BONHEUR: never as fortunate or unfortunate as we think, V: 49.

goodness, kindness, BONTÉ: [kindness is self-love's method of winning over other people, V: 236]; kindness often laziness or lack of willpower, V: 237; [dangerous to do too much good, V: 238; some wicked people less dangerous if they had no goodness, V: 284]; fool lacks substance to be good, V: 387; kindness merely weakness or politeness, V: 481; [kindness hard to tell from cleverness, I: 252; cannot be good if people think they can do us harm with impunity, I: 254].

good sense, BON SENS: grace is to body what good sense is to mind, V: 67; few sensible people except those who agree with us, V: 347.

GOÛT, *taste*: taste changes, inclination does not, V: 252; taste due to judgement more than intelligence, V: 258; give up interests rather than tastes, V: 390.

GOUVERNER, *rule*: harder to prevent ourselves being ruled than to rule others, V: 151.

grace, BONNE GRÂCE: grace is to body what good sense is to mind, V: 67.

gratitude, RECONNAISSANCE: gratitude keeps commerce going, V: 223; not all who show gratitude are grateful, V: 224; receive less gratitude than we expect, V: 225; ungrateful if too eager to discharge obligation, V: 226; [pride not willing to owe, self-love to pay, V: 228; respect evil from those who have done us good, V: 229]; gratitude is wish for greater favours, V: 298; gratitude puts friends in debt, V: 438; [limit gratitude more readily than hope, IV: 227].

GRAVITÉ, *solemnity*: solemnity is outward mystification to hide faults, V: 257.

[*greed*, AVIDITÉ: greed makes us run after least important things, V: 66.]

[GROSSIÈRETÉ, *uncouthness*: uncouthness can save you from being deceived, V: 129.]

own temper, v: 414; fortune and temperament rule world, v: 435; temper depends on little things, v: 488.

HYPOCRISIE, *hypocrisy*: hypocrisy is vice's homage to virtue, v: 218; different kinds of hypocrisy in sorrow, v: 233.

[IGNORANCE DE NOS FAIBLESSES, *ignorance of our weaknesses*: like Athenian madman, complain of those who cure us, I: 104.]

ills, evils, MAUX: philosophy triumphs over past and future ills, v: 22; never surprised to see evil in people, v: 197; should respect evil from those who have done us good, v: 229; less dangerous to do men evil than too much good, v: 238; pity is feeling of our ills prompted by ills of others, v: 264; pride and laziness make us ready to believe evil, v: 267.

IMITATION, *imitation*: good or evil deeds produce imitations, v: 230; [imitation always unfortunate, I: 245].

[IMPORTUNITÉ, *cadging*: often annoy others when think we could not, v: 242.]

INCLINATION, *inclination*: taste changes, inclination does not, v: 252.

[INCLINATION: FORCE DE L'INCLINATION, *strength of inclination*: man thinks he leads when he is led, v: 43; taste changes, inclination does not, v: 252.]

INCOMMODER, *annoy*: often annoy others when we think we could not, v: 242.

INCONSTANCE, *inconstancy*: one kind of inconstancy from fickleness, another from loss of taste, v: 181.

INDISCRÉTION, *indiscretion*: major indiscretions forgiven in love more than minor infidelities, v: 429.

INFIDÉLITÉ, *infidelity*: infidelities ought to extinguish love, v: 359; slight infidelities to us discredit more than greater ones to others, v: 360; self-inflicted injuries to remain faithful scarcely better than infidelities, v: 381.

INGRATITUDE, *ingratitude*: some men less guilty of ingratitude than their benefactors, v: 96; ungrateful if too eager to discharge obligation, v: 226; when we can do good, we find few ungrateful, v: 306; no great misfortune to oblige ungrateful men, v: 317.

INJURES, *insults*: men forget insults and reluctant to avenge, v: 14.

injuries, VIOLENCE: injuries to others less painful than to ourselves, v: 363; self-inflicted injuries to prevent love more brutal than beloved's cruelties, v: 369; least unbecoming violent passion is love, v: 466.

INNOCENCE, *innocence*: innocence protected less than crime, v: 465.

insults, INJURES: men forget insults and reluctant to avenge, v: 14.

intelligence, mind, ESPRIT: strength and weakness of mind are conditions of body, v: 44; judgement is magnitude of light within intelligence, v: 97; no one speaks well of his mind, v: 98; civility of mind thinks honorable things, v: 99; gallantry of mind flatters attractively, v: 100; things spring to mind absolutely finished, v: 101; mind always deceived by heart, v: 102; not all who know their minds know their hearts, v: 103; mind cannot act heart's role for long, v: 108; faults of mind grow worse, v: 112; intelligent man at loss without fools, v: 140; small minds talk much, say nothing, v: 142; mind

LARMES, *tears*: tears deceive us after deceiving others, V: 373.

laziness, PARESSE: laziness keeps us dutiful, V: 169; laziness dominates violent passions, V: 266; laziness makes us ready to believe evil, V: 267; laziness most tolerated of faults, V: 398; laziness keeps the mind to what is comfortable, V: 482; lazier in mind than body, V: 487; [laziness our most malignant passion, substitute for all good things, I: 290; lazy people put most pressure on others, IV: 90].

LIBÉRALITÉ, *generosity*: generosity is the vanity of giving, V: 263.

[*life, attachment to and disdain for*, ATTACHEMENT ET MÉPRIS DE LA VIE: philosophers' attachment or indifference to life a question of taste, V: 46.]

liveliness, VIVACITÉ: increasing liveliness with age not far from folly, V: 416.

look, MINES: pretended look to make person seem what he wants to be thought, V: 256.

LOUANGES, *praise*: we praise others to attract praise ourselves, V: 143; praise is subtle flattery, V: 144; we choose poisoned praise to reveal faults in those we praise, V: 145; we bestow praise to receive it, V: 146; few prefer useful criticism to treacherous praise, V: 147; some rebukes are praises, some praises slanders, V: 148; refusal of praise is desire to be praised twice, V: 149; desire to deserve praise strengthens virtue, V: 150; [some people praised to demean others, V: 198]; kindness does not deserve praise if no strength to be bad, V: 237; we praise only those who admire us, V: 356; no bad bargain to renounce the good said of us, provided no evil said either, V: 454; [modesty shuns praise to have it, I: 147; virtue never praised except from self-interest, I: 151; praise keeps us practising virtue, I: 155; praise enhances intelligence, valour, beauty, I: 156].

love, AMOUR: love is a hidden wish to possess after many rituals, V: 68; pure love unknown even to ourselves, V: 69; no disguise can hide or simulate love, V: 70; people ashamed of having loved when they no longer love, V: 71; love more like hatred than friendship, V: 72; few women have only one love affair, V: 73; only one kind of love, thousands of imitations, V: 74; love ceases to exist without hope or fear, V: 75; everyone talks about love, few have seen it, V: 76; love has no more relation to its alleged transactions than Doge has to Venice, V: 77; the more you love, the closer to hating, V: 111; making love is the least fault of lovemaking women, V: 131; people never in love if never heard love mentioned, V: 136; constancy in love is perpetual inconstancy, V: 175; constancy in love either due to finding new things, or a point of honour, V: 176; happier feeling love than inspiring it, V: 259; sacrifice beloved's peace more willingly than ours, V: 262; beloved not loved for her own sake, V: 374; hard to please when much in love or almost out, V: 385; first lover kept long if no second taken, V: 396; in love, first cured best cured, V: 417; young women look like flirts and elderly men foolish when they speak of love, V: 418; to women, friendship tastes insipid after love, V: 440; in love, happier in what we do not know, V: 441; true friendship even rarer than true love, V: 473; often pass from love to ambition, seldom return, V: 490; love less pleasurable than the ways it reveals itself, V: 501; [love is to lover's soul what soul is to body, I: 77; easier to fall in love than

out, I: 300; sure to be loved when you love little, I: 302; never at liberty to love or stop, IV: 71]; when weary of loving, pleased if beloved unfaithful, IV: 83.

love affairs, gallantry, GALANTERIE: few women have only one love affair, V: 73; gallantry of mind flatters attractively, V: 100; love rarely found in love affairs, V: 402; first love affair not counted until second, V: 499.

loyalty, FIDÉLITÉ: loyalty invented by self-love to gain people's confidence, V: 247.

[LUXE, *luxury*: luxury predicts national decadence, I: 282.]

lying, MENSONGE: aversion to lying is ambition to gain respect for our words, V: 63.

MAGNANIMITÉ, *magnanimity*: magnanimity disdains everything to gain everything, V: 248; magnanimity is pride's form of good sense, V: 285; [magnanimity is a noble effort of pride, I: 271].

MALHEUR, *misfortune*: never as unfortunate as we imagine, V: 49.

[MALIGNITÉ, *malignity*: if we had no faults, we would not be pleased by others', V: 31.]

manner, assured, AIR COMPOSÉ: assured manner usually turns into insolence, V: 495.

manner, middle-class, AIR BOURGEOIS: middle-class manner never shed at court, V: 393.

MARIAGE, *marriage*: good marriages, no rapturous ones, V: 113.

matters (of business), AFFAIRES: in great matters we should strive to profit from circumstances, V: 453.

MAUX, *ills, evils*: philosophy triumphs over past and future ills, V: 22; never surprised to see evil in people, V: 197; should respect evil from those who have done us good, V: 229; less dangerous to do men evil than too much good, V: 238; pity is feeling of our ills prompted by ills of others, V: 264; pride and laziness make us ready to believe evil, V: 267.

[*means of success*, MOYENS DE RÉUSSIR: eloquence in manner no less than words, V: 249.]

MÉDISANCE, *slander*: slander out of vanity, not malice, V: 483.

MÉMOIRE, *memory*: everyone complains of memory, V: 89; memory recalls what has happened, not how many times we have told it, V: 313.

MENSONGE, *lying*: aversion to lying is ambition to gain respect for our words, V: 63.

MÉRITE, *merit*: those who think they have merit treat misfortune as honour, V: 50; bad to disillusion a man preoccupied with his merit, V: 92; those who envy merit are forced to praise it, V: 95; nature creates merit, fortune displays it, V: 153; merits that leave a bad taste, V: 155; people whose sole merit is doing stupid useful things, V: 156; ability to use average talents wins more repute than real merit, V: 162; easier to seem worthy of positions you do not hold, V: 164; merits win respect from honourable people, V: 165; world rewards appearances of merit, V: 166; [kindness does not deserve praise if no strength to be bad, V: 237]; people whose only merits are useful

vices, V: 273; we overestimate friends' affection because we want our merit approved, V: 279; like fruits, virtues have their season, V: 291; when merits sink, tastes do, V: 379; people favour false merit more than misjudge true, V: 455; kings force us to take men at standard rate, not true worth, IV: 158.

mind, intelligence, ESPRIT: strength and weakness of mind are conditions of body, V: 44; judgement is magnitude of light within intelligence, V: 97; no one speaks well of his mind, V: 98; civility of mind thinks honorable things, V: 99; gallantry of mind flatters attractively, V: 100; things spring to mind absolutely finished, V: 101; mind always deceived by heart, V: 102; not all who know their minds know their hearts, V: 103; mind cannot act heart's role for long, V: 108; faults of mind grow worse, V: 112; intelligent man at loss without fools, V: 140; small minds talk much, say nothing, V: 142; mind better employed bearing misfortunes than anticipating them, V: 174; small-mindedness leads to stubbornness, V: 265; not fertile mind but lack of enlightenment makes us find various solutions, V: 287; do not long please if minds look only one way, V: 413; intelligence gives courage to do foolish things, V: 415.

minds, average, ESPRITS MÉDIOCRES: average minds condemn what is beyond their grasp, V: 375.

MINES, *look*: pretended look to make person seem what he wants to be thought, V: 256.

misfortune, MALHEUR: never as unfortunate as we imagine, V: 49.

mistrust, DÉFIANCE: mistrust justifies deceptions, V: 86; we do not show our hearts because we mistrust ourselves, V: 315; mistrust those who talk to us, but think they are more truthful with us, V: 366.

MODÉRATION, *moderation*: moderation comes from calmness given by good fortune, V: 17; moderation is fear of envy, display, and desire to appear greater than fortune, V: 18; moderation is laziness of soul, V: 293; moderation turned into a virtue to limit ambition, V: 308; [moderation is dread of shame or fear of losing, I: 18; moderation is like sobriety: you want more but are afraid, I: 21].

MORT, *death*: disdain for death is fear of facing it, V: 21; death endured mindlessly, V: 23; neither sun nor death can be looked at, V: 26; falsity of disdain for death, V: 504.

MORT: MÉPRIS DE LA MORT, *disdain for death*: falsity of disdain for death, V: 504.

[MOYENS DE RÉUSSIR, *means of success*: eloquence in manner no less than words, V: 249.]

names, famous, NOMS ILLUSTRES: great names demean those who cannot live up to them, V: 94.

NATUREL, *natural*: wish to look natural prevents us from being so, V: 431.

NÉGOCIATIONS, *negotiations*: abandon friends' interests in interests of successful negotiation, V: 278.

NIAIS, *silly*: silly people who use silliness cleverly, V: 208.

NOMS ILLUSTRES, *famous names*: great names demean those who cannot live up to them, V: 94.

NOUVEAUTÉ, *novelty*: novelty gives love an easily tarnished lustre, V: 274; novelty and habit prevent us from seeing friends' faults, V: 426.

OCCASIONS, *circumstances*: circumstances reveal our nature to others and ourselves, V: 345.

old age, VIEILLESSE: old people's good advice consoles for inability to set bad examples, V: 93; habit preserves tastes of old age, V: 109; mind's faults grow worse with age, V: 112; more foolish and wise as we grow old, V: 210; onset of old age reveals decline, V: 222; lukewarmness of old age opposed to salvation, V: 341; dangerous folly of old people to forget they are no longer attractive, V: 408; few know how to be old, V: 423; still living for pains, no longer for pleasures, V: 430; old age a tyrant forbidding pleasures of youth, V: 461.

old fools, VIEUX FOUS: old fools more foolish than young, V: 444.

OPINIÂTRETÉ, *stubbornness*: pride makes us stubbornly oppose accepted views, V: 234; small-mindedness leads to stubbornness, V: 265.

ORGUEIL, *pride*: [pride always finds some compensation, V: 33]; if no pride, would not complain of it in others, V: 34; all equal in pride, V: 35; nature gave us pride to spare us pain of deficiencies, V: 36; more pride than kindness in reprimands, V: 37; pride not willing to owe, V: 228; pride flattered when great people confide, V: 239; humility an artifice of pride, V: 254; pride makes us ready to believe evil, V: 267; pride rouses envy and mitigates it, V: 281; what we take away from other faults is added to pride, V: 450; pride makes us disdain good qualities we lack, V: 462; pride ourselves on jealousy, V: 472; [pride reveals self as arrogance, I: 37].

[*outward appearance*, EXTÉRIEUR: looks, gestures, tones make people pleasant or not, V: 255; outward appearance to make person seem what he wants to be thought, V: 256; solemnity is outward mystification, V: 257.]

PARESSE, *laziness*: laziness keeps us dutiful, V: 169; laziness dominates violent passions, V: 266; laziness makes us ready to believe evil, V: 267; laziness most tolerated of faults, V: 398; laziness keeps the mind to what is comfortable, V: 482; lazier in mind than body, V: 487; [laziness our most malignant passion, substitute for all good things, I: 290; lazy people put most pressure on others, IV: 90].

PARLER, *speaking*: little to say unless vanity makes us speak, V: 137; rather speak ill of ourselves than nothing, V: 138; small minds talk much, say nothing, V: 142; best to say little about wives, less about ourselves, V: 364.

PASSIONS, *passions*: no more control over passions than lives, V: 5; passion makes cleverest man a fool and vice versa, V: 6; great deeds the result of passion, V: 7; passions always persuade, V: 8; mistrust passions even when they seem reasonable, V: 9; downfall of one passion is rise of another, V: 10; passions engender opposites, V: 11; passions always seen through veils, V: 12; resist passions due to their weakness, V: 122; no more secure from

454; [modesty shuns praise to have it, 1: 147; virtue never praised except from self-interest, 1: 151; praise keeps us practising virtue, 1: 155; praise enhances intelligence, valour, beauty, 1: 156].

[PRÉCEPTES, *advice*: good advice consoles for inability to set bad examples, V: 93; philosophers' advice built up their pride, 1: 105.]

PRÉOCCUPATION, *preoccupation*: bad to disillusion a man preoccupied with his merit, V: 92.

pretence, AFFECTATION: qualities we have never make us as absurd as those we pretend to have, V: 134.

pride, ORGUEIL: [pride always finds some compensation, V: 33]; if no pride, would not complain of it in others, V: 34; all equal in pride, V: 35; nature gave us pride to spare us pain of deficiencies, V: 36; more pride than kindness in reprimands, V: 37; pride not willing to owe, V: 228; pride flattered when great people confide, V: 239; humility an artifice of pride, V: 254; pride makes us ready to believe evil, V: 267; pride rouses envy and mitigates it, V: 281; what we take away from other faults is added to pride, V: 450; pride makes us disdain good qualities we lack, V: 462; pride ourselves on jealousy, V: 472; [pride reveals self as arrogance, 1: 37].

PROCÉDÉ, *deed*: honorable deed may result from integrity or cleverness, V: 170.

PROMESSE, *promise*: make promises in hope, keep them in fear, V: 38.

PROPRIÉTÉS DES HOMMES, *characteristics of men*: men's characteristics revealed by chance, V: 344.

propriety, BIENSÉANCE: propriety the least law and the most obeyed, V: 447.

PRUDENCE, *prudence*: prudence cannot guarantee smallest occurrence, V: 65.

QUALITÉS, *qualities*: some innate good qualities degenerate, others never perfect when acquired, V: 365; born with great qualities if without envy, V: 433; judge merit by use made of great qualities, V: 437; no man thinks all his qualities inferior, V: 452; some bad qualities make great talents, V: 468; qualities indeterminate, at mercy of chance, V: 470.

[QUALITÉS: USAGE DES GRANDES QUALITÉS, *using great qualities*: know how to employ your merits, V: 159.]

QUERELLES, *quarrels*: one-sided quarrels would not last, V: 496.

RAISON, *reason*: not enough strength to follow reason, V: 42; reasonable if appreciate what is reasonable, V: 105; never desire passionately by reason alone, V: 469.

rebukes, REPROCHES: some rebukes are praises, V: 148.

RÉCONCILIATION, *reconciliation*: reconciliation is desire to improve ourselves or weariness of conflict, V: 82.

RECONNAISSANCE, *gratitude*: gratitude keeps commerce going, V: 223; not all who show gratitude are grateful, V: 224; receive less gratitude than we expect, V: 225; ungrateful if too eager to discharge obligation, V: 226; [pride not willing to owe, self-love to pay, V: 228; respect evil from those who have done us good, V: 229]; gratitude is wish for greater favours, V: 298; grati-

[TALENTS: DIVERS TALENTS, *various talents*: talents bear unique fruits, I: 138.]

taste, GOÛT: taste changes, inclination does not, V: 252; taste due to judgement more than intelligence, V: 258; give up interests rather than tastes, V: 390.

tears, LARMES: tears deceive us after deceiving others, V: 373.

[TEMPÉRAMENT, *temperament*: strength and weakness of mind are conditions of body, V: 44; temper more quirky than fortune, V: 45; opposite temperaments produce little and great things, I: 51.]

temper(ament), *(bodily) humour*, HUMEUR: temper more quirky than fortune, V: 45; temperament decides value of fortune's gifts, V: 47; happiness depends on temperament and fortune, V: 61; more faults of temperament than mind, V: 290; temperaments have attractive and unattractive sides, V: 292; body's humours play a part in deeds, V: 297; fools see things in light of own temper, V: 414; fortune and temperament rule world, V: 435; temper depends on little things, V: 488.

[*temperance*, SOBRIÉTÉ: temperance is love of health or inability, I: 135.]

TIMIDITÉ, *timidity*: timidity keeps us dutiful, V: 169; dangerous to rebuke timidity, V: 480.

TRAHISON, *betrayal*: betray from weakness more than plan, V: 120; betrayals arise from lack of cleverness, V: 126.

TRAVERS, *waywardness*: less trouble submitting to wayward minds than leading, V: 448; intelligence with waywardness tiresome, V: 502.

TROMPERIE, *deception*: no comfort when deceived by friends, yet happy to be deceived by ourselves, V: 114; easy to deceive ourselves without noticing, V: 115; often deceived if intend never to deceive, V: 118; deceived if think yourself more astute than others, V: 127; uncouthness may save from deception, V: 129; one who thinks he can do without others or vice versa is deceived, V: 201; less unfortunate to be deceived than disillusioned, V: 395.

truth, VÉRITÉ: truth does less good than its appearance does evil, V: 64; enemies' judgements nearer truth than ours, V: 458; [truth is basis and reason of perfection and beauty, I: 260].

[*truth, appearance of*, VRAISEMBLANCE: truth does less good than its appearance does evil, V: 64; disguised falseness imitates truth too well not to deceive, V: 282.]

[*uncouthness*, GROSSIÈRETÉ: uncouthness can save you from being deceived, V: 129.]

VALEUR, *valour*: valour caused by love of glory, fear of shame, etc., V: 213; soldiers earn living by valour, V: 214; many kinds of courage between perfect valour and cowardice, V: 215; valour is doing without witnesses as in front of world, V: 216; intrepidity is strength of soul, V: 217; men risk danger for honour, not for success of plan, V: 219; vanity, shame, temperament make up valour, V: 220; brave men strive to avoid death, V: 221; [intrepidity sustains in conspiracies, valour in war, I: 231; victory produced

timidity, V: 169; honorable deed may result from integrity or cleverness, V: 170]; virtues lose themselves in self-interest, V: 171; vices in composition of virtues, V: 182; disdain all who have no virtues, not all who have vices, V: 186; name 'virtue' useful to self-interest, V: 187; nature limits virtues at birth, V: 189; virtue would not go far without vanity, V: 200; hypocrisy is vice's homage to virtue, V: 218; self-interest puts virtues on display, V: 253; hard to make friend see his faults, V: 410; men dare not seem enemies of virtue, V: 489; [virtue is talent for seeming virtuous, I: 176; virtue is phantom given honorable name so we can do what we want, I: 179].

virtuous woman (see also *honorable man*), HONNÊTE FEMME: [women adorn beauty with austerity, V: 204; women's virtue is love of reputation, V: 205]; virtuous women weary of their occupation, V: 367; virtuous women safe because not sought, V: 368.

VIVACITÉ, *liveliness*: increasing liveliness with age not far from folly, V: 416.

[VOGUE, *popularity*: some people popular only for short time, V: 211; men judged by popularity or fortune, V: 212.]

VOLONTÉ, *willpower, wishes*: more able than willing, V: 30; do not know all our wishes, V: 295.

[VRAISEMBLANCE, *appearance of truth*: truth does less good than its appearance does evil, V: 64; disguised falseness imitates truth too well not to deceive, V: 282.]

waywardness, TRAVERS: less trouble submitting to wayward minds than leading, V: 448; intelligence with waywardness tiresome, V: 502.

weakness, FAIBLESSE: betray from weakness more than plan, V: 120; weakness is the only fault incapable of correction, V: 130; weak people cannot be sincere, V: 316; weakness more opposed to virtue than vice, V: 445; kindness is merely weakness, V: 481.

[*weaknesses, advantage of ignoring*, AVANTAGE D'IGNORER LES FAIBLESSES: like Athenian madman, complain of those who cure us, I: 104.]

wealth, RICHESSES: philosophers disdained wealth to compensate for lack of it, V: 54.

willpower, wishes, VOLONTÉ: more able than willing, V: 30; do not know all our wishes, V: 295.

wisdom, SAGESSE: easier to be wise for others than self, V: 132; more foolish and wise as we age, V: 210; wanting to be wise on own is great folly, V: 231; [hardly ever wise in things that matter, I: 132; refined folly from refined wisdom, I: 134].

wishes, willpower, VOLONTÉ: more able than willing, V: 30; do not know all our wishes, V: 295.

women, FEMMES: women adorn beauty with austerity, V: 204; women's virtue is love of reputation, V: 205; vanity, shame, temperament make women's virtue, V: 220; female temperament based on flirting, V: 241; women think they are in love when not, V: 277; woman's mind and heart well regulated only when it suits her temperament, V: 346; women mourn lovers to seem worthy of love, V: 362; to women, friendship tastes insipid after love, V: 440.

*The
Oxford
World's
Classics
Website*

www.worldsclassics.co.uk

- Browse the full range of Oxford World's Classics online

- Sign up for our monthly e-alert to receive information on new titles

- Read extracts from the Introductions

- Listen to our editors and translators talk about the world's greatest literature with our Oxford World's Classics audio guides

- Join the conversation, follow us on Twitter at OWC_Oxford

- Teachers and lecturers can order inspection copies quickly and simply via our website

www.worldsclassics.co.uk